ADDING ON

ADDING ON

HOW TO DESIGN AND BUILD
A BEAUTIFUL ADDITION
TO YOUR HOME

Edited by Roger Yepsen
and the
Editors of Rodale Do-It-Yourself Books

Rodale Press, Emmaus, Pennsylvania

OUR MISSION

We publish books that empower people's lives.

RODALE BOOKS

The editors who compiled this book have tried to make all of the contents as accurate and as correct as possible. Plans, illustrations, photographs, and text have all been carefully checked and cross-checked. However, due to the variability of local conditions, construction materials, personal skill, and so on, neither the editors nor Rodale Press assumes any responsibility for any injuries suffered or for damages or other losses incurred that result from the material presented herein. All instructions and plans should be carefully studied and clearly understood before beginning construction.

Printed in the United States of America on acid-free ♾, recycled ♲ paper

Library of Congress Cataloging-in-Publication Data

Adding on : how to design and build a beautiful
 addition to your home / edited by Roger Yepsen
 and the editors of Rodale Do-It-Yourself books.
  p. cm.
 Includes index.
 ISBN 0–87596–605–5 hardcover
 ISBN 0–87596–769–8 paperback
 1. Buildings—Additions—Design and
construction—Amateurs' manuals. I. Yepsen,
Roger B. II. Rodale Press.
TH4816.2.A33 1995
690'.837—dc20   94–38127
                                         CIP

Adding On Editorial and Design Staff
Editor: Roger Yepsen
Interior Book Designer: Barbara C. Snyder
Interior Illustrators: Vince Babak, Frank Rohrbach,
  and Ray Skibinski
Cover Designer and Illustrator: Frank Milloni
Cover Photographer: © Karen Bussolini
Photography Editor: Heidi Stonehill
Copy Editor: Carolyn R. Mandarano
Production Coordinator: Melinda Rizzo
Indexer: Laura Ogar
Administrative Assistant: Susan Nickol

Rodale Books
Executive Editor, Home and Garden:
  Margaret Lydic Balitas
*Managing Editor, Woodworking and
  Home Improvement Books:* Kevin Ireland
Art Director, Home and Garden: Michael Mandarano
Copy Manager, Home and Garden: Dolores Plikaitis
Office Manager, Home and Garden:
  Karen Earl-Braymer
Editor-in-Chief: William Gottlieb

Photographs on pages 175 and 204–205 © 1995
  by Stephen Cridland
Photographs on pages 188, 193, and 196–203
  © 1994 by Brian Vanden Brink, photographer

If you have any questions or comments concerning
this book, please write to:
  Rodale Press, Inc.
  Book Readers' Service
  33 East Minor Street
  Emmaus, PA 18098

Distributed in the book trade by St. Martin's Press
2 4 6 8 10 9 7 5 3 1 hardcover
2 4 6 8 10 9 7 5 3   paperback

CONTENTS

FROM DAYDREAMS TO BLUEPRINTS

DEFINING THE STRUCTURE

CLOSING IN

THE SHAPES OF DREAMS

THREADING THE UTILITIES

MAKING ROOMS

FINISHING UP

ACKNOWLEDGMENTS

Like the addition it describes, this book grew from concept to reality through the hard work of dozens of talented people. We'd like to thank each of the contributors listed below for the dedication they brought to this project. In addition, four people deserve special mention for the work they did behind the scenes. Assistant editor Tony O'Malley put in hundreds of hours researching and writing copy, conceiving tips, and gathering photos to ensure that we've provided the detailed information you need to tackle the project of your dreams. Copy editor Carolyn Mandarano meticulously examined every word to guarantee that our writing was clear and accurate. Illustrator Vince Babak labored long after all of us had gone home to produce the majority of the detailed drawings that grace these pages. Then Barbara Snyder brought all of the elements together to create a clear and compelling package. Thanks to each of them for enhancing the quality of this book.

Contributing Writers:
Roy Barnhart
Kenneth S. Burton, Jr.
Kevin Ireland
Anthony Noel
Tony O'Malley
David Schiff
John Wagner
Alasdair G. B. Wallace
Roger Yepsen
Robert A. Yoder

Technical Consultants:
Drew Benyo
Steve Bolt
Tom Budinetz

Technical Assistance:
Phil Gehret, Rodale Press Design Center
Fred Matlack, Rodale Press Design Center

Black-and-White Photographers:
Kenneth S. Burton, Jr.
Ed Landrock/Rodale Stock Images
Mitch Mandel/Rodale Stock Images
David Schiff
Alasdair G. B. Wallace
Kurt Wilson
Roger Yepsen

Color Photographers:
Karen Bussolini (pages 176–178, 180–181, 184–187, 190–191, 194–195)
Stephen Cridland (pages 175, 204–205)
Mitch Mandel/Rodale Stock Images (pages 179, 189, 206)
Robert Perron (pages 182–183)
Walter Smalling (page 192)
Brian Vanden Brink (pages 188, 193, 196–203)

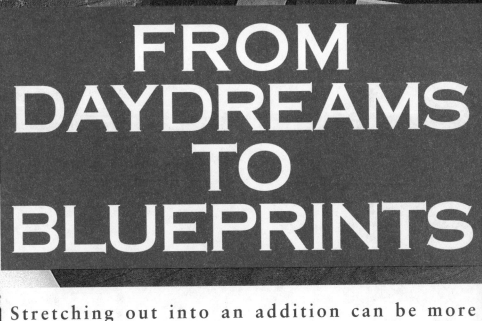

FROM DAYDREAMS TO BLUEPRINTS

Stretching out into an addition can be more satisfying than leaving the old place. Why? Because *adapting* is more challenging than *abandoning*. A well-planned addition is a triumph of problem solving. It represents the fine tuning of that most complex thing we'll ever own, a home. And then there's the creature comfort of a home you know intimately—broken in, like a favorite pair of shoes, and now extended to fit even better.

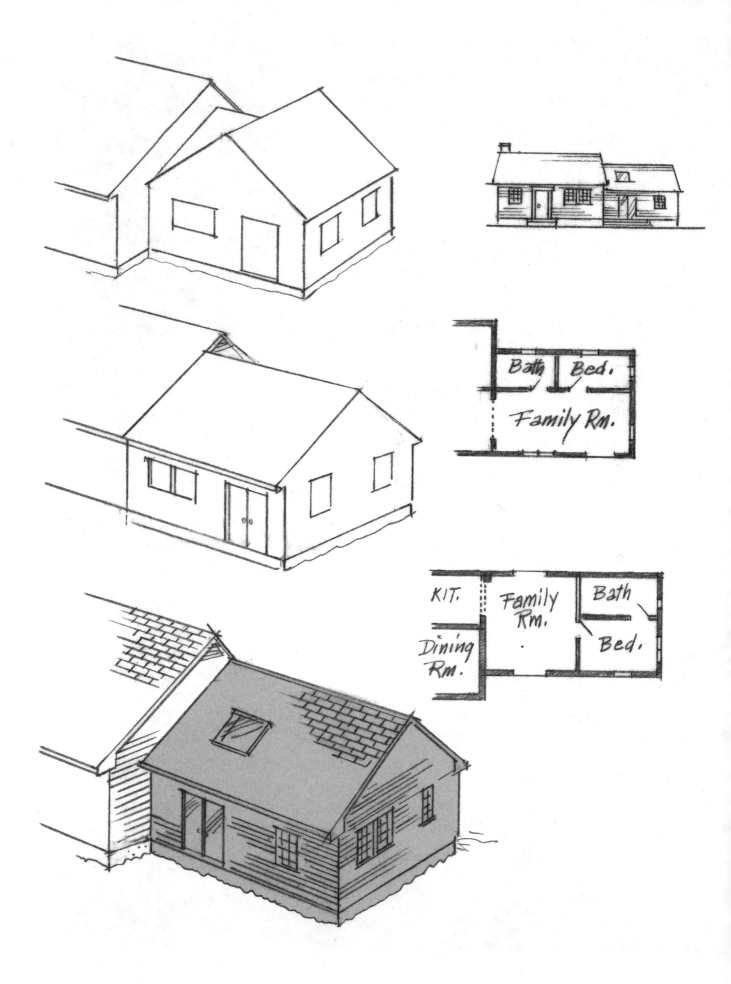

Bath

Bed.

Family Rm.

KIT.

Family Rm.

Bath

Dining Rm.

Bed.

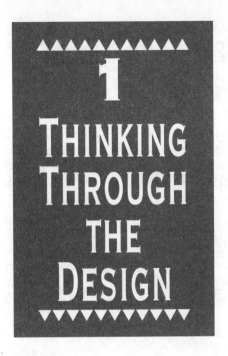

1

THINKING THROUGH THE DESIGN

You can leave, or you can work with what you've got.

These are the two options that face homeowners who find that their lodging has become too cramped for comfortable (or even sane) living. From the statistic that Americans sell their homes every eight years, on average, it's obvious that many choose to leave. We've all heard about the restless American psyche, and the sheer numbers of our real estate transactions suggest that's no myth. Increasingly, however, homeowners are deciding to stay put and invest their time and effort in the current address. Why?

The reasons often have to do with economics. It costs money to move—for taxes, banking fees, and real estate commissions. But beyond actual dollars, moving involves a human expense. It can be wrenching to leave the old neighborhood, with its network of friends, familiar businesses, and schools. That was the reason Jim and Carol Bailey decided to stay put. They opted to add on to their home in southeastern Pennsylvania rather than to pull up roots. An extension into the backyard would displace plantings and scrape away a brick patio. But after the Baileys tallied the pluses and minuses of relocating, moving across town to a new house looked less attractive than moving the back wall of the house 20 feet.

If, like the Baileys, you believe the reasons for staying put add up, this book will help you make the best of your decision, whether you're building up or building out. You can turn the entire job over to professionals—architect and contractor—and restrict your involvement to answering yes-or-no questions and writing checks. You can buckle on a carpenter's belt and wade right into the job, the ultimate do-it-yourself challenge. Or, like most homeowners, you can choose a middle course. That means considering your skills, aptitudes, free time, and budget, then getting involved in some areas of the job and delegating others.

The chapters that follow will help you decide how to do just that. They sketch what each step of the job entails—in tools, know-how, and hours. Armed with foreknowledge, you stand a good chance of making your project a successful one.

In fact, adding on can be one of the most exciting activities a family will share. And this *should* be a family adventure. Everyone's life will be affected by what will extend

▶ MEET THE BAILEYS AND THEIR CREW

Throughout the chapters ahead, you'll visit a backyard in Hatfield, Pennsylvania, as stakes driven into the lawn become a single-story addition. Jim and Carol Bailey recruited contractors Dennis Grim and Ted Currier, who in turn relied on carpenters Barry Frace and Dave Ackerman to do most of the construction. Because the Baileys felt their ideas were not that elaborate, they elected to have an architectural draftsperson produce working drawings rather than to work with a registered archi-tect. They limited their hands-on involve-ment to finish work at the tail end of this adventure.

Expanding their home held some sur-prises ("I never realized there'd be this much dirt," Carol sighed as she looked out over what had been a manicured yard). The finished structure needed some tweaking here and there before the Baileys were sat-isfied. But they ended up with a bright, ef-ficient space that quickly established itself as the new center of the home.

Carol and Jim Bailey

Ted Currier

Dave Ackerman

Barry Frace

into the yard or push up through the roof. So it is best to involve everyone from the earliest stages of planning. As a side benefit, children will have the experience of observing their shelter in the making. They'll see how thoughts are translated into two-dimensional drawings. Then as the project takes on a third dimension, the kids can watch as earth-moving machinery paws the backyard or as saws bite out a chunk of roof for a dormer. Another sort of magic takes place when spindly studs and rafters are filled out to create an intimate, cozy living space.

IMAGINING AN ADDITION

The first step in adding on may be the most challenging—getting a good idea of what you want and picturing how that space will look. Few of us have much experience in planning something this ambitious. So, from the beginning, it helps to be as concrete as possible in your thinking. Visit as many additions as you can. Call on friends and family who have been through the process. If you're comfortable doing it, drop in on people whose houses have recently expanded outward or upward. And while you're imposing, bring along a tape measure and a pad on which to record dimensions.

In time, you'll build a mental inventory of additions that will be more real to you than photos in any magazine or book, although these are worth keeping on hand. You'll learn what room dimensions *feel* like. Does a 10 x 12-foot bedroom seem cramped to you? At a height of 6 feet 6 inches, does the sloping roof of a shed dormer feel too close overhead? Would you be comfortable in a long, narrow room? Do living spaces with lofty cathedral ceilings feel liberating to you or cold and unwelcoming?

Next, pay attention to layout—the ways in which one room relates to another and in which the addition operates as a whole. Informal interviews help here. Ask the homeowners you're visiting how well the addition works. Are there certain rooms that people seem to avoid and others that invite them to congregate? Have there been pleasant surprises? Things they'd do differently?

Get in the habit of thinking of your addition in the context of the house, rather than as a little building that will be plopped down alongside it. These new rooms will do more than increase floor area. It is impossible to tack on an addition without changing the function and feeling of the house you know so well. This seems obvious, yet it is all too often overlooked by homeowners about to add on.

What is now an exterior wall with windows and doors might become an interior wall. Rooms now bathed in sunlight may become quite dark; and those that had been quiet havens may become thoroughfares of household traffic. Properly conceived, the addition can be an antidote to

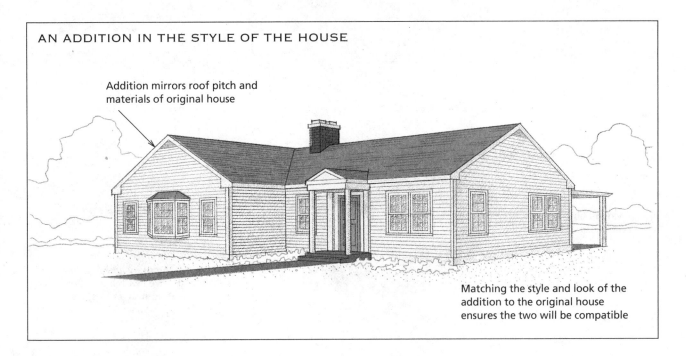

AN ADDITION IN THE STYLE OF THE HOUSE

Addition mirrors roof pitch and materials of original house

Matching the style and look of the addition to the original house ensures the two will be compatible

whatever ails your house. At this conceptual stage, you should feel free to shift walls in both the house and the addition or to remove them altogether. An eraser is as important a design tool as a pencil. For help in thinking through what an addition can do for you, see "Adding On Inventory" on the opposite page.

As you experiment with the inside of the addition, think about the exterior as well. You'll probably find that some projects strike you as ungainly—dormers that resemble solar collectors, wings that look like afterthoughts. Less-successful additions express a lack of care or at least a lack of a sense of design. It's easy to lift your nose at such efforts, and

architects routinely do. Architect Duo Dickinson wrote in his book *Adding On: An Artful Guide to Affordable Residential Additions* that additions not designed by architects are all too often "idiot cousins" and "cancers."

Some additions click aesthetically, for reasons that you might try to solve yourself. A couple of general strategies seem to work best. One is to have the addition's design, materials, and roof style and pitch conform closely to those of the existing house, as shown in *An Addition in the Style of the House* on page 5. This might strike you as restrictive and no fun, especially if the original house is no palace to begin with. It also might be a

difficult course if you have trouble buying materials that match the old. But it is the safer of the two options, in that you probably won't create too wild a mismatch.

The other tactic is to plan an addition that is a clear and intentional departure from the house, while echoing some of the original design elements or materials; see the illustration *Combining Old and New* below. You need some confidence in your design ability in order to improvise successfully. Many homeowners choose to rely on an architect for this aesthetic challenge.

An addition will fit in more gracefully if you pay attention to matching details that you might overlook at first glance.

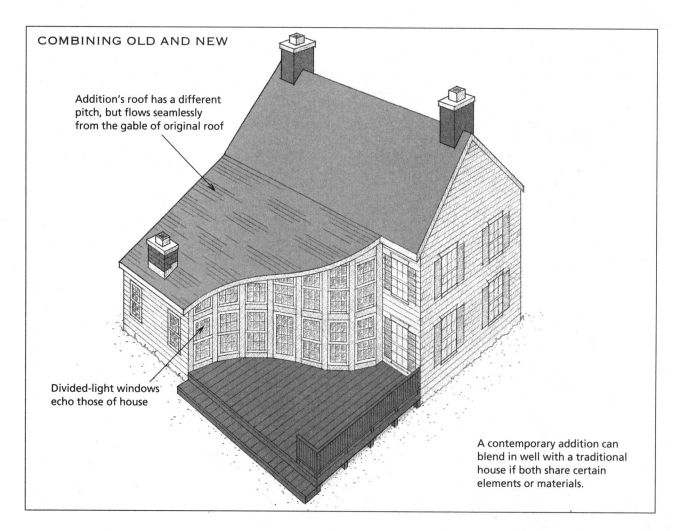

COMBINING OLD AND NEW

Addition's roof has a different pitch, but flows seamlessly from the gable of original roof

Divided-light windows echo those of house

A contemporary addition can blend in well with a traditional house if both share certain elements or materials.

ADDING ON INVENTORY

An addition can compensate for shortcomings your current home may have. Use this work sheet to inventory ways in which your home doesn't quite measure up.

☐ **Rooms too cramped.** Traditional houses tend to be segmented into many rooms, and modern tract houses often are warrens of tiny rooms.

The remedy may be an addition with at least one large, open, airy space. That large space can act as a pressure valve of sorts, making the older part of the house seem more livable.

A less-expensive way to fix cramped rooms is by remodeling—changing the existing structure rather than adding on. The Carter Way family of Saratoga Springs, New York, chose to rip out one wall and lavish money on details rather than bump out the back of their modest-sized house and build new walls. The kitchen is no bigger, but it feels expansive now that there's just a curbed counter separating it from what had been a small formal dining room.

☐ **Too little storage space.** A messy little house with stingy closets can make a family desperate for neatness and order.

If you are tired of living with coats tossed over chairs and recycling containers out in plain view, an addition can provide the storage space you need. However, adding on is an expensive way to get tidy. You owe it to your financial health to consider the alternatives. Investigate storage systems at your local home center and in the Hold Everything catalog (P.O. Box 7807, San Francisco, CA 94120-7807).

☐ **Too dark and dreary.** Some people, like cats, like to sit and even nap in pools of sunlight.

An addition can be designed with big windows and skylights to address this need; if the wall between the addition and original house is removed or perforated in some way, the darkness there can be dispelled as well.

☐ **No privacy.** Privacy means isolation from noise and visual distraction, from vibration (of kids' feet and stereo woofers, for example), and from intrusion (a knock on the door to borrow a stapler).

An addition can work wonders, in that it pushes away from the existing shell of the house. A room at the end of an ell will have a sense of being apart. A less-obvious haven can be made under the eaves with dormers and skylights.

☐ **Poor room layout.** Some houses just don't work well because of a poorly designed floor plan, for example, a living room that serves as the home's main thoroughfare; a kitchen that is a long haul from a carload of groceries; a family room that is so close to bedrooms that noise is a problem.

As you plan an addition, you have an opportunity not only to add new rooms but also to rethink the home's layout.

☐ **An uninteresting house.** Even if your home provides efficient, comfortable shelter, it may not offer the emotional warmth that comes from exceptional design and careful selection of materials.

Now is your chance to put your mark on an indistinguishable residence. A brief list of options for the outside includes cedar siding, unusual window treatments, stained glass, and bay or bow windows. Inside, consider wood floors, cathedral ceilings, built-in cabinetry, a stone or brick fireplace, recycled frame-and-panel doors, window seats, a slate window ledge for plants, wainscoting, and crown molding.

☐ **An unsellable house.** Concerned about resale value?

An addition can be planned with an eye toward what might attract potential buyers. Consult a real estate agent for advice on features that increase a home's value.

A SLIGHT SETBACK

A setback downplays a less-than-perfect match between materials

Examples are the profile of clapboard, the depth of roof overhangs, and molding along the roofline. If you anticipate trouble in matching the exact color of siding or roofing, differences will be less noticeable if the addition is set back slightly, creating a visual break between old and new; see *A Slight Setback* on the left. There is no functional value in this change in the home's perimeter. It merely formalizes the transition between old and new. If you have to live with a less-than-perfect match between materials on the addition and what was used on the house, a setback (and a few years of weathering) will help downplay the difference. A third alternative is to replace the siding or roofing on the house with the same materials you are using on the addition.

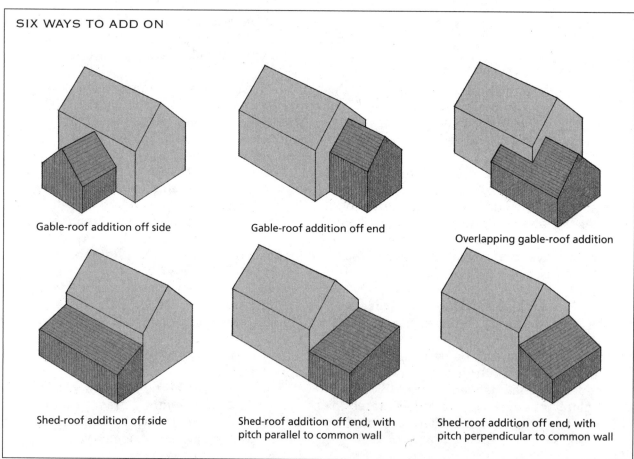

SIX WAYS TO ADD ON

Gable-roof addition off side

Gable-roof addition off end

Overlapping gable-roof addition

Shed-roof addition off side

Shed-roof addition off end, with pitch parallel to common wall

Shed-roof addition off end, with pitch perpendicular to common wall

THINKING THROUGH THE DESIGN

8

DESIGNING WITHIN YOUR LIMITS

Building an addition is fraught with many perils. From foul weather delays to subcontractors doing shoddy work, the ride is rarely free of setbacks. But none is more permanent or less remediable than a poor design. This is especially true for the addition's exterior; it goes up fast but is difficult and expensive to modify once it takes shape.

The ingredients for good design start with the house you already have—capitalizing on its strengths and playing down any weaknesses. Your budget imposes the next set of limits. Municipal regulations restrict how close a dwelling can come to the street and property lines. Other restraints include the location of septic system, well, valuable trees and plantings, and views from existing windows.

Beyond all that, additions are appended to houses in any of several ways, as shown in the photos here. There's no strict formula for success, but imagination, careful planning, and a dose of professional help where needed are surely part of the mix.

An addition can add an interesting wrinkle to an otherwise standard house; here, a bow window extends beyond the face of a two-story addition.

The ranch house, the nearly ubiquitous style of post–World War II America, can be coaxed into something bordering adventurous by adding on large windows and skylights.

If a house has an architectural pedigree, the safest course is to design an addition that works as a variation on the home's theme. This sunny addition uses similar materials and repeats the roof slope of the existing porch.

It can be a challenge to match materials, like the brick siding and asphalt roofing shown here, but weathering will help minimize the splice between old and new.

What's new and what's been added? If people can't tell the difference between new house and old, that's a sign that an addition was planned with care.

A "me too" addition may be the answer if you're already pleased with the looks and function of your house.

Additions are either one story or more. Beyond that, they are appended to the house in any of several ways and may or may not share the roof style of the existing house; see *Six Ways to Add On* on page 8 (bottom). Chances are, you won't have as many options as shown here. On conventional suburban lots, regulations limit how close a dwelling can come to the street and property lines. Before getting very involved in a particular design solution, check with your local zoning authority to learn if such laws will restrict your choices. Other restraints include the location of the septic system, well, valuable trees and plantings, play space in the yard, and great views from existing windows.

DORMER MAGIC

If your house has a gable roof, there may be potential living area tucked under the rafters. A low, dark, uninviting attic can be transformed by adding *dormers*. The term has its root in the Latin word *dormitorius*, meaning "for sleeping," and dormers were used traditionally in top-floor sleeping quarters. Indeed, a converted attic is a logical place to make new bedrooms. On a floor of their own, these rooms tend to be quiet and removed from the high-traffic areas of the house.

Even before-and-after photos can't convey how dramatic a change a couple of dormers make. There is something magical about carving a comfortable, well-lit living space out of what had been a repository for Christmas decorations and old clothes; see Chapter 7 for more information

on adding on with dormers. Because dormers don't enlarge the footprint of the house, they generally are cheaper than tacking on an addition. Chances are, heating and plumbing lines can be extended up from the existing top floor without much trouble. And insulating this new space will help keep the entire house more temperate.

Dormers are described by the style of their roofs, most commonly shed or gable, as explained in "Dormer Decisions" on the opposite page. Keep in mind that gable dormers, although more traditional in appearance, are a bit trickier to build and may add less living space. To coax the most out of an attic, you can *really* raise the roof with a shed dormer that runs the full width of the house.

As with a ground-level addition, dormers can either add to the appearance of a house or detract from it. Take note of dormers on houses in your area. Do they fit in with the house or

overwhelm it? Careful attention to roof pitch, materials, and window selection can make the difference.

ROOF WINDOWS

Perhaps the least costly way to increase living space is to saw out a section of the roof and cover the hole with a skylight. Suddenly, a gloomy attic becomes a cheerful place. And because the glazing of a skylight stands above the ceiling surface, headroom is increased—perhaps enough to allow tucking a bathroom under a low eave. These roof windows, as they're sometimes called, are nothing new. Slate roofs on old British houses are often pierced with modest-sized skylights. Thomas Jefferson even placed several in his home, Monticello.

The simplest sort of roof windows are fixed, or inoperable—they can't be

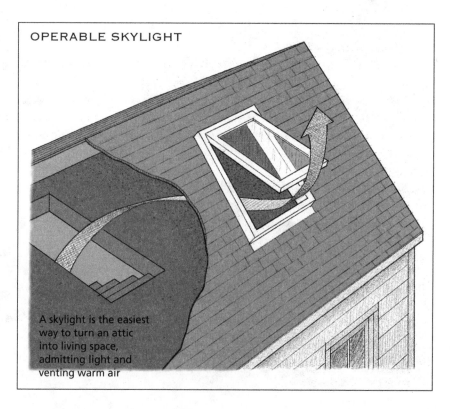

OPERABLE SKYLIGHT

A skylight is the easiest way to turn an attic into living space, admitting light and venting warm air

DORMER DECISIONS

Just as no one hat looks good on every head, some dormers will suit your house better than others. The higher and wider a dormer, the more living space it adds; but big dormers can overpower the rest of the house.

A narrow gable dormer looks traditional, even decorative, as shown in *Gable Dormer* on the right. This type of dormer adds relatively little living space. It does contribute light and ventilation, however, and that may be all you require in an attic with a relatively high roof line. You've probably seen exceptionally broad gable dormers without the side walls illustrated here. The closer the face of the dormer comes to the face of the house, the larger the enclosed space. Headroom in broad gable dormers is especially liberal, and there is plenty of area for windows.

As with a gable dormer, the higher and wider a shed dormer, the greater the space. Another consideration is that a lower pitch will allow more headroom.

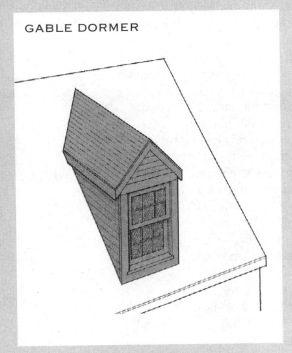

GABLE DORMER

The illustration *Shed Dormer* below also shows how you can make maximum use of your attic by stretching a shed dormer along the width of the roof.

SHED DORMER

opened. Operable skylights are somewhat more expensive but have a couple of advantages. First, and most obviously, they can be opened for ventilation. This is especially handy when high ceilings and attics collect hot air in the summer, as shown in the illustration *Operable Skylight* on page 10. Second, operable skylights from some manufacturers can be rotated, inside for out, so that both sides of the glass may be cleaned from within the house.

Options for skylights abound. You can buy them with screens, small auxiliary vents, custom shades, tinted glass, and long-handled cranks and motors for remote operation. For more on skylights, see Chapters 7 and 9.

PUTTING PENCIL TO PAPER

Armed with dimensions and mental pictures, you're ready to start drawing lines on paper. Get in the habit of conceiving of your project in a couple of ways—the inside world sketched by floor plans and the outside world of elevation views. An elevation drawing is a home as you'd see it from a strictly horizontal viewpoint; the convention is to show just one side, without the use of perspective to suggest a third dimension. Try to bring both the interior and exterior of the addition along at the same time. See *A Plan and an Elevation View* above.

As you refine a particular idea, add rough dimensions of the addition and the rooms within. These numbers will help anchor your fantasies in reality. You might be surprised at how hard it is to fit the rooms you

A PLAN AND AN ELEVATION VIEW

want within a reasonable-sized addition. Then take it to another level of detail—sketch in furniture. You may find that only a few items can be squeezed into the rooms of the plan. People your drawings with stick figures, again to make your renderings correspond with reality. For inspiration, try drawing a measured floor plan of an addition you've visited that seems particularly well thought out.

You can draw your plans

on plain paper, but graph paper with a ¼-inch grid is helpful. The grid ensures right angles without using a drafting triangle. And once you've assigned a scale—say, two squares to 1 foot—you can sketch away without a ruler. For detailed drawings, buy a large, blotter-sized pad of graph paper. Smaller pads will do for rough conceptual sketches.

A standard feature on architectural drawings is an arrow pointing north. It is

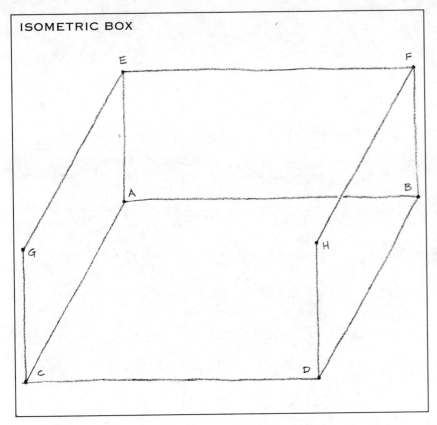

ISOMETRIC BOX

useful for noting the influence of sun and prevailing winds on the home. Depending on your climate, you may want the addition to either embrace the sun for more solar heat or turn away from it to lower heating costs. If your site is buffeted by cold, wet weather out of the Northwest, for example, it might be wise to specify fewer and smaller windows on the northwest wall and locate exterior doors elsewhere.

At this point, you can push your drawing to another level by sketching an isometric rendering. This, in effect, is a bird's-eye view; you are looking down at the project as if it were a dollhouse with the roof and closest wall removed. The point of this view is to bring your thinking a little nearer to studs-and-drywall reality.

For a straightforward rectangular addition, you would begin by drawing two parallel lines, A-B and C-D, as

illustrated in *Isometric Box* above; these represent the bottom edges of two exterior walls. Offset the lines, as shown, so that the closer line begins and ends to either the left or right of the line behind it. The farther apart these lines are, the higher the vantage point will appear to be.

▲▲▲▲▲▲▲▲▲▲▲▲

To quickly test variations of your design ideas, place tracing paper on top of your first drawing, trace the exterior walls, and then mark out your new ideas inside.

▼▼▼▼▼▼▼▼▼▼▼

Next, connect point A with C and B with D, completing a lopsided rectangle that describes the floor. To

establish the walls, draw vertical lines of equal length up from each corner. As illustrated, these lines end at four new points, E through H. Connect them as you did to define the footprint of the addition, but omit the line between G and H.

Now you're ready to turn the box into living quarters, as shown in *Filling In the Box* on page 14. Add interior wall partitions, doorways, windows, and fixed cabinets. In an addition with conventional right angles, nearly all of these features will be sketched with lines parallel to either the front and back walls or the side walls.

As you sketch, erase lines that would be hidden by walls. This makes the drawing clearer and more useful. If you do a good job, your mind will feel invited to occupy the space. And these graphic representations are an opportunity for household members to discuss what seems to be working and what doesn't.

Even a well-drafted sketch is limited, though. To make your ideas really come alive, construct a scale model. This is a standard tool of architects, both to explore ideas and to present them to clients. You can think of a scale model as a drawing in three dimensions.

A good material for your model is foam core board, sold in large sheets at art-supply stores. You'll also need a razor knife to cut the board, a metal-edged straightedge to guide the blade, and straight pins, model cement, or hot-melt glue to keep your little mock-up together.

Begin by picking a scale—a relation between the real-world dimensions of an addition and the downsized lines you'll be able to deal with on a tabletop. The scale should

13

Closet with
bi-fold doors

Door to driveway,
with transom
window

Utility room

Window above
sink

French doors
to deck

Pass-through
to dining room

14

yield a model large enough to see clearly and build easily, but not so large that it will be cumbersome. One-half inch to 1 foot might serve well. Working with the chosen scale, make measured elevation views and a floor plan. If you aren't sure what the dimensions should be, go outside your house and measure the heights of existing walls, including the height of the foundation and roof. Also measure out from the house to a point that is roughly where you think the addition might end.

Transfer the information on these drawings to the foam core, forming floor, exterior walls, and interior partitions. You can omit closets for the sake of simplicity. Make a roof if it involves design features you'd like to preview. Cut out windows, doorways, and skylights. Then assemble the pieces with pins or glue, as

shown in *Foam Core Model* on the opposite page. To strengthen joints, add strips of foam core along interior edges.

▲▲▲▲▲▲▲▲▲▲▲
Another way to anchor your dreams in reality is to go out onto the lawn and pound wooden stakes at what would be the corners of the addition. The stakes should be a bright color and high enough that you won't trip over them or fall on them.
▼▼▼▼▼▼▼▼▼▼▼

You can give a frame of reference to the little structure by adding the wall of the house to which it will be attached; if

you're really ambitious, make a model of the entire house.

A model is more than an interesting conversation piece. It puts your ideas to the test in a way that plan views cannot. It will be especially valuable if the addition involves unusual room shapes and ceiling heights. Cathedral ceilings, lofts, and dormers are difficult to convey on paper, but they come to life in a model.

A model also offers you a chance to try out exterior treatments—siding and roofing materials in different colors and textures. Do a representation of the treatment on paper, and attach the paper to the model with rubber cement or spray adhesive. Remember, this model is to be experimented with, so rearrange rooms and try different materials. And you can *really* play house by adding scaled-down furniture, either purchased or homemade. More simply, you can substitute squares or rectangles to approximate the space each piece would occupy.

FROM SKETCHES TO WORKING PLANS

Large, complex buildings have been constructed from nothing more than a thumbnail sketch. If you decide to do your own drawings, make sure you hire a contractor who is comfortable with the prospect of working from them. Some contractors enjoy the freedom to interpret drawings as the job unfolds; others may see only a potential for disagreement and expensive delays.

Homeowner's Plan on page 16 (top) is an example of a simple drawing that guided the construction of a top-floor renovation; this project included five dormers, two skylights, two rooms, a bath, and new stairs. The contractor agreed to work from this drawing, but the homeowner found it necessary to be on call daily to answer dozens of questions.

Even if you are conscientious about noting details in your drawings, it is nearly impossible to anticipate all of the design problems that will come up on the job. A pitfall of doing your own drawings is that you assume the contractor will know what you have in mind. Interior door styles, closet shelves, soffits, recessed lights, stair tread material, backing in the walls to support towel racks—these are just a few of the items that may be overlooked until the construction is underway. And you can expect a contractor to accommodate only so many

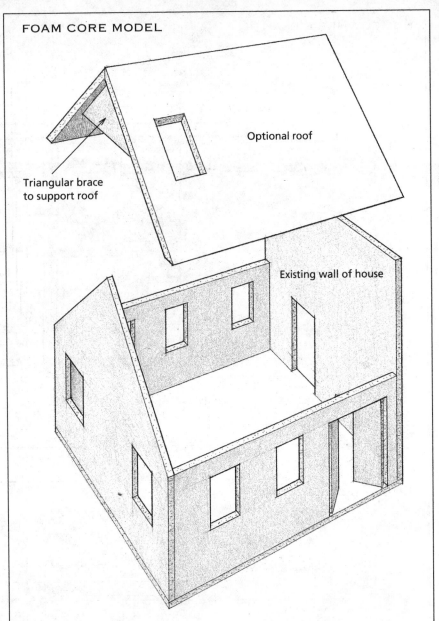

FOAM CORE MODEL

Optional roof

Triangular brace to support roof

Existing wall of house

penciled amendments to the plans before grumbling. Expect to be charged time and materials for such forgotten details, with an additional 10 percent or more tacked on for the contractor's time in administering the changes.

Depending on how ambitious your addition is and on how ambitious you are, you may or may not want help in designing your addition. As with building the structure, you can choose from a continuum of roles in the

design process—from being the check-writing onlooker to being the sole designer.

One big advantage of having a professional draft your sketches is that the information will be expressed in a universally understood code of lines and symbols, leaving as little as possible to chance and imagination. These documents will smooth the weeks ahead by making it clear what is to be done. You can confidently present these drawings to the building inspector when

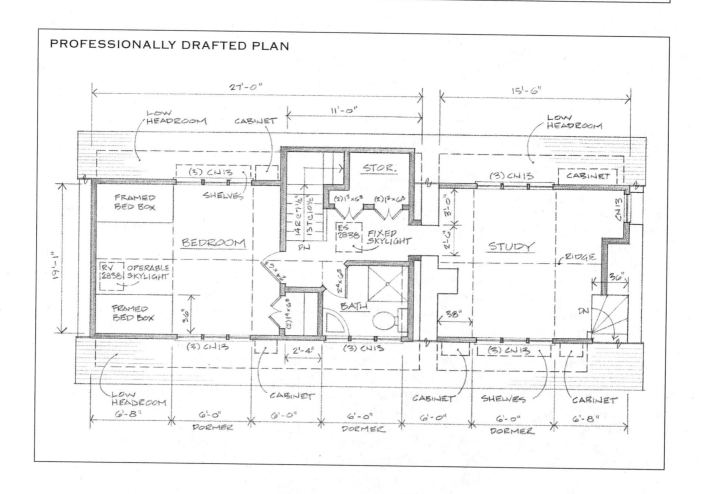

HOMEOWNER'S PLAN

27'-0" 11'-0" 15'-6"

19'-1"

Shelves — Cabinet   Cabinet

Framed bed box   Casements   Closet   Cabinet

Operable skylight   Dormer   Fixed Skylight   Casements   Dormer

Bedroom   Down   Study

Framed bed box   Dormer   Dormer   Down

Casements   Bath   Casements

Closet   Cabinet   Shelves   Cabinet

PROFESSIONALLY DRAFTED PLAN

27'-0" 11'-0" 15'-6"

19'-1"

LOW HEADROOM   CABINET   LOW HEADROOM

(3) CN13   STOR.   (3) CN13   CABINET

FRAMED BED BOX   SHELVES   (2)1³×6⁸ (2)1²×6⁸   CN13

RV 2858 OPERABLE SKYLIGHT   RS 2838   FIXED SKYLIGHT   STUDY   RIDGE

FRAMED BED BOX   BEDROOM   2×6⁸   36"

BATH   DN

(3) CN13   2'-4"   (3) CN13   38"   (3) CN13

LOW HEADROOM 6'-8"   6'-0"   6'-0"   6'-0"   6'-0"   6'-0"   6'-8"

DORMER   DORMER   DORMER

CABINET   CABINET   SHELVES   CABINET

THINKING THROUGH THE DESIGN

16

applying for a permit. And when you solicit bids, contractors may submit lower figures because they don't have to worry about the cost of unforeseen glitches. They'll also have a better idea of what you want and how they might be able to reduce costs with proper planning. *Professionally Drafted Plan* on the opposite page (bottom) is an architect's version of *Homeowner's Plan* on the opposite page (top).

You needn't hire an architect to design and manage the entire project in order to get professionally worked plans. You can hire an architect, designer, or draftsperson by the hour to go over your sketches and then produce the working drawings.

The package of working drawings might include a plot plan, which shows the location of the house and proposed addition on your lot, with dimensions of setbacks from property lines, easements, and utilities; a floor plan for each level; and elevation views.

Even in an age when people routinely hire experts to organize their closets and plan their weddings, many of us are reluctant to hire a professional to design an addition to our home. Perhaps that's because architects, as a group, are often seen as diffident, artsy, and expensive. Added to that is the sense that a stranger, no matter how skilled, cannot create the addition of our dreams out of mere studs and drywall.

In fact, good architects are able to coax half-formed ideas out of a client and translate them into sound designs. Architects are experienced in thinking about space in sophisticated ways that would be a stretch for those of us who find ourselves thinking of an addition in terms of a small box being stuck onto a bigger box.

Good-looking, serviceable additions have been built by homeowners without formal training, too. But the more complex the design challenges—odd angles, tricky roof intersections, steep grades, unusual carving up of space, passive solar technology, adding on to historic properties—the greater the contribution an architect can make.

But not just any architect. You face the challenge of finding someone who is sympathetic to what you want to do. You can begin your search by talking to friends and neighbors who have had happy experiences with an architect (or other designers who are not registered architects; see "Who Is an Architect?" below).

You can widen your talent search by visiting the regional office of the American Institute of Architects (AIA); consult your Yellow Pages. The office may be able to show you photographs of additions done by member architects. Once you find someone with whom you might like to work, arrange

17

 # WHO IS AN ARCHITECT?

Be forewarned that "architect" is a loosely used term, something along the lines of "therapist." Strictly speaking, architects are legally registered by the state in which you live. The training begins with either a five- or six-year undergraduate program or four undergraduate years followed by three in graduate school. Then follows a lengthy internship with an architectural firm, working both in the office and the field. The final hurdle is a rigorous registration exam that lasts a few days. The pass rates for this exam vary widely, with some states posting a low of 15 percent.

Other people plying the architectural trade include architecture majors who have graduated from four-year-degree programs; graduate students who have relatively little work experience; architectural draftspeople; and designers with or without formal training.

You can save some money by working with someone other than a registered architect. But as with any bargain, there are risks involved. For example, a graduate from a four-year school might be a gifted designer but might be short on technical knowledge, which your addition might demand. And a draftsperson's area of expertise might be too narrow to help you stretch your ideas of what your addition could be.

to meet at your house. Be prepared with sketches, rough plans, and photos of designs and details to suggest what you're after. If possible, provide the original drawings of the home. And try to arrive at a reasonable consensus among family members of what you want to achieve with the addition.

Lester M. Stein, an architect practicing in Bath, Pennsylvania, has found that many couples fail to talk through their ideas before calling an architect. "Often through initial discussions, we'll discover that a husband and wife are at odds," he says. "I tell them to go back and rethink. Usually they never come back."

Pay attention not only to the professional's design ability but also to his or her grasp of your needs. An architect who deals with residences is tapping into the intimate center of a family's life—or should be.

Your daily habits, rituals, and leisure time all may be factored into the design.

You should be ready to tell the architect how much you can spend. Some homeowners are reluctant to mention a dollar amount. The concern is that the architect, working on a percentage, will hand them a design that costs every penny of this maximum. But the architect has to know the limits to be placed on the job. It's up to the architect to state figures, as well—the fee for services and just what those services include.

If you haven't worked with an architect, a commission of 10 or 15 percent of the structure's total cost may sound like a steep price for a set of blueprints. But an architect charging that much is probably offering what is known as *comprehensive service* and will be doing far more than drafting plans. This soup-to-nuts

involvement begins with brainstorming about the addition and goes right through managing the construction. Here is a fairly standardized description of what this service involves.

• *Program analysis.* In talking with you and visiting your house, the architect gets an idea of what the project entails and whether or not your ideas can be accommodated within your budget. The architect then develops a "program of spaces," describing the size and anticipated function of areas in the house and addition, and a "program of context," covering the environment and site and how they affect the design.

• *Schematic design.* The architect works up preliminary sketches for you to review and arrives at a rough cost for the job.

• *Design development.* Drawings are taken to a more

 ## KITCHEN EXPERT

Unless you're planning a home chemistry lab, the kitchen will likely be the most sophisticated room in your new addition. Planning a highly efficient, storage-intensive kitchen—one you feel like working in—is a challenge. That's why a relatively new specialist, the kitchen designer, has earned a place in home design.

Fortunately for you, the kitchen designer's fee probably will not come directly out of your pocket. That's because this person usually works for a company that sells high-end cabinets and storage devices. In counseling you on which of the company's products to use, the designer earns his or her wage.

Is this silliness—having a professional tell you where to tuck your pot holders? Not if the new kitchen in your addition

will be a center of your home life and a productive work space. Even architects who orchestrate the whole design-and-construction show are apt to defer to the expertise of the kitchen design specialist. "Kitchen designers are great at figuring out which drawer is for bread and how to organize your silverware," says Daniella Holt Voith, president of the Philadelphia office of the American Institute of Architects (AIA). "You really don't want your architect doing that."

Another reason to go with a kitchen designer is that you'll have access to all sorts of cabinet styles and storage options that you won't find at your local home center. If it is important to you that your kitchen be a cut above the standard, investigate this route.

detailed level. The architect may consult with structural engineers or landscape architects in special cases or a kitchen designer to fine-tune the layout of this room; see "Kitchen Expert" on the opposite page.

• *Construction documents*. The architect prepares the final plans, including a written description of materials and utilities to be used.

• *Bidding*. Armed with the construction documents, the architect (or owner, if the architect's involvement ends here) is ready to solicit bids from contractors. These documents are much more informative than the drawings a homeowner is likely to produce, and bids tend to come in lower; the contractors are less apt to pad estimates if they feel they can clearly see what is involved in the job. "Many times the architect's fee is saved right there," says Stein. Your architect can set up an appointed time during which all prospective bidders visit your house and get a feel for the job. Once the bids are in, you interview the contractors and decide on one.

• *Construction administration*. The architect holds regular meetings at the site, answering the contractor's questions and monitoring progress. The architect checks with you before approving any changes and okays contractor payment requests before forwarding them to you.

▲▲▲▲▲▲▲▲▲▲▲

Hiring an architect will bring a serious bout of sticker shock—10 to 15 percent added to the project's cost. But unless you intend to manage the myriad tasks that an architect performs, from drawings and design decisions to overseeing construction, you probably need one.

▼▼▼▼▼▼▼▼▼▼▼

If you anticipate having trouble overseeing the construction, because you either haven't got the time or simply don't relish the thought, then the architect's involvement at this phase is well worth the added percentage—perhaps a total of 15 percent, compared to roughly 10 or 11 for stopping at the point of getting permits and soliciting bids. You should be clear from the outset on just what services will be provided during the building process.

An architect can also offer *limited service,* which describes any of several alternatives that fall short of seeing through the entire project. Payment may be by the hour or through a reduced percentage of the project's total cost. As an example, an architect might look at your drawings and your house, then offer ideas without putting pencil to paper. You could ask only for preliminary drawings if you have a contractor who is confident in working from them. Another alternative is to hire an architect to take your rough plans and make detailed working drawings from them. As with any other stage of building an addition—framing, roofing, or painting—you can choose your level of involvement and hire out the rest.

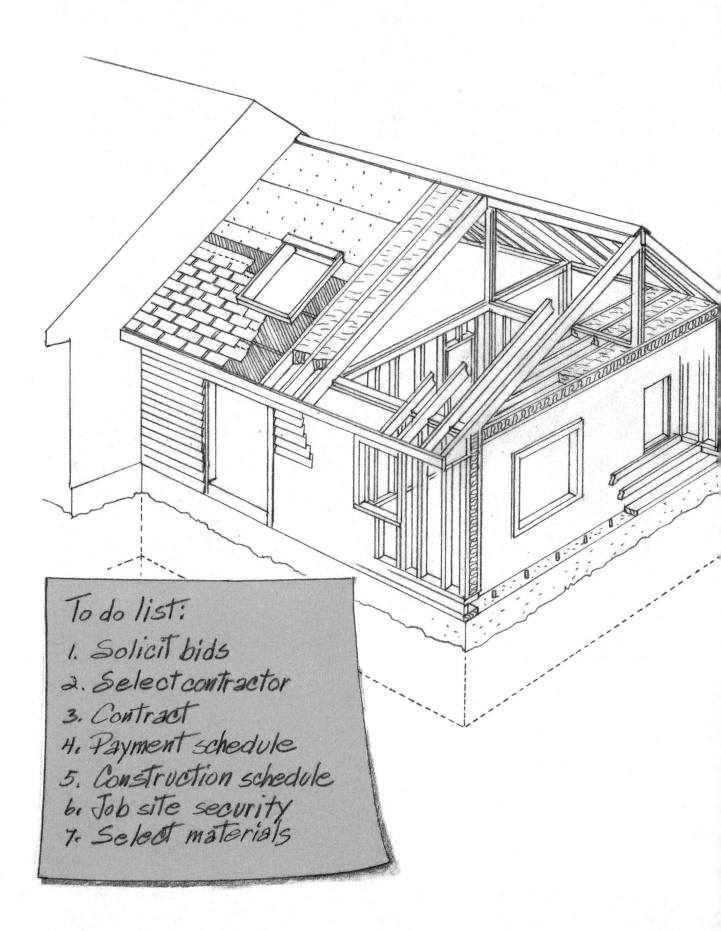

To do list:
1. Solicit bids
2. Select contractor
3. Contract
4. Payment schedule
5. Construction schedule
6. Job site security
7. Select materials

2 MANAGING THE PROJECT

Roaring saws and pounding hammers may give the impression that home construction is a matter of machines and muscle. In fact, the real heroics lie in the planning, improvising, and compromising done by whoever is managing the project.

The title of this person is *contractor* because the essence of the job is contracting with others to do the physical work of piecing the addition together. The contractor is a manager and may work with a cast of anywhere from a couple of people to dozens. Some are apt to be generalists who can do just about anything, and these people will be on the site from excavation through rolling paint over the drywall. Others are specialists of wires or pipe or tile who are lightning fast, highly organized, and gone before

you have had a chance to learn their names.

The contractor organizes the schedules of these players. One may not be able to begin his role until two or three others have finished theirs. In other cases, several parts of the job unfold side by side, and this, too, takes coordination. Self-employed tradespeople (or *subcontractors*) tend to be as independent as cowboys, and getting them to adhere to a schedule can take both pressure and diplomacy.

The contractor manages not only people but also materials. The stuff from which the addition is made must be delivered on time, according to specification, and in good shape; and it must be stored on site without loss to the elements or pilfering. Finally, the contractor manages contingencies— weather, illness, accidents,

unforeseen structural problems with the existing house, flawed working drawings, material shortages, and more.

It's a tough job. Most homeowners hire a pro who has been through this battle dozens of times. The reasons for letting someone else have the headaches are obvious. But others choose to be their own contractors.

THE HOMEOWNER AS CONTRACTOR

First, you may save money by hiring and managing the subcontractors yourself. A contractor earns a living either by making a *fixed-price bid* that factors in a percentage for management or by adding a percentage to the costs of *time and materials* (or *cost plus*), covering actual monies paid out to employees and for materials.

21

The contractor's cut varies greatly from one arrangement to another and from one job to another, but you might be able to spare yourself 10 to 20 percent of the total cost of the job if you serve as contractor.

How experienced should you be to manage the tradespeople who will build your addition? There are books that insist you don't have to know which end of a hammer smacks the screw. But imagine yourself in other managerial roles—walking into a school superintendent's office, climbing aboard a merchant marine ship, or hopping down the steps into a baseball dugout. No matter what the scenario, you'd want to be as prepared as possible.

Any type of human endeavor has its own lingo. In baseball, it's slider, change-up, Texas leaguer, fungo, suicide squeeze. In the building trades, it's float, darby, soffit, rabbet, dado, cripple, chalkline. You can get by without knowing this jargon, but communication becomes awkward; and communication is the essence of managing well.

Before taking on the role of contractor, you would be well served to have some hands-on experience with light construction. This could be a modest weekend project, like making a garden fence and gate or putting together a doghouse. And it's best if you've had the experience of walking up to the service desk of a building-supply store and placing an order for lumber. As simple as that sounds, it can be intimidating to find your way around a lumberyard. You might also visit electrical- and plumbing-supply firms that sell primarily to the trade. These businesses typically have a wide selection and can order almost anything imaginable; and if you have an account with them, you may be able to buy at a discount (see "Applying for an Account" below).

Another point to ponder as you consider hiring yourself as contractor is how well you'll deal with tradespeople. First you have to find them. If you don't have a list of dependable subcontractors you or friends have worked with, you are at a disadvantage. The Yellow Pages are a fine resource, but they don't tell you much about dependability and character. Even contractors, who give subcontractors (subs) repeat business, can have trouble getting someone to show up at the appointed time.

Think about the potential for stress. It's your money trickling away and your house being surgically altered. As homeowner, managing your own addition is a little like dentists drilling their own teeth—you may find you're too personally involved to do a good job.

The difficulty of acting as your own contractor is tied with the complexity of the addition. At the simple end of things, you'd be the contractor if you hired a carpenter to tack on a small deck out back, and you'd think little of it. But a large addition with several types of living space might involve subcontractors to handle the excavation, foundation, concrete floor, insulation, roofing, wiring, plumbing, heating system, tile, kitchen cabinets, each of two or three types of flooring, dry-walling, and painting. On top of this, you would be ordering and stockpiling building materials, itself a potential headache; see "Keeping an Eye on the Site" on the opposite page. A project of this scale requires that do-it-yourself contracting be treated as a part-time job.

You may find some management help from your architect, if you've hired one. An architect can oversee construction as well as provide design services (see Chapter 1).

THE HOMEOWNER AS WORKER

Instead of electing to be the brains of the project, you might want to be the brawn—or at least one of the laborers. You

 ## APPLYING FOR AN ACCOUNT

It's a rule of business that you pay less for buying in quantity. If you will be ordering materials for your addition, you should be able to get substantial discounts from suppliers—savings often not available to a customer walking into a supply house and buying a couple of items.

Qualifying for a discount usually involves opening an account with these firms. Unless you are an established contractor, that means providing credit references as you would if applying for a credit card. Allow time for the paperwork to be processed before placing your first order.

Your job site may be particularly attractive to others, especially young kids. "Kids are fascinated with construction and machinery," said Dennis Grim, contractor for the Baileys' addition. And they are rarely aware of how dangerous machines or a job site can be. So before Dennis starts a job, he writes to the client's neighbors asking for their cooperation in keeping children away from the project.

The building materials delivered to your yard may be attractive, too, for another reason—they're valuable. Stolen supplies are your liability. Talk to your insurance agent to see if any losses will be covered by your homeowner's policy.

If adding on means making big holes in your walls, the rest of your house will be more vulnerable to theft than usual. The contractor should take responsibility for securing your house as windows, doors, and walls are removed. This can be done by nailing plywood over openings and installing temporary locks.

could act as a subcontractor, taking over one area of the job that you would like to handle, such as roofing or drywalling. Or you could ask the contractor or a sub about signing on as one of the crew.

Some homeowners do it just for the experience. They want to make the most of this process and learn skills along the way (see "Tools for Your Big Adventure" on pages 24–25). Others expect to be remunerated. If you are being charged on a time-and-materials basis (an hourly labor rate plus the cost of building materials), then your contribution should show up in a lower figure for hours billed. If instead there is a fixed-price bid—a lump sum agreed upon at the outset—then you could ask to be paid a wage commensurate with your skill. Not all contractors will welcome the opportunity to have you join the crew. But some are honest in saying that they enjoy working alongside an outspoken homeowner.

Of the many roles in building an addition, which are best suited to the homeowner?

That depends on several factors, including how much time you can devote to a task, how handy you are with the tools or machines that will be used, and how much money you can save by doing the work yourself. There's a fourth factor as well: How much you're viewing this project as an opportunity to learn the building trade.

Working on an addition can help you to perfect skills that you can apply to later projects.

TO DIY OR NOT TO DIY

Just as with any job out in the workplace, the several distinct tasks of building an addition will appeal to some people and cause others to tremble, recoil, or simply yawn. Think carefully before assigning yourself any of the jobs described in this book. If possible, visit a house or addition in progress to see if you have the skills, tools, and temperament that are involved with each of the following tasks.

• *Excavation and foundation.* Mistakes made

here will be hard to cover up. There's no hiding a misaligned foundation or sagging footers by slapping on some trim. Renting a backhoe for a day may be an adventure, but an inexperienced operator shouldn't expect to save much, if anything, in the process. A good pro has developed the facility to use that steel claw like a third hand and can work quickly and accurately, with less threat to bystanders and the foundation of your existing house.

Stand back and enjoy the show. (And prepare a list of other projects the operator might do—dig a reflecting pool, holes for fruit trees, or evenly distribute gravel along the driveway, to suggest a few.) See Chapter 3.

• *Framing.* Workmanship is not so critical here. Dings and botches will be covered up later. The materials and tools will be familiar to most weekend dabblers in home repair. Erecting walls and lifting rafters into the sky do require help— family members, friends, or hourly wage carpenters. See Chapters 4, 5, and 6.

(continued on page 26)

TOOLS FOR YOUR BIG ADVENTURE

It often seems that the tools themselves, rather than the skills applied to them, are behind a person's decision either to embrace or avoid a particular homebuilding task. Some people are intrigued by the high-wire act that scaffolding promises; others might be drawn to sweating copper pipe with a torch. Here you'll find a quick survey of some equipment that might be called upon in the months ahead. One of the first tools on the site is a *builder's level,* which is used to lay out the addition and establish vertical measure-ments. A small telescope pivots on a stand to allow you to pick up a reading in one place and transfer it to another. This expensive, sensitive tool is a logical candidate for renting.

Another tool that gets called on early in the project is a *chalkline* (shown on the right). It is used to make long, straight lines between two points, a task that comes up often when laying out a project of this scale. A chalkline looks something like a fishing reel. The container holding the line also stores a supply of powdered chalk. As the line is drawn out, it is dusted with the powder. The line is then held taut between two points and plucked like the string of a musical instrument, leaving a faint—but unerringly straight—trace of chalk.

Chalkline

Scaffolding is the spidery metal framework that supports the platform that supports the workers. It is awkward to move, put up, and knock down, especially if you are working solo. But there is no good substitute for the combined jobs of framing; putting up roofing, siding, and gutters; and painting. Scaffolding also serves as a loading and staging platform for supplies. And it has spared the bones of roofers who have lost their purchase on a slippery pitch.

There are other ways to get a lift. *Pump jacks,* shown below (bottom), are metal brackets that travel up and down vertical poles made on site from doubled-up 2 x 4s. The jacks are raised by pumping a foot pedal. *Ladder jacks,* shown below (top), are brackets that attach to a pair of extension ladders and support a narrow platform. *Roof brackets* are nailed through to rafters and support a platform for workers laying down roofing; adjustable models can be adapted for a variety of pitches.

Ladder jacks

Pump jacks

It might seem that the hammer would be the least likely tool to be powered by technology, but *air-powered nailers* are the rule on many job sites. A compressor sends pressurized air through a hose to the nailer, and you pull a trigger to fire. The work goes faster than hammering by hand and is less fatiguing. Countering those advantages are a couple of drawbacks: The compressor is noisy when it kicks in to recharge the air tank, and a standard hammer will do a better job of drawing a joint tight as the nail is driven home. An air nailer and compressor are expensive tools; look into renting them.

A minor (but persistent) frustration of building an addition is that most of the work is done with electrical tools, yet there isn't a wall outlet to be had. A *cordless electric drill* (shown below) works independently of extension cords. Ongoing improvements in battery technology have made this a tool for serious work, especially models running on 12 volts or better. Buy a second battery pack so that you can keep on drilling as you recharge; or buy a "fast charger" that can get the drill back on the job in just 10 to 15 minutes.

Although a *screw gun* looks like the familiar variable-speed electric drill, it is a specialized tool that finds use in a dozen ways—whenever a screw would do a better job than a nail. Although a drill can be used to drive screws with a screwdriving blade in the chuck, a screw gun has the advantage of disengaging as the screw is driven home. This feature, made possible by a clutch, protects the motor from strain and prevents screws from penetrating too far—as when installing easily damaged drywall.

A *power miter saw,* shown below, can be used throughout the job, from cutting framing members to length to making angled (or "mitered") cuts on trim. On some models, the circular blade pivots as it is lowered through stock to be cut; on others, the blade is pulled forward, pivoted down into the wood, and then pushed away to make the cut. The blade can be swiveled to cut the stock at a variety of angles. And on compound-miter saws, the blade also can be tilted to make a cut that is mitered in two dimensions. This is useful for making tricky rafter and stud cuts and for fitting molding.

Miter saw

The plane, which produces curls of wood, is such a toolbox standard that it has become something of a logo for the woodworking trade. Today, however, a carpenter is more likely to plug in a *power plane,* a hand tool that is as fast as it is noisy (shown below). It can be used to straighten framing members, trim doors to size, dress old stock so that it looks new, and chamfer down the length of a board in seconds. This is a tool you may find yourself calling on long after the addition is done, so consider buying rather than renting.

Cordless drill

Power plane

• *Roofing.* This is a straightforward step in construction and difficult to foul up. But a steep pitch ups the ante—the more precipitous the roof, the more dangerous and the more fatiguing the job will be. See Chapter 8.

• *Siding, windows, and exterior doors.* Siding goes up without a lot of decision making, much like roofing but not quite so far from the ground. Just one person is needed to shingle walls, while clapboard is best handled by two. While vinyl siding seems as though it would be simplicity itself to install, the material expands a good deal with changes in temperature, and the panels may bind and buckle; traditional wood siding is more forgiving. Windows and doors are not difficult to install, but they may be awkward to handle without help. See Chapters 9 and 10.

• *Plumbing.* Local restrictions may prevent you from getting involved here. Check with your building inspector. Plumbing is not an abstract craft, as long as you're familiar with the effect that gravity has on water. But it is a nuisance tracking down the hundred and one fittings you'll need; a plumber will have them on his truck, while you'll be making repeat trips to the supply store.

Note that this job shares the tight space between framing members with two other activities, wiring and insulation. That means coordination is necessary between the trades. Promptness counts, too, because the honeycomb within the walls soon will disappear behind drywall. See Chapters 11 and 16.

• *Wiring.* Again, local restrictions may discourage you from doing much, if any, of this work. If you want to get involved, you should have a good sense of how electricity performs its wonders. You might take evening courses in theory and hands-on practice at your local vo-tech school. Another tack is to hire a licensed electrician to consult as you plan, rough in, and finish the addition's system. See Chapters 12 and 17.

• *Insulation.* If you choose fiberglass batts, the materials are easy to manage, though scratchy. Sprayed foam or cellulose should be handled by a contractor. See Chapter 13.

• *Heating and cooling.* This is heavy-duty work that will hold little appeal for most homeowners, as you'll learn in Chapter 14. Chances are you'll want to invest your time elsewhere. But be on hand when the systems are installed so you can get a quick course in operating and maintaining them.

• *Drywalling.* Drywall is cheap, fairly easy to handle, and won't leak water or voltage if you mess up. Still, even veteran contractors often hire this job out. Professional drywallers can get in and out of the addition in the time it would take you to learn to feather an edge of drywall compound. With this said, making those seams disappear can be among the addition's satisfactions if you're a patient perfectionist. And if you're not, you might hang the drywall and hire pros to come in and do the finicky work of spackling. See Chapter 15.

• *Flooring.* Sheet vinyl is not difficult to cut to fit a room, and it glues down with little fuss. Traditional wood flooring is an attractive material to work with, and the various species—pine, oak, walnut—fill the air with their distinctive incense as they are sawed and sanded; consider putting the floor down yourself, hiring out the tricky job of sanding, and then doing your own finishing. Wall-to-wall carpeting is usually installed by the retailer. See Chapter 18.

• *Interior finish work.* Aside from manufactured cabinets (see Chapter 20), the components are small and easy to manage. Ladders are short. And most, if not all, of the other workers will have completed their jobs and gone home by the time the work starts. That means you can hang the trim in peace and quiet—over the next five or ten years if you are like many homeowners. Because trim really isn't a system in any sense of the word, it's possible to work on it piecemeal and at your leisure. The job is particularly suited to weekend woodworkers with an interest in fitting one piece of wood to another. A power miter saw is a nearly indispensable tool for this job. See Chapter 19.

• *Painting.* Painting (covered in Chapter 21) requires relatively modest skills and a small outlay for equipment. You can do as good a job, or better, than most professionals, and most of the expense of hiring out the job goes to labor. Care with caulking, masking, and cleanup makes all the difference; it just happens to be time-consuming. As with interior trim, painting comes at the tail end of the project, so it is a logical choice for the homeowner's involvement.

HIRING A CONTRACTOR

Unless you have hired an architect to oversee the construction and act as a buffer between you and the day-to-day drama taking place at your home, you will be dealing with the contractor yourself. That can be either a memorably difficult relationship or one that you'll look back on as a pleasant part of adding on. You can help nudge the Fates in a favorable direction by researching contractors before accepting a bid.

The best way to find candidates is through personal referrals. As you gather the names and numbers of contractors, ask how these managers were to work with. Was the contractor there to keep the job moving smoothly and answer the owner's concerns rather than just dropping in from time to time? How many people were on the job? Was it enough to make gratifying progress or did the work seem to drag? Were the specifics on payment, changes in plan, and materials made clear? How did the contractor do in meeting deadlines and keeping within a budget? How were suggestions and changes received? Was the contractor receptive to dealing with both the man and woman of the house?

Once you've determined how well your potential contractors work, you can look at how much each one will cost. In order for you to compare bids, the contractors have to be dealing with the same conditions.

When you get in touch with contractors, ask them to bid on the same job with the same materials. That is, be specific about what the job entails. An architect's detailed plans and specifications should establish this; otherwise, it is up to you to supply the details. For example, state that you want beveled white cedar clapboard, if that's your preference, rather than wood siding.

When you settle on a bidder, the first order of business is to determine the *payment schedule.* How will the contractor be paid? This may already be laid out in the contractor's bid, but it is negotiable. In most cases, you are expected to make partial payments, or *draws,* at each of several stages of the project.

▲▲▲▲▲▲▲▲▲▲▲

Try to get between three and five bids for your job. Then, rather than pounce on the lowest one, consider each contractor's reputation and project how each would be to work with.

▼▼▼▼▼▼▼▼▼▼▼

This allows the contractor to purchase materials and pay the crew over the period of the job. See *A Sample Contract* on page 28.

As mentioned above, the bid will be expressed as either a simple fixed fee or an estimate based on projected time and materials. This estimate should be a maximum, worst-case figure, above which the contractor will not go; otherwise, you are entering into an open-ended relationship that could take you well beyond your budget. However, some contractors (and subs) resist placing a cap on an estimate, reasoning that if the job's unknowns eat up a lot of money, they may be donating labor and materials toward the end of the project. From your perspective, the contractor might cut corners to compensate for the shortfall.

Such miscalculations in bidding are more common with additions than with new construction because the contractor is not dealing with a blank slate; instead, your house has hidden flaws and idiosyncrasies. Before agreeing to an open-ended contract, you should know something of the person's record; and you'll want to monitor closely both the flow of money and the progress being made.

Money isn't the only sensitive commodity in a contract; another is time. The contract should specify a completion date or even a succession of dates by which major stages of construction are to be done. Any homeowner is anxious to have the project done, of course; but for the homeowner who is living in the middle of the job site, anxiety creeps to a higher level. Construction is noisy, dirty, and distracting. You are apt to have workers using the telephone and the plumbing, unless you've disallowed this in the negotiation stage.

To help ensure that the completion date is realistic, you can ask that yours be the only project a contractor takes on for the duration. If the crew is hopping between three or four sites, your project may drag on. The way in which payments are structured by the contract can put teeth in the stated deadline; if a relatively large payment is withheld until satisfactory

28

Form #401

Colin Ray
WOODWORK & DESIGNS
R. R. 4, 912 Centre Line,
Peterborough, Ont. K9J 6X5

CONTRACT PROPOSAL

To Mr. and Mrs. Allistair Wallace   Date November 8, 1983

45 Strickland Avenue

Lakefield, Ontario   KOL 2HO   652-8697

Dear Sir:

The undersigned proposes to furnish all materials and perform all labour necessary to complete all the work described below:

To finish attic per conversation and as outlined:

- Build 18' dormer with 7' exterior wall on south side with 4 Mason Awning windows 40 x 48" thermo-glazed and painted
- Ceiling dropped to 8' - joists built to 10" with 6" insulation throughout
- ½" underlay and carpet on floor at $15.00/yd installed
- attic to be divided into 2 bedrooms, each with a closet; 1 - 3 pc. toilet on raised floor; balance of attic to have 1 large clothes closet and 1 under-eave storage on north wall
- Electrical work to include 29 outlets and adequate thermostatically controlled baseboard heaters
- dormer to be clad in aluminum siding
- entire roof to be re-shingled with 210# asphalt shingles, special low slope roof at dormer - including 4 roof louvers
- eavestrough to be replaced on entire house, porches and dormer
- chimney brick seems to be quite sound
- access stairway to be built, and risers & TREADS covered with carpet, under-stair storage to be provided (total stairway made to conserve space in bedroom below.)
- Present wall between hall and bedroom removed and a wall with doorway and closet to be constructed at foot of stairs to complete the bedroom.
- all plaster work to be repaired and all trim made good   .../2

All of the above work to be completed in a good and workmanlike manner for the sum of _____
_____ ($ 25,597.00   ) Dollars.

Payments to be made as follows:

INCL. 30x55 VELUX + SCREEN.   FIRE ESCAPE
1/3 at start   ROPE LADDER
1/3 at rough plumbing stage
balance on completion

Any changes in the work and the price to be charged for same shall be made in writing.

This proposal is made on the basis of current material and labour costs. A delay in acceptance of more than _____
days will require a review of the proposal and re-dating before the agreement becomes binding.

Respectfully Submitted,

ACCEPTANCE

You are hereby authorized to furnish all materials and labour to complete the work mentioned in the above proposal, for which the undersigned agrees to pay the amount mentioned in said proposal, and according to the terms thereof.

Date _____   _____

Please sign and return one copy if you wish to proceed with this work.

COPYRIGHT   FORM 401   systemforms

completion of the job, the contractor has more incentive to wrap things up.

It's a given that you will be inconvenienced as the work goes on, but much can be done to minimize the migration of dirt, dust, cigarette smoke, and noise. Contractors or subs can be asked, or required through the contract, to take precautions.

Outside deliveries and parking can be restricted to one area to avoid savaging the entire lawn. Shrubs and planting beds around the construction site should be tarped. Valuable trees should be moved or protected where they stand with heavy wraps or simple nailed-up cages.

Inside, the addition should be sealed off from the house with polyethylene sheets, at the least. Plywood will do a better job of excluding noise, and it offers security as well. You can do your part by moving vulnerable furniture and carpets out of rooms adjoining the addition as much as possible.

WAYS TO PAY

Dennis Grim, one of the team of two contractors for Jim and Carol Bailey's addition, scheduled five points at which he would submit an invoice for the draws, each time showing the balance remaining. Colin Ray, a Peterborough, Ontario, contractor, scheduled just three for a top-floor addition—a third on signing, another third at the rough plumbing stage, and the final third upon completion.

"Completion" is a matter subject to interpretation. Who determines when the job is truly done, so that the last payment

is due and the crew can pack up and leave? A contract can be written to withhold 10 percent of the total payment to ensure that the job is done to the homeowner's satisfaction. As the project winds down, a contractor may ask you to prepare a *punch list*. This is your list of items that you decide still need to be addressed by the contractor, ranging from big (replacing a cracked toilet) to picayune (adding a daub of caulk here and there).

▲▲▲▲▲▲▲▲▲▲▲

Don't end the bidding process after choosing a contractor. You may be able to save substantial amounts of money by soliciting bids for many types of materials such as lumber, siding, plumbing pipe, and light fixtures.

▼▼▼▼▼▼▼▼▼▼▼

A contract can include *allowances*—stated sums that break out the costs of specific items. For example, the contractor may have prepared the bid with an allowance of $1,500 for carpeting. If you think this is an unreasonably low or lavish figure, say so before signing. Otherwise, you face the prospect of paying more later for a carpet you can live with or spending more than you can afford for carpeting.

To reduce the unknowns before signing a contract, you can do as the Baileys did and go to home centers and suppliers and pick out the fixtures yourself; note the cost and item

numbers, then relay this information to the contractor.

Careful planning will minimize surprises in the construction process. But plan as you will, you'll probably spot something that can be improved once work gets under way.

Change orders are formal requests a homeowner makes to alter the plans or specifications after the contract has been signed. As an example, it might occur to you that a recycled stained-glass window would look great in the wall above the kitchen sink. A nice idea—but you shouldn't expect the contractor to accommodate this extra detail without charging for the trouble.

The change order is a written agreement between you and the contractor that spells out what such an alteration will involve in time and materials; the contractor may also add a percentage for supervising this change. The order should be signed by both parties. Note that a change order might also involve a saving if a feature is omitted or simplified; in this case, the paperwork should make clear who is to benefit from the spared labor or materials.

Change orders, whether of your making or the work of chance, can add thousands of dollars to the figure you agreed upon at the bottom of the contract. The Baileys signed more than a half-dozen change orders as their addition was built; these covered the cost of adding wiring, lights, and windows to the original plan, hauling away the mountains of excavated dirt from the backyard, sealing up the walls of the entire house with Tyvek, upgrading the wall insulation, and—small, but significant—

adding a motion detector to the exterior floodlights. The better you can anticipate your needs and the requirements of the site, the smaller this unexpected surcharge will be.

Contractors, and subcontractors as well, may include in their contracts a term that protects them from extraordinary time and expense in the event of *unforeseen conditions*. Life is full of unforeseen conditions, and a few are probably lurking in your addition-to-be. A mammoth boulder might rest beneath the backyard lawn. The wall that your new wing is to adjoin may be devastated by termites. The responsibility for paying for setting such conditions straight is often left vague in a contract, with a clause stating only that owner and contractor should negotiate a fair arrangement.

The contract should require the contractor to carry insurance to cover both injury to workers and damage to your property. You should be protected by a clause stating that you will not be subject to *liens* from the contractor, subcontractors, or suppliers. A lien is a legal claim filed by someone who has not been paid for work or materials that went into the project. Contractors do go out of business; theirs is a speculative venture, vulnerable to the vagaries of weather, materials costs, clients, and bids that are well off the mark, and you don't want to be left liable for their unpaid bills.

Ask the contractor you choose to include in the contract a *waiver* of liens, protecting you from having to pay subcontractors and suppliers. The contract can provide that the contractor's final payment will be withheld until the contractor signs an affidavit stating that all parties have been paid in full. If an architect will be managing the project, he or she can help you secure a waiver.

To protect yourself against flaws in workmanship, there should be a clause in which the contractor warranties the work for at least one year after the date of completion.

DEALING WITH THE LAW

The building process is closely monitored by government agencies, more so in some areas than in others. Agencies want to be involved in your

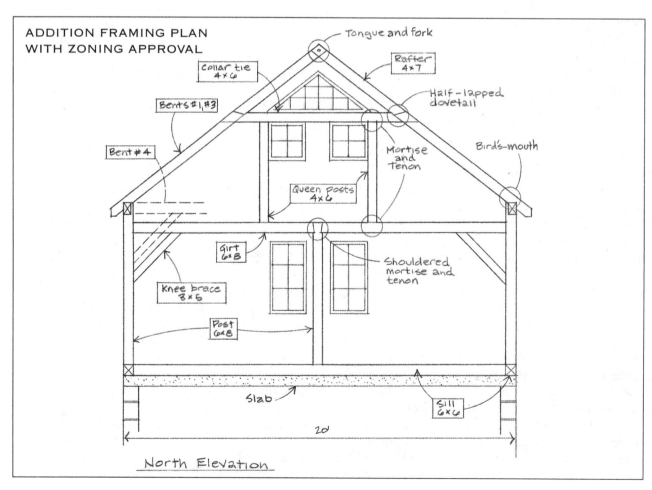

ADDITION FRAMING PLAN WITH ZONING APPROVAL

Tongue and fork

Rafter 4×7

Collar tie 4×6

Half-lapped dovetail

Bents #1,#3

Bird's-mouth

Bent #4

Mortise and Tenon

Queen posts 4×6

Girt 6×8

Shouldered mortise and tenon

Knee brace 3×5

Post 6×8

Slab

Sill 6×6

20'

North Elevation

addition for a couple of reasons. First, it is considered a matter of public health and safety that your building be soundly constructed. Second, an addition often is cause for a higher real estate tax assessment.

Be leery of running afoul of government regulations. Walls have been ripped apart because an inspector was not called in at the appropriate time to have a peek at the wiring.

To begin, you'll need to apply to the building inspector for a permit. The procedure of getting a permit is straightforward in more-rural communities, but may be confusing and time-consuming in cities; if neighbors report they had trouble getting through the legal maze, consider hiring an architect or contractor to take care of this stage for you.

Your application will have to be accompanied by other documents, which may include floor plans, an elevation view, and a site plan showing the setbacks of the project from property lines. Your plans will be examined to see if they meet the *building code* used by your local government. Building codes are concerned with construction and cover foundations, framing, wiring, and plumbing. Part of a homeowner's approved framing plan for a post-and-beam addition is shown in *Addition Framing Plan with Zoning Approval* on the opposite page.

To prove that your addition is being built according to code, you will have to schedule visits for the building inspector. The type

and number of these visits vary greatly from one locality to another; be clear at the outset what will be expected of you. Inspectors may want to see the excavation and forms before concrete is poured, rough electrical work, rough plumbing, rough framing, and final wiring, among other things. Local building departments may sell copies of the code for residences; bookstores are another possible source.

Construction is also governed by *zoning ordinances* covering such subjects as

minimum lot size, height of the dwelling, setback from the street, and minimum distances between dwelling and property lines. You may have to submit a map, based on one filed by the local government, on which you superimpose the distances from the proposed addition to roads and property lines; see the illustration *Setback Map* above. If an ordinance would make it difficult for you to build your addition as you wish, you can appeal to the local zoning board for a *variance*—an exclusion for that provision of the law.

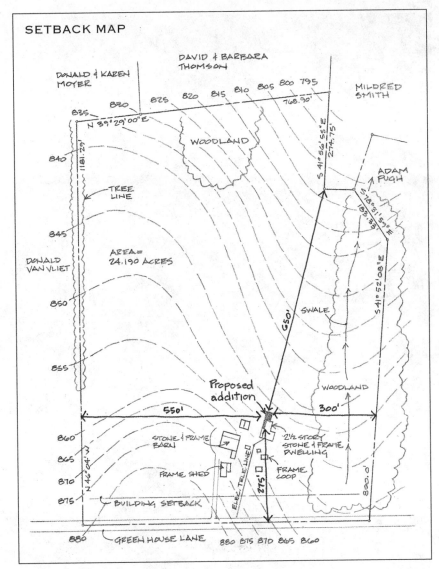

SETBACK MAP

DEFINING THE STRUCTURE

With the loud alchemy of hammers and saws, the abstract idea of an addition is first transformed into two-dimensional walls and then into a three-dimensional form as the walls are lifted into place. Well, not quite 3-D. Wind blows right through the studs and rafters, and the empty cagelike rooms put off their own clean, piney scent. The rough plywood platform sets the stage for the interconnected roles of tradespeople who will be visiting this site.

3
THE
FOUNDATION

It was almost noon when Dean Shellhammer pulled up in front of the Baileys' house with his excavating equipment in tow. More than 3 inches of rain had put other excavating jobs he had scheduled underwater, but Dean guessed that the ground at the Baileys' site would be dry once he had dug a foot or so below grade. The forecast called for good weather all week, and Dean was confident he could be in and out within two or three days.

All was normal at the front of the house, where Carol Bailey had her Halloween decorations in the windows. But behind the house, the backyard was about to be transformed. Dennis Grim had already laid out the addition with stakes, measuring out from the house the necessary distances. He

then spray painted lines on the ground between the stakes, showing Dean where to dig. This was the footprint of the Baileys' foundation.

Any structure, even a tree house, needs to be anchored to the earth in some way; see the illustration *Types of Foundation* on page 36.

The most common foundation is the *continuous wall*—all sides of a building rest on walls that extend below grade. These walls can be built from stone, brick, steel, wood, or clay tile, but most are of poured concrete or concrete block. For a poured foundation, forms are erected and filled with concrete. As the concrete cures, the walls become a single, monolithic mass. This is the foundation the Baileys would use. The job might also have been done with concrete blocks, stacked individually and held together

with either mortar between them or a coating on the outside.

With a *pier* foundation system, the building is supported on individual piers placed at intervals. The piers are usually made from poured concrete, brick, or concrete block. While a pier system is usually less expensive than a continuous wall foundation, it has two drawbacks: There is no way to include a basement, and the structure is less securely anchored against strong winds.

A type of pier system, the *pole* foundation consists of large poles sunk into the ground to carry the weight of the building. This is exceptionally strong and ideally suited to steep sites, where a masonry foundation would require extensive excavation. Pole foundations are also used along coastal areas and in flood

TYPES OF FOUNDATION

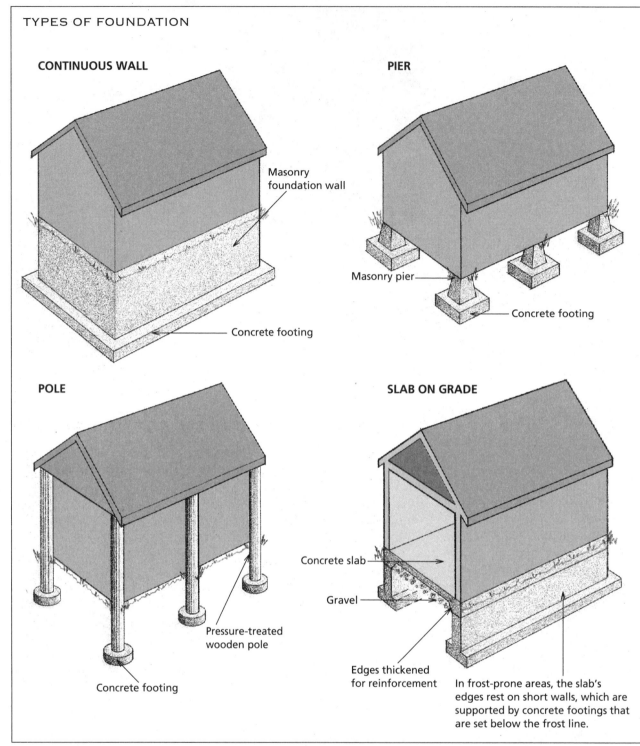

CONTINUOUS WALL

Masonry foundation wall

Concrete footing

PIER

Masonry pier

Concrete footing

POLE

Pressure-treated wooden pole

Concrete footing

SLAB ON GRADE

Concrete slab

Gravel

Edges thickened for reinforcement

In frost-prone areas, the slab's edges rest on short walls, which are supported by concrete footings that are set below the frost line.

plains, where codes call for buildings to be elevated above a certain level.

The poles can either carry a platform on which the building is framed conventionally or become a part of the frame itself, carrying the weight of the building from the roof down; with the latter method, the walls can be much less substantial because they only have to support themselves.

A *slab-on-grade* foundation is very economical because it eliminates the work involved in putting in a basement and takes the place of the first-floor deck. For this foundation, a concrete slab is poured directly over a layer of gravel spread on the ground to help dispel moisture and facilitate drainage. This foundation is particularly popular in areas where the water table is near the surface of the ground and in the southern parts of the country where the *frost line* is very shallow, if it exists at all. The frost line is the depth past which the ground in your area will not be expected to freeze. For more information, see "The Frost Line" below.

In frost-free areas, the edges of the slab are thickened for reinforcement, and the building is constructed on the slab. In areas where frost is a potential problem, the edges of the slab rest on short walls, and the walls in turn are supported by footings that extend below the frost line.

LAYING OUT THE FOUNDATION

Once you've determined where you want to put your addition, its position has to be laid out exactly. Most professionals use a *transit level*, or a less-complex builder's level, for this task. This pivoting telescope accurately transfers vertical measurements from one point to another and also establishes right angles with ease. It is an expensive precision instrument and can be rented for the short time it will take you to lay out the addition. Instructions for using a transit level may come with the rental tool, but they can also be found in general reference books on home construction.

A transit level isn't essential to laying out an addition. You can do just as well with string, a tape measure, a *plumb bob,* a *water level,* and a little high-school geometry.

For string, use mason's cord. It's stout enough to stand up well to the rigors of construction. Less-sturdy string might fray and stretch, distorting your careful work. Depending on how big your addition is to be, a 25-foot tape measure will probably serve your purposes well; longer ones are also available. A plumb bob is a pointed weight that is hung from a string to transfer points vertically. A water level is nothing but a length of ½-inch clear vinyl tubing. The tubing should be long enough to reach between any two points you want to compare without being stretched tight. For most residential building projects, between 50 and 100 feet of tubing will be adequate.

To use the tubing, leave both ends open to the air and fill it with water. As you raise one end, notice that the water is the same elevation in each end. This is the principle behind the device: Water will always seek its own level. To use the water level to transfer an elevation from one point to another, hold one end of the tubing at the first point and the other end at the second point. The water surfaces will be the same, as shown in the illustration *Water Level* on page 38 (top).

You can add food coloring to the water to make it easier to see. And if you're unlucky enough to be working in freezing weather, you can also add antifreeze to keep the level functioning. If you decide to add either substance, mix it with the water before filling the tubing; the fluid must be uniform to function correctly. Keep two rubber stoppers handy to plug the ends when the level is not in use.

To begin laying out the foundation, you first need to find the corners. Roughly lay them out with the tape measure. Measure out from your house to establish the back line of the addition, then locate the corners along this line and mark them temporarily by driving stakes in the ground. Run cord between the stakes and from

THE FROST LINE

Without a good foundation, even the best-crafted building is destined to fail. A foundation supports the weight of a building, keeping it from settling unevenly into the ground. At the same time, it anchors the building in place, protecting it from being blown away in the wind or racked by the freezing and thawing of the earth.

For a foundation to do its job, it must extend below the frost line—the depth below which the ground does not freeze in winter. Above this line, the ground expands and contracts as it freezes and thaws. The depth of the frost line varies across geographical regions, from the southern-most areas where the ground never freezes to far-northern climates where the ground is locked in permafrost. Your local building inspector can tell you how deep the addition's foundation must go.

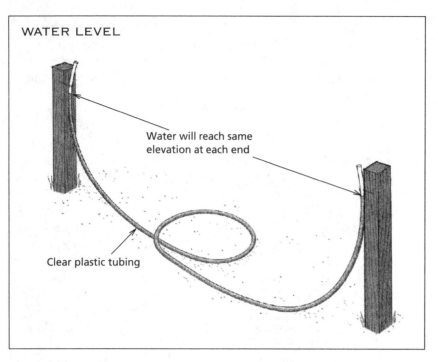

WATER LEVEL

Water will reach same elevation at each end

Clear plastic tubing

The same relationship is true for multiples of those numbers, such as 9-12-15 and 12-16-20.

Start by measuring 9 feet across the wall of the house from the point where one of the pieces of cord is attached and making a mark. Then measure 12 feet out from the house along this cord, as shown in *Using the 3-4-5 Triangle* below. (These two distances can be exchanged without altering the results.) Now measure the distance between the 12-foot point and the mark on the house. It should be 15 feet. If not, the angle at the house end of the cord is not 90 degrees.

Adjust the stake's location until the numbers work and you have a right angle. Check and adjust the staked layout lines in this way until all of the corners you've laid out are

the stakes to the wall of the house, then check the lines for square using the 3-4-5 triangle method. This is where high-school geometry comes in. A right triangle with legs that are 3 and 4 feet long will have a hypotenuse that is 5 feet long.

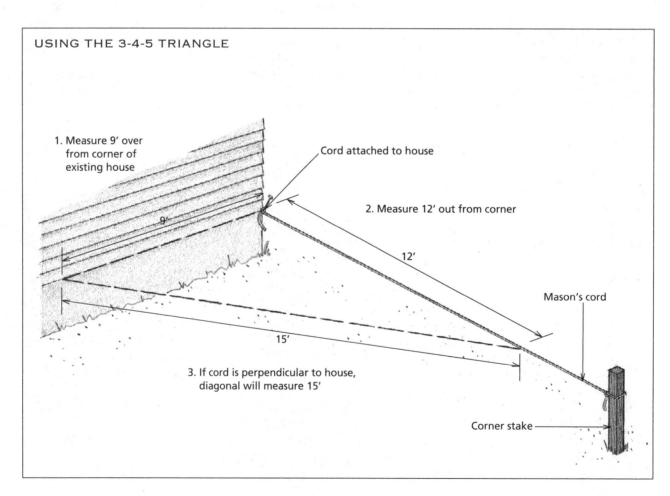

USING THE 3-4-5 TRIANGLE

1. Measure 9' over from corner of existing house

Cord attached to house

9'

2. Measure 12' out from corner

12'

Mason's cord

15'

3. If cord is perpendicular to house, diagonal will measure 15'

Corner stake

square. To double-check the stakes on a square or rectangular foundation, measure across opposite corners. If the measurements are equal, then the corners are square.

These stakes are temporary and will come out once the excavation begins. Each point represented by a stake becomes permanently established with the help of *batter boards*. These look like little fences and are erected about 4 feet beyond the outline established by the stakes. The boards hold the layout lines as the foundation is being built.

Make batter boards from sturdy scrap lumber and set them firmly in the ground; if they come loose after the layout stakes have been removed, your reference lines will be gone. To make sure the lines don't shift, notch the horizontal boards with a saw, as illustrated in *Batter Boards* on the right.

DIGGING IN

At the Bailey house, Dean fired up the track loader and rumbled around the house to begin work. He faced two immediate problems. The first was a large brick patio right in the middle of the dig. The Baileys wanted to save the bricks for later use. But as Dean skimmed the bricks with his bucket, he found that they had been resting on top of a concrete slab; see *Photo 3-1* on page 40 (top). He broke this up as well, and dumped both concrete and brick off to the side for the Baileys to sort through later.

The other challenge was a good-sized tree. It was Jim Bailey's pet, planted eight years before and nursed through a few tough seasons. The tree

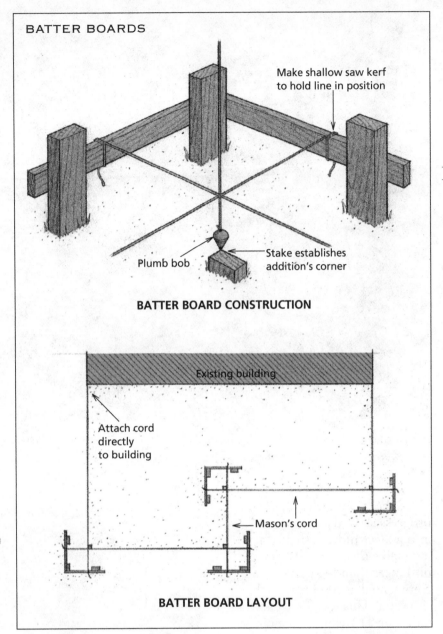

BATTER BOARDS

Make shallow saw kerf to hold line in position

Plumb bob

Stake establishes addition's corner

BATTER BOARD CONSTRUCTION

Existing building

Attach cord directly to building

Mason's cord

BATTER BOARD LAYOUT

was flourishing, but it happened to be smack-dab within the lines sketching the addition's footprint, as shown in *Photo 3-2* on page 40 (bottom). Since the cost of having the tree professionally transplanted was prohibitive, Jim asked Dean to see what he could do with his equipment. After wrapping the trunk heavily with old blankets to keep the bark from being damaged, Dean dug out the tree and carefully chained it to the

loader's bucket. He moved it to a hole he had prepared alongside the garage and staked it upright.

As Dean worked, diesel exhaust mingled with the scent of freshly dug earth. The sod wrinkled up like a shaggy green carpet in front of the loader's bucket. Dean skimmed it away along with the topsoil, saving both for regrading. Then he tore into the subgrade, removing bucket after bucket of red earth.

Photo 3-1. *A track loader assaults the Baileys' brick patio. Before an addition can begin, something of value invariably is lost.*

About 3 feet down, progress slowed as Dean ran into a layer of hard shale. "It looks like this is going to take a bit longer than I expected," he commented as he surveyed the situation. This turn of events didn't upset Dean. Like most excavators, his contract included a "rock clause," stating that his fee goes up if he hits rock and has to spend more time than estimated on the job.

Fortunately for the Baileys, the bucket didn't hit a monolithic rock that would have called for dynamite or a change in the addition's design. Dean did what he could with the loader, then brought in a backhoe to finish the job.

Once the hole was dug, Dean wouldn't return to the site until the foundation was ready to *backfill*, which involves

Photo 3-2. *Favorite plants, like this tree planted by Jim Bailey, often can be plucked from the job site and moved elsewhere in the yard. Ask your excavator to help you move your plants to another site that you've picked out.*

Photo 3-3. By the time the excavation was finished, Jim and Carol Bailey had a new mountain range in their backyard. Luckily, they found someone nearby who needed fill and so were able to dispose of most of the unwanted dirt without having to pay too much for hauling.

adding earth around the foundation walls to bring the site up to grade.

As Dean left, Carol Bailey stood looking in dismay at the hole and the piles of dirt on what had been a beautifully manicured lawn (see *Photo 3-3* above). It was just amazing, she said, how much dirt can come out of a relatively small hole.

THE FOOTINGS

There are two major parts to a standard masonry foundation: the footing and the walls. The footing is at the very bottom, as shown in *Foundation Section View* on page 42 (top), and serves to distribute the weight of the building onto the ground. This lowest level of the addition must be below the frost line.

Steel reinforcing rods, known as *rebar,* usually run through the footing. A slot in the top, called a *keyway,* helps connect the footing with the walls to be added above. (A keyway isn't used for block walls.) The keyway can be made by setting lengths of 2 x 4 into the wet concrete after the footing has been poured. The boards should first be beveled to the profile illustrated so they will come out of the concrete easily once it has hardened; they are not a permanent part of the foundation.

The footing can often be poured into simple trenches around the perimeter of the foundation. Short stakes and lines strung along the outside edge of the trench indicate the top of the footing; the earth itself constitutes the bottom

and sides of the form. It may be necessary to make forms from wood if the footing is aboveground or if the bottom of the excavation is very rocky and digging trenches would be impossible. The latter was the case at the Baileys' site. Ted Currier and Dennis Grim stood 2 x 10s on edge along the layout lines and staked them to hold them upright, as illustrated in *Form for Footing* on page 42 (bottom). Form ties and spreaders helped keep the 2 x 10 form boards in position.

If the first floor of your addition will incorporate a beam supported by piers or Lally columns, you'll need to add an individual footing or pad for each pier or column. These footings are formed in the same manner as the wall footings. A fireplace will require its own footing. If you're in doubt about how to design your addition's foundation, consult a local structural engineer or architect.

Once the footing forms are complete, you can lay rebar in the holes. Rebar is an important part of concrete work because concrete has a flaw: While tremendous pressure is required to crush it, comparatively little force is necessary to pull it apart. Steel, on the other hand, has great tensile strength. Combining concrete and rebar creates a footing that can withstand the stresses that footings normally face.

To work properly, rebar should be covered in all directions by at least 3 inches of concrete. That means the rods must be located within the body of a footing, not resting on the bottom. Use specially made foundation *chair-wire brackets*, which hold the rebar the required distance off the ground.

Once the rebar is in place, the forms are ready to be filled with concrete. The most economical source of concrete

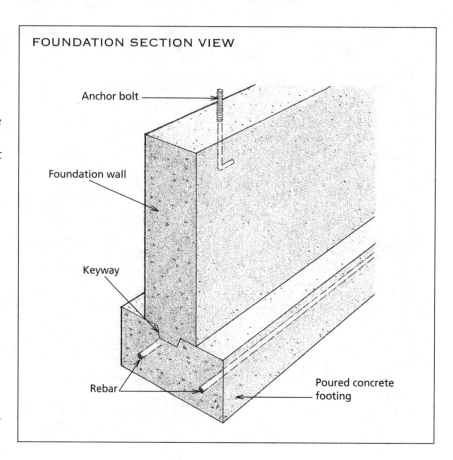

FOUNDATION SECTION VIEW

Anchor bolt

Foundation wall

Keyway

Rebar

Poured concrete footing

in large quantities is a ready-mix company that will deliver it right to the job site.

Concrete is comprised of two active ingredients—water and portland cement—and two fillers—a fine aggregate such as sand and a course aggregate such as gravel. The proportions of these ingredients determine the characteristics of the mix. A higher percentage of water or sand improves workability but detracts from strength.

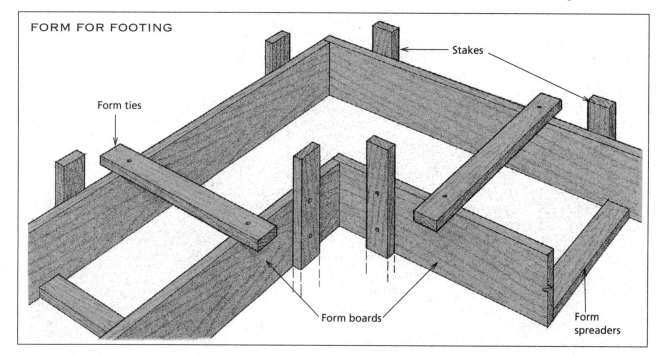

FORM FOR FOOTING

Stakes

Form ties

Form boards

Form spreaders

Likewise, using less water will strengthen concrete but make it harder to pour and smooth.

Formulating concrete for specific qualities is a science. Your local supplier can help you determine what kind of a mix you need for a given situation. Give the supplier a call and describe the job and any special engineering requirements well before you will be pouring the concrete.

You might also want to talk about access to your site. Most ready-mix trucks have an extension chute to carry concrete across a short span between the truck and the foundation site. But if the truck cannot get fairly close, you may have to ask that a pump truck deliver the goods. You can also rely on a low-tech alternative: Enlist the help of burly friends to transfer the heavy, gray mud in wheelbarrows. It is best, though, to have the concrete poured directly into your forms if possible; you will have less work and will avoid weakening the concrete by doing a good deal of hoeing and shoveling.

Several days before you intend to pour, call your supplier to place your order. Be sure to provide good directions so the drivers know exactly where to go; a lost concrete truck can spoil your day. You'll need to state how much concrete is needed in units of a cubic yard (and fractions thereof).

To calculate how many cubic yards are in your pour, multiply the width by the length by the depth of the footings (all in feet), then divide that number by 27. If at all possible, take your measurements from the forms themselves rather than from your drawings.

Craters left by tree roots and other obstacles can eat concrete, so it's best to compensate for them ahead of time.

Round your numbers up rather than down. It is a real disaster to run out of concrete and only a minor problem to have a little too much.

▲▲▲▲▲▲▲▲▲▲

The foundation may not take quite all of the concrete you've ordered, so consider other uses for the leftovers. If you have a need for well-anchored posts, dig the holes and have the posts ready to go prior to the pour.

▼▼▼▼▼▼▼▼▼▼

Most suppliers allow you a certain amount of time to dispense the concrete, after which they charge overtime. Make sure you have enough help on hand to get the concrete out of the truck within the allotted time. This isn't simply a question of money. Under average conditions, concrete can sit in a truck for about an hour before water has to be added to keep it workable. Adding water weakens the mix. Concrete still on the truck after 90 minutes is pretty much useless.

You'll want to keep this time in mind if your delivery has to be made by several trucks (most carry a maximum of about 8 yards). Ideally, the trucks should arrive so you can continue the pour uninterrupted.

On the day of the pour, call to confirm your order. If the forecast is for bad weather, reschedule. Pouring concrete is stressful enough without worrying about rain and mud.

As the concrete is poured, the top of the footing is *screeded* if there are form boards. Screeding is a lot like leveling off flour in a measuring cup with a table knife. The excess material is scraped off with a screed board, often simply a straight 2 x 4 that is slid along the tops of the form boards. Although a single person can screed a narrow pour such as a footing, the job is a lot easier with someone at each end of the screed board. If you intend to pour your foundation walls rather than build them from block, create a *keyway* by pressing 2 x 4 keys into the footing after it has been screeded but before it has hardened.

Once the concrete has hardened, the form boards and keys are removed, leaving a crisp, gray footing to await the foundation walls.

THE FOUNDATION WALLS

For the homeowner who wants to get involved, building the foundation can be a source of savings since about half of the cost is in labor. Forms for poured concrete are available for rent, sparing the time it would take to build your own; block walls don't require forms. You can even rent a backhoe; see "Borrowing a Backhoe" on page 44. And a fairly new way of laying up block without mortared joints, called surface bonding, is suited for the inexperienced mason; see "Surface-Bonded Blocks" on page 45.

Still, building the foundation is not a task to be

taken lightly. It's hard, demanding work, and a mistake can jeopardize everything that follows. Unless you're confident that you can handle the task, concentrate your efforts on aboveground parts of the building and leave the foundation to professionals.

Even though the Baileys' original house was made with block foundation walls, Dennis decided to go with poured concrete for the addition.

There is little difference in overall cost: The materials required for traditionally laid block walls are cheaper than those for poured concrete, but the labor associated with block offsets the lower material cost. There is a considerable savings with surface-bonded block, however, as it doesn't require nearly as much time to lay. The problem is finding a contractor who will attempt it. Many contractors, Dennis included, prefer to use techniques they are familiar with. Poured concrete had worked successfully for Dennis on other jobs, and he chose it here for that reason.

It was cold and gray when a professional four-man crew arrived to install the forms for the foundation walls. They first checked that the footing was square using the 3-4-5 method. Dennis and Ted had done a good job forming the footing, so no corrective measures were needed. The crew snapped chalklines along the footing to establish the outside of the foundation walls, then they started unloading the ribbed steel forms. These forms are sophisticated cousins of the 2 x 10s Ted and Dennis used for the footing. They're part of a modular system that has been developed to speed the process of pouring concrete.

The standard ribbed steel form is 2 feet wide and a little over 8 feet tall. Each unit interlocks with the next to form a continuous wall, as shown in *Photo 3-4* on page 46 (left). One line of forms creates the outside of the wall; another line runs parallel to it to define the inside wall. Metal ties hold the sides together, keeping them from bowing out under the weight of the concrete. Once the forms are removed, the ties can be broken off flush with the walls.

As the forms were set in place, a worker sprayed them with diesel oil to keep the concrete from sticking to them when they were removed. Clean forms are a sign of a good foundation contractor;

▶ ## BORROWING A BACKHOE

For most do-it-yourselfers, the prospect of excavating for a foundation can be daunting. Hand digging the trenches for even a modest addition will mean hours of back-breaking work. And a backhoe is an expensive piece of equipment that few of us have waiting in the garage. But there are tool-rental centers that will rent you almost anything you're brave enough to ask for, from wheelbarrows to backhoes.

If you think you can handle heavy equipment like this, you can arrange to have a rental center deliver a machine directly to your site, show you how to operate it, and return to pick it up when you are finished. A backhoe will handle almost any excavating you're likely to do yourself, and you should be able to pick up the basics of operating one in an hour or two.

Is it worth it? You may save money over hiring a professional excavator—the daily rental charge for a full-size backhoe is roughly half of what you would pay a pro for a day's work. But the pro can almost certainly work faster than you can, and the pro will have the experience to handle tricky situations, like cutting into a steeply sloped site or digging a full basement close to an existing house, where one slip on a lever could punch a hole in your house. Most pros also carry insurance to cover any damage they might do.

If you opt to tackle the job yourself, call your local utility companies to find out what might be underground before you start digging. The last thing you want to do is cut into a buried pipe or utility line. Many states have a toll-free number to call for information.

SURFACE-BONDED BLOCKS

For homeowners determined to build their own masonry foundation, the best option may be walls made from surface-bonded blocks. This technology requires none of the skill associated with a traditionally laid block wall, and it is stronger to boot.

The process is simple. Concrete blocks are stacked up dry, without mortar in the joints. (Only the first course of blocks is laid in a bed of mortar.) Once the walls are up, a layer of surface-bonding mix—a stucco-like coating—is troweled on both sides, locking the blocks together. The secret is in the mix's ingredients. Chopped fiberglass is mixed in with the cement and sand, bridging the joints between the blocks and reinforcing the wall. (It's interesting that the glass strands are only about ½ inch long—too short to bridge the mortar joints of traditionally laid walls.)

Use 8-inch-wide blocks for walls 5 feet or shorter and 12-inch-wide blocks for anything taller. You may have to adjust the lengths of your walls somewhat. Standard 16-inch blocks are actually only 15⅝ inches long to allow for a ⅜-inch mortar joint. So you can't count on the standard 16-inch module to calculate the length of a wall.

When you build a surface-bonded block wall, you have to cast lengths of threaded rod into the footing. As shown in *Surface-Bonded Wall* below, the rods run up through the blocks at corners, into reinforcing columns called pilasters, at openings, and at intervals of 4 to 6 feet along the wall. The mudsill is anchored to the footing with these rods as well.

After the walls are laid, it's time to coat them. Water is added to the bonding mix, then the mix is applied with a plasterer's trowel, which is distinguished by a triangular steel blade.

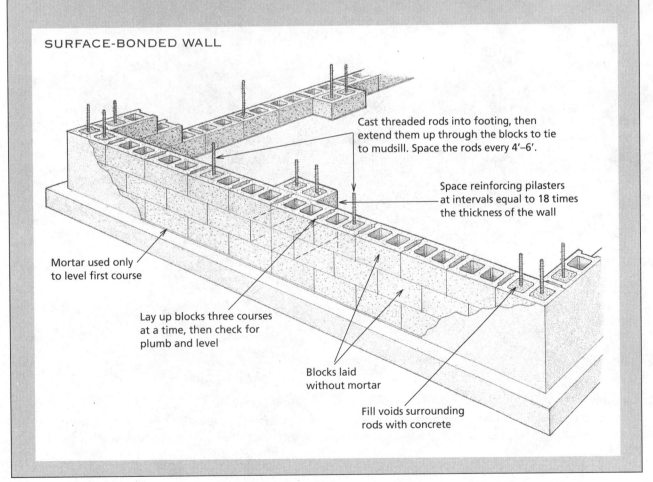

SURFACE-BONDED WALL

Cast threaded rods into footing, then extend them up through the blocks to tie to mudsill. Space the rods every 4'–6'.

Space reinforcing pilasters at intervals equal to 18 times the thickness of the wall

Mortar used only to level first course

Lay up blocks three courses at a time, then check for plumb and level

Blocks laid without mortar

Fill voids surrounding rods with concrete

although they don't affect the strength of the job, clean forms make smoother and straighter foundation walls. The crew leader was very proud of the fact that, despite almost daily use, their forms were not caked with old concrete.

An odd-sized gap where the new foundation had to tie into the old couldn't be filled by a form. "Here is where the crew has to get creative," said Ted, observing the work in progress. The crew began by drilling holes into the existing block wall with a carbide-tipped masonry bit mounted in a heavy-duty hammer drill, as shown in *Photo 3-5* below right.

The crew stuck lengths of rebar into the holes to reinforce the joint after the concrete was poured. The forms were brought up as close to the building as possible and braced in place, then the gap was filled in with pieces of scrap wood. Around the perimeter of the foundation, 2 x 4 braces were run diagonally from the top of the steel forms to stakes in the ground to push or pull the walls plumb, as shown in *Photo 3-6* on the opposite page.

Shortly after the forms were completed, the ready-mix trucks began to arrive. With the weather so unpredictable in late October, calcium had been added to the mix at the concrete plant to keep the mix from freezing. Concrete that freezes before it cures can lose up to 50 percent of its strength.

The concrete poured down the chute and quickly filled the forms. Then the crew pushed ½-inch-diameter, L-shaped *anchor bolts* into the still-wet walls, leaving about 2½ inches exposed. The wooden frame of the house would be attached to these bolts, forming a vital link

Photo 3-4. Modular steel forms have revolutionized the process of pouring concrete. Here a worker sets one piece of the form wall in place.

Photo 3-5. A worker drills holes in the old foundation for lengths of rebar that will help to reinforce the connection between the new concrete and the existing block wall.

Photo 3-6. *Once the walls are assembled and straightened, they are pushed into plumb and held with braces running diagonally to the ground.*

in the structure. The bolts were plumbed so it would be easy to slip the sill plates over them.

When the concrete crew returned the next day, they stripped away the forms, leaving the foundation ready for the next step: A waterproof foundation coating applied to the outside of the concrete walls. This coating is a sticky, black, asphalt-based mixture formulated especially for keeping out moisture.

At this time, the exterior of a basement wall can also be insulated with tongue-and-groove, 4 x 8-foot sheets of rigid foam insulation, which are simply placed up against the wall. The sheets will be held in place by backfilled soil.

Another part of keeping the basement or crawl space dry is to lay plastic pipe along the footing as a foundation drain. The pipe is first covered with several inches of gravel to allow water to percolate around it, and then it is covered over with filter fabric and backfill. For information on this piping, see "Foundation Drains" on page 50.

THE BASEMENT FLOOR

The basement floor, or slab, is prepared for a pour of concrete with a layer of gravel about 4 inches thick. If the slab lies above ground level, it is set apart from the outside wall with rigid insulation that extends from the top of the floor to below the gravel; see the illustration *Aboveground Slab* on page 48 (top). The basement floor is edged by an isolation joint, as shown in *Belowground Slab* on page 48 (bottom). This joint allows the floor to expand and contract with changes in temperature independently from the walls. In either case, the slab is separated from the gravel with sheets of 6-mil polyethylene as a vapor barrier.

At the Baileys, Dennis set up the transit level in the center of the basement and, together with contractor Dave Ackerman, struck a level chalkline around the foundation walls to indicate the top of the slab. They used the height of the slab in the existing basement as a reference so that the surfaces of the two floors would be in the same plane; an opening would later be made in the old foundation, connecting old basement with new.

The transit level was also used to set a row of reference pins in the center of the new slab. The pins, made from lengths of rebar, were driven

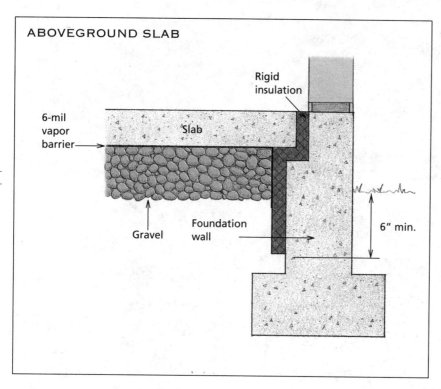

ABOVEGROUND SLAB

Rigid insulation

6-mil vapor barrier

Slab

48

Gravel

Foundation wall

6" min.

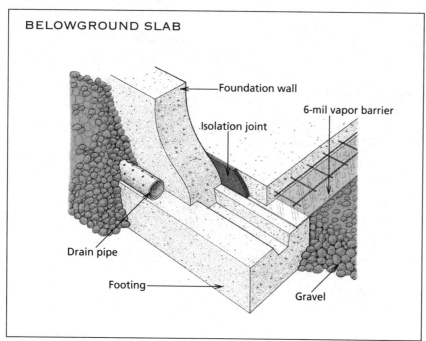

BELOWGROUND SLAB

Foundation wall

Isolation joint

6-mil vapor barrier

Drain pipe

Footing

Gravel

extra measure of water was added to make it easier to work the slab to a smoother finish. The driver backed the truck along the house and got the chute set up to dump the mud through the basement window.

In this case, the slab was poured after the joists and flooring were installed across the foundation walls. If you have a choice, it's much easier to pour before this work is done, since you can move the chute to direct the concrete where you want it.

"How wet do you want it, Bud?" the driver called down. Dennis said they'd start with the mix just as it came off the truck to see how well it would work. He didn't want to compromise the final strength of the slab with added water unless it was absolutely necessary. The gray mud slid down the chute into wheelbarrows manned by Dave and contractor Barry Frace. After distributing several barrows of mud, Dennis had the driver add just a touch of water to improve the way the concrete handled.

A *mason's hoe* was used to spread the piles of concrete. (The hoe looks much like a garden hoe, except for two holes through the blade that help mix the concrete as you hoe it, preventing the ingredients from separating.) The mud was screeded with a long board, as was done on a smaller scale with the footers; see *Photo 3-7* on the opposite page (top). Then, a *float* was worked back and forth over the surface, as shown in *Photo 3-8* on the opposite page (bottom), to smooth away the ridges left by screeding. Dave proceeded across the slab toward his escape route so he didn't have

into the gravel base at roughly 8-foot intervals so the concrete workers could screed the concrete to the rebar to establish the height of the slab pour. Dennis and Dave used the transit level to align the tops of the pins with the lines around the walls.

For the isolation joint, the

men cut 1-inch-thick rigid foam insulation into 4-inch-wide strips and placed these along the foundation walls, even with the chalkline.

As the men were finishing up, the first ready-mix truck rumbled up out front. This would be a different mix than that ordered for the footings; an

Photo 3-7. *A worker levels the slab with a long screed rail—the first step in finishing the concrete.*

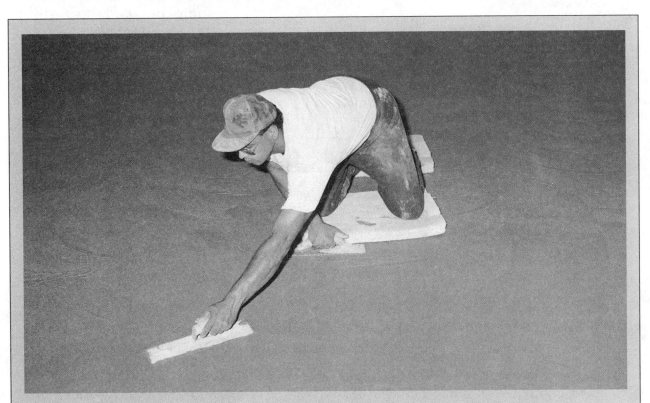

Photo 3-8. *Once the basement floor has been screeded, it is finished with a magnesium hand float that further smooths the surface.*

FOUNDATION DRAINS

If water collects under a foundation, it can make your basement damp. Worse, it can erode the soil under the footings, causing the foundation to settle severely. This is especially true if the property is in a low-lying area that receives runoff or on a slope. You should take steps to make sure water will drain away from the addition. In some soils, the water may drain on its own. In others, you have to provide a means of channeling water away. The easiest way to do this is with a foundation drain.

shown in *Foundation Drain* below, 4-inch-diameter perforated pipe is laid on a bed of gravel along or slightly below the footing. It is then covered with more gravel and a layer of filter fabric before the foundation is backfilled. The filter fabric, which is available from most building-supply centers, keeps the drain and gravel bed from clogging with sediment from the soil.

The pipe should be pitched at least 1 inch in 20 feet with its perforations facing down. When groundwater rises, it enters the pipe through the perforations and is conveyed away from the foundation. Cleanout pipes that run to the surface can be installed to keep the system free of obstructions. You can run an auger down into the system to clean it out should it become plugged up with roots or other debris.

At the lowest point of the drain, the water can be piped to a *drywell,* a hole lined with concrete block and filled with coarse gravel. Water drains into it and slowly dissipates into the surrounding soil. Other alternatives are to send the water to a drainage ditch, evacuate it with a sump pump, or connect the drain directly to a storm sewer system if one is accessible from the property.

Foundation drains divert water that's already below the ground. Be sure to divert rainwater away from the addition at ground level by grading the soil slightly away from the walls. If rainwater pools close to the walls instead of being carried away by the slope of the ground, the soil around the foundation and the basement walls will stay wet.

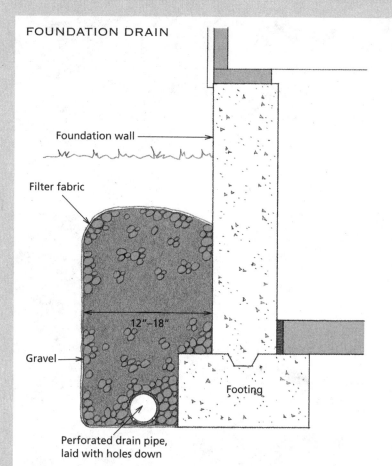

FOUNDATION DRAIN

Foundation wall

Filter fabric

12"–18"

Gravel

Footing

Perforated drain pipe, laid with holes down

A foundation drain is simply a pipe laid outside the foundation where water can collect and be diverted away from the building. The traditional material used for this was clay pipe in short sections laid end to end but with a gap between the sections. Perforated plastic pipe has made the job much easier and less expensive. As

to move back over the freshly smoothed surface. The float also brought a slurry of sand and water to the surface. Producing this pastelike substance is important to forming a smooth, hard surface. See *Tools for the Slab* below.

As the surface is finished with the float, joints are cut in the wet concrete with a *groover,* a special trowel-like tool with a ridge on its underside. A groover cuts partway through a large slab to create a weak place so the concrete will crack inconspicuously, rather than randomly, as the surface cures and shrinks.

As concrete cures, it loses some of its water to evaporation. This water will initially rise to the surface and puddle, giving the concrete a slight sheen. When the water has evaporated, it's your cue to finish the slab. Keep in mind that there is a limited span of time in which the concrete can be worked.

To finish a slab, kneel on boards that distribute your weight and keep you from sinking into the hardening mud. Using a magnesium *hand float,* work with a sweeping motion to both smooth and level the slab. Finally, repeat the process with a steel trowel. This is

something like sanding wood with coarse and then fine sandpaper. The magnesium float does the bulk of the smoothing, and the steel trowel puts on the finishing touches. Plan your work so that you don't have to walk over the area you finished and mar the slab as you leave.

At this point, the only thing left for you to do is allow the slab to cure. Concrete cures very slowly—and it should—taking at least a month to reach its rated strength. To ensure a slow cure, keep the slab wet for up to a week following the pour by either spraying it or keeping it covered with wet burlap.

TOOLS FOR THE SLAB

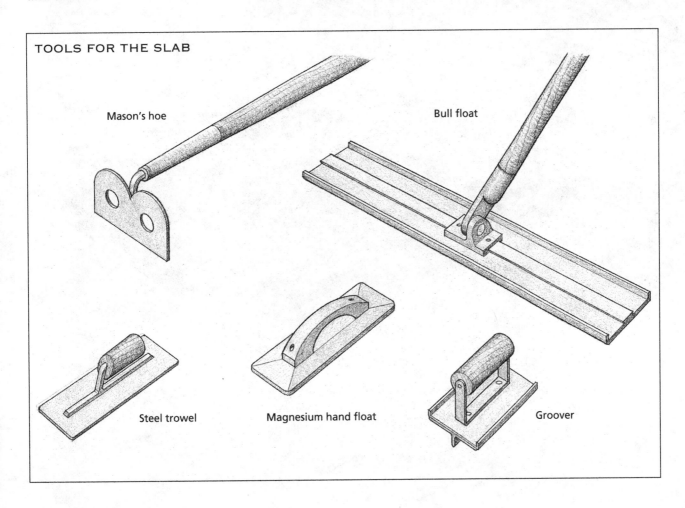

Mason's hoe

Bull float

Steel trowel

Magnesium hand float

Groover

4
FRAMING THE FLOOR

The Baileys' addition was framed by Barry Frace and Dave Ackerman. Barry, the head carpenter, was the quieter of the pair. He was thinking as he worked—keeping ahead of the job, mapping out the next step as he sank nails into the board at hand. Dave, his helper, was thinking ahead, too, anticipating Barry's moves. "Plumb this," Barry would tell him. "Just did," Dave answered, moving into place for the next operation.

Just two people can handle a residential addition because of the nature of the materials. In home construction, the frame is usually of wood—relatively thin, lightweight pieces, much of it no thicker in dimension than the 2-by stock used to make picnic tables.

FRAMING, LIGHT AND BEEFY

House frames weren't always the fine-boned cages made today. Traditional post-and-beam construction used massive mem-bers, as described in "The Post-and-Beam Alternative" on page 54. Each sturdy element repre-sented the heart of a tree. Sides were often squared by hand, and rafters might have been left with some of their bark.

The technology of framing has evolved, but the material is still the same. Wood is strong, light, and beautiful. It's easy to cut and easy to fasten. We have yet to concoct a replacement for this renewable resource. Today, a frame is usually pieced to-gether from rather slender pieces of construction lumber,

as shown in *Conventional Framing* on page 55.

Conventional framing (also known as platform framing) begins by spanning the foundation with *joists* and cov-ering them with a rough sub-floor. This platform, or deck, provides a level stage on which to assemble the first-floor walls and raise them in place. Each wall that is built looks some-thing like the side of a crib, with top and bottom horizontal pieces (called *plates*) and verti-cals between (called *studs*).

If your addition will have a second story, this same process begins again once the first-floor walls are up. Joists are placed across the top plates of these walls, and second-story walls are assembled from this elevated platform.

The roof is framed with

THE POST-AND-BEAM ALTERNATIVE

Two-by lumber is the near-universal choice for framing wooden dwellings. But for centuries, heavy hardwood posts, beams, and rafters did the work. These post-and-beam structures have fewer pieces; that's because each piece is stronger and can do more work.

Stronger, but also heavier and more expensive. A child can pick up almost any wooden component of a conventional addition, but it takes a crew of supple-backed adults to lift an oak 8 x 10 into place. And that hunk of hardwood will probably cost more than the several mass-produced 2-bys that do the same job today. Nevertheless, post-and-beam construction has enjoyed a modest revival.

There are a few reasons for this surprising return to an all-but-forgotten bit of technology. First, you get to know wood on a personal basis—surfacing it, making joints at either end, and wrestling it into place. In contrast, it's hard to develop a relationship with a damp, sticky, look-alike stud dumped off a truck.

Second, these old-time frames lend themselves to the modern technique of attaching a seamless insulating skin around the outside of the structure. In standard construction, individual pieces of insulation are placed between studs and rafters, leaving potential gaps every 16 inches.

Then there is the impressive appearance of those lunking, over-engineered timbers (see *The Bones of Post-and-Beam Construction* below). Most modern post-and-beam builders celebrate the frame by leaving it at least partly exposed on the inside. Given a chamfer or decorative bead and an oil finish, these timbers can look as handsome as an antique corner cupboard.

Putting up a post-and-beam structure takes special skills. If you can't find local workers to do the job or work with you, look into companies that specialize in this construction method (check out the ads in homebuilding magazines). Some companies will help design the addition and then bring precut timbers to the site for quick assembly.

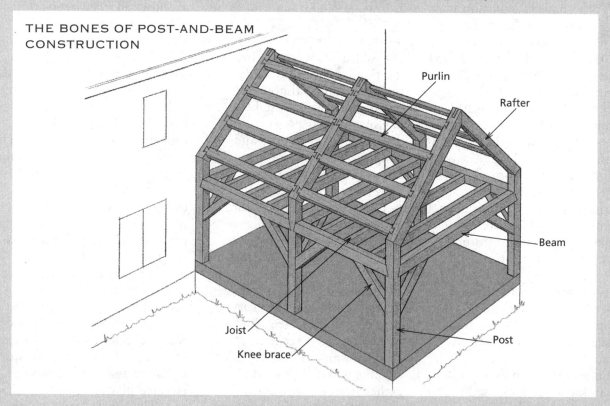

THE BONES OF POST-AND-BEAM CONSTRUCTION

Purlin

Rafter

Beam

Post

Joist

Knee brace

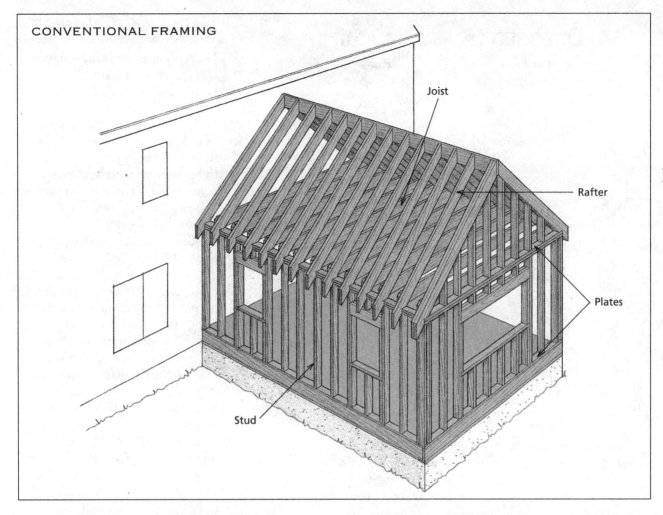

Joist

Rafter

Plates

Stud

rafters, which function something like the joists in a floor.

The handiwork of a conventional frame will be all but invisible once the addition is done. The outside will be sheathed, and the inside surfaces will be clad in drywall or paneling. You can glimpse the skeleton if you look up at the floor joists from the basement or if you view the rafters in an unfinished space under the roof.

SOFTWOOD LUMBER

The basic framing material of a conventional frame is softwood construction lumber. It is sold *dressed,* which means it has been planed to a standard width, thickness, and

length. Over the years, the standard width and thickness have changed; curiously, the *names* of those sizes have not. A 2 x 6 (or two-by-six), for example, is a piece of wood that measures 2 by 6 inches in

name only—this is the *nominal* size of the lumber. The board might have started out that way, when rough cut and still wet as a sponge. But both planing and drying conspire to produce a skinnier board.

▶ ORDERING LUMBER

Shop around before ordering lumber, and don't be afraid to call suppliers outside of your immediate area. You may be able to get a price break by including your plywood and sheathing with an order of lumber, even if you want them delivered separately. When placing your order, mention its intended use to double-check that you've specified the right item. Ask if the truck will have a boom or even a forklift for unloading heavy materials. If the supplies have to be moved by hand, ask if you can expect the driver to help.

DRESSED SOFTWOOD SIZES

Nominal	Actual
1 × 2	¾" × 1½"
1 × 3	¾" × 2½"
1 × 4	¾" × 3½"
1 × 6	¾" × 5½"
1 × 8	¾" × 7¼"
1 × 10	¾" × 9¼"
1 × 12	¾" × 11¼"
2 × 2	1½" × 1½"
2 × 3	1½" × 2½"
2 × 4	1½" × 3½"
2 × 6	1½" × 5½"
2 × 8	1½" × 7¼"
2 × 10	1½" × 9¼"
2 × 12	1½" × 11¼"
4 × 4	3½" × 3½"
6 × 6	5½" × 5½"

SOFTWOOD GRADES

Class	Grade	Characteristics
Select (or Clear)	B and Better	Practically clear on both sides; no knots; virtually no blemishes
	C	Slightly more blemishes than B and Better; perhaps a few very small knots
	D	One side is finish quality; recognizable defects on back
Common (or No. 1)	Construction	Smooth grain; evenly distributed knots no more than 2" in diameter; no knots near edges
Standard (or No. 2)		Similar to Construction, except knots up to 3" in diameter in wide boards

The table "Dressed Softwood Sizes" above (top) gives nominal and actual sizes for softwood lumber.

Rest assured that there is not as much confusion with length. When stating the specifications, length is given last—a 2 x 4 x 10 refers to a 10-foot-long piece of 2 x 4. Lumber is usually available in 8- to 16-foot lengths in 2-foot increments. Lengths over 16 feet often require a special order. The pieces you get will usually measure a little longer than their stated length. An exception is precut studs.

HARDWOOD LUMBER

Hardwood is the other general classification of lumber. Hardwood is taken from broad-leaved trees that lose their leaves each year, including such species as oak, maple, cherry, and walnut. These woods continue to be used for post-and-beam construction, and their attractive appearance and strength recommend them for floors, molding, and decorative details of a home—if they are used at all. Hardwood usually costs more than softwood, sometimes dramatically so, and its use is often restricted to accents. In the Baileys' addition, the only piece of hardwood was to be a slab of oak for the fireplace mantel.

Hardwood isn't sold in an array of precut sizes. Instead, you'll find it sawed to a certain thickness and to random widths. It is priced by the *board foot*. To calculate the number of board feet in one piece, multiply the thickness and width in inches by the length in feet, then divide by 12. For example, a board 2 inches thick by 6 inches wide and 10 feet long would compute this way:

$$\frac{2'' \times 6'' \times 10'}{12} = \frac{120}{12} = 10 \text{ board feet}$$

Hardwood thickness is usually described in quarters of an inch before stock is planed. That means you have to order thicker stock than what is specified for a job. If you need 1½-inch-thick cherry for shelves, for example, you would ask a sawmill for 8/4 (called eight-quarter) boards. The boards will be roughly 2 inches thick and must be planed smooth. Home centers usually sell hardwood stock already planed, but the boards are described (and priced) as if they were still in their full rough thickness.

WOOD GRADES

Wood is described not only by its size but also by its appearance and structural strength. Again, softwood and hardwood have their own systems. The tables "Softwood Grades" on the opposite page (bottom) and "Hardwood Grades" on the right give typical descriptions; you may run into regional variations from one area to another.

Softwood structural lumber is termed Select if it is strong and especially good in appearance. Most framing lumber is of a lower appearance grade, called Construction, that nevertheless is straight and strong. The lowest class you'll encounter—standard—sacrifices strength for lower price.

Grading information is marked on the stock; *Lumber Grade Stamp* on the right

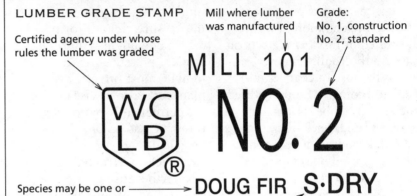

HARDWOOD GRADES

Grade	Characteristics
Firsts and Seconds (FAS)	Usually at least 6" wide and 8' long; over 83⅓ percent clear on both sides
Select	At least 4" wide and 6' long; one side as good as FAS
No. 1 Common	Narrower and shorter than Select; 66⅔ percent clear
No. 2 Common	50 percent clear

LUMBER GRADE STAMP

Certified agency under whose rules the lumber was graded

Mill where lumber was manufactured

Grade:
No. 1, construction
No. 2, standard

MILL 101

NO. 2

WC LB ®

DOUG FIR S·DRY

Species may be one or a group of species having similar characteristics

Moisture content (MC):
S-GRN = MC 20% or more (should not be used for framing)
S-DRY = MC 19% or less
MC 15 = MC 15% or less

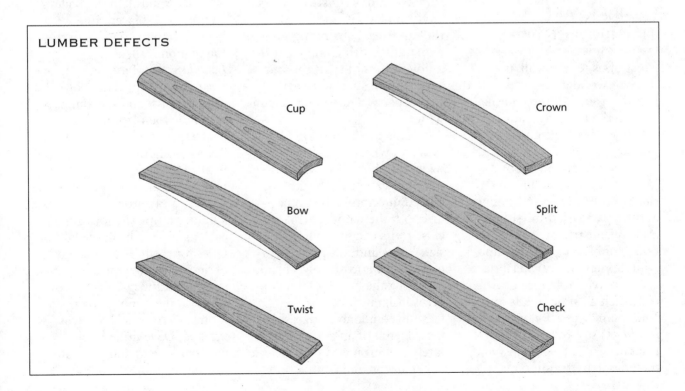

LUMBER DEFECTS

Cup

Crown

Bow

Split

Twist

Check

shows a typical grading stamp as it would appear on the end of a softwood board or stud. Examine the grading stamps upon delivery of an order of wood *before* it comes off the truck. If the wood is not what you ordered or if it appears warped, stand firm and reject it. Once the wood is off the truck, it's your headache.

Be aware of defects that are not covered by the grading rules. Most of these are a variation on a single theme: warping. Some of the more common flaws are illustrated in *Lumber Defects* on page 57 (bottom). Lumber warps because of changes in moisture content. Properly dried and stored lumber is less likely to be affected; once stock is delivered, keep it under cover and well supported on scrap wood or concrete blocks.

The grading system of the National Hardwood Lumber Association also recognizes that knots are a liability (see "Hardwood Grades" on page 57).

LUMBERYARD TERMINOLOGY

Most of us tend to call any piece of wood a "board," but in fact this is one of three terms used in the building trade to describe broad categories of lumber.

Boards are pieces of lumber sawed to a nominal thickness of less than 2 inches, and they are used for siding and finish carpentry, including door jambs, sills, soffits, and trim. Somewhat thicker boards are also available for specific uses such as stair treads and deck planking. *Dimensional lumber* is sawed to a nominal thickness of 2 to 4 inches and includes 2-by framing mem-

bers such as studs, joists, and rafters. Finally, *timbers* are usually described as having a nominal thickness of at least 4 inches and are most often used as posts and beams.

Since posts typically will be anchored in or near the ground, they are widely available as *pressure-treated* stock, permeated with chemicals under pressure to prevent decay and insect infestation. Boards and dimensional lumber can also be purchased in pressure-treated form.

Code might require that you use pressure-treated lumber, most often for sill plates. It's also a wise choice for permanently exposed structures such as porches, decks, and sheds.

Pressure-treated lumber is heavier because of the chemicals forced into it. Note that these chemicals are in the sawdust, as well, so you should avoid inhaling the dust when sawing.

As an organic, once-living thing, wood is sensitive to its environment. It refuses to stay the same size, shrinking and expanding with changes in the ambient humidity. Rain and even humid summer weather will cause wood to increase in width.

This can be a particular problem with the relatively wide, thin boards used for indoor finish work. The sealed, heated interior of the home dries out the wood, shrinking it close to its original kiln-dried size. Splits and unsightly gaps may result. Fortunately, shrinkage along the length of a member is insignificant, and the framing components that sketch the skeleton of an addition are rarely compromised by this cycle of expansion and contraction.

BOLTING THE MUDSILL

Back at the Baileys on one cold, clear Friday in November, Barry and Dave began working on the *mudsill*, the first wooden element of the Baileys' addition. The mudsill is usually a 2 x 6, laid flat and bolted on top of the foundation wall. Pressure-treated lumber is usually chosen to resist rot and turn away termites.

Installing the mudsill is a straightforward job, yet this step deserves a lot of care and precision. It's the nature of foundation walls to be rarely dead-on true. Your best chance of compensating for this is installing the mudsill level and square. Otherwise, you are apt to pay for your lack of precision throughout the building process. Every subsequent job—from creating level floors to adding molding—may become a struggle. Installing square kitchen cabinets or bathtubs in a trapezoidal house is nothing less than a nightmare.

The mudsill in the Baileys' addition was placed roughly ½ inch from the outside of the foundation wall, as shown in *Installing the Mudsill* on the opposite page (top). This ledge allows the plywood sheathing to sit on the foundation wall.

Dave started by laying 2 x 6s along the foundation walls. He worked as the "cut man," marking the pieces at the corners and cutting them to length. Noting the location of each anchor bolt, Barry laid out holes for them by drawing pairs of lines square to the edge, as shown in *Laying Out Anchor Bolts* on the opposite page (bottom). As each 2 x 6 was marked, Dave drilled holes ¼ inch oversize to allow for adjusting the mudsill for square.

Next, the crew laid out the location of the sills on the foundation by marking a ½-inch space for the sheathing. Dave held a chalkline taut at one end while Barry snapped the string to establish the outside edge of the mudsill. (If you won't be attaching sheathing and there will be no offset for it, you should snap a chalkline to define the *inside* edge of the mudsill.)

In laying out the two adjoining walls, Barry didn't assume that the foundation was square to the house. He snapped lines on the side walls that were square to the line on the addition's back wall. He made sure the lines formed a right angle by using the 3-4-5 measurement method described in Chapter 3.

Before the crew bolted the mudsill in place, a sill sealer was installed to fill gaps between the foundation wall and the mudsill. In the old days, this was accomplished by laying the mudsill in a bed of mortar. (Masons call mortar "mud," which probably explains the term mudsill.) Modern sill sealer takes the form of spongy plastic. The material comes off its roll ¼ inch thick but will compress to ¹⁄₃₂ inch under a building's weight.

Barry unrolled the sealer along the foundation wall, pulling it down until it was punctured over each anchor bolt. The carpenters then slipped the mudsill over the bolts, topping them with washers and nuts. If you live in an area with severe termite problems, place a metal shield between the sealer and the mudsill. The carpenters aligned the outside edges of the 2 x 6s with the chalklines. As they tightened the nuts, they checked the mudsill with a level. In a few places, they shimmed up low spots with wedges between the seal and the mudsill.

INSTALLING THE MUDSILL

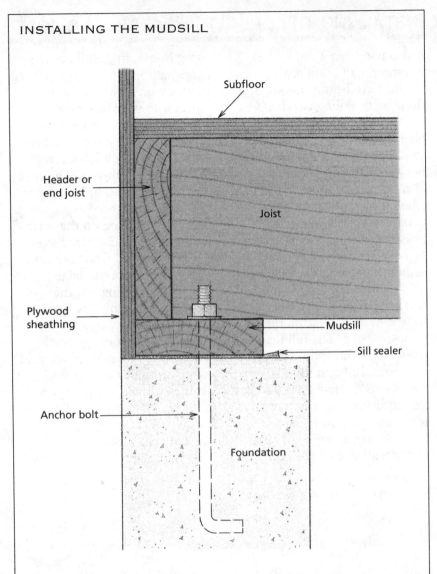

Subfloor

Header or end joist

Joist

Plywood sheathing

Mudsill

Sill sealer

Anchor bolt

Foundation

LAYING OUT ANCHOR BOLTS

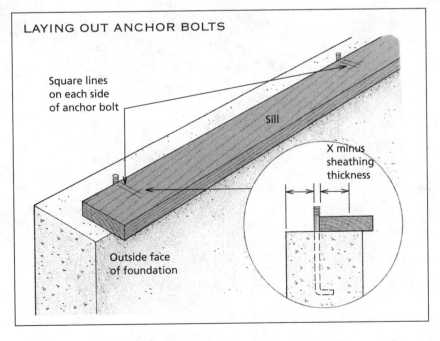

Square lines on each side of anchor bolt

Sill

X minus sheathing thickness

Outside face of foundation

FRAMING THE FLOOR

If this had been a new freestanding building, you would have begun framing the floor by installing two *headers* on opposing foundation walls. Headers sit on the mudsill, as shown in *Typical Floor Framing* below. Joists run between the headers and support the floor when it's installed. In order to make the span as short as possible, the joists usually run across the width of the building rather than its length. The ends of each joist rest on the mudsill and are nailed to a header, as shown in *Photo 4-1* on the opposite page. The full load of the walls is transferred directly to the mudsill and foundation.

Unlike a new house, a typical addition has only three new foundation walls. If the addition's joists run perpendicular to the wall shared with the existing house, this wall needs a *ledger,* a horizontal strip of 2-by stock on which the joists will rest in metal joist hangers. The ledger is secured to the house first with nails and then with ⅜ x 3½-inch lag screws that will reach through the wall and into the framing members; you'll hit either an end joist or a header, depending on the orientation of the house's framing; see *The Baileys' Floor Framing Plan* on the opposite page.

Before laying out the ledger, you'll probably need to remove some existing siding. Barry and Dave made quick work of this by using a scaffold set up on the basement floor; neatness didn't count here because the back wall of the house would be removed after the addition was closed in.

Using an 8-foot level to ensure accuracy, Barry established where the 2 x 12 ledger would go. He first marked a point 11¼ inches above the mudsill, representing the top of the ledger (a 2 x 12 is actually 11¼ inches wide). Then he drew a line on the sheathing across the back of the house.

In picking lengths of 2 x 12 for the ledger, look for the straightest boards you can find. Irregularities here will be telegraphed throughout the entire structure.

Dave first drilled 5/16-inch-diameter pilot holes at 2-foot intervals through the ledger and into the house framing, ensuring that there would be one screw between every other joist. He then slipped washers over the screws, and drove the screws into the holes.

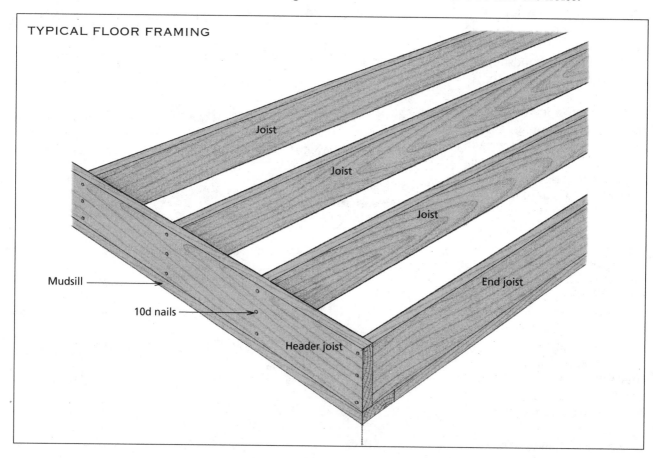

TYPICAL FLOOR FRAMING

Joist

Joist

Joist

End joist

Mudsill

10d nails

Header joist

Photo 4-1. *Dave uses an air nailer to attach the joists to the header.*

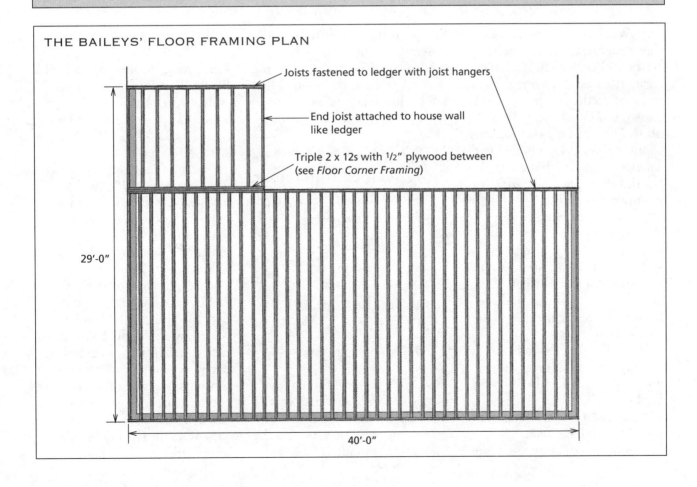

THE BAILEYS' FLOOR FRAMING PLAN

Joists fastened to ledger with joist hangers

End joist attached to house wall
like ledger

Triple 2 x 12s with ¹/₂" plywood between
(see *Floor Corner Framing*)

29'-0"

40'-0"

FRAMING THE FLOOR

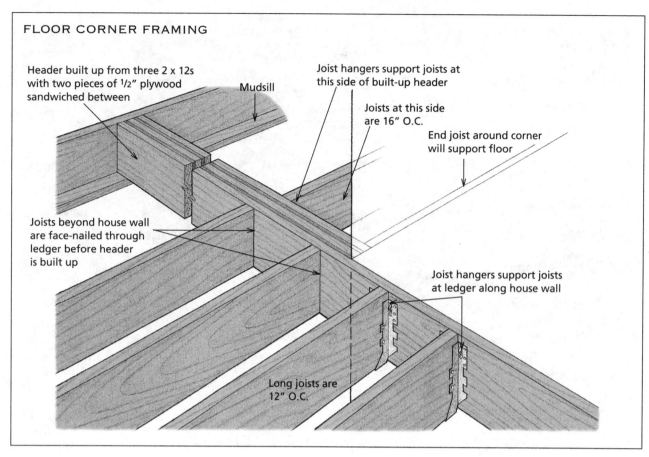

FLOOR CORNER FRAMING

Header built up from three 2 x 12s with two pieces of 1/2" plywood sandwiched between

Mudsill

Joist hangers support joists at this side of built-up header

Joists at this side are 16" O.C.

End joist around corner will support floor

Joists beyond house wall are face-nailed through ledger before header is built up

Joist hangers support joists at ledger along house wall

Long joists are 12" O.C.

When the ledger reached the corner near the garage, Barry and Dave continued it straight ahead so that it spanned to the end joist, as shown in *Floor Corner Framing* above. Barry laid a level on this spanning piece. He nodded with satisfaction as the bubble centered. Careful mudsill work was paying off already.

The extended section of the ledger, spanning from the back wall of the house to the side wall of the addition, isn't typical construction. This corner of the addition had the longest space for the joists to span—nearly 26 feet.

Ordinarily, joists this long are supported underneath by a girder, as explained in "Girders for Long Spans" on page 64. But putting a girder under the joists would have reduced headroom, and Barry knew the

Baileys wanted a clear 7-foot basement ceiling. So he extended the ledger instead, using it as a brace for the joists. He later reinforced the extension with plywood and 2 x 12s.

▲▲▲▲▲▲▲▲▲▲▲

A detailed framing plan that has been approved by your local building inspector and careful workmanship are essential ingredients for a sound floor frame.

▼▼▼▼▼▼▼▼▼▼▼

This solution gave the Baileys plenty of headroom and was, in Barry's words, "plenty strong enough." It was also the first mistake made in con-

structing the Baileys' addition.

The building inspector, Ken Amey, stopped by and told Barry the ledger didn't meet code. "A tripled 2 x 12 is allowed to span something less than 10 feet," he said. "This span is 11 feet."

Contractor Dennis Grim was told that a girder would have to be installed under the built-up header. Dennis decided to use an 8-inch-high steel girder; it would eat up less headroom than its wooden equivalent. Because no girder pockets had been cast into the foundation, the girder would be supported by steel Lally columns on each end. The lesson behind Barry's minor misadventure is to consult span tables and your building inspector well in advance of each aspect of the job.

With the ledger in place, the crew working on the Baileys' addition was ready to install the header and end joists, all of which sit on the mudsill and form the outer edges of the floor framing.

Barry started flipping through his stack of 2 x 12s, looking for header and end joist candidates that were both as straight as possible and close to a consistent 11¼-inch width. If you ignore variations in width along the length of these members, you may wind up with an uneven floor despite all of your careful mudsill work.

With the boards trimmed, Barry put one end joist in place on the mudsill and checked for level. Then he and Dave toe-nailed the end joist to the mudsill, nailing from both sides and making sure the outside face of the header was flush with the outside edge of the mudsill. They continued around the foundation wall, installing the header and the other end joist. For a short course in nailing, see "Face-Nailing and Toenailing" on page 84.

LAYING OUT THE JOISTS

Now it was time to mark where the joists would meet the ledger and header, as shown in *Laying Out Framing Members* on the right (top). With a square, Barry drew a line representing the left side of each joist, adding an X to make clear which side of the line the joist should be on. The most typical spacing you'll find in framing is 16 inches *on center* (O.C.). This means that there is 16 inches between the center of each joist or other framing member (and, of course, 16 inches between the left side of one framing member and the left side of the next).

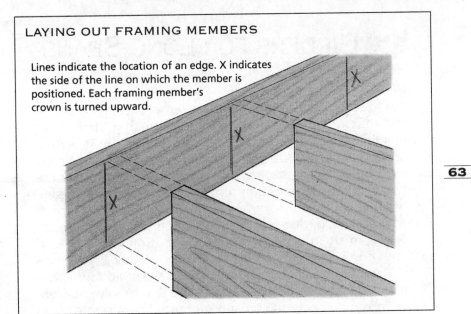

LAYING OUT FRAMING MEMBERS

Lines indicate the location of an edge. X indicates the side of the line on which the member is positioned. Each framing member's crown is turned upward.

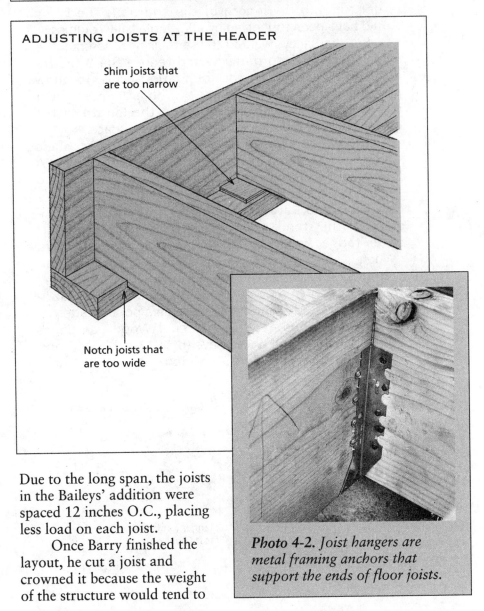

ADJUSTING JOISTS AT THE HEADER

Shim joists that are too narrow

Notch joists that are too wide

Photo 4-2. Joist hangers are metal framing anchors that support the ends of floor joists.

Due to the long span, the joists in the Baileys' addition were spaced 12 inches O.C., placing less load on each joist.

Once Barry finished the layout, he cut a joist and crowned it because the weight of the structure would tend to

GIRDERS FOR LONG SPANS

The longer the distance a joist must span, the beefier the joist must be—that's common sense. A simple way to cut that distance in half is to run another structural member, called a *girder,* across the middle of the structure and perpendicular to the joists. To do its work, a girder must be unusually strong. A site-built answer is to nail up two or three pieces of 2-by lumber. Or you can use a beam of steel or laminated wood. Because they carry a great deal of load, girders must be well supported at either end. They can sit in pockets cast in foundation walls or rest atop posts, as shown in *Girders and Posts* below.

When the floor framing for the Baileys' addition was planned, the first thought was to use 2 x 10 joists spaced 16 inches on center (O.C.) and supported by a single steel girder running the length of the addition. The beam would have been supported by adjustable Lally columns.

But the Baileys wanted to use their new basement as living space. A deep girder would reduce the 8 feet of headroom provided by the foundation walls. To allow more headroom, they could get by with a skimpier girder if more columns were placed along the length of the girder, but they didn't want to break up the space.

The solution was to use beefy joists and space them close together, doing away with the need for a girder. A look at joist span tables showed that 2 x 12s were needed for the joists, header, and ledger. As required by the tables, Barry and Dave spaced the joists 12 inches O.C. instead of the standard 16 inches. This made economic sense, too, according to Ted Courier, one of contractors. "When I priced the girder and 2 x 10s and compared this with the 2 x 12s, I realized the girder wouldn't have saved the Baileys much money." Ted also looked at prefabricated wood I-joists, which have become a popular alternative to solid wood. (See "Engineered Wood" on pages 78–79.) "But they still would have to be 12 inches O.C. and that would mean no savings," said Ted.

flatten it. He set one end on the mudsill and positioned it against the header. Dave held the other end against the ledger. They checked the joist with an 8-foot level, and Dave toenailed through the top of the joist and into the ledger using an 8d nail. They checked for level again, and Dave made slight adjustments by tapping his end. Barry then drove 16d nails through the header into the joist, while Dave toenailed another 8d nail on either side of the joist.

Satisfied that the initial measure for the length of the joists was correct, Barry cut several more joists, and the carpenters installed them. Some joists will turn out to be wider or narrower than the header. To remedy the wide ones, Barry notched them slightly, as shown in *Adjusting Joists at the Header* on page 63 (bottom). (This illustration also shows how to shim joists to raise them.)

Once all the joists are installed, the connection between joists and ledger must be reinforced with joist hangers, as shown in *Photo 4-2* on page 63. Hangers for each joist can be put up as you go. But Barry explained that it's easier to do one job at a time. More important, he said, "Without the hangers, it's easier to adjust the joists for level after a few are in place." With just a few nails in a joist, you can bang on the top or bottom near the ledger to adjust the joist's height slightly.

INSTALLING BRIDGING

Additional support for the floor frame, called *bridging,* is installed between the joists, both to keep the joists from twisting and to make the floors stiffer. Bridging was routine in

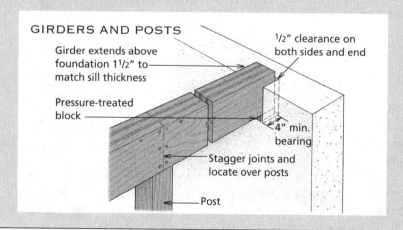

GIRDERS AND POSTS

Girder extends above foundation 1½" to match sill thickness

Pressure-treated block

½" clearance on both sides and end

4" min. bearing

Stagger joints and locate over posts

Post

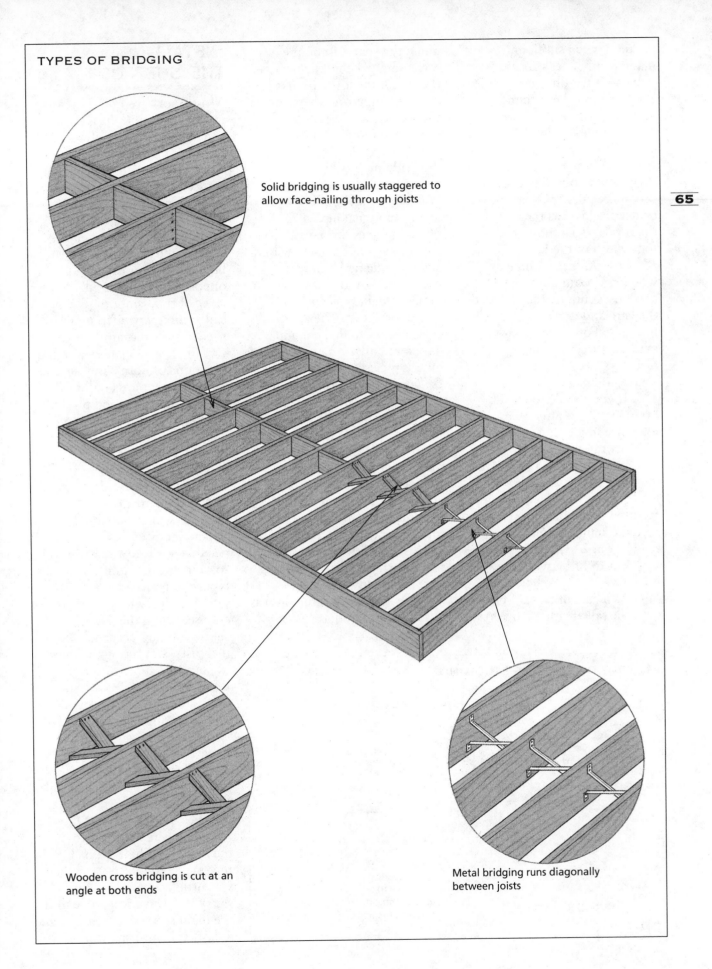

Solid bridging is usually staggered to allow face-nailing through joists

Wooden cross bridging is cut at an angle at both ends

Metal bridging runs diagonally between joists

the days when subfloors were made from boards. These days, you can often omit bridging because it has been found to add little stiffness to floors sheathed with plywood.

However, long, wide joists will tend to twist, even under plywood, so building codes usually require that they be bridged. This was the case for the 2 x 12s spanning the 20-foot width of the Baileys' addition. An exception is wooden I-beam joists, which don't twist no matter how wide they are and don't require bridging. For more about manufactured framing members, see "Engineered Wood" on pages 78–79.

If you decide to install bridging, do so after all of the joists are in place. Your options are illustrated in *Types of Bridging* on page 65. Solid and diagonal bridging are both made on site from wood; manufactured metal bridging comes ready to nail up. Solid bridging, made from 2 x 12 scraps that were cut to fit between the joists, was Barry's choice.

As a rule of thumb, bridging is installed either halfway along the span or about every 8 feet. Snap a chalkline across the top of the joists to mark your bridging run, then stagger the blocks on either side of the line. This allows you to face-nail through the joists and into the bridging blocks.

A disadvantage of solid bridging is that you'll have a harder time snaking wires and plumbing lines through it. You won't have this problem with diagonal bridging because it is used in pairs and sawed from thinner stock, typically 1 x 3s, 1 x 4s, or 2 x 2s. The angled cuts are easy to make if you have a radial arm saw or power miter saw. *Laying Out Cross Bridging* below shows how to determine the cuts.

Metal bridging also goes up in pairs. The pieces should stand apart from each other so they won't make noise or wear if the joists deflect from load. If you use either metal or diagonal bridging, attach only the top end of each piece until after you've nailed down the subfloor. In this way, the bridging won't fight any shifts in the flooring system, and the floor is less likely to be squeaky.

INSTALLING THE SUBFLOOR

Most floors are built in two layers. The *subfloor* is usually tongue-and-groove plywood (although a single layer of substantial wood flooring may be used instead if the joists and flooring will be visible from living quarters below). The subfloor supports the *finished floor*. If the finished floor will be tile, vinyl, or carpet, as opposed to solid wood, another layer of thin, smooth plywood, called *underlayment*, may be needed over the subfloor.

Increasingly, however, the functions of both subfloor and underlayment are combined into a single plywood product, known by a variety of brand names; see "A Look at Plywood" on page 68. This product is sanded smooth enough to act as underlayment and has tongue-and-groove edges to stiffen the floor. The Baileys' addition would be carpeted, except for the bathroom, so ¾-inch-thick subfloor of this type was specified.

Whatever first layer you choose, install the 4 x 8-foot sheets running perpendicular to the joists, staggering the joints to help stiffen the floor. *The Baileys' Subfloor Layout* on the opposite page shows how Barry and Dave applied these rules.

The main part of the Baileys' addition measures 20 x 40 feet. As shown in the layout drawing, Barry was able to cover the entire area with 25 full sheets of plywood. Only two cuts were needed—to make the four 4 x 4 half-sheets for the staggered joints—and there was little waste. As a result, Barry and Dave were able to do the main subfloor in about half a day. (It helped that the addi-

LAYING OUT CROSS BRIDGING

Space between joists

Joist depth

Second cut is parallel to first

Blade

Tongue

Bridging stock

Carpenter's square

Outside edge of tongue indicates angle of first cut

THE BAILEYS' SUBFLOOR LAYOUT

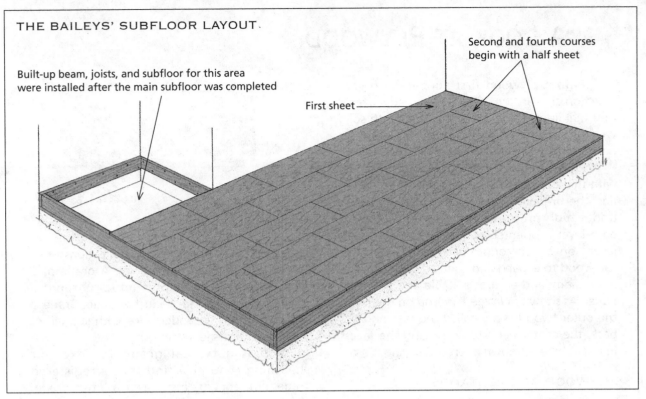

Built-up beam, joists, and subfloor for this area were installed after the main subfloor was completed

First sheet

Second and fourth courses begin with a half sheet

Photo 4-3. *Construction adhesive can be applied along the tops of the joists as an adjunct to nailing the plywood subfloor in place.*

tion had been designed in 4-foot increments.)

Barry and Dave used construction adhesive and nails to attach the subfloor. The contin-uous bond provided by the ad-hesive makes the floor even stiffer. As the joists dry out and shrink, the adhesive will main-tain contact between them and the subfloor, and this goes a long way toward preventing squeaks. Dave used 32-ounce tubes of adhesive, as shown in *Photo 4-3* above.

A Look at Plywood

Before plywood first appeared on construction sites in the 1930s, the broad surfaces of a building's frame were sheathed with solid wood boards. Today, plywood (or one of its newer relatives) is usually chosen to do the job.

Plywood is a wood sandwich, typically with thin plies of solid wood for both the meat and the bread. The layers are glued together under high pressure. The grain direction of each layer is oriented perpendicular to the adjacent ones; this counteracts the tendency of the wood to expand and contract with changes in humidity and ensures a stable and balanced panel. As shown in *Inside Plywood* on the right, the outer two plies are called the face and the back, the center ply is the core, and the layers in between are known as cross banding.

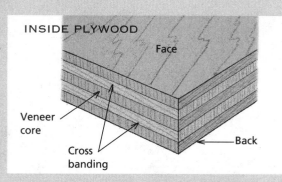

INSIDE PLYWOOD

Face

Veneer core

Cross banding

Back

commonly used for interior applications, such as cabinets and built-in shelves. A grade of C allows defects that don't impair strength, including knots up to 1½ inches wide. Grade D is found on an unsanded face with still larger knots and offers less strength.

CD is a typical grade for exterior sheathing. You may find that a registered trademark appears instead of a letter grade. This means the panel is designed for a specific use. The photo on the left shows the grade stamp for Unifloor, a product intended for subflooring.

The second line gives the structural spanning capacity of the panel, such as 24 O.C. This tells you the maximum spacing of the framing members on which it can be used. When only one span number appears, it refers to rafter spacing, and the panel is rated only for roof or wall sheathing. When two numbers appear, such as 24/16, the first gives maximum rafter spacing and the second gives maximum joist spacing. Joist spacing and plywood selection should be planned simultaneously, since wider spacing may require thicker plywood. Plywood thickness is stated on the grading stamp as a fraction—¼ or $^{15}\!/_{32}$, for example.

Plywoods are further designated for either interior or exterior use, depending on the glues used in their fabrication. The distinction is important because a plywood made with interior glue will eventually delaminate (the plies will separate) if used outdoors. Some interior plywood grades use an exterior glue; this combination is particularly useful if the installed sheets will be temporarily exposed to direct moisture, as in a subfloor. Exterior plywoods often carry their own exposure rating; Exposure 1 allows the longer exposure time.

PLYWOOD GRADE STAMPS

C-D
24/16
INTERIOR
PS 1-74
EXTERIOR GLUE

APA
000

STURD-I-FLOOR®
24oc
T&G
23/32 INCH
INTERIOR
000
EXTERIOR GLUE

APA

This grade stamp identifies a trademarked subflooring material.

Plywood Grade Stamps above shows the grading information placed on each sheet, stating where and how a particular grade can be used. The first line gives the grade of the face and back veneers, expressed by letters. N is a smooth veneer surface intended for transparent finishing and has no visible defects. Grades A and B are smooth and paintable, with minor repairs allowed. N, A, and B are most

Photo 4-4. *The tongue on one plywood sheet of the subfloor is intended to slip into the groove on the adjacent sheet, but coaxing is sometimes necessary.*

Beginning at one corner of the house, Barry laid the first course of plywood with the tongue facing the existing house wall. If you use square-edged plywood and will be placing carpeting or tile on top, you'll have to back up the edges with 2 x 4 blocking between joists.

The instructions on the adhesive tube said the stuff would set up in 15 minutes. So to get the flooring positioned and nailed within that period, Barry and Dave installed two sheets at a time. Dave put a ¼-inch bead of adhesive along the tops of the joists where the two sheets would go. They put the sheets in place, and Barry hammered in a few nails by hand to secure

their position. Then the men quickly snapped lines across the sheets to ensure that nails would sink into the middle of the joists. Dave finished with the power nailer, spacing the nails about 6 inches apart.

But he delayed nailing the outside edges of each sheet until the adjoining sheet was slid into place. This made it easier to get the tongues into the grooves. Nevertheless, as revealed in *Photo 4-4* above, force occasionally was necessary. Dave stood on the joint between sheets while Barry rapped the opposing edge with a sledge hammer. A scrap of 2-by along the edge prevented the heavy head from crushing the groove.

COMPLETING THE SUBFLOOR

When the main subfloor was completed, a small section remained by the garage. Barry built up the ill-fated header shown in *Floor Corner Framing* on page 62, then he and Dave continued the ledger around the corner of the house and along the back of the garage wall. They used joist hangers to install short joists between the built-up header and the garage wall. Since the span was short, Barry spaced the joists 16 inches O.C. After installing the remaining subfloor, the carpenters headed for lunch at the local pizzeria.

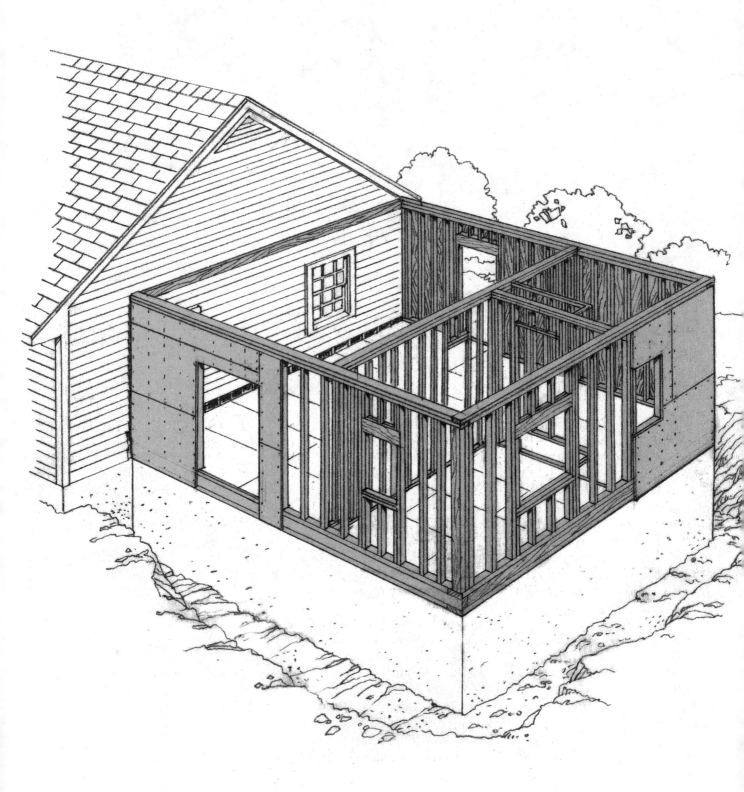

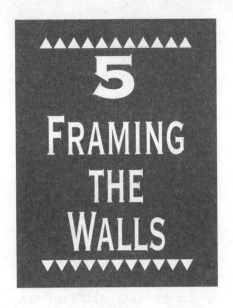

5
FRAMING THE WALLS

The subfloor was down. Barry and Dave were ready to begin framing walls. Carpenters usually assemble the walls "on the flat"—that is, with the walls lying flat on the platform provided by the subfloor. Once each wall is assembled, it is raised into position. (Now, before the subfloor is used to assemble the walls, is a good time to test the fit of rafters for a gable roof; see "Cutting the Gable Rafters" on page 96.)

Some carpenters like to sheathe each wall before putting it up. Putting the sheathing on first keeps the whole wall more stable and square. It's simpler to nail the sheathing when it's down on the ground, too. But other carpenters find it easier on their backs to lift unsheathed walls into position, especially if only a couple of crew members are doing the

lifting. And by putting off sheathing walls until the roof is up, the addition and any supplies can be more quickly protected from wet weather. (In areas prone to high winds or earthquakes, code may prohibit sheathing on the flat.)

Fortunately for Barry, Dennis Grim happened to be backfilling around the foundation on the day the long back wall had to go up. Barry tied a rope from the top of the wall to Dennis's backhoe so that the muscle of the machine could be enlisted to pull the wall into position.

But framing is an activity subject to weather. A stiff breeze came up, and the sheathed wall acted like a huge sail with a mind of its own. Barry was forced to cut it in half and raise it in two sections. He took out a stud where two plywood sheets met and cut

through the plates with a circular saw. After the two halves were in place, he replaced the stud and renailed the plywood to it.

ANATOMY OF A WALL

The components of a wall are of three kinds—horizontal lumber, vertical lumber, and sheathing. As illustrated in *Parts of a Wall* on page 72, horizontal pieces called *plates* are on the top and bottom. The sole plate is nailed to the sub-floor, while two top plates establish the top of the wall. The top plate is doubled to create lap joints at corners that tie the walls together and to help support rafters and joists. Stock chosen for the top plate should be sound and relatively free from knots, and the longest stock should be used so that fewer joints need to be staggered.

Common studs are the wall's main load-bearing elements. They run the full length between the sole plate and top plate and are typically placed 16 inches O.C. When the run of studs is interrupted with door and window openings, the load-bearing job of these studs is taken on by a horizontal *header*. For openings up to 36 inches wide, a header made of two 2 x 4s on edge does the job. For wider openings, the header requirement depends on the load above. As an example, some partition walls carry no load, while others are *bearing walls*. Among bearing walls, gable end walls carry less weight than those on the side that support the ends of rafters.

Headers are supported by *trimmers,* sometimes called *jack studs.* These studs define the width of the rough opening. For door openings, trimmers always run from the bottom of the header to the sole plate. For windows, carpenters sometimes run trimmers all the way to the sole plate, as shown in the illustration. Other carpenters, Barry included, prefer to stop trimmers at the top of the *rough sill.* The decision doesn't affect the strength of the wall. As you'll find a little later, it's just a matter of how a carpenter likes to work. Nailed against each trimmer is a full-length *king stud,* which stiffens the opening.

The rough sill defines the bottom of a window opening. It carries no building load, so it's usually just a single 2 x 4 laid flat. However, if your plan calls for a wide molding under the window, you may want to double the rough sill to give yourself more wood to nail into.

Cripple studs, also called cripples, support the rough sill and give you something to which you can attach drywall. If trimmers stop at the rough sill, there will always be cripples under each end of the rough sill. Otherwise, cripples are located to continue the 16-inch O.C. nailing pattern for the sheathing and drywall. Carpenters may use cripples between the header and top plate, but time can be saved by filling the space with a wider header than needed for the load.

CORNER FRAMING

Before laying out and building walls, you need to decide how they'll be tied together at the

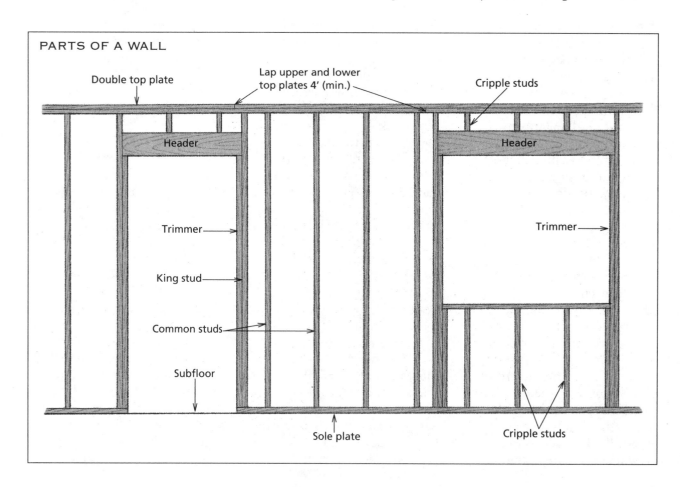

PARTS OF A WALL

Double top plate

Lap upper and lower top plates 4' (min.)

Cripple studs

Header

Header

Trimmer

King stud

Trimmer

Common studs

Subfloor

Sole plate

Cripple studs

CORNER FRAMING

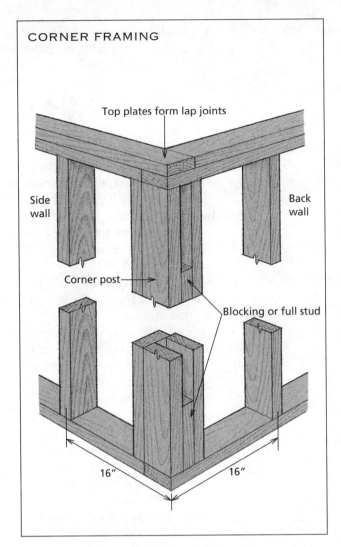

Top plates form lap joints

Side wall

Back wall

Corner post

Blocking or full stud

16" 16"

ALTERNATE CORNER FRAMING

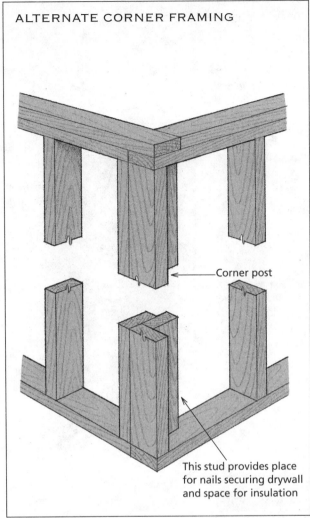

Corner post

This stud provides place for nails securing drywall and space for insulation

corners. The corner connections are crucial to the strength of the frame; unless walls are linked securely, you'll be building something like a house of cards. Corners are formed where the ends of two exterior walls meet and where an interior partition wall meets the run of another wall. In all cases, corners are designed to provide wood to which you anchor interior wall coverings.

For the Baileys' addition, Barry favored the most common method of joining ends, as shown in the illustration *Corner Framing* above left. He laid out the plates so that the long back wall ran the full 40 feet of the addition, with the side walls butting into it.

First, Barry nailed three studs together to form a corner post. The first stud of the side wall was nailed to this post, tying the walls together and providing a base for attaching drywall in both directions. Barry used full 2 x 4s, although he could have substituted three or four blocks of scrap 2 x 4s for the middle 2 x 4 in the post. "It's just a matter of what I have lying around," Barry said. "I didn't have much scrap when I made these corners. A couple of 2 x 4s weren't going to break the budget."

Another approach is shown in *Alternate Corner Framing* above right. This configuration saves a stud and

lets you stuff fiberglass insulation into the corner. Make sure code in your area allows this method before you use it.

Where a partition wall met an exterior wall, Barry used the standard construction shown in *Partition Wall Corner* on page 74. With this method, a stud is turned so that its face will meet the face of the last stud in the partition wall, then two studs are positioned in the usual way and nailed to either side of the center stud. These two studs will provide a place to nail the drywall.

Note that in all three methods of corner construction, the upper top plate from one wall overlaps the lower top plate of the other wall.

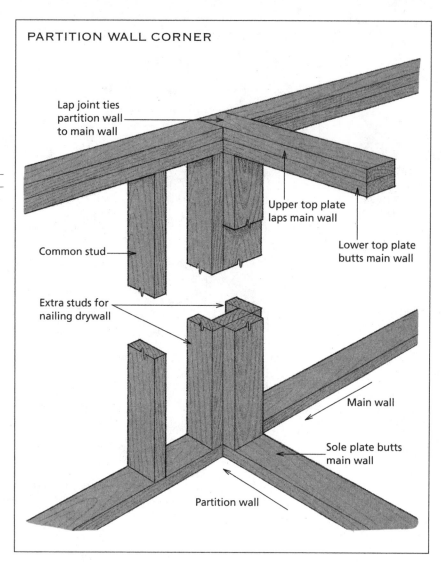

PARTITION WALL CORNER

Lap joint ties partition wall to main wall

Upper top plate laps main wall

Common stud

Lower top plate butts main wall

Extra studs for nailing drywall

Main wall

Sole plate butts main wall

Partition wall

LAYING OUT AND PLATING

Constructing a wall begins with two steps: laying it out, which involves transferring dimensions from the floor plan drawing to the plywood subfloor, and plating, which is the process of marking the lower top plates and sole plates to show where studs and other framing elements will be placed.

To lay out where the walls in the Baileys' addition would go, Barry snapped chalklines across the subfloor. (If the subfloor was to serve as a full-scale pattern, it would need to be swept especially well.) Because the edge of the platform

probably wasn't true, lines were snapped for the outside walls as well. The walls of the Baileys' addition would be framed with 2 x 4s, so the line was snapped 3½ inches from the edge to establish the inside of the plate.

Then, it was a matter of picking which wall of the Baileys' addition to build first. Common practice is to begin with the longest walls, then butt shorter walls into them. In this case, it meant starting with the 40-foot back wall, adding the side walls, then moving on to the interior partition walls that defined the family room, master bedroom, closet, and bath.

The crew placed two

layers of 2 x 4s along the back wall. These would become the sole plate and the lower top plate.

Barry placed the end piece of the sole plate flush with the left corner of the floor. He tacked it to the floor by driving a nail only partway at both ends; this plate would be removed later to build the walls on the flat. He butted other 2 x 4s to complete the sole plate; see the illustration *Laying Out Plates* on the opposite page (top).

Consulting his plans, Barry marked the sole plate for the positions of the studs, also noting the shorter cripples and trimmers that would go around door and window openings; see the illustration *Laying Out Studs* on the opposite page (bottom).

Next, Barry placed lumber for the lower top plate against the inside of the tacked sole plate, making sure that the joints of the lower top plate fell where they would be supported by a stud. (Local building codes may require this extra step, and if you don't attend to it now, you may have to add extra studs later.) The upper top plate was then placed alongside the lower top plate; the joints of the two upper plates were staggered, with the first piece of the top started at the opposite corner.

At this point, the upper top plate could have been nailed directly into the lower top plate. Instead, Barry chose to add the upper top plate once the walls were up.

Photo 5-1 on page 76 and the illustration *Laying Out Studs* show how to translate the information on the plans into a stud and cripple layout directly on the plates. Start by laying out the stud spacing along the entire length of the wall. Don't worry about window or door openings at this point. If this is a main wall that will run through, include the two extra studs that will form the corner.

Now check your plans and mark the centerlines of windows and doors. Measuring from each centerline, add trimmer locations that will give you the door and window openings you need and label each location with a T. Add a king stud to the outside of every trimmer. Every stud inside the

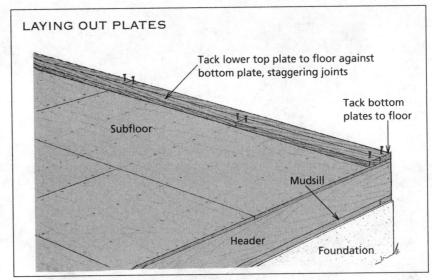

LAYING OUT PLATES

Tack lower top plate to floor against bottom plate, staggering joints

Tack bottom plates to floor

Subfloor

Mudsill

Header

Foundation

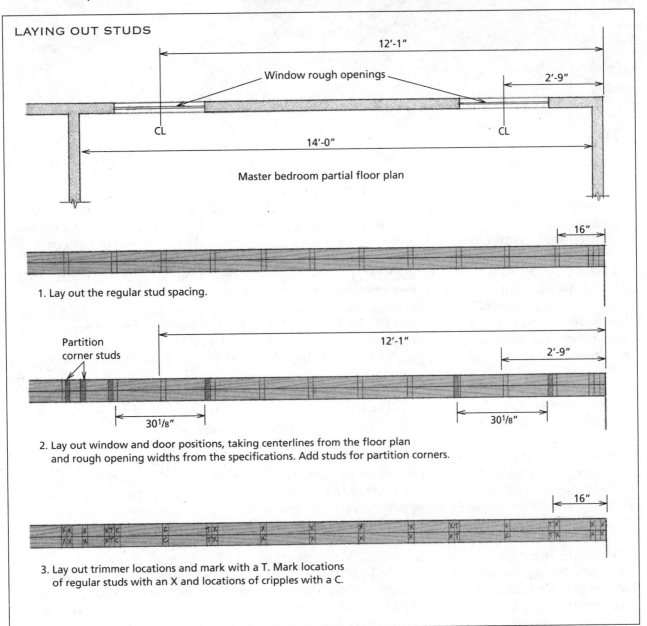

LAYING OUT STUDS

12'-1"

Window rough openings

2'-9"

CL

CL

14'-0"

Master bedroom partial floor plan

16"

1. Lay out the regular stud spacing.

Partition corner studs

12'-1"

2'-9"

30 1/8"

30 1/8"

2. Lay out window and door positions, taking centerlines from the floor plan and rough opening widths from the specifications. Add studs for partition corners.

16"

3. Lay out trimmer locations and mark with a T. Mark locations of regular studs with an X and locations of cripples with a C.

Photo 5-1. The plates are marked to show where studs will be nailed in place.

trimmers will be a cripple, and the locations of these short studs should be marked with a C. If there will be partition walls, mark the locations of the two extra studs for each partition corner. If code requires that breaks in the top plate be supported and they haven't been planned to fall atop studs, then mark these spots for additional studs.

By now, any location that hasn't been lettered should be a full-length stud, whether it be a king or regular stud. Mark these locations visibly with an X.

Sometimes a trimmer location may overlap the 16-inch O.C. layout for a regular stud. That's not a problem. Just slide the stud over to make room for the trimmer, promoting the regular stud to a king stud. For practical purposes, your layout has only two goals—to create the rough opening widths you need while providing something to nail into every 16 inches.

MAKING THE HEADERS

As mentioned, you can design your header for the load, then cut cripples to fit between the header and lower top plate. Or you can make a wider header to fill the space.

For the Baileys' addition, Dave made headers by sandwiching a piece of ½-inch-thick plywood between two lengths of 2-by set on edge, as shown in *Solid Wood Header* on the opposite page. This brought the headers to the same 3½-inch thickness as the walls. Dave assembled the sandwich by driving 16d nails at an angle from both sides, then nailed it in place, as shown in *Photo 5-2* on the opposite page.

You can build up the header to the width you need by adding layers of 2 x 4s, laid flat, to the top or bottom of the sandwich, which saves the trouble of ripping lumber to fit. Barry used three different combinations to get the headers he needed for the Baileys' addition.

A disadvantage of wide headers is that they may shrink significantly across their width. You can sidestep this problem by using one of a variety of manufactured wood products that are more stable (as explained in "Engineered Wood" on pages 78–79).

No matter how you choose to build your headers, you need three pieces of information to size them: rough opening width, rough opening height, and the distance from the subfloor to the bottom of the lower top plate. Because headers span king studs and rest on trimmers, the headers will be 3 inches longer than the rough opening width.

Today, most walls are built with precut studs that don't require being trimmed to length. Inquire locally to find what lengths are available.

The studs delivered to the Baileys' site were 92⅝ inches long. Adding 4½ inches for the combined thicknesses of the three plates resulted in a subfloor-to-ceiling joist height of 8 feet 1⅛ inches. This allowed a margin for a ceiling of either ½-inch- or ⅝-inch-thick drywall and meant that 8-foot-long drywall panels (or two courses of 4-foot-wide panels) would fit comfortably on the walls.

Your plans may be very specific about header height. Or, as with the plans for the

Baileys' addition, you may only have a rough idea based on a scale drawing of the outside walls. The illustration *The Baileys' Rough Openings* on page 80 shows the three header combinations used in the Baileys' addition. All of the interior doors required standard 6-foot, 10-inch

(continued on page 80)

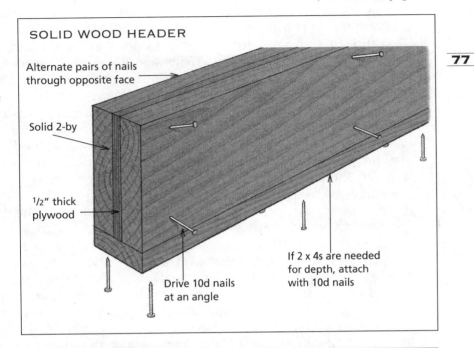

SOLID WOOD HEADER

Alternate pairs of nails through opposite face

Solid 2-by

½" thick plywood

Drive 10d nails at an angle

If 2 x 4s are needed for depth, attach with 10d nails

Photo 5-2. *Headers must be sturdy so that they won't bend and interfere with the operation of the window or door below.*

77

▶ ENGINEERED WOOD

The ubiquitous 2 x 4 is the building block of housing construction. Along with its stouter siblings, dimensional lumber continues to provide architects and builders with a reliable set of standardized parts for designing and building every manner of house. Dimensional lumber is strong, stable, and easy to use. But it is not without its problems.

First of all, it moves. All wood expands and contracts with changes in humidity. The wider the stock, the more movement there may be. A 2 x 12 header covered with drywall can shrink considerably during its first dry indoor winter. The drywall won't shrink, but it *will* crack.

Second, wood tends to warp. As stock twists, bows, cups, splits, or goes crooked, it becomes less usable. These problems usually come out during drying and milling, and most of the bad stuff is culled. Still, every carpenter has to be on the lookout for warped lumber.

A third limitation of softwood lumber is its strength. Used to frame a 2 x 12 floor, with 2 x 12 joists spaced 12 inches O.C., dimensional lumber can span no more than 24 feet.

Finally, softwood lumber is a limited and dwindling natural resource. It takes many trees to produce a house frame worth of 2-by stock. No matter how well this finite resource is managed, demand for wood products is likely to always exceed supply. And this means prices will continue to rise.

For all of these reasons, engineers, architects, wood scientists, and forestry managers have worked to develop alternatives to standard dimensional lumber. Compared to solid lumber, the following alternatives are relatively stable dimensionally, and they can span greater distances.

A *glue-laminated structural timber,* shown below (left), is made by sandwiching thin laminations of dimensional lumber with special glues under pressure. This is a good alternative to solid lumber where an exposed beam is called for. Timbers can be made to order for arched roof frames.

A *box beam,* shown below (right), combines the best features of 2 x 4s and plywood. It is commonly used for door and window headers. Box beams can be bought manufactured, or you can make your own.

Trusses, shown on the opposite page (top), are rigid frameworks of 2-by stock designed to replace larger dimensional stock. Trusses can be cut and assembled on the job site, or they can be bought ready-made. Manufactured trusses are assembled either with plain butt joints that are scabbed on both sides with a toothed plate of steel or with plywood gussets. A trussed header is an alternative to a built-up header since it can be made from 2 x 4 stock alone. Floor trusses don't require bridging. Roof trusses are another application. Truss manufacturers offer the same hanging and joining hardware used with conventional lumber.

I-joists, shown on the opposite page (bottom), are manufactured I-beams used primarily for floor joists. The flanges are either milled lumber or parallel-veneer lumber. Plywood or waferboard panels are

GLUE-LAMINATED STRUCTURAL TIMBER

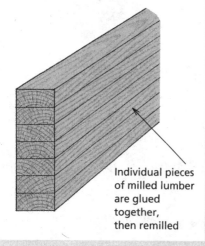

Individual pieces of milled lumber are glued together, then remilled

BOX BEAM

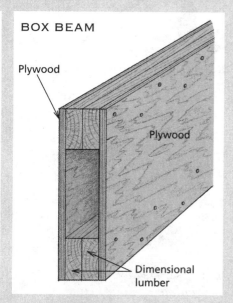

Plywood

Plywood

Dimensional lumber

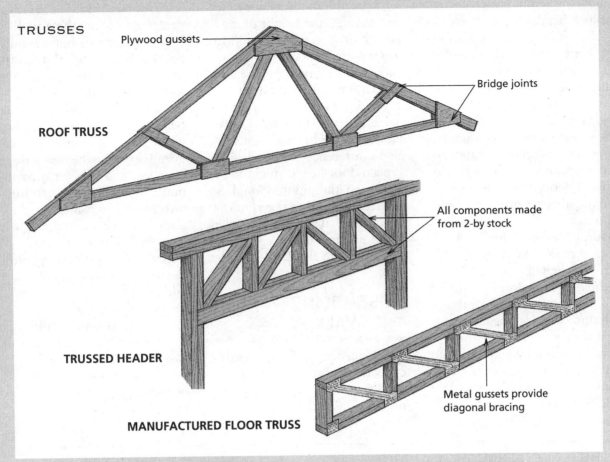

Plywood gussets

Bridge joints

ROOF TRUSS

All components made from 2-by stock

TRUSSED HEADER

Metal gussets provide diagonal bracing

MANUFACTURED FLOOR TRUSS

used for the webbing. At least one manufacturer provides perforated punch-outs for running pipe and duct. Most I-joists eliminate the need for bridging, but check your building codes. With lumber prices on the rise, I-joists have become competitive, particularly when longer floor spans are needed.

Laminated-veneer lumber is a composite wood lumber product that is similar to glue-laminated wood timbers but uses very thin layers of veneer rather than dimensional

lumber. Unlike plywood, all the veneers in this product run parallel with each other. Defects in any single piece of veneer cause no strength reduction in the laminated stock. Beams and girders of great length are available; 3½-inch-thick stock is commonly used for solid headers.

Parallel-strand lumber is composed of long strands of wood glued parallel with the length of the stock. The strands come from small-diameter second-growth trees. This product is used like laminated veneer lumber but has a shorter spanning capacity.

Oriented-strand lumber is made almost exclusively from aspen, one of nature's fastest growing trees and a species otherwise unsuitable for dimensional lumber. The logs are sliced into random-shape chips or wafers, which are completely coated with glue. The strands are organized so they all run lengthwise, giving the product a structural grain direction. The oriented-strand process was first used to make sheathing panels, called oriented-strand board (see "Sheathing Options" on page 88). Oriented-strand lumber is used for large structural members and headers.

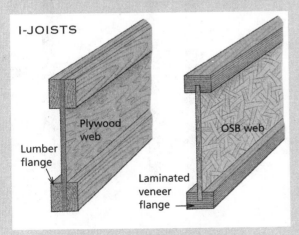

I-JOISTS

Plywood web

OSB web

Lumber flange

Laminated veneer flange

headers. Barry subtracted this 82-inch header height from the 94⅛-inch height of the lower top plate and found he needed 12⅛-inch-wide headers. By sandwiching a 2 x 10 between two 2 x 4s, Barry got a header width of 12¼ inches, close enough for a rough opening.

The only new entrance into the addition was to be a pair of French doors, which would require a rough opening height of 6 feet 8 inches. So Barry made a header of one 2 x 10 with three 2 x 4s. This gave him a header height of 6 feet 8⅜ inches—again, close enough.

As a general rule of design, window and door headers look best if they are at the same height, especially when they are in the same room and on the same wall. Otherwise, the addition may take on a haphazard look. But Barry decided that the height of the French door header would look too low for windows under a cathedral ceiling. If he brought the windows up just another 1½ inches to the standard door height, they'd still look too low. He also thought that such a slight difference from the French door height might look awkward and unintentional. So he elected to bring the window headers up to 6 feet 11⅜ inches by adding just one 2 x 4, rather than three, to the 2 x 10 header.

ASSEMBLING THE WALLS

The sequence for wall assembly can vary according to your crew size, equipment, and preferences.

As mentioned, Barry preferred to sheathe a wall before raising it, but wouldn't add the upper top plate until after the walls were up. This is just a matter of personal preference—would you rather bend over to drive the nails or work from a ladder? (You can even leave out the headers, cripples, and sills for now to make the walls easier to lift into place.) In a modest addition like the Baileys', with only eight connections between walls, Barry wouldn't have saved much time by adding the upper top plate before raising a wall.

If you choose to add the upper top plate while the wall is still lying flat, plan on lapping partition top plates over main wall top plates for easier installation.

THE BAILEYS' ROUGH OPENINGS

Interior door

6'-9⅞"   92⅝"

3'-0"

French door

9¼"

6'-8⅜"

6'-0"

Window

48¼"

30⅛"

94⅛"

Photo 5-3. Few pieces of lumber will appear perfectly straight to the eye, so it's good to get in the habit of sighting down each piece to find its crown, or high point.

The method described here—using trimmers that run to the rough sill instead of all the way to the sole plate—is a common approach. Start by pulling the temporary nails out of the plates. Put the sole plate and the lower top plate on edge, about a stud's length apart with the layout marks turned in. Now put full-length common studs and king studs in position.

If a common stud will be located less than 14½ inches from a king stud, leave that common stud out for now to allow room to nail headers. Also leave out common studs that fall near the two extra studs for each partition wall corner. You'll need room to nail the extra studs to the stud that is placed sideways between them.

Crown the studs, as shown in *Photo 5-3* above. Place them with the outside of the curve facing up, so they won't rock as you work with them and so the wall will be more consistent.

▲▲▲▲▲▲▲▲▲▲▲▲

Before raising a wall, double-check that the center of a stud falls every 48 inches. It's easier to adjust or add a stud now than to finagle with drywall cuts later on.

▼▼▼▼▼▼▼▼▼▼▼▼

With 16d nails in his nail pouch, Barry was ready to frame. The illustration *Assembling a Wall on the Flat* on page 82 shows the sequence he followed for walls that were framed on the flat. First, he nailed the lower top plate to the studs using two nails per stud and working from one end of the wall to the other.

To do this, Barry started a pair of nails into the plate. Then he clamped the stud to the floor by stepping on it with one foot. His free hand held the plate against the stud while he hammered in the nails. When the lower top plate was nailed in place, he did the same for the sole plate.

At window openings, Barry nailed the short cripple studs to the sole plate just as he did the common studs. Using 10d nails, he attached the end cripples to the king studs. Then he nailed the sills to the cripples, again relying on pairs of 16d nails at each joint. Next, with a hand from Dave, Barry cut and fit the headers, rested them on the trimmers, and nailed them in place through the king studs. If there are

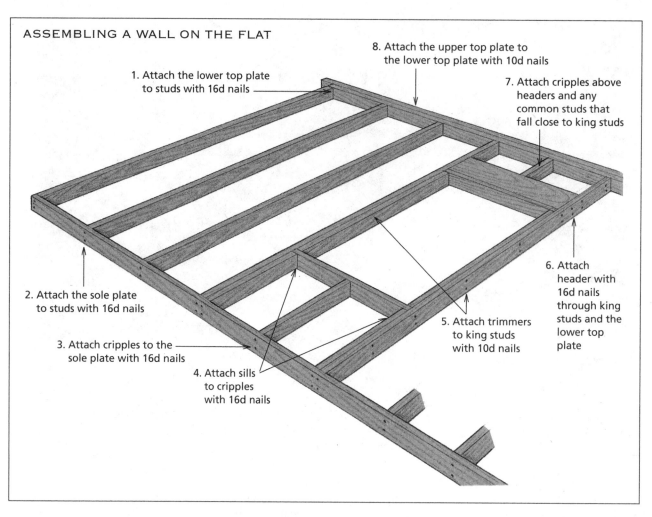

ASSEMBLING A WALL ON THE FLAT

1. Attach the lower top plate to studs with 16d nails

8. Attach the upper top plate to the lower top plate with 10d nails

7. Attach cripples above headers and any common studs that fall close to king studs

2. Attach the sole plate to studs with 16d nails

3. Attach cripples to the sole plate with 16d nails

4. Attach sills to cripples with 16d nails

5. Attach trimmers to king studs with 10d nails

6. Attach header with 16d nails through king studs and the lower top plate

cripples over the header, fasten them to the lower top plate with pairs of 16d nails. If the header is solid, drive 16d nails through the lower top plate and into the top of the header. Finally, Barry attached the upper top plate to the lower top plate with 10d nails. (See "Face-Nailing and Toenailing" on page 84 for tips on anchoring nails securely. "Air Nailers" on page 87 is an introduction to the high-speed power nailers that are widely used for framing carpentry.)

If you have decided to sheathe walls on the flat, remember to stuff insulation behind the sideways stud at the corner of any partition wall; see "Installing Sheathing" on page 86. *Photos 5-4 through 5-7* on the opposite page show an alternate sequence for framing openings after the wall is raised.

RAISING THE WALLS

If this is the first wall you are raising, you'll need to hold it up temporarily with braces, so have a couple of 12-foot 2-bys handy (three if you're raising a long wall), as well as scrap blocks of wood to nail to the floor, as shown in *Photo 5-8* on page 85. To keep the wall from sliding off the platform when lifted, nail several floor stops along the platform's edge as a sort of curb. These floor stops can be vertical scraps of 2-by stock, 18 to 24 inches long, with about 6 inches showing above the surface. Finally, assemble your crew. Plan on

having one reasonably well-conditioned person per 8 feet of wall, plus another person to wield a hammer.

Shove blocks of wood under the top plate to make it easier to grip. With helpers spaced along the wall, grab the top of the wall and tip it up. As the helpers hold the wall steady, the free person should first check that the sole plate is against the line that was snapped before the plates were marked and then attach the plate with a 16d nail between each stud, nailing close to king studs. Sections of the sole plate under doorways don't get nailed; they will be cut out later.

Then attach a brace at each end, plus a third in the middle to support a long wall. Run the braces at roughly a 45

Photo 5-4. *After the header is attached, the trimmers are nailed to the king studs.*

Photo 5-5. *The sill is nailed to the trimmers from underneath.*

Photo 5-6. *The cripple is anchored by nailing through the sill.*

Photo 5-7. *The cripples are toenailed to the bottom plate.*

FACE-NAILING AND TOENAILING

Whether you're driving nails manually or with an air nailer, there are two basic ways to nail one board to another: face-nailing and toenailing. *Face-nailing* involves driving a nail perpendicular through the face of one piece of wood and into the end, edge, or face of another piece. *Toenailing* can refer to any nail driven at an angle, but the most frequent use is for a face-to-end joint, in which the face is not accessible (as when a joist is connected to a ledger). *Face-Nailing and Toenailing* below shows common applications.

Face-nailing is the easiest method of joining two pieces of wood with nails; often it's the only sensible way. In face-to-face and face-to-edge nailing, for example, the nail penetrates the wood perpendicular to the wood grain. This provides the best holding power (or withdrawal resis-

tance) a nail can give. Nailing into end grain, such as when a nail is driven up through a bottom plate to anchor a stud, offers very little withdrawal resistance.

While the best method of nailing may be obvious, the type of nail to use often is not. The common nail serves adequately for all framing jobs, but most other nails are designed for a specific use.

Galvanized common nails don't rust; use them when they'll be exposed to the weather. Common nails bend easily in the dense yellow pine used for pressure-treated lumber, so choose a hardened deck nail for this material. A spiral shank imparts greater holding power to a nail; use this type for decks, siding, and wood shingles. The broad head of a roofing nail holds flat, often brittle, materials from being lifted by the wind.

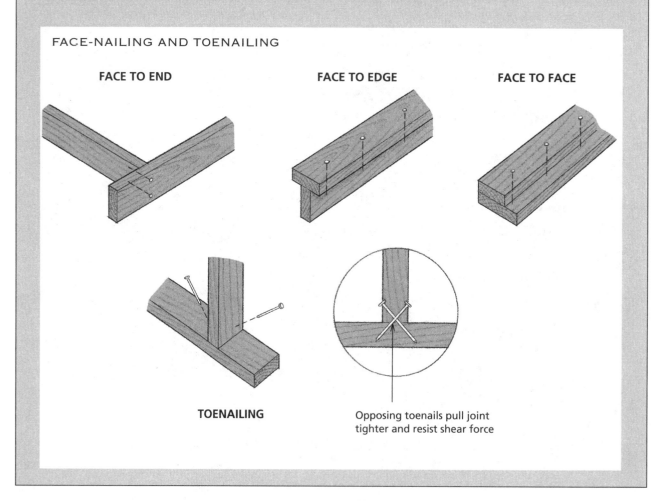

FACE-NAILING AND TOENAILING

FACE TO END

FACE TO EDGE

FACE TO FACE

TOENAILING

Opposing toenails pull joint tighter and resist shear force

Photo 5-8. Newly erected walls are kept in place with braces nailed temporarily.

degree angle from the top of the wall to the subfloor, where the braces are backed up with scrap blocks nailed to the floor. Nail each brace into the side of a header or stringer joist. Just eyeball to get the wall roughly plumb for now.

If there will be a main wall running perpendicular to the first one you raised, then assemble, raise, and brace that wall now. Nail the sole plate into place, then fasten the top plate lap joint with a piece of the upper top plate and two 16d nails. Don't nail the corner studs together yet.

Now is the time to make sure the walls are plumb. If you didn't sheathe them on the flat, it's also time to make sure they are square. Check both sides of the corner for plumb with a 4-foot or 8-foot level.

Barry found that the main wall leaned out a bit. The illustration *Plumbing and Squaring a Wall* on page 86 shows how he remedied the situation.

▲▲▲▲▲▲▲▲▲▲▲
When checking a wall for plumb, a long level provides a more accurate reading than a short one. Extend a short level by holding it against a longer wood straightedge.
▼▼▼▼▼▼▼▼▼▼▼

He tacked a temporary diagonal brace to the top plate of that wall. Then he climbed a step ladder and pushed on the top of the main wall while Dave pulled on the brace. When the level read plumb, Barry called out, "Nail it, buddy!" Dave drove a nail through the opposite end of the brace and into the bottom of a stud.

Barry checked again that both walls were plumb. If adjacent walls are plumb, they should be square, too, but it's always smart to double-check. Barry grabbed a framing square to make sure the studs were at right angles to the headers, sills, and plates. Dave tacked the brace to a few more studs to hold the wall in position until it would be sheathed.

With all of the exterior walls raised and plumbed, the men turned their attention to the interior partition walls. These would divide the large new space into smaller rooms— a master bedroom with a walk-in closet, a bathroom with a small linen closet, and a family room.

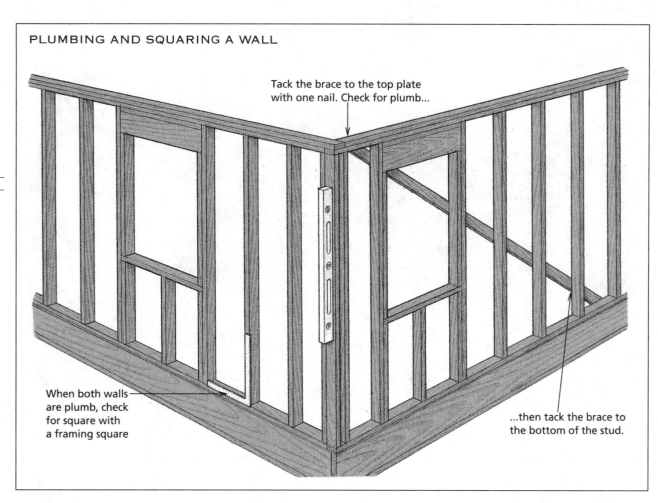

Tack the brace to the top plate with one nail. Check for plumb...

When both walls are plumb, check for square with a framing square

...then tack the brace to the bottom of the stud.

Partition walls are either bearing or nonbearing; bearing walls help to carry the structural load of the ceiling or floor joists above, while nonbearing walls support only their own weight. As mentioned earlier, an opening in a nonbearing wall requires a less-beefy header than one in a bearing wall, but otherwise the construction is identical.

There's no critical sequence for raising interior walls, but some builder's logic can be applied. One rule is to assemble and raise the longest walls first. Putting short walls up first may seem inviting, especially near the end of a long day, but it cuts into the deck space needed for assembling larger walls.

A second rule is to work from one end of the addition to the other. This ensures that, as often as possible, you'll be adding new walls perpendicular to walls already in place and avoiding the need to shoehorn a length of wall between two parallel walls.

But the more practical issue when raising the interior walls is their connection to the exterior walls. Ideally, the upper top plate should extend over the exterior walls at the intersection, as shown in *Partition Wall Corner* on page 74. If you attach the upper top plate to your exterior walls before raising them, you'll need to leave a 3½-inch gap at each intersection—a cumbersome approach, especially if there are numerous intersections. This is another good reason for adding

the upper top plates after all of the walls are assembled.

INSTALLING SHEATHING

As with floors, walls in old houses were sheathed with boards. Today, sheet goods are the overwhelmingly preferred choice, and plywood is the most common among them. It lends strength to the structure, making the walls rigid and usually eliminating the need for cross bracing. CDX plywood is made with exterior glue so that it will hold up to weather in the time it takes you to get the siding on. For other materials, see "Sheathing Options" on page 88 and "Rigid Insulating Sheathing" on page 91.

AIR NAILERS

Many of us associate the sound of a claw hammer with putting up a house. And many of us have had the pleasure of cleanly sinking a 16d nail with a 20-ounce hammer. But if you visit a construction site during framing, you are apt to find that the rhythmic tatoo of hammers has been replaced by the incessant thud and ping of air-driven nailers.

Air nailers work something like staple guns. A trigger-activated piston pushes a single nail through a tip and into the wood. Instead of a simple spring, however, compressed air provides the force to drive the nail. All nailers have a safety device to prevent accidents and injury; as shown in *Air Nailer* below, the work-contact element surrounds the tip and prevents the gun from firing unless firmly placed against something. This is not a fail-safe mechanism, though, so use the tool with due caution.

Nailers employ either a coil magazine or a strip-loading mechanism. Coil magazines carry more nails than strip loaders, but the coils generally take more time to reload. Besides these differences, consider heft and balance before renting or buying an air nailer. It is rather heavy, so the better the balance, the easier the tool will be to use. Versatility is something else to keep in mind. Determine the range of nail sizes you're likely to use, then review the capacities of various nailers. For example, a framing nailer is used to drive large nails when putting up a frame, but it may also be suited to nailing on sheathing. But don't expect a single gun to conquer every job in an addition. Another model will probably be needed to handle the smaller nails used with roofing and finish trim.

Firing an air nailer is as easy as pulling the trigger. Nevertheless, it takes a little practice to get a feel for the tool. Start with single-shot nailing. After some experience, you can try "bounce nailing," letting the tool's recoil hop it from one shot to the next. Either way, the work will go quickly.

Unless your building plans include more than an addition, consider renting a nailer as you need it. Buying a nailer also means acquiring an air compressor, lengths of hose, and fittings to connect the parts.

AIR NAILER

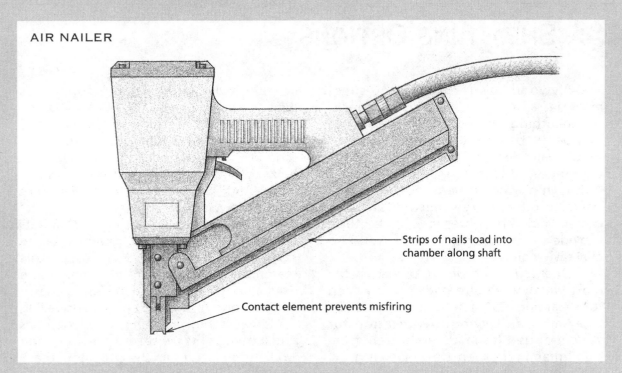

Strips of nails load into chamber along shaft

Contact element prevents misfiring

Photo 5-9. Sheathing can be run right over openings and cut out later (being done here with a reciprocating saw), sparing the trouble of laying out the openings on the sheathing.

 ## SHEATHING OPTIONS

Plywood was the first large-sheet material to replace solid wood boards for sheathing floors, walls, and roofs. It may be the best all-purpose sheathing material available; see "A Look at Plywood" on page 68 for more information. Although plywood is hard to beat, several newer products serve specific functions better. Some are lighter in weight; others provide better insulating value. You also may save money.

Oriented strand board, or OSB, is the most widely used alternative to plywood for sheathing. OSB is performance rated by the American Plywood Association for structural use. It's made exclusively from small-diameter aspen trees, which grow quickly but are unsuitable for use as lumber.

OSB works like plywood for wall and roof sheathing. Available with square or tongue-and-groove edges in 4 x 8 sheets, it holds nails and can be glued as well as plywood. And OSB costs from 30 to 50 percent less than plywood.

The biggest complaint about OSB is its tendency to absorb moisture and swell up far more than plywood does. For this reason, many builders are reluctant to use it as a subfloor, particularly under hardwood flooring, where even a little swelling could cause big problems, or in kitchens and bathrooms, where a serious leak would completely ruin the OSB altogether.

How thick should the plywood be? That depends on the spacing of the studs and on the siding material. Your code may allow using ⅜-inch plywood over studs spaced on 16-inch centers. This also will probably suffice if you are using wooden clapboards and 16-inch stud spacing: The clapboards add strength, and you don't need sheathing thick enough to hold nails since the clapboards can be nailed into framing.

But ½-inch plywood is the standard. You'll need it for vinyl siding, which adds no strength and must be nailed to something between structural members. Ask your building inspector about sheathing thickness requirements in your area.

How long should the sheets be? The width is standard 4 feet, but lengths run 9 feet, 10 feet, and even 12 feet, as well as the common 8 feet. With longer sheets, you can avoid cutting extra pieces

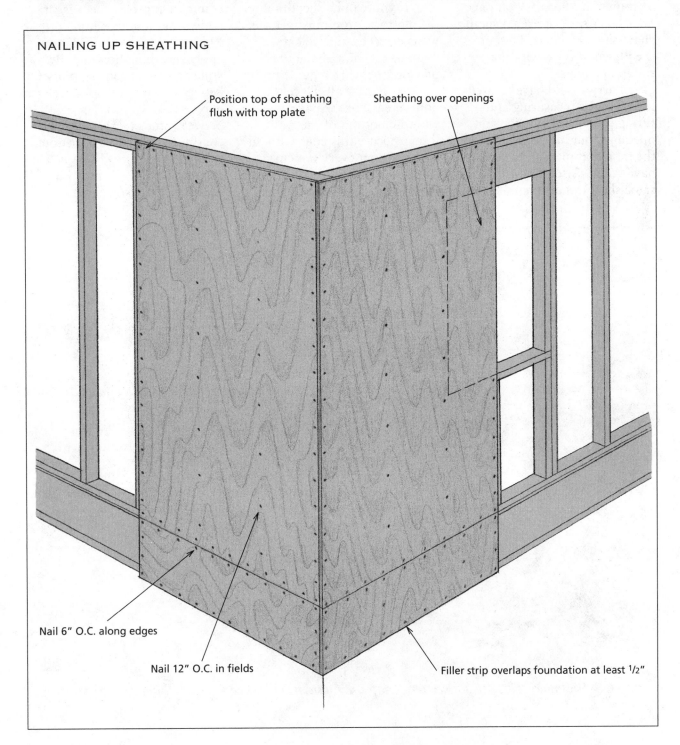

NAILING UP SHEATHING

Position top of sheathing flush with top plate

Sheathing over openings

Nail 6" O.C. along edges

Nail 12" O.C. in fields

Filler strip overlaps foundation at least ½"

to cover the mudsill and top plates. And extra-long panels can save you the work of making filler strips to cover the header and stringer joists.

Like many carpenters, Barry ran the plywood sheets over the window and door openings, which would be cut out later. A reciprocating saw, as shown in *Photo 5-9* on page 88 a saber saw, or even a small chain saw can be used to cut the plywood flush with the rough openings.

Barry would have created less scrap by measuring and fitting pieces around the openings, but his method saved the time that measuring would have taken. Also, because the same sheet ran around

openings, as shown in *Nailing Up Sheathing* on page 89, the walls were tied together better. However, Barry didn't sheathe completely over the opening for the French doors because it didn't make sense to sheathe over large openings where most of the sheet would be hanging in air.

If you will be sheathing on the platform, you must get the walls perfectly square before you raise them. Use the first plywood panel as a guide to square up the wall. Place the bottom edge of the panel flush with the bottom of the wall frame. Secure this edge with an 8d nail about every 6 inches. Check that the adjacent edge of the sheet is flush to the first

stud. Put a nail through the lower top plate to hold the wall square. Now continue nailing every 6 inches through all of the framing.

Plywood sheathing can be applied horizontally or vertically. On the Baileys' addition, Barry ran the panels vertically; this is the most common approach because it allows continuous nailing on every edge of the sheet. If you apply sheathing horizontally, you should stagger the joints between courses. Also, code may require you to block between studs to provide continuous nailing for the long sides of the sheets. There is one advantage to horizontal sheathing: The strongest

Photo 5-10. *Filler strips are added to overlap the foundation if sheets of sheathing aren't sized to extend past the mudsill.*

▶ RIGID INSULATING SHEATHING

A variety of insulating composite panels can be used for sheathing purposes, either by themselves or in conjunction with structural sheathing. Rigid sheathing adds to the overall thickness of the walls. Be sure the frames on your doors and windows are deep enough to allow for this.

Foil-faced fiber-ply panels have several advantages over other types of sheathing. Used instead of plywood, these panels increase structural strength. The foil membrane acts as both vapor barrier and insulator. The panels are lightweight, and using them requires no framing or finish siding modifications.

Extruded and expanded polystyrene *(bead board)* are similar in their insulating value. They provide little structural strength, so they must be accompanied by diagonal metal bracing on the framing when used as sheathing. The bracing is T-shaped and is let into a groove cut across the edges of the studs, then nailed to each stud. Finish siding can then be nailed directly to studs.

Polyurethane and polyisocyanurate panels are similar to fiber-ply panels and bead board, but they have a higher R-value (a measure of the resistance to the flow of heat) and cost more. All four of these insulating sheets are flammable and give off highly noxious fumes when burned, so most building codes require that a fire-rated sheathing be installed over them.

veneers in plywood run along the length of the sheet. Running these veneers at a right angle to the studs increases the strength of the wall.

For a rigid wall, full sheets of sheathing must cover the sole plate and the lower top plate. Depending on the length of the studs you used, the sheathing may not reach the upper top plate, but this makes no difference structurally.

At the Baileys, Barry made the bottom edges of the sheathing flush with the bottom of the sole plates. With 92⅝-inch-long precut studs, this meant the sheathing panels covered ⅜ inch of the upper top plate.

If you apply the sheathing after raising the wall, drive a couple of nails partway in between the sole plate and the floor. Rest a sheet of plywood on the nails to make it easier to adjust its position, then nail it in place.

Finally, filler strips made to overlap the foundation by at least ½ inch are needed unless you use extra-long sheets of plywood. Barry and Dave needed to use filler strips, so they used a portable table saw to rip scrap plywood to 11¾ inches wide, then they nailed the strips in place, as shown in *Photo 5-10* on the opposite page.

If you are building a two-story addition, you may want to sheathe the first-story walls before you go on to the second story, then install filler strips around the second-floor header and stringer joists to support the sheets on this level as you nail the sheets in place.

6

FRAMING THE ROOF

A cross much of North America, the most common roof style is the *gable,* a peaked roof with triangular gable walls at either end. Also familiar is the *shed* roof, with just one slope. Both roofs are widely used for additions. The Baileys' addition was to be something of a hybrid of the two. It uses a low gable roof that in effect becomes a shed roof where it intersects the house; see *The Baileys' Roof* on page 94 (top).

The choice of roof type is based partly on aesthetics and partly on practical matters. Steep gables are associated with the colonial Northeast and have roots in the traditional architecture of northern Europe. If you have a gable-roof house, an addition may fit in better if it has a gable roof of the same *pitch,* or steepness. Beyond its looks, a steep gable roof en-

courages snow to slide off, thereby reducing the load on rafters.

Shed-roof additions tend to look more contemporary and may be suited for relatively new suburban houses with their modestly pitched gable roofs. Perhaps the most famous and venerable of additions adds a shed to a gable, as shown in *Saltbox-Style House* on page 94 (bottom). The shed-roof addition continues the slope of one side of the gable roof, although not necessarily at the same pitch. Refer back to Chapter 1 for more information on roof design.

Both gable and shed roofs present challenges. A gable uses more materials—there's more roof than on a simple shed, and that means more rafters, more studs, and more sheathing and shingles. In return, the space under that peak may yield more living space, either now or when you again feel the need to

expand. But it can be argued that a shed roof makes more efficient use of space—there are no low-overhead eaves.

The terminology of gable and shed roofs is based on a right triangle, as shown in *Roof Geometry* on page 95 (top). The gable is two right triangles; the shed is one. The length of the base of the triangle is the *run* of the roof. The distance from the right-angle corner to the peak is the *rise*. As you can see, the span of a shed roof equals the run. The span of a gable roof is twice the run, usually; a saltbox has two different runs.

The pitch of a roof is described by the number of inches of rise per 12 inches of run. For example, a 6-in-12 roof rises 6 inches for every 12 inches of horizontal run. That information is compressed in carpenter's jargon, and you might hear

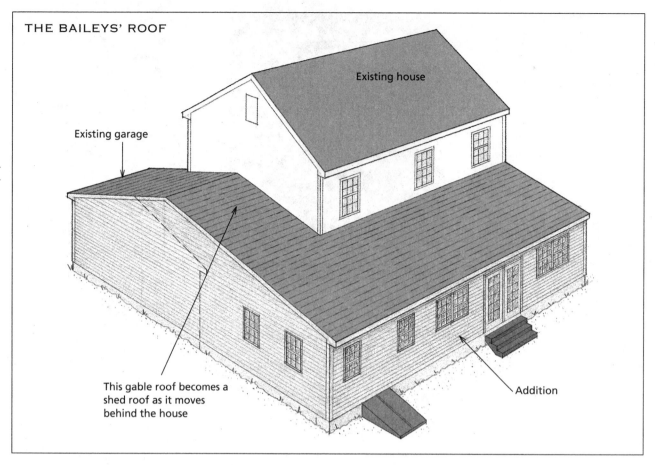

THE BAILEYS' ROOF

Existing house

Existing garage

This gable roof becomes a shed roof as it moves behind the house

Addition

someone on the job say, "That roof's a 6." Building plans include a symbol that gives the roof pitch; see *Roof Geometry* on the opposite page (top).

The *rafters* form the hypotenuse of the triangle—the pitched part of a roof. They support the roof the same way joists support a floor.

On a gable roof, pairs of rafters ascend to meet at the *ridge*. A *ridge board* may run along the top to intercept the ends of the rafters; in traditional construction, rafter pairs may be attached to one another without a ridge.

On a standard shed roof, there is just one set of rafters. The rafters on a shed addition are supported at the high end by a doubled plate if the wall is new or by a *ledger* if the wall is part of the existing house. For a very long shed roof, the rafters

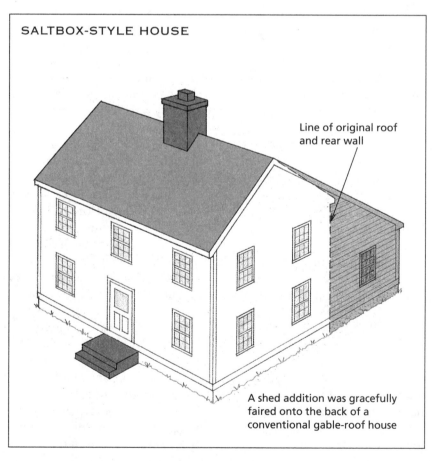

SALTBOX-STYLE HOUSE

Line of original roof and rear wall

A shed addition was gracefully faired onto the back of a conventional gable-roof house may have to be overlapped and supported by an interior wall, as shown in *Supporting a Long Shed Roof* on the right (center). Rafters usually run past the outside wall of the addition, creating an overhang that protects the house from sun and rain.

A gable roof involves additional framing members. Ceiling joists serve not only to support a ceiling and perhaps a floor above but also to resist the outward thrust of the opposing rafters. Collar beams may be used to tie pairs of rafters together and to help counter this force. See *Joists and Collar Beams* below. Collar beams are especially vital if the joists do not run parallel to the rafters; alternately, a heavy, structural ridge board can be supported by posts that in turn rest on bearing walls.

If you want to have a cathedral ceiling without looking at ceiling joists, as the Baileys did, you can substitute a structural ridge beam for the standard thin board and support the beam with posts at either end. As shown in *Cathedral Ceiling* on page 96, this beam must be supported by load-bearing walls.

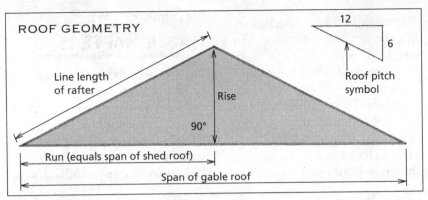

ROOF GEOMETRY

Line length of rafter

Rise

90°

Run (equals span of shed roof)

Span of gable roof

12

6

Roof pitch symbol

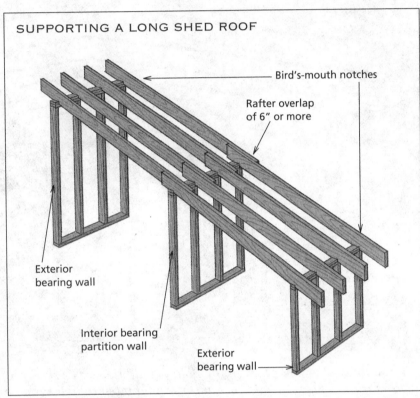

SUPPORTING A LONG SHED ROOF

Bird's-mouth notches

Rafter overlap of 6″ or more

Exterior bearing wall

Interior bearing partition wall

Exterior bearing wall

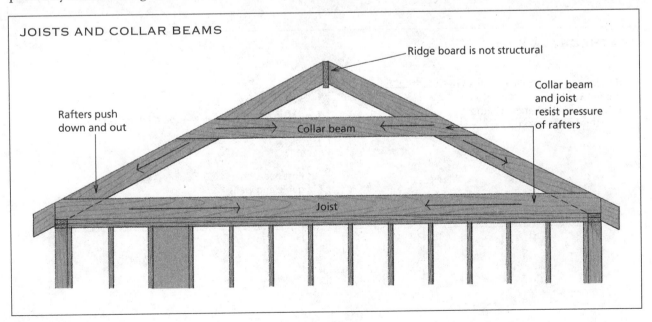

JOISTS AND COLLAR BEAMS

Ridge board is not structural

Collar beam and joist resist pressure of rafters

Rafters push down and out

Collar beam

Joist

FRAMING THE ROOF

The rafters may be notched to fit over the beam to place their weight directly upon it.

For their living room ceiling, the Baileys chose a hybrid: Barry and Dave installed a set of false rafters under the shed roof rafters to create a cathedral ceiling. This unusual system is shown in *Photo 6-1* below.

CUTTING THE GABLE RAFTERS

On a simple gable or shed roof, most framing members are ordinary *common rafters* that run the full length of the pitch. Matters get more complex when roofs meet at an angle, but these framing challenges

are beyond the scope of this book.

Either plumb cuts or notches are made at either end of the rafter where it meets the ridge or ledger. These cuts are shown in *Rafter Parts* on the opposite page. The *rafter tail* may be cut plumb, square (at a 90 degree angle), or with still

Photo 6-1. The major part of the Baileys' addition has a shed roof, but you wouldn't know that from the inside. False rafters frame a second pitch to make this cathedral ceiling.

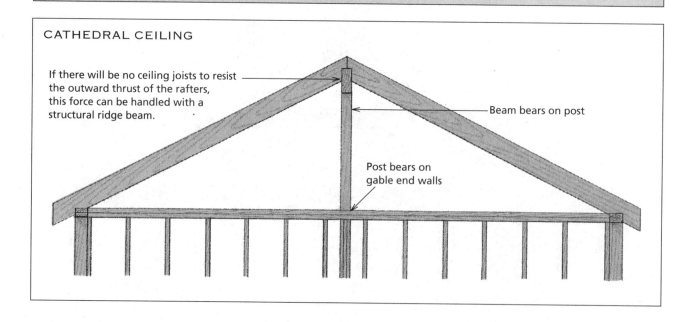

CATHEDRAL CEILING

If there will be no ceiling joists to resist the outward thrust of the rafters, this force can be handled with a structural ridge beam.

Beam bears on post

Post bears on gable end walls

another shape, depending on the design of the overhang. This lower end of the rafter is notched with a *bird's-mouth,* so that it fits over the outside of the top plate and sits on top of the plate. The top end of a shed rafter also receives a bird's-mouth if it will rest on a plate.

In the Baileys' addition, the top end of the rafters was supported by a 2-by ledger attached to the house; since the roof had a very shallow pitch, the rafters were not notched for the ledger. If your shed roof will have a shallow pitch—less than 2 in 12—the rafters do not need to be notched.

Once you know the run and pitch of your roof, you can use the framing square to "step off" the rafter length and cuts. The illustration *Stepping Off Rafters* on page 98 shows the procedure using a 5-in-12 roof with a run of 10 feet as an example. To calculate the cuts for a gable roof, subtract half the thickness of the ridge board if there will be one.

The number of "steps" you lay out is equal to the number of feet in the run plus one odd step to make up the remainder. In our example, you'll have nine steps plus a 10½-inch odd step. This doesn't include steps for the rafter overhang.

Select your straightest piece of rafter stock and use it to lay out a pattern rafter. Crown the rafter and position it so the crown will be up. Start by laying out the plumb cut at the top of the rafter. Align a framing square with the top edge of the rafter so that the measurement on the tongue of the square equals the rise and the measurement on the blade equals the run. Mark the line for the plumb cut. Now mark

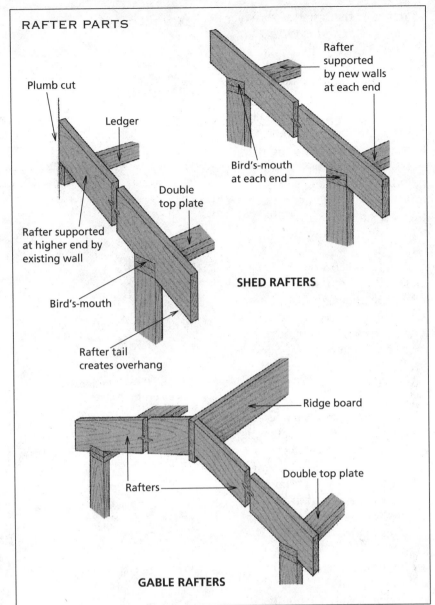

RAFTER PARTS

Plumb cut

Ledger

Double top plate

Rafter supported at higher end by existing wall

Bird's-mouth

Rafter tail creates overhang

Rafter supported by new walls at each end

Bird's-mouth at each end

SHED RAFTERS

Ridge board

Double top plate

Rafters

GABLE RAFTERS

the length of the odd step along the blade.

Slide the framing square down until the outside of the tongue aligns with the odd step mark. Again, align the square so the measurement on the tongue equals the rise and the measurement on the blade equals the run. Now mark 12 inches along the blade to establish the length of the first full step. Repeat this for each step (eight more times for the rafter in our example).

Mark a plumb line on the last step. This plumb line

corresponds to both the building line and the plumb cut of the bird's-mouth. Flip the square over and align it with this plumb mark to find the horizontal part of the bird's-mouth. As a rule of thumb, make the horizontal cut as long as the width of the top plate plus the sheathing. That would be 4 inches for a 2 x 4 wall.

Finally, lay out the rafter tail. *Stepping Off Rafters* shows a tail of 20 inches as measured along the top of the rafter. Flip the framing square so the blade is on top of the rafter, as shown in step 3 of *Stepping Off Rafters*. This way the tongue of the square will lay across the entire rafter. Step off another full step using the same rise and run marks on the square. Then lay out the partial step, in this case 8 inches, to yield the desired overhang, and mark the rafter tail plumb cut. This may be a little easier if you have an extra framing square to mark the partial step, as shown in the illustration.

All the repeated measuring involved in stepping off rafters can result in a significant accumulated error. Use care and a sharp pencil or you may find that your pattern rafter doesn't fit. You can ensure accuracy and save time with a pair of stair-gauge fixtures that clip to the framing square's blade and tongue; they automatically align the square to the rise and run.

A problem with stepping off is that it doesn't reveal how long the rafters need to be until after you've laid one out. But a framing square blade holds the answer. Under each inch mark for the unit rise you'll find a column of numbers. For example, look at the numbers under the 5-inch mark. The top figure is the rafter length per 12 inches of run for a 5-in-12 roof (hence the positioning of this column below the 5-inch mark). You can see that 13 inches of rafter length are required per 12 inches of run.

Our example roof, running 10 feet with a 20-inch overhang, requires 12 steps. (You can count the two odd steps as full steps for the purpose of ordering lumber.) Multiply 12 by 13 and you get 156 inches, or 13 feet. The lower numbers in the column are lengths for rafters in more-complex roofs.

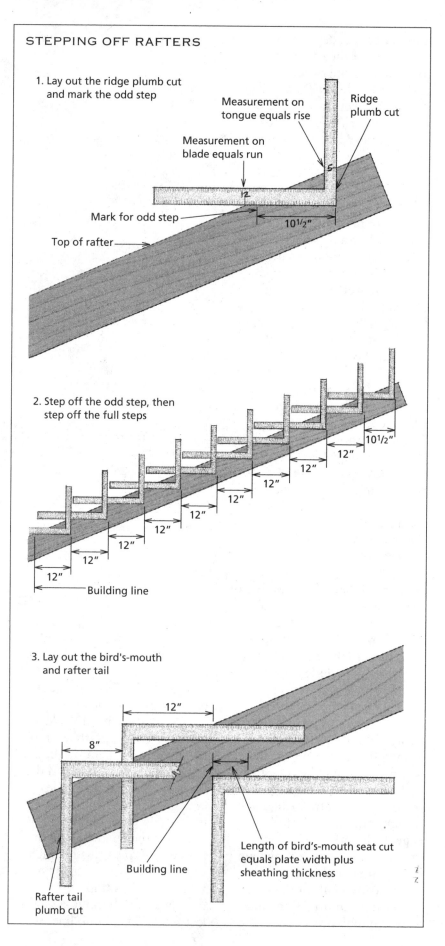

STEPPING OFF RAFTERS

1. Lay out the ridge plumb cut and mark the odd step

Measurement on tongue equals rise

Ridge plumb cut

Measurement on blade equals run

5

12

Mark for odd step

10½"

Top of rafter

2. Step off the odd step, then step off the full steps

10½"

12"

12"

12"

12"

12"

12"

12"

12"

12"

12"

Building line

3. Lay out the bird's-mouth and rafter tail

12"

8"

Length of bird's-mouth seat cut equals plate width plus sheathing thickness

Building line

Rafter tail plumb cut

CALCULATING THE BAILEYS' RAFTERS

If you were designing a new building, you'd pick a roof pitch based on style, climate, and how space within the roof framing will be used. An addition brings with it certain restraints, however. Because you are adding on to an existing building, its roof design may influence your thinking on how the new roof should look. And there are structural considerations as well, since the new roof intersects the existing structure with its windows, doors, and roof.

According to the plans for the Baileys' addition, the roof pitch was to be roughly 2 in 12. To Barry, though, the more important fact was that the new roof had to meet the existing house no higher than 2 inches below the upstairs windows for roof flashing.

▲▲▲▲▲▲▲▲▲▲▲

When cutting the bird's-mouths on your rafters, you can save time and improve accuracy by making all of the cuts at once. Clamp the rafters together on edge, then run a circular saw across the rafters to cut each side of the bird's-mouth.

▼▼▼▼▼▼▼▼▼▼▼

"I need to leave a couple of inches under the windows for roof flashing," Barry said.

He found that the distance from the subfloor of the addition to the bottom of the windows, less the 2 inches for flashing, was 12 feet 5 inches. The rafters had to travel from this height to the back wall of the addition, which was 20 feet away.

Rather than try to calculate the rafter cuts, Barry relied on his chalkline, framing square, and tape measure. He laid out the rafters on the subfloor, using it as a huge blackboard, as shown in *Making a Full-Scale Rafter Layout* below. He snapped a line representing the rafter run, subtracting 3½ inches for the thickness of the addition's back wall and 1½ inches for the thickness of the rafter ledger. Then he snapped perpendicular lines at each end representing

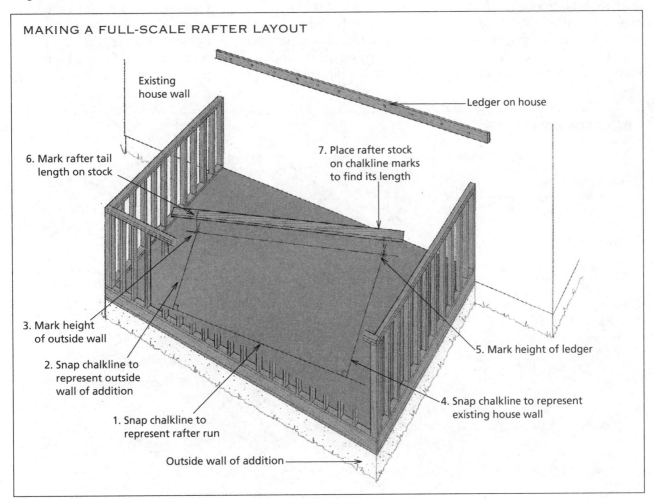

MAKING A FULL-SCALE RAFTER LAYOUT

Existing house wall

Ledger on house

6. Mark rafter tail length on stock

7. Place rafter stock on chalkline marks to find its length

3. Mark height of outside wall

2. Snap chalkline to represent outside wall of addition

1. Snap chalkline to represent rafter run

5. Mark height of ledger

4. Snap chalkline to represent existing house wall

Outside wall of addition

the outside wall of the addition and the back wall of the existing house. He marked the wall height of 8 feet 1⅛ inches on the outside wall line. On the line representing the existing house wall, he marked 12 feet 5 inches.

Barry selected a straight piece of rafter stock to serve as his pattern. He calculated that the outside edge of the bird's-mouth seat cut should be about 15 inches from the lower end of the rafter by adding 4 inches for the seat cut to the 10½-inch rafter tail length.

Next, the carpenters placed the rafter stock on the chalklines. Barry aligned the 15-inch mark with the outside wall, then Dave aligned the other end on the line for the existing house wall. The snapped wall lines were then extended onto the rafter to get the angle and position of the plumb cuts. By measuring and marking from both ends of the

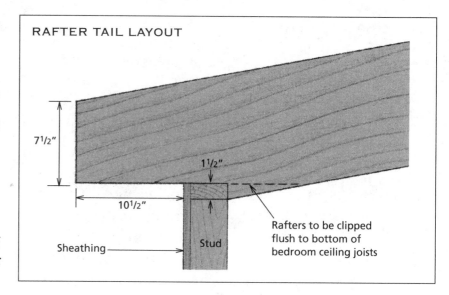

RAFTER TAIL LAYOUT

7½"

1½"

10½"

Sheathing

Stud

Rafters to be clipped flush to bottom of bedroom ceiling joists

bird's-mouth plumb cut line, Barry marked and drew the tail cut. Aligning his framing square to the bird's-mouth plumb cut, he drew in the seat of the notch. The resulting rafter tail and bird's-mouth layout is shown in *Rafter Tail Layout* above.

The pitch of the new roof needed to meet the front pitch of the existing garage roof. As shown in the illustration *Side*

Elevation below, the new roof would overshoot the front of the garage, and Barry had to extend the front of the garage roof up to meet the new rafters.

Finding this new garage roof ridge was easy. Barry and Dave removed most of the siding from the side of the house that meets the garage roof. Dave held a chalkline on the juncture of the front garage

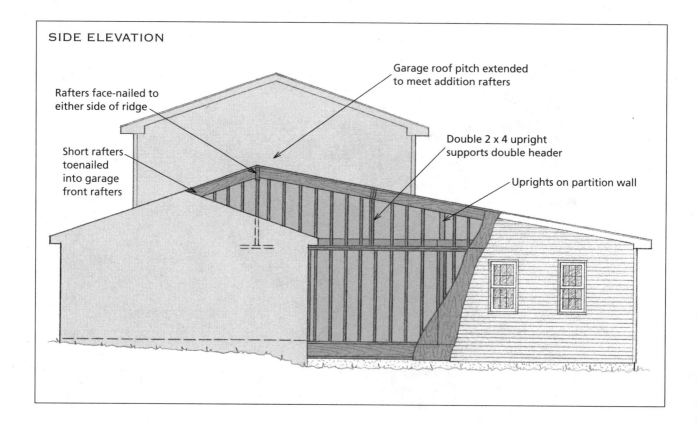

SIDE ELEVATION

Rafters face-nailed to either side of ridge

Short rafters toenailed into garage front rafters

Garage roof pitch extended to meet addition rafters

Double 2 x 4 upright supports double header

Uprights on partition wall

FRAMING THE ROOF

roof and the side of the house. Following the garage roof pitch, Barry unreeled several feet of line past the garage roof ridge until he knew it was more than high enough to meet the new rafters. Then he snapped the line against the tar paper on the side of the house. Later, after installing rafters across the back of the house, he would snap a line extending the new pitch. The intersection of the two lines would define the new ridge.

CEILING JOISTS

As with floor joists, the lumber size required for ceiling joists depends on the species of wood and the span and spacing of the joists. For ceiling joists, though, there's another factor to consider. If the space above the ceiling will be inaccessible, you don't have to make the ceiling strong enough to carry a *live load*. Designing for a live load, as for floor joists, means accommodating for the weight of people and objects that might be in the room.

Because the space above the ceiling joists in the Baileys' addition would be inaccessible, the joists only needed to carry a *dead load,* the weight of the joists themselves plus drywall, without sagging.

Ceiling joists are installed in much the same way that floor joists are installed. The only major difference between ceiling joists and floor joists is that ceiling joists don't meet headers. So instead of these joists being face-nailed into headers, they are toenailed into the top plate with a 16d nail, then the rafters are face-nailed to the joists with three 16d nails; see the illustration

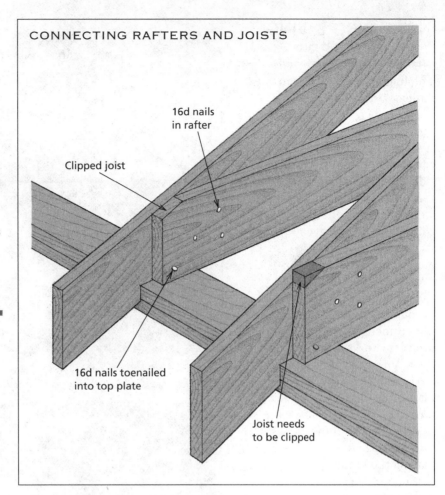

CONNECTING RAFTERS AND JOISTS

16d nails
in rafter

Clipped joist

16d nails toenailed
into top plate

Joist needs
to be clipped

Connecting Rafters and Joists above.

For a gable roof, the joists run between opposing outside walls, so you can use this procedure for both sides. But shed roof rafters and joists usually join an existing wall. In most of these cases, you'd attach the ceiling joists to a ledger, just as for the rafters above and the floor joists below. Or, for a short run carrying a dead load, you might just toenail the rafters into the end joist or header of the existing house. This is what Barry did for the two short ceiling joists that run over the bedroom and linen closet to the back wall of the existing house.

However, Barry used a different method of attaching the ceiling joists that were to run to the garage back wall.

Because the new roof was to pass over the back pitch of the existing garage roof, Barry didn't have to worry about tearing off some of the roofing and sheathing to expose the top plate of the garage back wall. That way, the ceiling joists could land on this wall.

As it happened, the garage top plates were $1\frac{1}{2}$ inches higher than the addition top plates. So Barry made a $1\frac{1}{2}$-inch-deep notch in one end of the joists. He could safely notch the joists because they would only carry a dead load. (If you come across a similar situation with load-bearing members, think twice before notching them. Realize that you will be reducing the load-bearing strength along the whole length of those pieces.)

INSTALLING LIVING ROOM RAFTERS

102

The living room rafters in the Baileys' addition went up quickly once Barry cut a pattern rafter; see *Photo 6-2* on the right and *Photo 6-3* below. The carpenters began by removing siding that was in the way, then they installed a 2 x 12 ledger along the back of the house. Unlike the floor ledger, this one would carry a lighter load, so it didn't need lag screws. Instead, it was attached through the sheathing using three 16d nails in each stud. Barry then marked the 16-inch rafter centers on the top plate and the ledger.

With the ledger in place, Barry and Dave set their sawhorses next to a pile of 24-foot 2 x 12s. They put each piece of rafter stock on the horses in turn and crowned it before placing the pattern rafter on top. Cut lines were scribed on both ends, then the cuts were made. Once the rafters were done, Barry and Dave anchored them with 10d nails at either end.

Because the cathedral ceiling in the Baileys' living room ceiling would be nailed to the rafters, not ceiling joists, Barry had installed the outermost rafter 3½ inches in from the outside wall, as shown in the illustration *False Cathedral Ceiling* on the opposite page (top). In this way, the end rafter would provide a place to nail the ceiling drywall.

The last step in framing the roof was to install the false rafters to complete the pitched cathedral ceiling. Barry and Dave made these rafters out of 2 x 12s, the same stock used for the main rafters. While false rafters help to brace the roof, they didn't need to be from such wide lumber. "They were actually meant to be 2 x 8s,"

Photo 6-2. *The rafter stock for the living room is marked for cuts with a pattern rafter.*

Photo 6-3. *While a circular saw will take care of the rafter's end cuts, the bird's-mouth cuts can be made with a saber saw.*

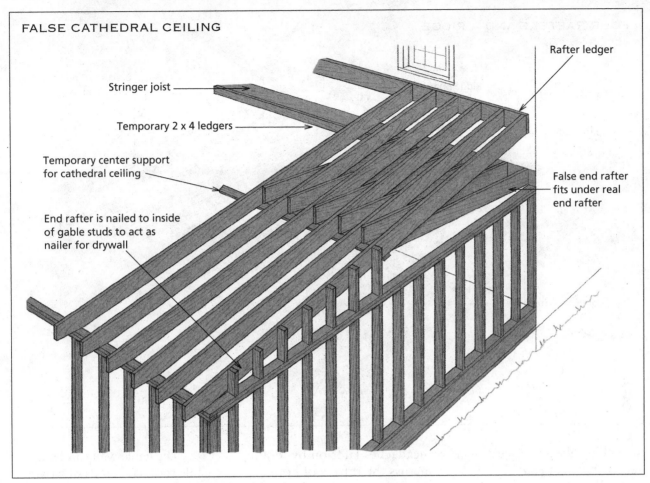

FALSE CATHEDRAL CEILING

Stringer joist

Temporary 2 x 4 ledgers

Temporary center support
for cathedral ceiling

End rafter is nailed to inside
of gable studs to act as
nailer for drywall

Rafter ledger

False end rafter
fits under real
end rafter

Ted Currier said. "But the lumberyard delivered 2 x 12s instead. That's okay—the larger stock will just make the rafters beefier."

Making and installing the false rafters was simple. As shown in *False Cathedral Ceiling* above, the first false rafter was cut to fit under the first rafter. The remaining rafters were nailed to the sides of the real rafters.

LAYING OUT A GABLE ROOF

In contrast to a shed roof, a gable roof has two planes and two sets of rafters. Another part of the job is framing the triangular sections of a gable wall; this is often put off until after the roof is framed. See the

illustration *Framing a Gable with a Window* below.

Thrust up against the sky, the spindly rafters and ridge look impossibly wobbly at first. And they are wobbly, until sheathed and supported by gable walls. You'll need some way of reaching the ridge—

either an improvised platform or scaffolding. For a working stage, lay down lumber or plywood if the joists won't be covered with decking. And provide hard hats for the crew.

You begin by putting up the ridge with two rafter pairs acting like legs. This first stage will look

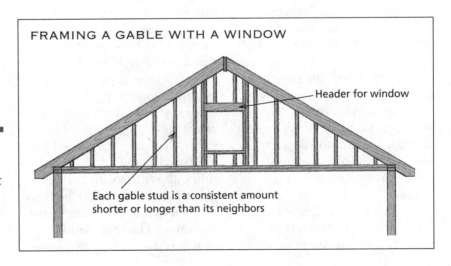

FRAMING A GABLE WITH A WINDOW

Header for window

Each gable stud is a consistent amount
shorter or longer than its neighbors

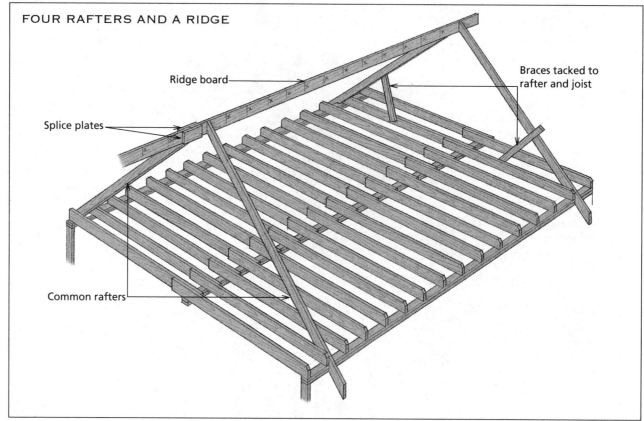

FOUR RAFTERS AND A RIDGE

Ridge board

Braces tacked to rafter and joist

Splice plates

104

Common rafters

something like a backyard swing set, as shown in *Four Rafters and a Ridge* above. Place plywood on the joists to make a platform on which to work. Lay the ridge board flat on the platform and nail the two rafters to one side, choosing locations close to the ends. Gingerly lift this partial assembly so that the bird's-mouths catch the top plate and the rafters meet the appropriate ceiling joists. With the ridge close to its proper height, toenail the rafters to the plate with 16d nails, then add 10d nails through the rafters and into the joists.

Now attach the opposing pair of rafters in the same way. To help stabilize this assembly, you can run braces flush against the ridge board and down to short lengths of 2-by nailed temporarily atop the ceiling joists.

Check the ridge board for level and the gable ends for plumb. You can spare yourself

headaches later on by looking across the rafters of both pitches to see that they are in line with one another.

If there will be an overhang at the gables, typical practice is to omit the rafter at each gable wall and add a *fly rafter* to define the cantilevered edge of the roof, as shown in the illustration *Gable with Overhang* on the opposite page (top). The fly rafter is like the other rafters, except that it doesn't have a bird's-mouth. Each pitch of the overhang is framed with *ladder rafters,* short horizontal rafters running something like rungs between the last standard (or common) rafter and the fly rafter. These rafters typically are spaced 14 or 16 inches O.C. In place of a rafter above the wall plate is a gable plate, which may be fitted into a notch in the ridge board, as shown. The short ladder rafters rest on the gable plate.

The gable walls under a gable roof have studs of varying length. Matters are made simpler by the fact that each stud is a given length longer or shorter than those on either side of it, as long as the stud spacing remains the same; see the illustration *Framing a Gable with a Window* on page 103 (bottom).

As illustrated in *Gable without Overhang* on the opposite page (bottom), the studs are placed directly above the wall studs and are usually notched to fit the end rafters.

In the Baileys' addition, making a low gable wall was part of the job. To lay out the length of each gable stud, Dave held a piece of stock plumb where the shortest stud would go. He scribed for the top and bottom edges of the rafter to establish the notch. The seat of the notch for the first stud was 4 inches from the bottom, while the mark for the second stud

GABLE WITH OVERHANG

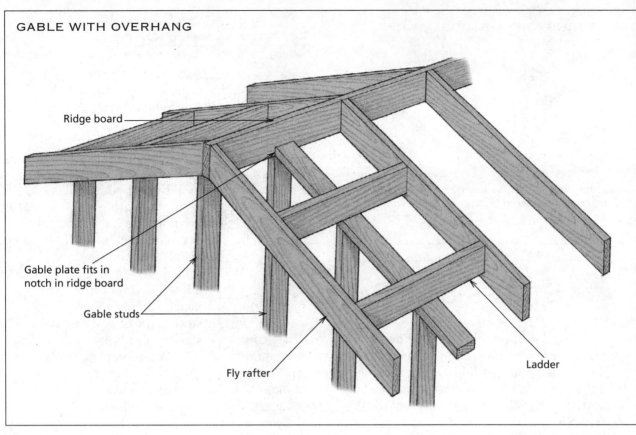

Ridge board

Gable plate fits in
notch in ridge board

Gable studs

Fly rafter

Ladder

GABLE WITHOUT OVERHANG

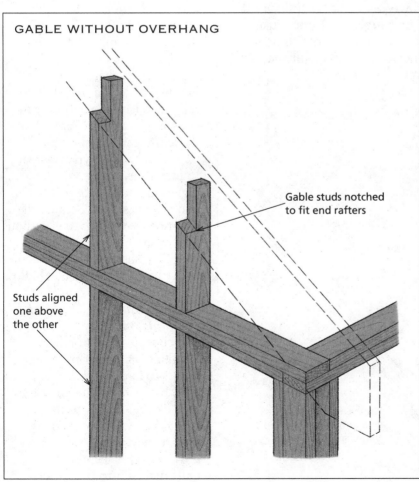

Gable studs notched
to fit end rafters

Studs aligned
one above
the other

measured 7 inches. This meant
that each successive gable stud
would be 3 inches longer than
the last. Laying out the cuts went
more quickly once that measurement was known. Dave made
the angle cuts, as shown in
Notching Gable Studs on page
106. He set his circular saw for a
2-inch-deep cut along the scribed
line on each stud. Then he reset
his saw to its full depth and cut
in from the end of the upright to
make the notch's vertical cut.
The studs were ready to install.

Your local building code
may require collar beams to keep
pairs of rafters from spreading.
These typically are of 1 x 6
stock, nailed to the rafters and
spaced as called for by code. But
collar beams may make the space
under the roof unusable; an
alternative is to nail thin steel
strapping bands over the top of
rafter pairs; check with your
building inspector to learn if they
are allowed.

NOTCHING GABLE STUDS

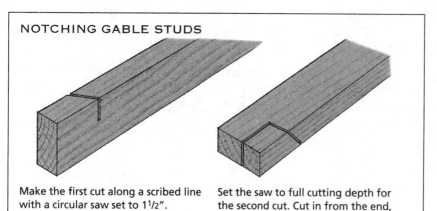

Make the first cut along a scribed line with a circular saw set to 1½".

Set the saw to full cutting depth for the second cut. Cut in from the end, then finish the notch with a handsaw.

STRESS-SKIN PANELS

Stress-skin panels are a sandwich of layers that can include a finished or rough ceiling below, foam insulation in between, and a nailing surface for shingles on top. There are all sorts of panels on the market, with a choice of interior materials (including drywall for the interior face, as shown in *Cutaway of Stress-Skin Panel* below) and a range of R factors. Manufacturers have come up with several ways to fit the panels together snugly, including using splines and mechanical cams. If a building-supply company cannot get information on panels for you, consult home-construction magazines for names of suppliers.

CUTAWAY OF STRESS-SKIN PANEL

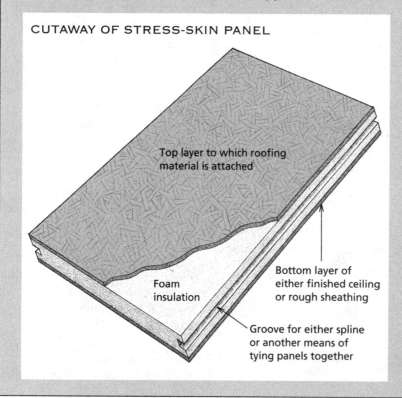

Top layer to which roofing material is attached

Foam insulation

Bottom layer of either finished ceiling or rough sheathing

Groove for either spline or another means of tying panels together

SHEATHING THE ROOF

Most of the sheathing will be done with plywood, unless this layer will be visible from a living space below; in this case, consider using tongue-and-groove or shiplapped boards above the rafters.

Even if you will be sheathing with plywood, boards are normally substituted at the overhang if its underside will be visible from outside. Use tongue-and-groove plywood for a low-pitch roof if water penetration is a worry; on steeper roofs, you can use square-edged plywood.

When ordering plywood, keep in mind the span index printed on each sheet. The first part of a two-number code, such as 32/16, tells you that the sheet can be used to sheath rafters of no more than 32 inches O.C.; the second number refers to joist spacing. No matter what the numbers say, check your local building code before ordering. (Plywood isn't the only way to go; see "Stress-Skin Panels" on the left for an alternative.)

Thicknesses typically are ½ inch for square-edged plywood and ⅝ inch for tongue-and-groove sheets. Because the square-edged plywood is without support at its top and bottom, adjoining sheets are held together with plyclips (also called H-clips, for their shape), as shown in *Clipping Square-Edged Roof Sheathing* on the opposite page. The clips save the trouble of installing nailing strips between rafters to back up these edges.

Begin sheathing at the eave's edge. Check to make sure that the rafter ends are in line; if they aren't, trim them now. Attach sheets with 8d nails driven into the rafters

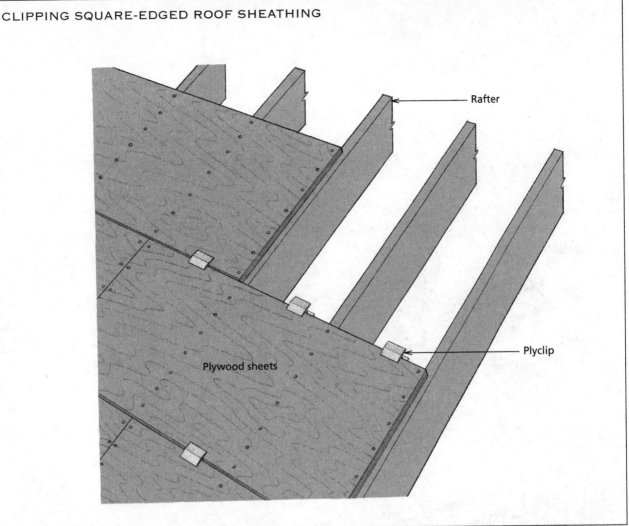

Rafter

Plyclip

Plywood sheets

every 6 inches along the edges and every 12 inches into intermediate rafters. Use plyclips along the upper edge of the sheet. Work your way across the first course of sheets. Start the second course with a partial sheet (the cutoff from the last sheet of the first course might do). Continue staggering seams for each course.

When you reach the ridge on the first pitch, this final course should overlap. Trim the edge flush with the opposing rafters. Then sheath the other pitch, overlapping its last course as well. Trim these top sheets flush with the sheathing on the first side. Finally, trim the plywood along the sides of the roof so the edges are flush with the end rafters or fly rafters.

7

▲▲▲▲▲▲▲▲▲▲
ADDING UP WITH DORMERS
▼▼▼▼▼▼▼▼▼▼

If you can't add on, perhaps you can add up. Extending the dimensions of your home involves a new foundation, new walls, and new tax assessment, but you can avoid at least the first two by making the top floor—the attic—habitable.

The challenge is that attics tend to be less than habitable. Traditionally, they have been a low-rent district of the home—barely accessible, arcticlike in winter, and tropical in summer. To that, add dark and cramped. But making an attic livable is not as daunting as it once was, thanks to improved insulation and air conditioning technology. Also, the high cost of new construction makes that space under the rafters look all the more attractive.

The best arguments for making high-quality living space out of your attic are before-and-after photos of other people's experiences with adding up. The "Shapes of Dreams," beginning on page 174, gives some evidence; another example is shown in *Photos 7-1 and 7-2* on page 110. Perhaps you can visit the houses of friends and neighbors who have added up from the top floor and have done it well.

Not every house lends itself to having the top floor reworked. First, the house must have a certain kind of "lid"—in most cases, a gable or hipped roof. And there must be enough salvageable space to make the project practicable.

Although the Baileys' original house had a gable roof, the very low pitch (common to much post–World War II housing) wouldn't offer the necessary headroom. So adding on was the only option.

Another impediment to adding up is an attic floor that isn't meant to carry the load of added furniture, wall partitions, bathroom fixtures, and people. Beefing up a floor can involve new joists and reinforced walls on the floor below—a technical challenge that requires consultation with a professional.

THE TOP SIX REASONS FOR ADDING UP

An informal survey of homeowners who've made something of their top floors turned up these advantages to building up rather than out.

• *Economics*. For starters, you skip the expense of an excavation and foundation. And it costs less to expand within existing walls and roof.

• *Speed of construction*. It usually takes less time to redo the top floor than to expand the footprint of the house.

Photos 7-1 and 7-2. Before-and-after shots show how an uninhabitable top floor can be dramatically transformed. This 200-year-old attic had previously been used for smoking meat.

• *Privacy.* The top story of a house can feel like a world apart, especially if there's a door to the stairway and a substantial floor. Consider moving bedrooms, a study, or a music room to the top floor.

• *Insulation dollars do double duty.* When you do a good job of insulating and sealing the top floor, the house benefits in both summer and winter.

• *The yard isn't compromised.* You don't lose any lawn by adding up, and that can be important to an active family with a small lot.

• *The house's appearance isn't altered significantly.* If you like the way your house looks now, dormers will contribute living space without calling much attention to themselves. See *Photos 7-3 through 7-6* on the opposite page.

Is your house a candidate for an attic upgrade? Head up there with a flashlight and a tape measure. A key dimension is from the center of the floor to the highest point—the under-side of the ridge in a house with a gable roof. Some references say that you shouldn't bother with an attic that measures less than 10 or 11 feet to the ridge, but perfectly good top-floor additions have been tucked under ridges less than 8 feet high.

Headroom is at its maximum in the center and tails off toward the eaves, as illustrated in *Attic Cross Section* below. The rate at which you lose headroom to either side is a function of the roof's pitch. The steeper the pitch, the quicker the space under the roof becomes more difficult to use. To help visualize the possibilities and limitations of your attic,

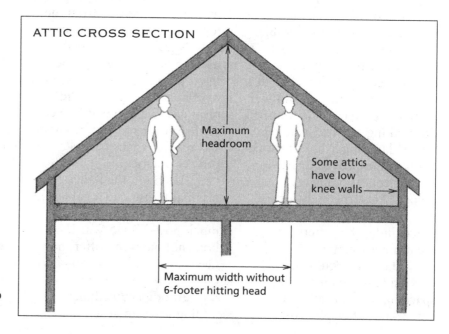

ATTIC CROSS SECTION

Maximum headroom

Some attics have low knee walls

Maximum width without 6-footer hitting head

Photos 7-3 through 7-6. Despite the dramatic contribution they make to the living space within the home, dormers change the exterior of most any type of house relatively little.

transfer the attic dimensions to a sheet of graph paper, using a scale that will allow a cross section of the roof to fit on one page. You'll need to know the width of the attic, the height at the ridge, and the height of the knee walls, if your attic has them. Once you get the measurements on paper and draw lines between them, you should have a clear representation of the roof's pitch.

To see what will fit under the existing roof, draw in a person's outline. A 6-foot-tall person is used in the illustration here, but you may want to substitute a shorter or taller figure if your family members vary from the norm. Note that you can squeeze in a bit more headroom by building a new insulated roof on top of the rafters, as illustrated in *Exposed Rafters* on the left (top), rather than by insulating between them and then applying a finished ceiling. This is an especially attractive option when the rafters are attractive—hand-hewn or just old and rough-sawn.

To support the weight of a new, well-insulated roof, you may need to replace the rafters with more substantial ones, and this gives you the opportunity to use handsome rafters of either new or recycled stock. Still another possibility, if you have headroom to spare, is to add attractive false rafters to the underside of a ceiling that conceals the true structural rafters. These faux rafters needn't be full thickness; a couple of inches will suffice and won't compromise the living space by much.

If you don't have all the space you need under the existing sloping roof, modify your cross-section drawing with dormers on one or both sides. Dormers usually have either shed or gable roofs.

Attic Cross Section with Shed Dormer on the left (bottom) shows how the first option affects headroom. You can gain more space by decreasing the pitch of the dormer roof and moving its outside wall toward the wall of the house—even out to the edge of the eave for an overhanging dormer.

EXPOSED RAFTERS

112

Roofing

Insulation

Finished ceiling

Exposed rafter

Headroom between rafters

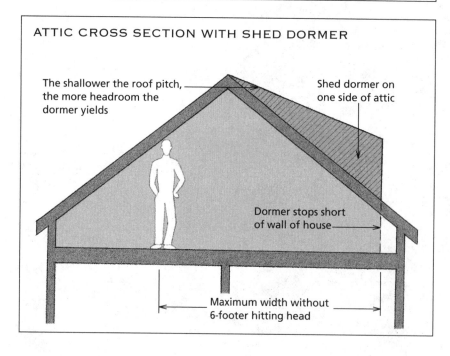

ATTIC CROSS SECTION WITH SHED DORMER

The shallower the roof pitch, the more headroom the dormer yields

Shed dormer on one side of attic

Dormer stops short of wall of house

Maximum width without 6-footer hitting head

Special consideration must be given to a roof with a low pitch because snow and rain aren't as efficiently removed by gravity.

Why aren't all shed dormers built for maximum space? A high, large dormer may overwhelm your house visually. To see if this might be the case, either make sketches to scale or superimpose sketched dormers onto a large elevation photo of your house; better still, make a foam core model of your house, as described in Chapter 1, and top it with dormers. Small dormers are less obtrusive, yet they can yield an amazing amount of usable space.

The illustration *Attic Cross Section with Gable Dormer* on the right suggests that this style of dormer offers more space than the shed-roof version. The ridge of the dormer's roof extends horizontally out from the existing roof. But unlike the space afforded by a shed dormer, this space is compromised by the fact that the gable dormer has a sloping roof with two pitches. That becomes

obvious in *Elevation View of Shed and Gable Dormers* on the bottom. You can see that the headroom created by the shed dormer extends its full width. In both examples of gable dormers, occupants may have to duck toward either side.

As you make your sketches, think about uses for the low space under the eaves. It can be left open or closed off with knee walls. See "Making the Most of Knee Walls" on page 114.

HOW BIG AND HOW MANY?

Once you've settled on the style of your dormers, you can turn next to deciding how large to make them and how many to specify. There is no substitute for visiting other houses and seeing how space has been expanded and illuminated by dormers.

The size, number, and placement of dormers will have a lot to do with how you'd like

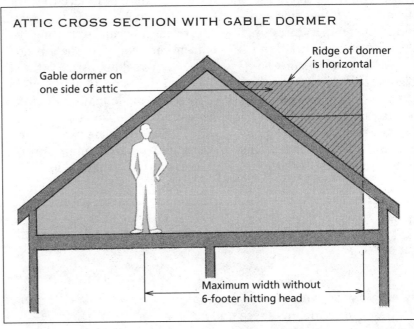

ATTIC CROSS SECTION WITH GABLE DORMER

Gable dormer on one side of attic

Ridge of dormer is horizontal

Maximum width without 6-footer hitting head

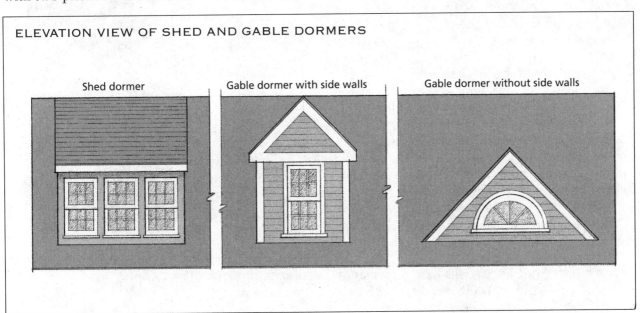

ELEVATION VIEW OF SHED AND GABLE DORMERS

Shed dormer

Gable dormer with side walls

Gable dormer without side walls

to lay out the rooms on this floor. You'll want at least one dormer per room, unless a skylight or generous gable windows will suffice. (For more on skylights, see Chapter 9.)

Consider placing a dormer or skylight over a stairway as well; if the window of the dormer or the skylight can be opened, it will help to ventilate the house below, and it will light up the steps. Consider also that rooms just under a roof tend to be the warmest part of the house, and dormers on either side will moderate temperatures by creating cross ventilation.

Dormers shouldn't be placed without regard to the exterior of the house. If possible, arrange them over windows or doors. Failing that, try for a pleasing symmetry that works well with the rest of the house.

GETTING INVOLVED IN THE PROJECT

Because adding up requires fewer tasks than building an addition, homeowners may find it easier to get involved in the construction. Unlike a ground-level addition, though, this project takes place well above the ground.

For the sake of safety and convenience, scaffolding should be erected alongside the house. Scaffolding serves as staging for workers and as a place to stack building materials. It also provides a means of getting from the ground to the job site without tracking through the house; this is particularly vital if there are inadequate stairs to the attic or no stairs at all.

Shed dormers, with their straightforward framing, are easier to build than gable

dormers (see "Gable Dormers" on page 116) and are the more popular choice for adding up. The job begins with doubled-up trimmer rafters on either side of the opening. A board of similar dimension is nailed to each of these rafters. Then, on the outside, chalklines establish the outline of the dormer. To locate these chalklines, transfer the rafter layout to the roof surface; do this by drilling holes from the attic along the inside edge of the reinforced rafters.

You don't have to peel off the entire area of roof that will be covered by the dormer. For now, you need only remove as much at the eave (lower) end as necessary to erect posts, as described here.

Use either a circular saw or reciprocating saw to cut the opening. Cut through only the

---

▶ MAKING THE MOST OF KNEE WALLS

At some point in planning your attic renovation, you'll be confronted with how best to use the low space under the eaves. It can be left open, especially if the eaves are above the floor. But there are a few good reasons to enclose this space with knee walls.

First, the new attic rooms may seem less cramped if the low eaves are concealed. Second, knee walls are excellent places for storage, as shown in the photo on the right. The closer you bring in the knee walls, the more space they provide and the higher the room tends to feel. (In turn, of course, you sacrifice the room's width.) You can build in bookshelves and cabinets or even plywood boxes for beds. More simply, leave low doors, behind which you can store seldom-used things in boxes and chests in traditional attic fashion.

Note that knee walls may also play a structural role; if built sturdily, they can

To make the best use of nooks and crannies in an attic room, storage bays were built into the knee walls.

help support thin or widely spaced rafters that might not otherwise be sufficient to bear the weight of the new roof.

finished roofing material and the sheathing below it. Leave the rafters intact. Once this initial section of roofing has been lifted off and discarded, you can temporarily nail up 2-bys to make sure the dormer you have in mind will look right from the outside and create satisfactory headroom within.

The pieces representing rafters are attached to the posts, and their ends at the ridge can simply rest on the roofing, as shown in *Dormer Mock-Up* on the right (top). The main variable in where you want to place the rafters is the height at which these temporary rafters meet the posts at the front edges of the dormer; the higher this point, the less steep the roof pitch and the greater the headroom.

You also might adjust how close the dormer's window wall comes to the eave; this point can be set back from the wall of the house below, stand in line with the wall, or extend past it. To make it easier to visualize the dormer, you can clad this temporary framework with thin plywood or even cardboard sheets stapled in place.

Once you are satisfied with the dormer dimensions, permanently install corner posts. A dormer that extends to the wall of the house will have the existing top plate as the base of these posts, as shown in *Dormer Framing* on the right (bottom). If the dormer is set back from the wall, its posts are placed on a new plate attached to the attic floor. To extend the dormer out past the house wall, beams in the walls or built-up floor joists must transfer the load to the exterior wall below. After stabilizing the corner posts with temporary braces extending to the roof, run the dormer top plate across them.

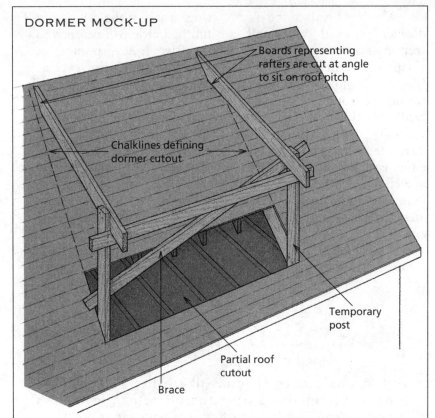

DORMER MOCK-UP

Boards representing rafters are cut at angle to sit on roof pitch

Chalklines defining dormer cutout

Temporary post

Partial roof cutout

Brace

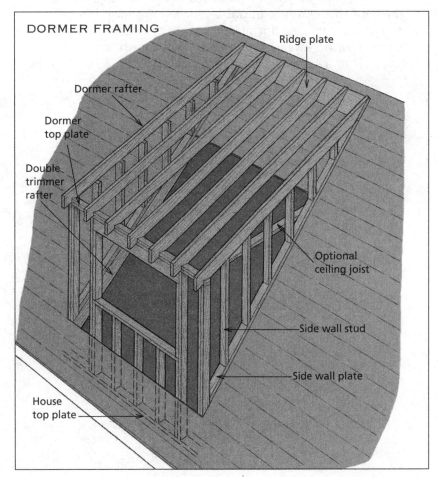

DORMER FRAMING

Ridge plate

Dormer rafter

Dormer top plate

Double trimmer rafter

Optional ceiling joist

Side wall stud

Side wall plate

House top plate

The front wall of the dormer is framed like a small section of house wall; see Chapter 5. Rafters are then run from a ridge board and rest on the dormer top plate with a bird's-mouth notch. The side walls are framed with studs that have somewhat tricky cuts at either end; the lower end is angled to meet the side wall plate, and the upper end has an angled notch to fit behind the end rafter.

At this point, the roof covered by the dormer is removed—all the way up to the ridge board if the ceiling of the finished attic will be open to the ridge. If headroom in the attic is plentiful, however, a lower, flat ceiling can be made by running horizontal ceiling joists from some point on the shed rafters across the width of the attic. In this case, the roof would be removed only as far as necessary to run these joists.

Finally, house rafters are cut away to complete the opening, and the dormer is then sheathed and insulated like conventional walls and roof.

GABLE DORMERS

A gable dormer looks like a little gable-roof doghouse emerging from the plane of the home's shingles. The framing of its roof is somewhat complex. Note the cuts on the dormer rafters where they intersect the roof of the house in *Gable Dormer Framing* below. As suggested for shed dormers, it is best to mock up a gable dormer with 2-bys, right on your roof, before committing yourself to a set of dimensions.

GABLE DORMER FRAMING

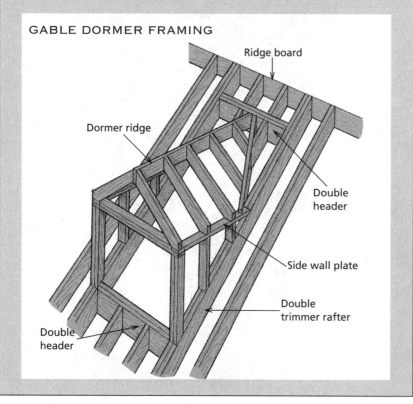

Ridge board

Dormer ridge

Double header

Side wall plate

Double trimmer rafter

Double header

A FAMILY ADDS UP

For many of us, the prospect of sawing holes in the roof is daunting. Even the handiest of homeowners tend to call in professionals to minimize the period during which their living space will be open to the elements. That was the approach of Alasdair and Wendy Wallace, who had enjoyed doing smaller projects on their Lakefield, Ontario, home.

When the Wallaces bought their three-bedroom, two-story structure, it offered them just what they were looking for—mature trees, veranda, bright kitchen, pine paneling, hardwood floors, 12-inch baseboards, and high ceilings, with substantial construction throughout. Their daughters, Elizabeth and Margaret, could share a small bedroom on the second floor, but the elder Wallaces were thinking ahead. They had their eyes on the unfinished third floor, a dry and spacious attic accessible only by a ladder tucked in a closet.

When Elizabeth and Margaret entered their teens, the house seemed cramped. It was time for them to have their own bedrooms, and the family needed a second bathroom. The Wallaces faced a common decision: move or expand.

The family had come to feel very much at home in their house in Lakefield. They liked the quiet shade of its garden, the community, and the proximity of schools, shops, and employment. The Wallaces took a closer look at the untapped space on the third floor, as shown in *Photo 7-7* on the opposite page. As Alasdair and Wendy considered how the attic could be turned into living quarters, they conferred often

Photo 7-7. This large, uninterrupted space became the Wallaces' "aerie." A skylight, full-length mirrors, and glass-paned door at the head of the stairs were added to help make this a bright and cozy living area.

with the principal beneficiaries, their daughters. Rather than the open floor plan the parents favored, the girls preferred two separate bedrooms, with a large, bright common room for entertainment, ballet, and music. And there was just enough room for a small bathroom. For their part, Alasdair and Wendy insisted that the third floor include a large walk-in closet to accommodate and organize things that would be displaced from the old attic.

Even as Alasdair and Wendy talked and planned, they projected ahead several years to when the girls would leave home. The layout they had in mind would lend itself to conversion into a studio and two spare rooms.

The Wallaces didn't neglect the exterior. "It was important to us that we retain the house's profile as seen from the front," Alasdair said. "But the back of the house looks over a large garden and woods, and we were willing to compromise the rear profile."

The decision remained as to what sort of dormer to use. At first, the Wallaces reasoned that a row of three gable dormers would be aesthetically satisfying. Instead, they opted for a more-practical shed dormer, which would accommodate larger windows and provide greater headroom.

CHOOSING A CONTRACTOR

In looking for a contractor, the Wallaces visited several additions in the area that they found particularly appealing. In

every case, the owners spoke positively about the quality of the work and their relationship with the contractor. The Wallaces decided to invite each contractor to their house to describe the project and request a bid.

The first contractor insisted that a circular stairway was the only practical solution in such a confined space, and he submitted a ballpark estimate that covered only framing, roofing, flooring, wiring, and plumbing. Everything else would be extra. The second contractor, whose work the Wallaces especially liked, took six weeks to finalize his estimate and even then wasn't sure when he could begin.

The third builder, Colin Ray, arranged for subcontractors to visit the house within a few days. He listened

Photo 7-8. *Removing a large swath of roof is the first step in a dormer project. The bigger the opening, the more dramatic the transformation will be to the new living space.*

attentively to the family's needs and submitted an all-inclusive estimate within a week.

The Wallaces were impressed with his initiative and guessed they could work with him comfortably. They liked his ideas, too. Colin suggested that the existing attic floor be extended out to the edge of the soffit, 24 inches beyond the wall of the house below; this extension would be supported by cantilevered beams and added 2 feet to the width of both bedrooms. He also recommended incorporating a skylight to brighten a new common room, later termed the "aerie" by the family, which otherwise would have only a small double window.

The real selling point was Colin's commitment to work solely on the Wallace job until its completion. Often, a contractor will have two or more projects underway at the same time, ensuring a steady flow of work and perhaps a dry, roofed site for rainy days. This can mean unsettling delays for homeowners waiting to have their lives return to normal. Despite the fact that Colin's quotation came in the highest, Alasdair and Wendy hired him.

ROUGHING IN

The job began in early November, so the approaching winter added some urgency to the project. A large industrial waste container arrived in the Wallace driveway the day before the south side of the roof was torn off. Wendy appreciated the temporary framework that was erected to protect her shrubs.

The Wallaces' dormer would replace almost the entire roof surface on one side. To retain the roof profile, rafters were removed to within one of each gable end, as shown in *Photo 7-8* on the opposite page. Once the roof was off, a cherry picker hoisted lumber, drywall, a shower stall, toilet, and flooring through the opening, as shown in *Photo 7-9* on page 121 (top). The materials were placed around the perimeter of the attic to distribute their weight.

▲▲▲▲▲▲▲▲▲▲▲

If you're renovating an attic floor, contain the dust from top-floor construction by installing a temporary 2-by stud wall on the second floor around the opening to the attic. Cover the wall with 6-mil plastic. For access, cut a 5-foot vertical slit between studs.

▼▼▼▼▼▼▼▼▼▼▼

The new roof was supported at each end and within each partition wall on either side of the stairwell by posts. These posts were laminated from 2 x 6s, the bottom ends of which rested on the existing wall plate. These, in turn, supported cantilevered beams within the walls and partitions, which would carry the dormer extension out past the face of the house below. Laminated from 2 x 10s, the beams transferred the weight of the dormer wall to the second-floor plate.

As Ontario winters can be very harsh, Colin's first task was to frame in the shed dormer and seal the attic space against the weather. Low-slope shingles

would be installed in the spring when they would seal more readily under the warm sun, but roll roofing sufficed for this first winter. It was applied none too soon. The day after the dormer was sealed, Lakefield experienced its first blizzard of the season.

FINISHING THE JOB

Even as the attic space was enclosed, the Wallaces continued to refine their design. They placed boards on the floor to indicate where walls and doors would go. This full-scale floor plan made it easy to try out variations of the original drawings (see *The Wallaces' Floor Plan* on page 120). For instance, it had been a challenge to know exactly where to place knee walls until the Wallaces visualized just how their location would influence room sizes.

As with many top-floor additions, the layout of the floor below would be affected. Getting ready access to the attic meant losing some space on the second floor for a new stairway. The girls' former bedroom had to be slimmed down by 36 inches; the balance of the stairway was accommodated by the existing hall closet. The stairs themselves would be 30 inches wide, rather than the standard 36 inches, only minimally reducing the capacity of the closet. (This space-stingy stairway limited the size of furniture that could be moved upstairs.)

A dormer window at the turn in the stairway would brighten what had been a dark second-floor hall. A 24-inch-wide sill over the soffit would

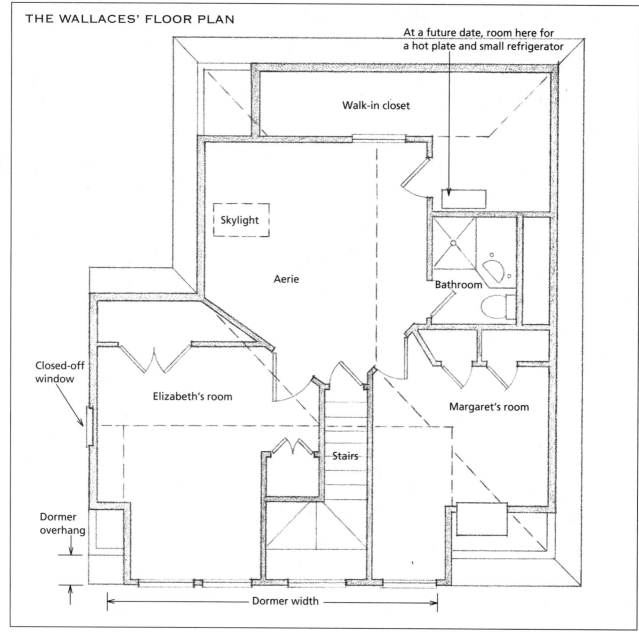

THE WALLACES' FLOOR PLAN

At a future date, room here for a hot plate and small refrigerator

Walk-in closet

Skylight

Aerie

Bathroom

Closed-off window

Elizabeth's room

Margaret's room

Stairs

Dormer overhang

Dormer width

accommodate some of Wendy's many plants, giving the illusion of summer during long winter months.

After the partition walls and knee walls had been roughed in, plumbing and wiring were installed; the existing stack box running from the basement to the attic accommodated both. Years earlier when he was rewiring the house, Alasdair had run five circuits through the stack with expansion in mind, but this proved inadequate for the attic's electrical requirements. Colin added three more.

To avoid the attic joists being cut into to accommodate plumbing, the attic bathroom floor was raised 3 inches; an alternative would have been to lower the ceiling in the room below, allowing pipe to make its way to the soil stack.

Because top-floor additions carve space out of nonstandard areas, improvisation is often necessary. For example, the ceiling configuration at the Wallaces permitted a door height of only 70 inches to one bedroom—and that happened to be adequate for this rather short family. An existing gable window looked fine from the outside, but it would have interfered with the interior layout. So the crew kept the window in place and tacked a dark sheet of plywood inside the new wall, giving the illusion from the outside that the window was still functional.

The completed third floor was a success. Alasdair built furniture to fit the idiosyncratic spaces, as shown in *Photo 7-10* below. The contractor's suggestion to add a skylight worked well; the common room was flooded with light and proved to be a welcoming place.

The daughters since have gone off to college. Wendy has modified the common room to realize her dream of an attic studio. Looking back, the decision to expand up was wise. "The girls developed responsibility and independence," Alasdair said. "And because we all gained personal space, family sanity and compatibility benefited immeasurably."

Photo 7-9. A cherry picker is used to lift building materials through the new opening in the roof, sparing a good deal of back-breaking labor.

Photo 7-10. Dormers leave you with interesting spaces. Using the spaces fully may require custom-fitted cabinets or furniture.

ADDING UP WITH DORMERS

CLOSING IN

As the addition is clad in logo-covered plywood sheets and bright house wrap paper, it begins to look more like a huge cereal box than a place to live. The great view from within is obscured, chunk by chunk. But this gawky stage doesn't last for long. Roofing and siding are nailed up, and the door and window openings are formed. Visually, the addition has become part of the house—even if the insides are still a shambles of extension cords, scraps, and sawdust.

8 ROOFING

Perhaps the most peculiar pieces of equipment used on the Bailey job were left-handed cotton workgloves with the fingers cut off. That's what Barry and Dave pulled on the morning they began roofing. It was the last week in November, and in Pennsylvania that tends to mean cold mornings followed (with luck) by brisk, sunny afternoons. The idea was to leave free only those fingers that would be fishing for nails and holding them while hammering.

Actually, the optimal weather for roofing is a cool day with good cloud cover and no precipitation. For most roofers, hot midsummer days are the worst time to be caught on the roof.

Putting on a finished roof involves challenges other than the weather. Most obviously, there's the height off the ground—a matter of no consequence for some of us, and a lifelong bugaboo for others. There's the weight of the roofing material—about 3 pounds per square foot for asphalt shingles. Finally, there is the monotony. Perhaps no other job in building an addition is so repetitive.

And yet there are aspects of roofing that recommend it to the homeowner who wants to get involved. Asphalt- and wood-shingle roofs are relatively straightforward to install. The work goes quickly. And once you get acclimated to the height and the pitch of the roof, the view is exceptional. Even if you don't feel up to running this part of the show, consider signing on as a helper.

Covering the plywood roof deck is an important stage. Once you have a weather-tight cap on the addition, the work inside can proceed with less worry about the elements. A rainy day will no longer bring work to a standstill. What's more, the roof is usually the first part of the addition to be finished, and therefore it represents turning a corner in this long process of enlarging your home.

CONSIDERING ROOFING MATERIALS

The appearance of the roof tends to be overlooked by builders and homeowners alike. Inexpensive and inobtrusive are the standards. And yet that big expanse of roof can do a lot to define the addition. Just as a good haircut plays up facial features, a carefully chosen roofing material contributes in a subtle way to the appearance of a house.

In choosing a roof, you'll find a fairly good correlation between dollars and durability. That is, the more a material costs, the longer it tends to last. However, the longevity of a roof will be influenced by the steepness of the pitch, the angle and intensity of sunlight, wind, and rain, and the frequency of hail and freeze/thaw cycles, among other factors.

The most common choice for roofing, and the one used on the Baileys' addition, is *asphalt shingles*. These look something like large, heavy place mats and are a yard long and a foot high. They are made from asphalt, a petroleum product, impregnated with felt or fiberglass. The shingles usually are covered with a sprinkling of fine mineral particles. The asphalt makes the shingles waterproof; the mineral contributes protection from the sun and lends color and texture.

The color of roofing material is part aesthetic and part practical. You'll want a shade that fits in with the addition and existing house, without drawing too much attention to itself. Beyond that, a light-colored roof will absorb less heat from the sun, and this is particularly important if the space just under the roof will be inhabited.

Asphalt shingles come in a range of weights, with the heavier products costing the most and holding up the longest. They go on quite quickly and easily with either nails or staples. The back of the shingles usually has a pattern of tar applied to it, a simple but clever device; as the sun beats down on the installed roof, the tar softens and further bonds the shingles to each other.

Wood shingles are particularly suited to traditional-style houses and contribute a texture and range of soft, weathered colors that asphalt shingles can only approximate. A wood shingle is narrower than a strip of asphalt shingle and takes more time to put up. Shortages of the wood from which shingles are sawed—cedar is used most frequently—can drive up prices and even make them impossible to purchase.

▲▲▲▲▲▲▲▲▲▲▲

The lower the roof pitch, the quicker the shingles will wear. So on a roof pitched lower than 5 in 12 (5 inches of rise for every 12 inches of run), use a higher grade of shingles to get the most life out of your roofing job.

▼▼▼▼▼▼▼▼▼▼▼

Expect the price of wood shingles to be at least double the price of standard asphalt shingles; in return, you can expect a longer service life.

Wood shakes are made from split wood rather than sawed wood; the result is a rougher look that may or may not be to your liking. Shingles and shakes are attached with nails.

Clay and concrete tiles are a traditional roofing material in areas of the southwestern states and Florida. Their use harkens back to the Spanish colonial era. The tiles are fireproof and durable, but costly and too tricky for

installation by homeowners.

Another long-lasting, fireproof alternative is *slate*. Slate blocks are cleaved into thin shingles with square or ornamental edges. Depending on where the stone is quarried, colors range from gray to muted reds and greens. A slate roof is immediately distinctive, but the material is expensive— roughly twice the cost of cedar shingles—and requires special techniques for installation.

The sound of rain falling on a *metal roof* is musical— and like any kind of music, some people care for the sound and some don't. Plated and enameled steel are the most common choices. The service life of the roofing depends on the quality of the coating, and the cost varies accordingly. Metal is often used on low-pitch roofs because there are few if any horizontal seams to admit water.

A *built-up* or *tar-and-gravel* roof is not a do-it-yourself project. Layers of roofing felt are bonded into a highly waterproof layer with applications of hot asphalt or tar. This process is suited to roofs with a very low pitch. A modern (and less messy) version is the *single-ply* roof, laid down in one sheet. That sounds simple, but most manufacturers limit its installation to licensed contractors.

ESTIMATING MATERIALS

The coverage of roofing materials is described in *squares,* with one square equaling 100 square feet. When you order a square of shingles, this unit of measurement compensates for

126

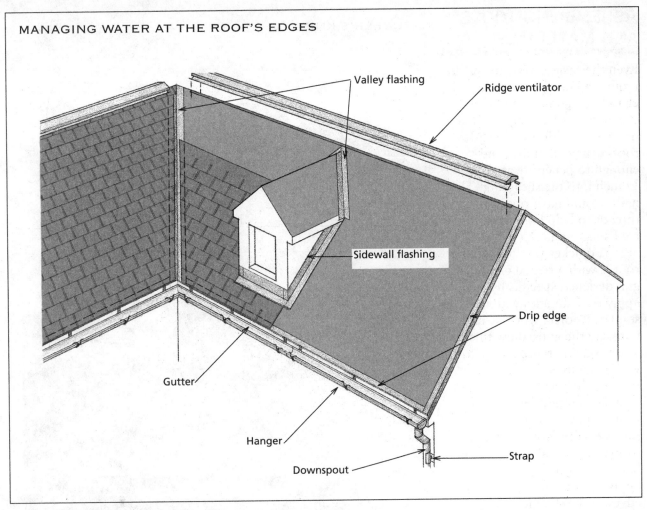

Valley flashing

Ridge ventilator

Sidewall flashing

Drip edge

Gutter

Hanger

Downspout

Strap

the fact that the shingles have to be overlapped to make a weatherproof barrier. The amount of overlap for wood and slate shingles will vary with the pitch—the steeper the roof, the less overlap you need for a secure roof. An old rule of thumb advises adding another 10 percent when you order roofing to allow for waste.

Most types of roofs require an underlayment for complete weatherproofing. The standard material is *roofing felt,* also called roofing paper or tar paper. This is asphalt-impregnated felt, sold in 36-inch rolls in weights of 15 and 30 pounds per square. Plan on applying two layers over the entire roof. Heavier felt will be

more durable and is particularly recommended under wood shakes. For added protection against ice dam formation, you may want to install a 3-foot-wide horizontal course of *water-and-ice-shield membrane* on the edges of roofs that have a very gentle slope. Apply it directly to the plywood deck along the eaves.

A roof is more than shingles or tiles. It also involves means of directing water away from vulnerable places. A *drip edge* is a metal strip nailed to the edges of a roof along eaves and rakes. Its purpose is to protect the edges from water and ice damage. *Flashing* is a lining used to channel water where roof pitches meet to form a valley and where the

roof meets a wall, chimney, or skylight. Valleys may be flashed with roll roofing or, for greater durability, metal. Flashing between the roof pitch and a vertical plane (such as a wall or chimney) may take the form of individual pieces, or steps.

You may want to consider a *ridge ventilator* to permit a flow of air under the roofing; this helps keep the house cooler and carries off potentially damaging water vapors from below the roof. Finally, after the roofing is completed, gutters and downspouts take the runoff from the roof and divert it away from the walls and foundation. See the illustration *Managing Water at the Roof's Edges* above.

Assembling Tools and Materials

Even the easiest roofs to shingle require a ladder, tape measure, chalkline, hammer, and metal shears to cut flashing. Stock a nail apron with broad-head roofing nails that are long enough to penetrate at least ¾ inch into the sheathing. The nails should have rings or threads to help hold them in the roof sheathing.

A quicker way to install a roof is with a rented pneumatic gun designed specifically to apply roof shingles with nails or staples. Roofers who use nail guns say the guns allow them to work roughly twice as fast as with a hammer.

Asphalt roll roofing and shingles can best be cut with a roofer's knife. In addition to this specialty tool (illustrated in *Roofer's Knife* above), have on hand a trowel or putty knife for applying roof cement along cut edges of the shingles.

Wear soft-soled work shoes that won't mar the shingles or cause you to slip as you work. If the roof has a fairly steep pitch, you'll need roofing jacks and planks for secure footing; see *Photo 8-1* on the right. Roofing jacks are metal brackets that are temporarily nailed through the sheathing and into the rafters. They can be rented for the week or two you'll need them.

Then there is the felt and shingles themselves. The easiest way to get these backbreakers to the roof surface is to have the supplier lift the material onto the roofing deck with a cherry picker or conveyor. Any extra charge will be well worth the money. See "Minding Your Shingles" on page 130. If you have been

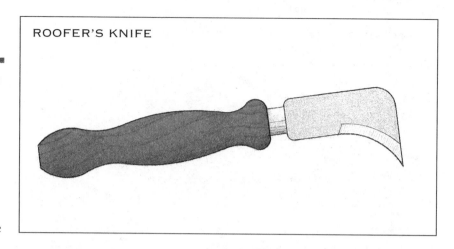

ROOFER'S KNIFE

Photo 8-1. Roofing jacks provide a base for a secure platform from which to work.

using pump jacks to support a scaffolding of lumber, these can be enlisted to lift materials to roof level.

READYING THE ROOF DECK

At the Bailey site, Dave used a household broom to clear scrap wood and loose nails from the plywood deck to ready it for roofing. The first item to be nailed down was the drip edge along the eaves. *Drip edge* is usually made from aluminum and attached with aluminum nails. It protects the perimeter of the roofing material from water damage and nesting insects; see the illustration *Drip Edge* on the right (top). (The drip edge is placed along the roof's sloping edge, or rake, after the roofing felt is down.)

Once the drip edge was down on the eaves, Barry and Dave began installing the first course of roofing felt at the lower left-hand corner of the roof. Barry opened the roll and carefully positioned the felt even with the corner of the rake and eaves, as shown in *Installing Felt* on the right (bottom). Note that the nails are more closely spaced along the eave and rake than along the top of this first strip.

Barry and Dave worked their way across to the other rake, taking care to avoid tearing the felt by staying off of it until it was nailed securely. Then they trimmed the felt at that edge flush with the plywood sheathing.

With the first course of felt in place, Barry and Dave proceeded to cover the roof. For a single layer of underlayment, they would have

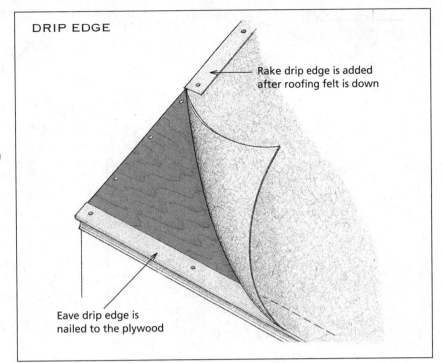

DRIP EDGE

Rake drip edge is added after roofing felt is down

Eave drip edge is nailed to the plywood

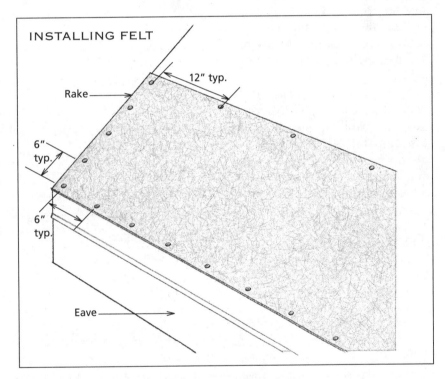

INSTALLING FELT

12" typ.

Rake

6" typ.

6" typ.

Eave

overlapped each course just 2 inches, leaving 34 inches exposed. But the roof on the Baileys' addition had a low pitch (between 2 in 12 and 4 in 12), so they created a double layer by letting just 17 inches show. Whenever the crew started a new roll of felt in midcourse, they allowed at least 6 inches of overlap. (Rolls are printed with guidelines to assist you in overlapping evenly. It isn't necessary to drive nails along the very top of the second and succeeding courses.)

Once they reached the ridge, Barry and Dave overlapped the last course past the top, allowing a minimum of 9 inches to run beyond the ridge. Then they repeated the process on the other side of the roof.

With the felt in place, Barry and Dave installed drip edge along the rake of the roof, placing the strips on top of the underlayment.

ATTACHING FLASHING

Flashing, the means of directing water away from joints in a roof, is largely put in place before the shingles go down. But step flashing is done as shingles are attached, and flashing along hips and with certain ridge treatments may be attached after the shingles are in place.

Flashing can be made from either roofing felt or, for greater durability, one of several metals. Care must be taken when nailing down metal flashing. By mixing metals, one for the flashing and another for the nails, you can cause corrosion. Examples of pairings to avoid include either aluminum or copper

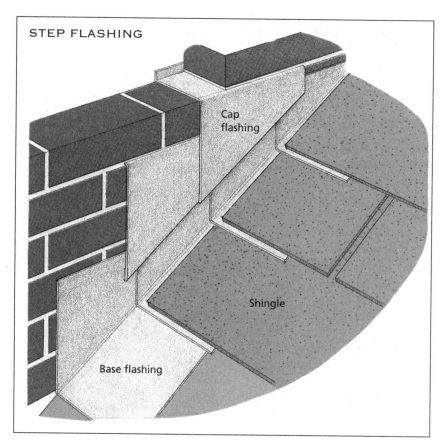

STEP FLASHING

Cap flashing

Shingle

Base flashing

▲▲▲▲▲▲▲▲▲▲▲

Flashing is essential anywhere a roof line ends or is broken: valleys; eaves; around chimneys, stack vents, and fans; and where the roof intersects a wall.

▼▼▼▼▼▼▼▼▼▼▼

flashing and steel nails. If nails aren't of the same material as the flashing, they should be separated with neoprene washers to reduce conductivity.

To use metal to flash a valley, where pitches meet at an inside corner (see *Managing Water at the Roof's Edges* on page 127), you need to start with metal strips at least 14 inches wide. The strips should

 ## MINDING YOUR SHINGLES

If you can't have shingles delivered directly to the roof surface, the best on-site storage method is to stack the bundles up to 4 feet high on wood pallets. Cover the bundles with a tarp. When it comes time to carry the shingles to the roof surface, you won't have to deal with wet wrappers and sloppy shingles.

The first few bundles from the top of the stack will be easy to guide onto your shoulder. Bend your knees and use your free hand to hold the side of the ladder as you climb. Use your legs, not your back, when picking up bundles from lower in the stack. You also want to protect the shingles from long-term exposure to intense sun, which can activate the dabs of tar and make the shingles difficult to separate.

STRIP SHINGLES

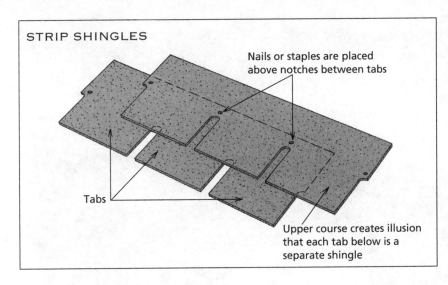

Nails or staples are placed above notches between tabs

Tabs

Upper course creates illusion that each tab below is a separate shingle

STARTER COURSE

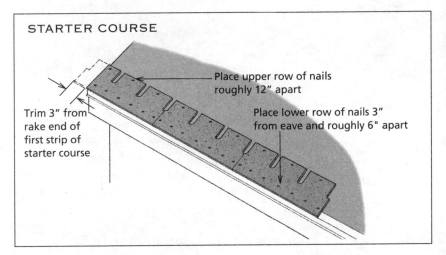

Place upper row of nails roughly 12" apart

Trim 3" from rake end of first strip of starter course

Place lower row of nails 3" from eave and roughly 6" apart

SHINGLE PATTERN

Seventh course is 3 tabs

Fifth course is 1 tab

Third course is 2 tabs

First course is 3 tabs

Rake

Sixth course is 1½ tabs

Fourth course is 1½ tabs

Second course is 2½ tabs

Eave

be as long as the valley, plus a minimum of 4 inches per overlap between pieces and another 12 inches to extend over the ridge at the top and past the eave at the bottom. The strip is attached to the ridge with nails. Roofing cement should be run along the edges to seal them.

Where a brick chimney or wall interrupts the new roof, you need to flash in a two-step process. The first step is to attach base flashing—pieces of metal bent into an L-shape—around the perimeter. Overlap the pieces from bottom to top, as shown in *Step Flashing* on the opposite page. Next add a course of cap flashing. The top edge of the cap flashing must be made watertight. It can be bent over before it's installed and tucked into masonry joints; on a new chimney, the mason should put the cap flashing in place as the brick is laid. On a wall with lapped siding, the cap flashing is not bent, but simply slipped between boards and nailed in place.

SHINGLING THE ROOF

Once the flashing is in place, the shingles can go down. The most common asphalt version is the strip shingle. When the courses are in place, each strip will appear to be three separate shingles in a row, as shown in *Strip Shingles* on the left (top).

The truck delivering the roofing to the Bailey job was equipped with a conveyor to whisk the heavy stacks of shingles up to the roof. As the stacks came off the conveyor, Barry and Dave distributed them across the roof so the shingles would be close at hand as they worked back and forth with each course. If yours is a solid-colored roof,

Photo 8-2. The asphalt shingles on the Baileys' addition were attached with a power nailer.

even slight differences in appearance between lots may show up on the completed job, so it is best to take shingles alternately from several stacks as you work to avoid unsightly variations in color.

Begin with a starter course of inverted shingles—tab side up. This course will be covered. As illustrated in *Starter Course* on page 131 (center), cut 3 inches from the first strip where it meets the rake, using a roofing knife on the back side of the strip with a carpenter's square for guidance. Nail the shortened strip so that the nail heads won't show through the notches in the first regular course of shingles, and follow with strips to run the width of the eave. Space the nails following the illustration.

Apply a course of shingles atop the starter course, tabs now facing down, as shown in *Single Pattern* on page 131 (bottom). Trim the first strip slightly, and place it to allow a ½-inch overhang at the eave and rake. Run full strips to complete the remainder of this course, tacking them tempo-rarily to see if you come out with a full tab at the far rake. If not, make adjustments along the course.

The pattern illustrated arranges the shingles so that the notches of the strips you are applying are centered over the tabs below. The second course begins with a strip cut to two-and-a-half tabs long, the third with a strip just two tabs long, the fourth with a one-and-a-half tab strip, and so on, as shown. The seventh course will begin with three tabs, as did the first, and the procedure is repeated.

Typical exposure for each course—the height of shingle left showing—is 5 inches. As you lay courses up the roof, snap chalklines parallel to the eave to maintain this exposure. To ensure tabs are aligned, snap lines perpendicular to the eave.

Continue adding courses, as shown in *Photo 8-2* above, until you come to the ridge, but stop short of overlapping it. This may mean that the last course overlaps the one below it

INSTALLING RIDGE VENTILATORS

Most ridge ventilators are designed as units that can be linked together and cut as necessary. Consult the directions that come with the model you purchase. Chances are that you will have to add connectors for each joint, as well as two end caps.

To prepare to add a ridge ventilator, shingle both sides of the roof up to the final two courses. Snap a chalkline for guidance, then use a circular saw to cut a 2-inch-wide vent slot through the felt-clad plywood at the peak, avoiding damaging the rafters below. Next, finish the last courses of shingles and trim the shingles to reveal the slot in the plywood. Finally, nail the ventilator in place and complete the shingling.

SHINGLING THE RIDGE

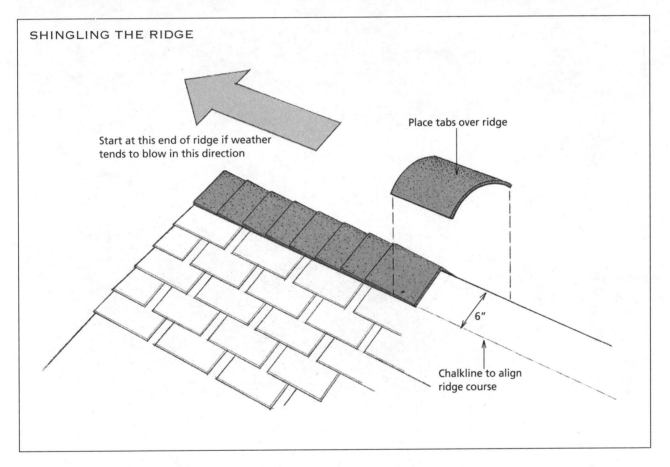

Start at this end of ridge if weather tends to blow in this direction

Place tabs over ridge

6"

Chalkline to align ridge course

by a greater margin than you've allowed for the other courses. (If you will be topping the roof with a ridge ventilator, omit the last two courses on each pitch; see "Installing Ridge Ventilators" above.)

Cap the ridge with single-tab-wide strips run vertically; see *Shingling the Ridge* above. Snap a chalkline 6 inches from the ridge, and align the strips with the chalkline, leaving 5 inches of each strip exposed. Shingle the ridge from either left to right or right to left, depending on the direction of the prevailing winds; work left to right, for example, if wet weather blows in from the right.

When you've shingled all the way to the far end of the ridge, cut the tab from a shingle and use that for the final piece; be sure to dab roofing cement on all exposed nail holes.

9
WINDOWS, SKYLIGHTS, AND EXTERIOR DOORS

There are a few decisive landmarks in building an addition. The foundation strikes a solid footprint, defining the perimeter of a new structure. The completed frame gives the structure a three-dimensional shape. With the installation of windows and exterior doors, you have yourself a shelter. And providing shelter, no matter how grand your plans and expectations, is the primary purpose of any living space.

That's why closing in an addition brings a sigh of relief from all of the participants. The owners cross a psychological threshold that assures them, perhaps for the first time, that they will actually be able to live in the new space. The building's interior is now protected from the elements. Tools and materials find safekeeping. And workers gain a place of retreat from cold wind, rain, or baking sun. Both owner and builder will definitely sleep a lot better once the addition is closed in.

The first night after the Baileys closed in their addition, they considered rolling out sleeping bags to camp in their new domestic frontier. There was a small problem, though. Heat had not yet been installed, and December temperatures had dropped below freezing. The family settled for a celebratory pizza instead, enjoying it in what would soon become their new family room.

LOCATING WINDOWS

Locating and selecting windows requires a careful balance of form and function. Windows simultaneously affect both the inside and outside of an addition. From outside, they are visual focal points, giving pattern and texture to the facade. They may help blend the addition with the existing house, or they may boldly announce that the new space is just that—new and different. On the inside, windows bring light, air, and a view.

We tend to prefer rooms that are bright with natural light and offer a view of the outdoors. Recent research has shown that improving lighting in homes and workplaces often leads to a general improvement in health and mood for the inhabitants. Consider also how an addition's windows can bring light to the adjoining rooms of the house.

Remember that each wall of your addition will receive a different amount of direct sunlight. North- and east-facing walls get less exposure and will need more window area to provide the same amount of light as south- and west-facing walls.

Along with light comes heat. If you live in a colder climate, using solar heat from windows can reduce energy costs. In warmer climates, and elsewhere in summer, you'll want to reduce the heat from sunlight with shading devices or to counteract it with air conditioning. Of course, any window can be shaded to increase privacy. Skylights, even small ones, admit plenty of light without infringing on privacy. They're also the most efficient way of using light for solar gain.

Window location will also influence how air travels through your addition, as shown in *Window Placement and Air Flow* below. Windows on opposite sides of a room provide the best cross ventilation. If you place a window where it will receive the prevailing wind directly, consider adding an eave to deflect wet weather.

It goes without saying that window placement determines the view you'll have and the privacy you may be giving up. Window height should be considered carefully. Dining room windows are best set for viewing from a seated position. Bedroom, bathroom, and hallway windows typically are placed to provide a view when standing. Family rooms, with their range of activities, often combine low and high windows. For a clean design, the tops of windows are usually aligned with the tops of exterior doors, 80 inches above floor level, but sill heights can vary from room to room and even within a room.

The quality of the view from the windows shouldn't be overlooked. Before the addition walls are framed, stand where the various rooms are planned and sample the views in each direction. A small lateral adjustment in a window's location may make the difference between seeing your neighbor's garage and enjoying the fields and woods beyond it.

Building codes add another consideration to window planning and for good reason. In the event of fire, windows become potential escape routes and sources of lifesaving oxygen. Bedrooms, in particular, are required to have a window big enough to escape through. Sill heights must be low enough to reach easily.

Most building codes require that every room in a residence have at least one window that opens for ventilation. As a rule of thumb, the total area of window surface should be about ten percent of a room's square footage; four percent of the square footage should be ventilating window. For example, in a room measuring 10 x 10 feet (100 square feet), 10 square feet of window area is needed; 4 square feet of ventilating window is called for. This is a general rule of residential construction. Your

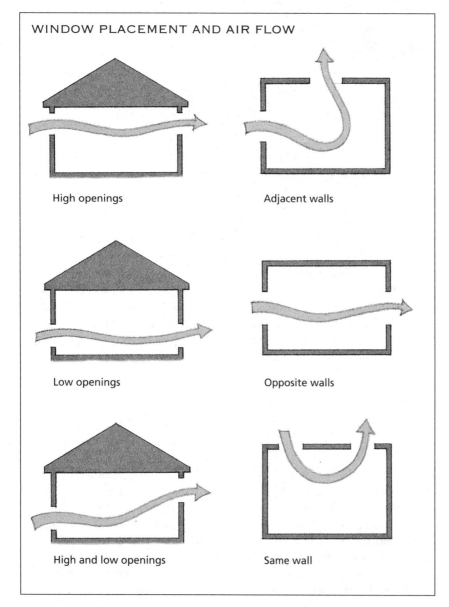

WINDOW PLACEMENT AND AIR FLOW

High openings

Low openings

High and low openings

Adjacent walls

Opposite walls

Same wall

136

local building code will provide specific requirements.

Don't forget that window locations will affect where you can place furniture. Certain pieces can only go against a wall. If your addition includes a dining room that has to accommodate your grandmother's heirloom breakfront, be sure the window locations leave a wall that it will fit against.

SELECTING WINDOWS

Buying windows deserves patient shopping. The choices are many, with a wide range of materials, designs, and even types of glass. Most manufacturers design their windows for easy installation by homeowners. Accessory and trim kits provide everything you'll need for typical framing conditions. Design assistance and detailed installation instructions are geared toward the first-time installer. Compare window suppliers according to price, warranties, and service, and examine the products.

Traditionally, windows have been made of wood, which offers some insulating value and can look attractive. But wood needs to be painted or sealed regularly to protect it from the weather, and wooden windows are more likely to stick because they expand from moisture.

Steel and aluminum extrusions are ideal for windows, but they are poor insulators. Solid vinyl windows combine lower manufacturing costs with modest insulating value. Aluminum and solid vinyl come in relatively few colors, fade over time, and may not be painted with good results.

Many windows combine a wood core with an aluminum or vinyl exterior. This provides a maintenance-free exterior, the insulating value of a wooden frame, and the option to change finishes on the interior.

You may have options in glazing as well. Standard clear glass lets nearly all the light in and a lot of the heat out. You'll find *low-E* glass (the E stands for emissivity) offered as an option in most lines of stock windows. Low-E glass is coated with a microscopic layer of metal oxide, which admits light but restricts heat passage. In winter, more heat stays in, while during summer, heat is kept out.

▲▲▲▲▲▲▲▲▲▲▲

You might save money by purchasing windows from local manufacturers rather than from national companies. Just make sure the low price doesn't come at the expense of quality and service.

▼▼▼▼▼▼▼▼▼▼▼

Double-pane insulating glass is another common feature in windows. Creating an air space between multiple panes of glass increases *resistance* to heat loss, known as *R-value*. Filling the sealed space between two panes with an inert gas like argon adds still more R-value. Tinted glass reflects some ultraviolet rays, keeping rooms cooler in summer and protecting wood and fabrics from fading.

To judge the quality of windows, start with appearance. Aluminum and vinyl windows are made from extrusions, which means the parts are molded when the material is in liquid form. Better products will have smooth welds and crisply mitered corners. Wooden windows should have clean joints, too. If the moldings are unfinished, check that they are smooth and ready for varnish or paint.

Whether you choose aluminum, vinyl, or wood, examine a window's operating features thoroughly. Don't buy a window until you have put it through its paces. Unlike the clunky, 30-year-old windows you may be putting up with in the rest of the house, new models should operate smoothly and with minimal effort. If a sliding window seems unduly troublesome to open and close in the showroom, it probably won't be any easier in your house. Tilt-out mechanisms should be uncomplicated and sturdy. Check that locks engage precisely and with minimal slack.

Before shopping for windows, familiarize yourself with the terminology. The *frame* is the outer structure that you fit into the rough opening. As shown in *Parts of a Window* on page 138, the frame includes *side jambs*, a *head jamb*, and an outside *sill*. The inside sill, or *stool*, is installed as part of the interior trim. This trim also includes three pieces of *casing* and *apron* molding under the sill.

The *sash* is the frame containing the glass. Sashes can be divided into smaller panes of glass, known as lights, with *muntins*, strips of wood, dividing them. False muntins can be fitted over a single large pane, giving it the appearance of a divided sash at a lower cost.

Windows can be grouped according to how they open; several common types are shown in *Types of Windows* on page 139.

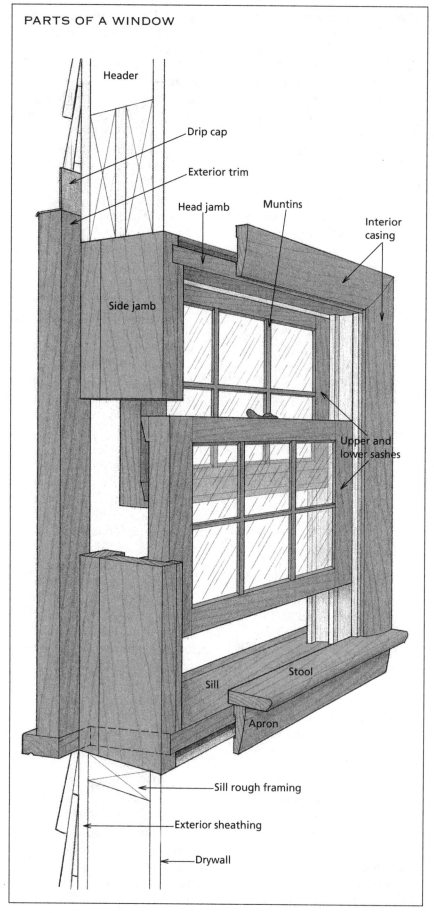

PARTS OF A WINDOW

Header

Drip cap

Exterior trim

Head jamb

Muntins

Interior casing

Side jamb

Upper and lower sashes

Sill

Stool

Apron

Sill rough framing

Exterior sheathing

Drywall

138

A *double-hung* window is composed of two sashes that slide up and down in separate channels in the side jambs. Each sash is held in place by counterweights, springs, or compression weather stripping. Look for sashes that can be either completely removed or pivoted inward for easy cleaning. Some tilt-in mechanisms work better than others, so try the brand you're considering at a showroom.

Sliding windows are much like double-hung windows, except the sashes slide horizontally and are often supported by rollers. This arrangement works well for larger windows and is used with glass patio doors. Like double-hung windows, sliding windows provide only half of their surface area for ventilation.

Casement windows are hinged on one side. Most are operated with a hand crank or lever and open outward to provide the best weather stripping seal between sash and frame. The full window area opens for ventilation.

Awning windows are hinged at their top edge and open outward, while *hoppers* are hinged along their bottom edge and open inward. A *fixed* window, as you might guess, doesn't open at all. Accent windows of many shapes are available as fixed sashes.

Additionally, there are specialty and hybrid windows. A *jalousie* window is made of small bands of overlapping glass mounted horizontally in a frame. Windows adjacent to a door are called *sidelights*, while those above are called *transoms*. Windows and doors with an arched top are called *circle heads*. A *bay* window projects out from the wall, providing a wider view and

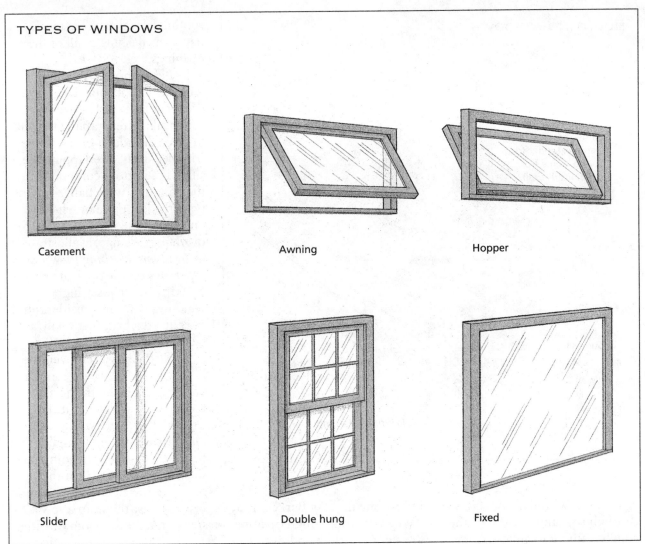

Casement

Awning

Hopper

Slider

Double hung

Fixed

admitting more light. A *bow* window is a bay that appears curved, but both bays and bows are usually made up of a series of smaller sashes.

Whenever you assemble a group of windows, you can mix and match types for the sake of both appearance and function. Bay windows, for example, often combine fixed sashes with casements.

The Baileys selected vinyl-clad double-hung windows for their addition. The design also called for two quarter-round accent windows flanking the fireplace in the family room. French doors were installed as the new main entrance into the back of the house.

INSTALLING WINDOWS

Rough openings for windows are specified by the manufacturer, so it's critical to have the specs in hand during wall framing. See Chapter 5 for more information on rough openings. If an opening is too small, you'll be tearing out studs—and perhaps your hair as well. If an opening is too big, you might be able to add stock and bring the opening down to size. However, a gap any larger than ½ inch requires longer screws and is difficult to insulate properly.

There are two methods for attaching a window frame to the wall, as shown in the illustration *Mounting Windows*

on page 140. If the frame has a flange that registers against the exterior sheathing, simply nail through the flange and sheathing into the studs. Some windows come with the exterior casing preattached to the jambs instead of a flange. When the casing is wood, nailing it to the trimmer studs anchors the window.

Other windows float in the opening, and you have to position the inside edge of the jambs so they will be flush with the finished drywall. Since the drywall is usually put up after a window is installed, you have to position the window with a spacer the same thickness as the drywall you will be using.

Once in place, the window

140

If necessary, add jamb extender to bring frame flush with inside wall

Align

Shim space

Rough sill

Drywall or spacer

Mounting flanges register against sheathing

Exterior sheathing

is attached with nails or screws through the jambs and into the rough framing members. Some windows use metal clips that are attached to the frame with screws, then bent into place against the siding after the window is positioned.

If the wall is thicker than the window frame is wide, you'll need to add *jamb extenders*, as illustrated above. Make these from wood strips that match the thickness of the frame material; they should be flush with the interior wall surface.

Installing windows is a two-person operation. One person is responsible for holding onto the window, while the other adds shims and then secures the window in place with nails or screws.

Barry and Dave installed all of the Baileys' window units

in just one day. As Barry put it, "When all your rough openings are right on, the windows just pop into place."

▲▲▲▲▲▲▲▲▲▲▲

If insulating around windows or doors with aerosol foam, spray a foot-long test bead of foam on a piece of scrap to gauge how much the brand you bought will expand.

▼▼▼▼▼▼▼▼▼▼▼

Window and door openings are particularly susceptible to leaks. After all, each one starts out as a big hole in the wall. To protect the wooden framing, plan on installing a layer of

roofing felt (also called tar paper) as flashing at all of the openings.

Before hoisting each window into its opening, Dave draped a layer of felt over the rough sill. After stapling the felt in place, he added pieces to the trimmer studs, overlapping the sill at the bottom corners. Since the windows were flange-mount type, the last piece of felt—the one across the head—needed to overlap the flange, as illustrated in *Applying Flashing to Window Openings* on the opposite page.

If you are inserting windows with the outside trim already attached, first apply a heavy bead of exterior caulk.

Next, Barry removed the lower sashes. This gave him a better grip on the frame and reduced the weight of it. He decided to set the windows in place from inside by angling the frame through the opening, as shown in *Photo 9-1* on the opposite page. The other option was to hoist them up a few steps on a ladder from outside, a more precarious operation.

As Barry held the window in place, Dave headed outside to tack the window in place and check for level (shown in *Photos 9-2 through 9-5* on page 142). Dave instructed Barry where to insert shims between the windowsill and rough sill to raise and lower the window. Once the window was level, Dave began nailing the flange. Since nailing could have twisted or bent the window frame, Barry installed the sash he had removed earlier and checked that the window opened and closed properly as Dave nailed it in.

Before installing the interior trim on windows and doors, Barry filled the space between the frame and studs with insulation. The best types

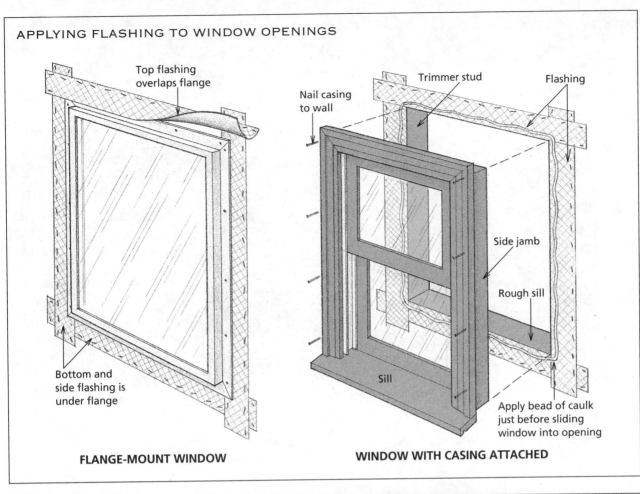

APPLYING FLASHING TO WINDOW OPENINGS

Top flashing overlaps flange

Bottom and side flashing is under flange

FLANGE-MOUNT WINDOW

Nail casing to wall

Trimmer stud

Flashing

Side jamb

Rough sill

Sill

Apply bead of caulk just before sliding window into opening

WINDOW WITH CASING ATTACHED

Photo 9-1. Barry and Dave lift a window frame through its opening from the inside of the addition rather than struggle with it while on a ladder outside the addition.

Photo 9-2. *With the window in place, Dave holds on to it while Barry goes outside to secure it with nails.*

Photo 9-3. *Barry checks the window frame for level, then calls out his readings to Dave, who is inside.*

Photo 9-4. *Dave inserts shims under the sill. When shimming the sides, be sure not to bow the jambs.*

Photo 9-5. *As the mounting flange is nailed, it's a good idea to check that the window continues to operate properly.*

FRAMING NONRECTANGULAR WINDOWS

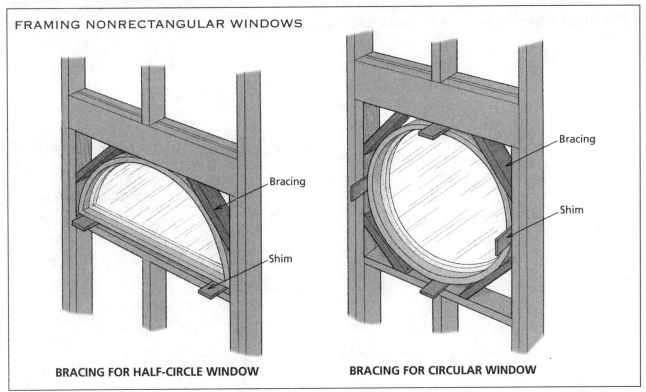

Bracing

Shim

BRACING FOR HALF-CIRCLE WINDOW

Bracing

Shim

BRACING FOR CIRCULAR WINDOW

of insulation are fiberglass or Styrofoam sprayed from a can. Be sure not to overfill the space with foam, as its expanding action can bow the frame.

Windows with arches work well to enliven a broad expanse of siding. Even a small window can add a strong visual punch. That's just what the Baileys needed along the north wall of their addition, where they flanked the mantle with two quarter-round fixed windows.

Arched and other nonrectangular windows are installed in much the same way as regular windows. The manufacturer will specify a rectangular rough opening, but you may have to add stud bracing, as shown in *Framing Nonrectangular Windows* above. The studs support the window frame and provide a nailing surface for the casing. The Baileys' small quarter-round windows required just a single brace nailed at a 45 degree angle, as shown in *Photo 9-6* on the right.

Photo 9-6. If windows are not rectangular, you may have to add framing members to anchor them, as Barry is doing here.

FRAMING A SKYLIGHT IN A CATHEDRAL CEILING

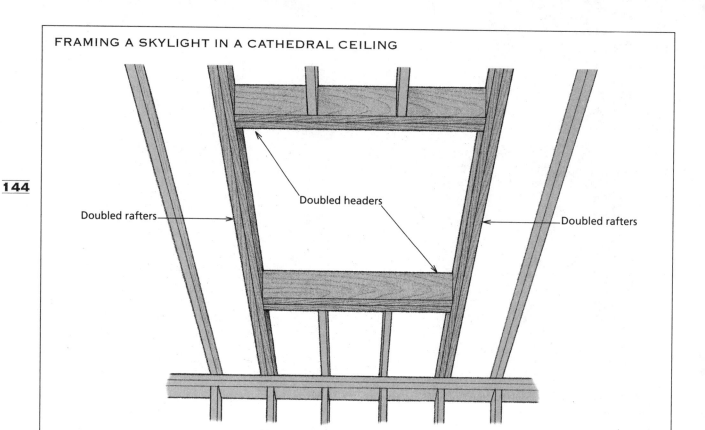

Doubled rafters

Doubled headers

Doubled rafters

FRAMING A LIGHT WELL

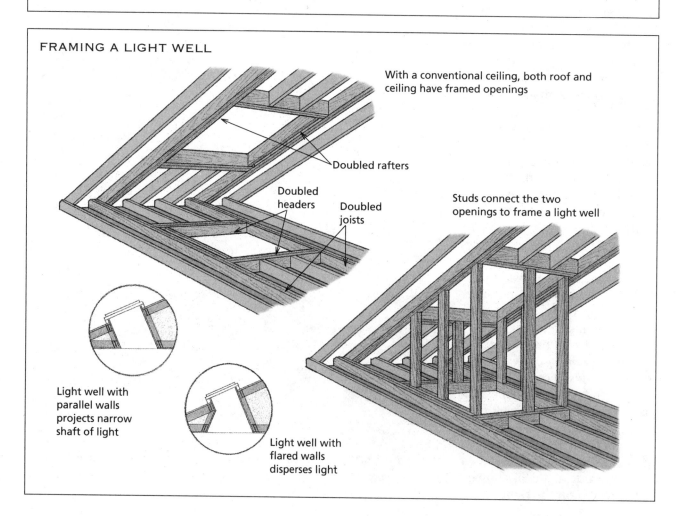

With a conventional ceiling, both roof and ceiling have framed openings

Doubled rafters

Doubled headers

Doubled joists

Studs connect the two openings to frame a light well

Light well with parallel walls projects narrow shaft of light

Light well with flared walls disperses light

WINDOWS, SKYLIGHTS, AND EXTERIOR DOORS

INSTALLING SKYLIGHTS

Like windows, skylights come both fixed and operable. They require adding either a finish frame or light well to bridge the area between the ceiling and roof opening.

If the ceiling is attached to the rafters, as on a cathedral or vaulted ceiling, skylight framing is straightforward and similar to window framing. See *Framing a Skylight in a Cathedral Ceiling* on the opposite page (top). If the roof and ceiling are framed separately, each requires a rough-framed opening. The two frames are structurally connected with framing stock, as shown in *Framing a Light Well* on the opposite page (bottom).

Light wells can have either parallel or flared walls. Flared light wells are harder to build, but they spread light over a much wider area. On the other hand, the shaft of concentrated light cast by a light well with parallel walls may be just the striking effect you want.

Because they are set in roofs, skylights are more prone to leaks than windows. Most skylights include a flashing kit designed to ensure a watertight seal. Some designs (particularly of nonopening skylights) require that you build a shallow curb from 2 x 4 stock for the skylight to rest upon. The flashing is then installed in conjunction with the roofing material. The sequence for this is critical, so follow the manufacturer's instructions carefully.

Like roof flashing, skylight flashing is installed from the bottom up to resist water as it runs off the roof. The flashing along the bottom edge is first laid over the roofing, and the side flashing is then installed. Finally, the head flashing along the top edge is covered by the roofing.

For easier installation, some skylights come with a heavy-gauge rubber bib that is overlapped by roofing. There is no additional flashing except along the bottom edge, where a narrow strip lays over the roofing.

CHOOSING EXTERIOR DOORS

An entry door needs to be both accessible and attractive. Doors instruct visitors how to approach your home, so a main entry deserves more visual prominence than a side or secondary door. If the addition opens onto a deck or patio and the doors will get heavy and frequent use, consider sliding glass doors. A more formal look may call for French doors. Or get the best of both designs with sliding French doors. Consider also how a new doorway will create traffic patterns through the addition and into other parts of the house.

Doors can be used like windows for increasing

FRAME-AND-PANEL CONSTRUCTION

Panel

Mullion

Rails

Stile

Panels expand and contract freely within grooves

ventilation. But in the winter, they should seal tightly against the weather. If possible, avoid placing a door where it will face prevailing winds, unless it will be shielded by a vestibule, awning, or roof overhang.

The most time-tested door is the wooden frame and panel. In fact, frame-and-panel construction is the only reliable method of making a large, flat, and stable structure out of solid wood.

Wood expands and contracts as it absorbs and gives off moisture; the wider the board, the more extreme the movement. A door made from solid lumber glued edge to edge might expand as much as ½ inch, making it a challenge to operate and seal against the weather.

As shown in *Frame-and-Panel Construction* on page 145, a structural frame of *stiles* and *rails* allows the panels to expand and contract freely, without affecting the size of the frame.

A *French door* has intersecting stiles and rails that hold glass *lights* instead of wooden panels. Often used in pairs, French doors admit lots of light and provide a view. But they have less R-value than wooden doors and offer less security against a break-in. You can get the look of a French door in a single-pane insulated glass door with false muntins. Both true divided-light and single-pane doors are available with insulated glass.

Flush wooden doors are either solid or have a hollow core, as shown in *Flush Door Construction* below. Solid-core flush doors are made from surface layers of veneer laminated to a core of flakeboard or particleboard. Hollow-core doors are made from a lightweight wooden grid or cardboard honeycomb, clad with layers of thin plywood. In both, a border of solid wood provides secure anchoring for hardware and allows for trimming the door if necessary.

Wooden doors suffer the same drawbacks of wooden windows: They deteriorate from exposure to the elements if not sealed or painted regularly. But there are plenty of worthy alternatives to wooden doors. Insulated doors are made from a core of rigid insulating foam with sheet steel, aluminum, vinyl, or, most recently, fiberglass. These doors provide greater resistance to heat loss than insulated wooden doors, but they come in fewer styles.

Every door, no matter what the style, starts with a rough opening and ends with finish trim. You can purchase a door without a surrounding frame, then tackle these tasks yourself. Or you can use a prehung door.

At the very least, a prehung door includes an assembled frame and a hung door with hinges mortised into both the frame and the door edge. Prehung kits may also include the interior or exterior casing, doorstop, weather stripping, threshold, and installation bores (called *mortises*) for a standard lockset. The more complete the package, the greater the cost—and the less time and trouble for the installer.

Home centers stock a small selection of prehung doors, but will custom order other styles and sizes. Most specialty window stores also supply doors, and there are stores that sell nothing but doors.

Once you've decided on a door style, you need to

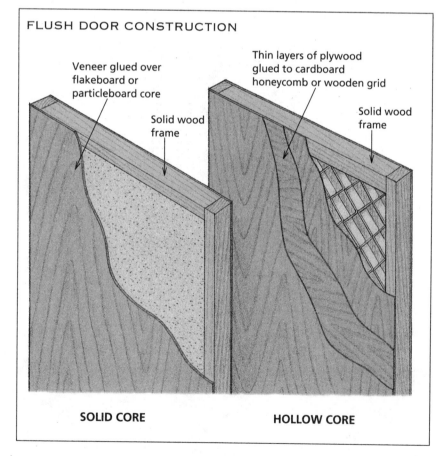

FLUSH DOOR CONSTRUCTION

Veneer glued over flakeboard or particleboard core

Solid wood frame

Thin layers of plywood glued to cardboard honeycomb or wooden grid

Solid wood frame

SOLID CORE

HOLLOW CORE

determine the size. The standard size of an entry door is 1¾ inches thick, 36 inches wide, and 80 inches high. Anything smaller will limit your ability to bring furniture and appliances through the door.

To determine the rough opening for a door, you need to know the thickness of the side and head jambs—usually ¾ inch. Rough opening width equals door size plus twice the thickness of the side jambs plus ¾ to 1 inch more for shimming. Rough opening height equals the door height plus the thickness of the head jamb plus ½ inch for shimming plus the allowance for finish flooring or threshold.

The thickness of your walls determines what jamb width you should order. Standard width is 4⁹⁄₁₆ inches. If you buy a stock prehung door and the jambs are narrower than your walls are thick, you can extend the jambs by gluing on strips of wood. Door manufacturers may supply jamb extension kits for this purpose. As shown in *Split Jamb* on the right (top), some prehung doors come in a two-piece jamb, with a tongue-and-groove joint that allows you to adjust the jamb width to your wall thickness. Split jambs usually have the casing attached on both sides, as shown.

A final specification concerns direction of swing. Be extra careful here; if you order the wrong swing, you'll be sending the door back and probably incurring a charge if it was a custom order. Residential entry doors open into the house, so the hinge barrels are always on the inside of the door. Beyond that, unfortunately, there are different conventions for describing a door as left- or right-handed, depending on whether you're ordering a

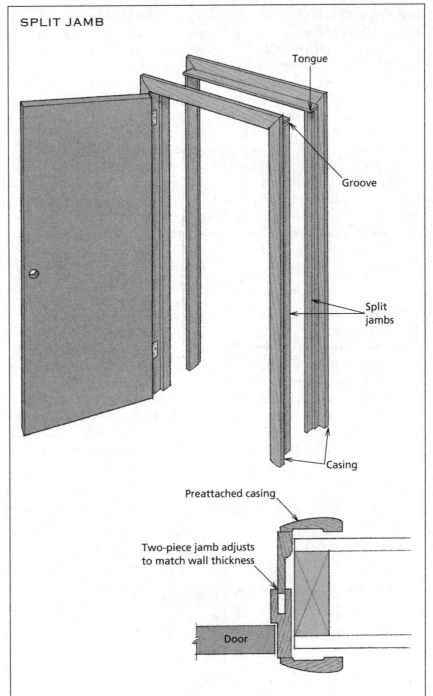

SPLIT JAMB

Tongue

Groove

Split jambs

Casing

Preattached casing

Two-piece jamb adjusts to match wall thickness

Door

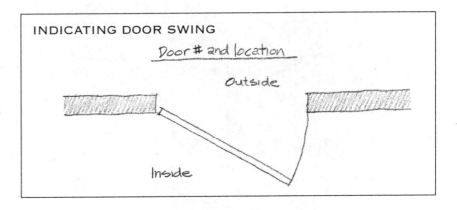

INDICATING DOOR SWING

Door # and location

Outside

Inside

prehung with or without a lockset. Pairs of doors complicate the picture still further. Some carpenters use the handled edge as a reference, while others use the hinged edge.

To avoid confusion, make a simple plan view drawing of every door you order and let a salesperson translate your drawing into company convention. Give each door a number. Show which side it's hinged and handled on and the direction of swing. See *Indicating Door Swing* on page 147 (bottom).

INSTALLING EXTERIOR DOORS

If you take delivery of your doors before you're ready to install them, store them upright in their jambs or on edge if they are not hung. Make sure they are not racked or twisted, since a twist in the frame will eventually show up in the door. Protect wooden doors from excessive moisture; for example, don't store them in a room that will receive wet work like plastering or one that isn't closed in yet. If possible, let a prehung unit acclimate to the humidity of its intended site for at least a couple of days before installation.

The first step in installing an exterior door is to flash the rough door frame members with roofing felt. Next, move on to the sill—the angled block of wood or metal that drains water away from the base of the door. The sill should project out beyond the siding; the inside edge should be nearly flush with the finished floor, as illustrated in *Doorsill* below. Install a threshold to bridge the gap and any height discrepancy between the sill and the finished floor.

Most prehung units include the sill or a combination sill and threshold as part of the frame. Using one of these will save you a lot of time and trouble, since all that's left is to fit the whole frame into the opening. If your door unit does not include a sill, you can buy it separately and cut it to fit between the trimmer studs. Then, cut the bottoms of the jambs to match the taper of the sill—they're left long for this purpose. You'll then need to trim the door bottom so it closes snugly against the threshold or weather stripping.

Once you've accounted for the sill, you can set the frame into the opening. Leave the door in the frame to keep the unit square as you shim the frame in the opening. At this point, you could spend a lot of time trying to plumb the jambs. However, it's more important with a prehung that the door operate properly in its frame under existing conditions, even if the jambs are a little out of plumb.

Shimming a Door Frame on the opposite page shows where to locate the shims around the frame. Start at the head, applying shims at the corners and the middle. This should wedge the frame enough to free up your hands. Check the edges of the frame on both sides—it should be flush or just a little proud of the inside and outside wall surfaces. If the frame is wider by more than $1/16$ inch, set the hinged side flush; trimming this edge would require removing the hinges and might interfere with hinge operation.

When using tapered shims, it's always best to overlap a pair, with each shim coming in from an opposite side of the jamb. This may not be an option if one side of the door frame has the casing attached. In that case, you can only work around the open

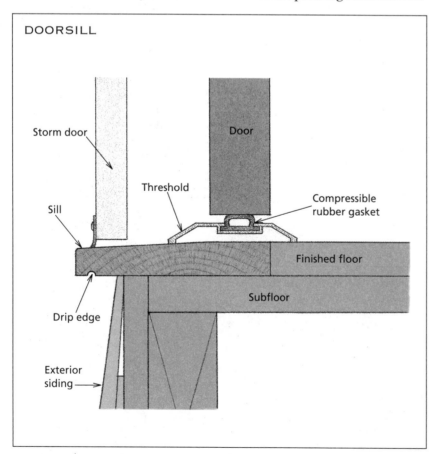

DOORSILL

Storm door

Threshold

Sill

Compressible rubber gasket

Door

Finished floor

Subfloor

Drip edge

Exterior siding

edge of the frame, so use shortened shims that won't hit the casing on the far side. Tapping in tapered shims from one side only is risky because the jamb can twist when it's nailed into the trimmer studs. To prevent this, nail closer to the shimmed edge instead of in the middle of the jamb, as shown in the illustration detail.

Proceed to insert shims directly behind the hinges on the hinge side and in the corresponding locations on the lock side. Open the door about 90 degrees and slide a wedge or a few shims underneath to keep it open. Using 10d or larger finish nails, secure the hinge-side jamb first. Place the nails above or below the shims for now, so that you can adjust the shims in or out if necessary.

As you nail, check the gap around the door, and don't hammer the nails all the way home yet. With the hinge side of the jamb secured, open and close the door a few times and check that the jamb is not twisting, which would indicate the door is binding at some point in its swing.

Next nail the lock side of the jamb. Nailing usually compresses the shims a bit and widens the gap between door and jamb. Close the door after installing each nail and check the gap. Simply tap the shims in farther until the gap is consistent.

If the door came with a lockset, make sure it is engaging properly. If you're installing the lockset, do it now—minor adjustments in the fit of the frame are often needed to help the lockset function perfectly. See "Installing a Lockset" on pages 150–151 for instructions.

Once you're confident that the door is operating properly, add a nail through each set of

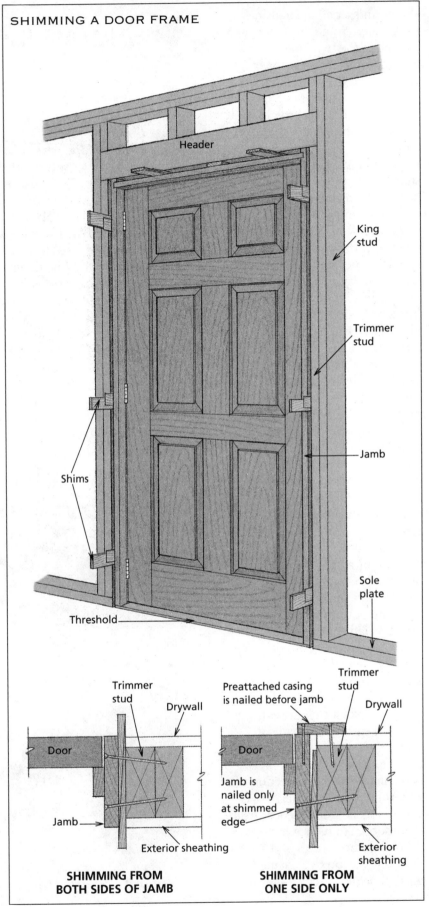

SHIMMING A DOOR FRAME

Header

King stud

Trimmer stud

Jamb

Shims

Sole plate

Threshold

Trimmer stud

Door

Jamb

Drywall

Exterior sheathing

SHIMMING FROM BOTH SIDES OF JAMB

Preattached casing is nailed before jamb

Trimmer stud

Door

Jamb is nailed only at shimmed edge

Drywall

Exterior sheathing

SHIMMING FROM ONE SIDE ONLY

shims, and set all the nails below the surface. Some carpenters like to replace the two hinge screws closest to the center of the jamb with longer screws, tying the door to the wall framing itself. There may still be a little bounce in the door frame, but that's okay—the finish casing will reduce that considerably. Cut the shims flush with the wall using a handsaw, or snap them off after scoring them with a razor.

After you've installed your door, seal the gap between the rough frames and finish frames with insulation. Strips of foam or batt insulation will work, but the most weather-tight alternative is to spray expanding polyurethane foam from a can. However, be careful to avoid overfilling the space—too much foam can cause the door frame to bow.

If your prehung exterior door isn't sold with weather stripping already in place, consider buying one of the systems at your home center. Foam, felt, rubber, and thin strips of metal are among the materials used to seal the sides and top of an exterior door against drafts. As shown in the illustration *Doorsill* on page 148, the bottom of the door gets specialized treatment; many exterior thresholds include a weather strip. Additionally, you may want to add a sweep to the door bottom to help make a tighter seal.

An entry door made of wood, unless fully shielded from direct exposure to wind, rain, and sun, needs the protection of a storm door. Even steel, vinyl, and fiberglass doors benefit from storm doors to reduce heat loss. A combination storm-and-screen door allows you to exchange the glass panel for a screen in warm weather.

▶ INSTALLING A LOCKSET

A *lockset* typically includes knobs or handles, lock, latch bolt, and a strike plate that will fit in the door frame to hold the bolt. There are variations of locksets for use in different parts of the house. A *passage set* has no lock mechanism and is used for children's bedrooms and closet doors. *Privacy sets,* most commonly used on bathroom doors, can be locked from one side only with a push button or twist knob. An *entrance set* is lockable from both sides, with a key on the outside and a button or twist knob on the inside. A *dead bolt* is a cylinder lock used in conjunction with an entrance set for extra security, and it usually is operated from the outside with a key and from the inside with a latch.

Unless your door has already been mortised for a lockset, you will need a large-diameter drill bit or hole saw for the lockset and a smaller bit for the latch unit. Additionally, you'll need a hammer, chisel, and an awl or other sharp marking device.

A template is provided with the lockset to ensure that the two holes are bored properly. First, measure and mark the height of the handle; 36 inches is standard, but feel free to adjust the height a few inches either way if you're taller or shorter than average (the knob height can be set to either favor or discourage young children). Locate the template at the desired height against the outside face of the door, as shown in the photo below.

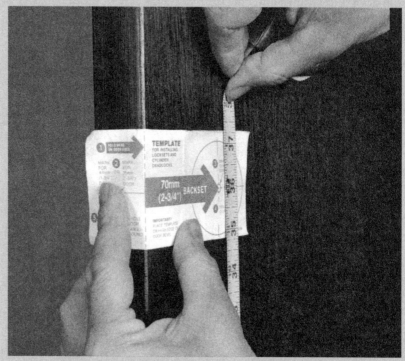

The manufacturer supplies a template to assist you in laying out holes for a lockset and latch unit.

Fold the paper template over the door's outside edge, then use an awl at the center points on the template to locate the holes for the lockset and latch unit.

A try square helps to ensure that the drill is held perpendicular to the surface of the door.

To help guide the bit for both bores, begin by drilling ⅛-inch pilot holes at the points you've marked. It's crucial that the pilot holes be square to the face of the door, so use a try square as a guide for the drill, as shown in the photo above.

Next, make the lockset hole, drilling roughly halfway from each face, as shown in the photo below.

The hole for the latch unit must be square to the edge of the door and parallel with the faces; otherwise, the bolt might bind up. With both holes drilled, install the lockset and check the fit. If the bolt doesn't spring freely, use a wood rasp to widen its hole slightly.

The pilot hole guides the large hole saw, keeping it square to the door. Drill halfway from each face.

The latch unit faceplate must be flush with the door edge, and this requires making a mortise. Predrill for the faceplate, then temporarily attach the latch unit to the door edge with screws. Trace around the faceplate with the awl to mark for the mortise, then remove the latch unit. Start the mortise by deepening the score marks *slightly* with a chisel. Cut across the end grain with a series of shallow cuts, then cut along the grain to clean out the material, as shown in the photo below. Use a chisel just a little narrower than the width of the mortise. Remount the latch unit and check that it still operates smoothly.

The strike plate must line up with the latch bolt. Here's how to get it right the first time. Close the door so that the bolt rests against the jamb. Mark along the bottom and top of the bolt to establish the vertical position of the strike plate hole, and bore it with the bit used for the bolt hole in the door.

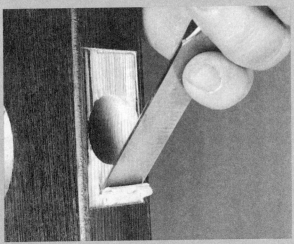

The edge of the door is mortised for the latch unit faceplate.

The strike plate itself, not the hole behind it, determines how accurately the bolt catches. Carefully measure the distance between the flat side of the bolt and the outside face of the door. Set the strike plate with this distance between its flat edge and the doorstop. Predrill for the strike plate, then attach it temporarily. If the bolt catches properly, mark and mortise the jamb as you did the door edge. If the doorstops are not fully nailed in place, you can set the strike plate and then adjust the stops snugly against the door.

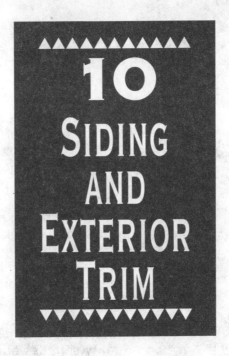

10 SIDING AND EXTERIOR TRIM

Although siding may be only millimeters thick, it can make or break the appearance of your addition, not to mention the overall look of your house and property. If you make a poor choice here, you (and your neighbors) will have to live with it for years to come.

You have several options for siding. Most obviously, you can try to match the siding of your addition to whatever clads the old house. But this isn't as simple as it seems. It's all but impossible to match new siding to siding that has faded under the constant onslaught of weather and sunlight.

Another option is to choose a complementary siding as a contrast. If you live in an old stone farmhouse, for example, you might choose to side the addition with stucco or natural-finished wood.

The Baileys took a third route, putting new siding on the existing house at the same time the addition was sided. That ensured the addition looked like part of the house.

Whatever your decision, you'll find there are several types of siding available, ranging from modern maintenance-free products to traditional wood.

SYNTHETIC SIDING MATERIALS

In recent years, wood and wood-based siding have largely been supplanted by vinyl siding and aluminum siding in new construction. Vinyl is especially popular with contractors and homeowners who are looking for a long-lasting, low-maintenance siding that is quick to install and looks traditional—from a distance, at

any rate. In fact, vinyl siding is chosen twice as often as any other type of siding.

Made from extruded polyvinyl chloride (PVC), this siding often was criticized for looking fake when it was first introduced. But the manufacturers have become better at mimicking the look of wood. As well as the siding itself, manufacturers make corner boards, vinyl soffit panels, and door and window trim. The industry now produces some siding from recycled stock, but the quality isn't quite as good as first-run vinyl.

Because the butt joints in the siding advertise that this is a plastic product and not real wood, some manufacturers now produce sections of vinyl up to 40 feet long to reduce the number of joints. The thickness of the vinyl ranges from 0.035 to 0.048 inches. The beefier grades hold up better when assaulted by children, baseballs, or golf balls. Top grades cost twice as much as the lower grades. On average, vinyl siding costs slightly more than hardboard and half as much as beveled redwood or cedar.

One of the best things about vinyl siding is that it never has to be painted, and most brands are guaranteed for the life of the homeowner, if not for the life of the house. Maintaining vinyl siding means spraying it down with the garden hose when it gets dirty.

Vinyl siding isn't quite as permanent as stone, however. It will fade, though less so if the manufacturer included a relatively high amount of titanium dioxide in the mix, as is often the case in more costlier grades. Darker-colored vinyls are especially vulnerable to fading.

Since it is so thin and flexible, this siding can't be nailed too tightly or it will flex near the nails; then, when the sun hits those impressions from just the wrong angle, the siding will look odd. Also, vinyl expands and contracts with changes in temperature, so you have to allow for this movement during installation.

Aluminum siding has largely been supplanted by vinyl. It can cost up to twice as much as vinyl siding, and aluminum is vulnerable to denting. On the positive side, aluminum siding expands and contracts less than vinyl siding, so you rarely see aluminum buckling because of poor installation. It also fades less than vinyl, and this may be a help if you are trying to match new siding to old. Most siding suppliers still carry a selection of aluminum siding.

 # WOOD SHINGLES

Many century-old houses still have their original shingles, grayed and pitted but still doing their job. Shingles are installed in courses, like clapboard, although the pieces are much smaller. That means more handling, but one person can do the job alone, whereas long strips of siding really require two people. Shingles come in 16-, 18-, and 24-inch lengths and random widths from around 3 to 14 inches. The narrowest widths should be used sparingly because of their relatively small coverage.

Much of the cutting and fitting of shingles is done with a shingler's hatchet, which serves the purpose of a hammer and hatchet all in one tool. It is used to split and pare shingles, hammer nails, and pull nails that have gone astray.

Single-course shingles, discussed here, have one layer of good-quality shingles applied to each course. Roof shingles are applied in a single course, and this is the traditional method for installing shingles. Sometimes shingles are installed in a double course. In double-course installation, two layers of shingles are installed for each course—a lower-grade shingle is installed first with a better grade on top. Double-course shingles stand out from the wall and have a more rustic look.

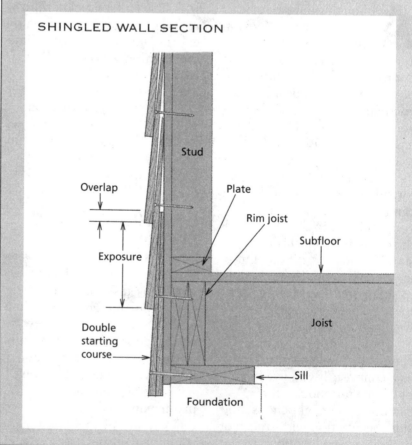

SHINGLED WALL SECTION

Stud

Overlap

Plate

Rim joist

Subfloor

Exposure

Joist

Double starting course

Sill

Foundation

SHINGLE POSITION

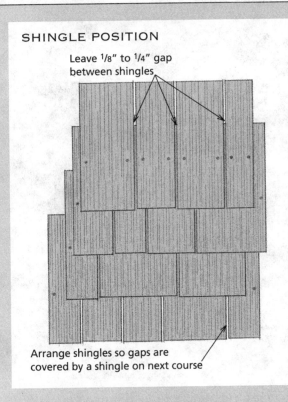

Leave 1/8" to 1/4" gap between shingles

Arrange shingles so gaps are covered by a shingle on next course

determined, lay out the courses at the corners of the walls, and snap a line at the bottom of the first course. As with clapboard siding, it is best to have the lower edges, or butts, align with the tops of windows; you can arrange this through a careful layout of courses.

Instead of running a starter strip as you do with board siding, you begin with a double course of shingles, as illustrated. Nail the first course in place, then snap a chalkline for the next course. Nails that hold the later courses in place are positioned so that they will be covered and protected by subsequent courses.

Because the shingles will expand and contract across the width of the wall, they should be spaced 1/8 to 1/4 inch apart, as shown in the illustration *Shingle Position* on the left. The gaps in one course should always be lapped by shingles in subsequent courses.

At corners, shingles can be met by corner boards or be woven, as shown in *Shingle Corner Treatments* below. To weave a corner, one wall's course overlaps the other wall's course, and the overlapping shingle is chopped off to make an even edge. This overlap alternates from wall to wall with each subsequent course.

To install shingles, first determine the desired *exposure*, or surface area of a shingle that will be seen after installation. As shown in *Shingled Wall Section* on the opposite page, this procedure will arrange the shingles so they are at least two layers thick. When the exposure has been

SHINGLE CORNER TREATMENTS

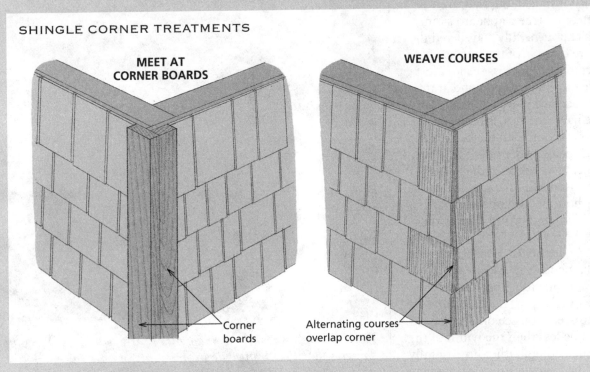

MEET AT CORNER BOARDS

WEAVE COURSES

Corner boards

Alternating courses overlap corner

WOOD SIDING

One of the best things about wood siding is that it has the look and texture of wood. Unfortunately, as our old-growth forests dwindle, the prices of quality wood products continue to climb. Wood siding

156 is one of the more expensive cover-ups for an addition. Also, keep in mind that wood siding will be very durable only if it is installed and maintained properly. Unless you choose a wood that can go without paint or stain, you face an ongoing routine of repainting—and some prep work as well.

If you choose to side your addition in wood, you'll find a number of softwood sidings available, including spruce and pine (which need paint) and cedar and redwood (which can go without paint).

Wood commonly is milled as *clapboard* or *beveled siding*, as shown in *Photo 10-1* on the right (top). These two siding types look virtually the same when installed, but they are different. True clapboard siding, which is generally considered the more durable of the two, is rectangular in cross section, just like most boards you find at the lumberyard. Beveled siding, as the name implies, is beveled in cross section with the bottom edge being wider than the top edge. In either case, the boards are installed horizontally with the bottom edge of each board overlapping the top edge of the one below it.

Clapboard or beveled siding comes in widths from 4 to 12 inches. Since the boards are overlapped, the *exposure*, or face area, you see on each board will be less than the width of the actual siding. Other horizontally applied sidings are illustrated in

Photo 10-1. Wood clapboard was often the standard siding used on older houses.

Photo 10-2. Shakes (right) have more surface texture than sawn shingles (left). Both provide protection and a traditional look.

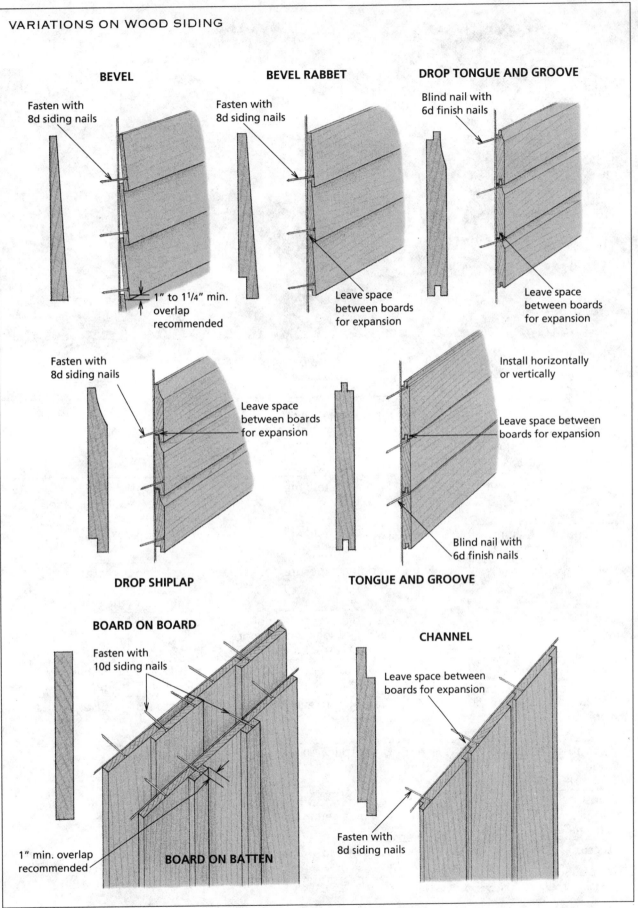

BEVEL

Fasten with 8d siding nails

1" to 1¼" min. overlap recommended

BEVEL RABBET

Fasten with 8d siding nails

Leave space between boards for expansion

DROP TONGUE AND GROOVE

Blind nail with 6d finish nails

Leave space between boards for expansion

DROP SHIPLAP

Fasten with 8d siding nails

Leave space between boards for expansion

TONGUE AND GROOVE

Install horizontally or vertically

Leave space between boards for expansion

Blind nail with 6d finish nails

BOARD ON BOARD

Fasten with 10d siding nails

1" min. overlap recommended

BOARD ON BATTEN

CHANNEL

Leave space between boards for expansion

Fasten with 8d siding nails

Photo 10-3. The grainy split face of shakes adds a rustic texture to a house.

COMPARING SIDING

Material	Cost	Life (years)	Care	Pros	Cons
Vinyl	Low	50+	None	Easy to install; many styles and colors	Color may fade; no fire resistance; easily damaged by heat, like that from gas grill
Aluminum	Medium	30	None	Easy to install; high fire resistance	Dents easily; color may fade
Hardboard	Low	30	Paint	Variable exposure; looks like solid wood	Susceptible to moisture damage; very heavy; conforms to defects in the wall
OSB	Low	30	Paint	Variable exposure; looks and feels like solid wood; more stable than solid wood	Susceptible to moisture
Plywood	Low	20	Paint; stain	Quick and easy to install; can double as sheathing	Short life; susceptible to moisture damage
Horizontal wood	Medium to high	50	Paint; stain; none*	Traditional; several styles available	Slow to install; susceptible to moisture
Vertical wood	Medium	50	Paint; stain; none*	Quick to install	Susceptible to moisture
Wood shingles and shakes	High	50+	Stain; none*	Long life; traditional looking; low maintenance	Very slow to install; expensive
Stucco	Medium	50	None	Long life; low maintenance	Susceptible to moisture; may crack or bulge

*Cedar and redwood will weather but won't rot.

Variations on Wood Siding on page 157.

Shingles and *shakes* are another way of cladding a home in wood. See *Photo 10-2* on page 156 (bottom). They were probably first used as a roof covering, which attests to their weather-resisting powers.

You can find a 100-year-old house still clad in its original shingles or shakes. The siding will be pitted and worn by years of wind and heavy weather, but the shingles or shakes will still be intact and protecting the house.

Shingles are sawn wedges that are available with the faces rough-sawn or sanded. Shakes differ from shingles in that the faces are split, not sawn. As shown in *Photo 10-3* on the opposite page, splitting produces a rustic, grainy face. Neither shingles nor shakes are difficult to install, but the process is time-consuming since they have to be installed one piece at a time. To speed up installation, some siding companies sell shingles and shakes preinstalled on plywood backing panels that can cover as much as 14 square feet.

MANUFACTURED WOOD SIDING

Manufactured wood siding includes plywood siding, hardboard siding, and oriented strand board (OSB). Standard panels of manufactured wood are quite featureless, but sheets intended for siding are often patterned in some way. Texture 1-11 (called T1-11), shown in *Photo 10-4* below, is a well-known trade name of plywood siding; it has vertical grooves cut in the face veneer to simulate individual boards.

Plywood panels can be installed faster than any other siding, and they also save time by doubling as sheathing. Panels come in a wide range of prices depending on the veneer that covers the face. Products with a veneer of Douglas fir or yellow pine can cost as little as one-third of those with cedar veneer. In fact, cedar-veneered plywood can be as costly as the most expensive solid wood siding, but the price may be offset if this product saves installation labor and the need to use sheathing.

Hardboard siding is made of wood fibers that are bonded together with phenolic resin or a linseed oil emulsion. The resulting product is rather heavy, so plan on at least two strong backs for installation. You can buy hardboard siding that resembles clapboard or beveled siding and has either a smooth or wood-grained face. Hardboard is the least expensive siding available. On the down side, it is very susceptible to water damage even though it comes from the factory already primed. You'll need to apply at least two coats of exterior paint and repaint periodically.

OSB siding is made up of strands of wood arranged in layers of alternating grain direction and held together with a phenolic resin adhesive. The wood used to make OSB generally comes from quick-growing aspen trees, a plentiful resource. As with hardboard, OSB's face layer can be ordered smooth or textured to imitate wood. OSB is stiffer than hardboard, yet not as heavy; it costs only slightly more. Relative to solid wood, OSB is more stable and resists splitting. But it must be sealed with a couple of layers of quality exterior house paint and periodically repainted for proper maintenance.

Photo 10-4. T 1-11 is the most common type of plywood siding, and it's speedy to install.

MASONRY SIDING

Stucco and veneers of stone and brick also have a traditional look. Veneers require little maintenance, but they are quite expensive initially. Also, installation is a job for the pros. Laying brick and stone isn't nearly as forgiving as working with wood and many other building materials.

Stucco is a thin layer of a special type of cement. The cost falls somewhere in the middle of other siding options. It is usually applied over metal mesh, called lath, as shown in *Photo 10-5* on the right. The lath is attached to the sheathing, then stucco is troweled over and through it. A few coats are applied, and the finish coat may be left natural or colored. Applying stucco is an involved process and relatively time-consuming.

Photo 10-5. Stucco is troweled over and through metal lath, which has been attached to the sheathing.

Photo 10-6. House wrap covers exterior walls and keeps the wind from whistling through the many seams in the walls. The barrier is simply unrolled and stapled on quickly.

Photo 10-7. *Openings like windows and doors are cut out after the house wrap has been applied.*

Photo 10-8. *To hold the house wrap tight at openings, it is pulled against the rough framing and stapled.*

INSTALLING VINYL SIDING

Jim and Carol Bailey looked at the many siding options and decided vinyl siding was their best choice, mainly because it was inexpensive enough that they could afford to re-side their entire house, replacing the existing tired-looking asbestos siding.

Barry and Dave stripped the old siding off the house, then wrapped all the walls with Tyvek, DuPont's brand name for a fibrous synthetic house wrap. This wrap works as a barrier to keep cold winter winds from whistling through the many tiny seams in walls.

Dave loaded a stapler with zinc-coated staples that resist corrosion, and with Barry's help, applied the house wrap vertically against the sheathing; see *Photo 10-6* on the opposite page (bottom). They didn't worry about openings; they just rolled the house wrap right around the addition.

Once the house wrap was in place, Dave took out his utility knife and cut openings for the doors and windows, as shown in *Photo 10-7* on page 161 (top). Instead of cutting right up to the edges of the openings, he left about a 5-inch flap all around the perimeter. He then made diagonal slits at the corners so he could fold and staple the edges, as shown in *Photo 10-8* on page 161 (bottom). This provided a weather-tight seal around door and window openings.

When the house was wrapped and trimmed like a big birthday present, Dave and Barry began installing the vinyl trim, which would help support the vinyl siding and soffit.

There are eight basic forms of trim, as illustrated in *Siding Trim* on the right. These include *starter strip,* which hooks into the bottom of the first course; *inside and outside corner posts,* which hide the ends of the siding at the corners; *F-channel,* often called soffit track, which is designed to house the edges of vinyl soffit panels; *J-channel,* called door and window trim, which catches the ends of the siding at the sides of doors and windows; *undersill trim,* which is designed to catch the top edge of the siding panels; *fascia cover,* which weatherproofs the fascia and rake; and *window and door drip cap,* which diverts water away from the tops of doors and windows.

Each type of vinyl trim has one or more built-in nailing strips. Vinyl siding is not completely standardized from one com-pany to another, so the elements shown here may differ from those that you choose.

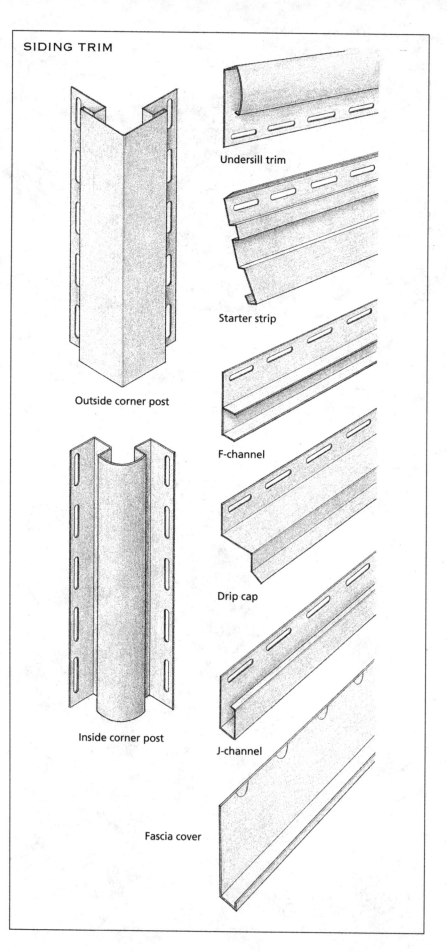

SIDING TRIM

Undersill trim

Starter strip

Outside corner post

F-channel

Drip cap

Inside corner post

J-channel

Fascia cover

162

SOFFIT TRACK INSTALLATION

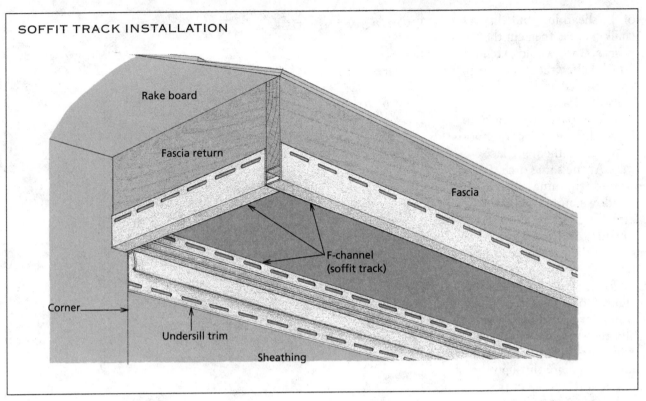

Rake board

Fascia return

Fascia

F-channel
(soffit track)

Corner

Undersill trim

Sheathing

CORNER POST DETAIL

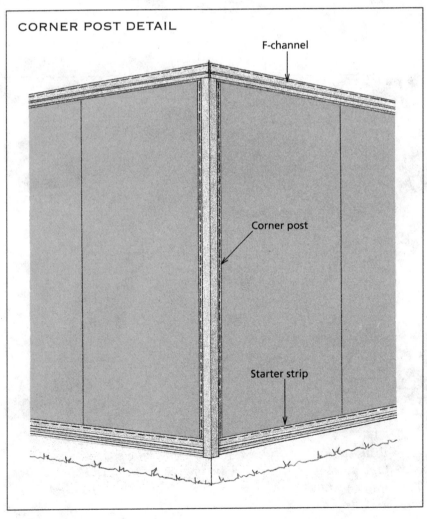

F-channel

Corner post

Starter strip

On the Baileys' addition, Barry first installed the soffit track; see *Soffit Track Installation* above. Barry nailed a strip of the track at the bottom of the fascia. Aluminum or galvanized nails were used to resist corrosion. Next, Dave snapped a chalkline along the wall level with the bottom edge of the soffit track Barry had attached to the fascia. Barry then nailed the soffit track to the wall above the chalkline.

Meanwhile, Dave nailed a strip of undersill trim along its bottom edge. The upper edge of the top siding panels would be hidden under the lip of the undersill trim. At the outside corners of the roof, Barry nailed a short piece of soffit track below the fascia return, as shown in *Soffit Track Installation*. He drove the nails in the middle of the slots in the nailing strips so that the vinyl would be able to expand and contract freely.

The starter strip was next. Dave attached it to the bottom

of the sheathing guided by a chalkline. He then cut the corner posts so they would extend 1 inch below the starter strip when butted at the top against the soffit track; see *Corner Post Detail* on page 163 (bottom). Dave plumbed the corner posts as he nailed them in place.

164

At the same time, Barry started trimming out the windows and doors by attaching J-channel to the outside of their casings, drip cap on their tops, and undersill trim below, as shown in *Window Trim Detail* on the right. Not long before quitting time, Barry and Dave cut and slid the vinyl soffit panels, which are perforated to allow air to circulate through the eaves, into the soffit track.

The next morning, Dave and Barry were ready to begin nailing up the siding on one wall.

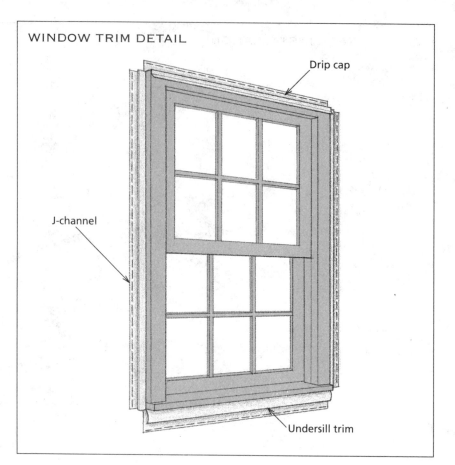

WINDOW TRIM DETAIL

Drip cap

J-channel

Undersill trim

Photo 10-9. Vinyl siding is secured to walls with nails driven through the nailing strip and sheathing and into a stud. The head of the nail should touch the nailing strip but not press against it. This will allow the vinyl to expand and contract freely.

Photo 10-10. *Each course of siding is snapped into the one below it, then it is nailed in place.*

Barry picked up a siding panel, snapped it into the starter strip at one corner, and slid its end into the corner post. Since the temperature was about 50 degrees, Barry backed the panel away from the corner by ⅜ inch; under a hot summer sun, the vinyl would need room to expand into the corner. Barry then proceeded to attach the panel to the wall by nailing through the nailing strip and sheathing into the studs, as shown in *Photo 10-9* on the opposite page. After he finished the starter course, he put the next courses in place, snapping each into the one below, as shown in *Photo 10-10* on the left.

At the ends, Barry overlapped the panels by about 1 inch. Most vinyl siding comes with the nail strip offset on the right-hand end of each panel to allow for this overlap. Barry

Photo 10-11. *Vinyl siding can be trimmed with tin snips to fit around obstacles.*

was careful to leave a gap between the nail strips at the overlap. "If you butt the nail strips together," he said, "the panels will definitely buckle when the weather warms up."

As Barry encountered water spigots, windows, and doors, Dave cut panels to fit, using tin snips and a utility knife, as shown in *Photo 10-11* on page 165 (bottom).

Sometime after the crew's coffee break, Ted Currier arrived to wrap the fascia and rake boards in vinyl fascia cover to protect them from the weather. He started by nailing undersill trim even with the top edge of the fascia and rake boards.

When the undersill trim was in place, Ted put the J-shaped vinyl fascia cover panels on the fascia. He fit the top edge of the fascia cover up into the undersill trim and hooked its bottom below the F-channel. Ted pushed the leading edge of each fascia cover panel about 1 inch underneath the lower edge of the one above it. This would keep water from seeping into the joints, he said.

When he got to the corner of the roof, Ted cut and bent a small piece of fascia cover to go around the corner, as illustrated in *Fascia Cover Corner Piece Detail* above. He cut a 90 degree notch out of the bottom of the J so it could fold around the corner. Ted then continued by covering the fascia return, as shown in *Photo 10-12* on the right. Since the undersill trim angled off toward the roof peak, Ted hammered a couple of nails into the top edge of the piece to keep it in place. The nails would be covered later when he wrapped the rake board.

Ted started wrapping the rake board at the peak and worked his way down to the

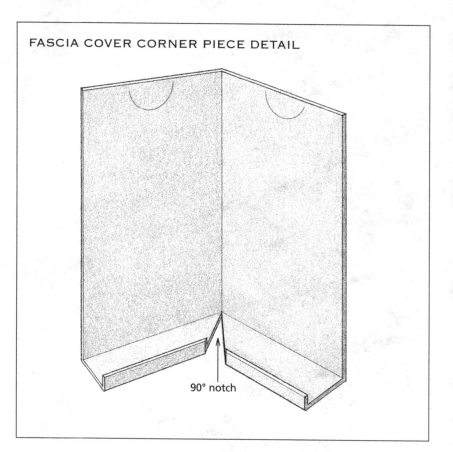

FASCIA COVER CORNER PIECE DETAIL

90° notch

Photo 10-12. Ted Currier wraps the fascia return on the Baileys' addition with fascia cover.

Photo 10-13. *Rake boards are wrapped with vinyl fascia cover. The panels are snapped into undersill trim that has been applied at the top edge of the rake boards.*

Photo 10-14. *Siding is cut at an angle with tin snips to fit the addition's gable end.*

Photo 10-15. Siding at the gable is fit into J-channel, which is attached below the rake boards.

corners of the roof. He marked the last piece of fascia cover where its lip met the already covered fascia return. Then he cut off the lip so the end of the last piece of fascia cover could slip alongside the fascia return, as shown in *Photo 10-13* on page 167 (top).

When Ted was finished with the fascia cover, he was ready to nail the J-channel under the rake board to accept the ends of the siding at the gable. Because of the angle of the roof, the end of each course of siding had to be cut at a sharp angle with tin snips, as shown in *Photo 10-14* on page 167 (bottom). Ted then slid the angled ends behind the J-channel, as shown in *Photo 10-15* above.

All told, it took Barry and Dave, with occasional help from Ted, a little better than three days to install the vinyl siding.

INSTALLING WOOD CLAPBOARD OR BEVELED SIDING

Vinyl siding can approximate the look of clapboards, but it won't match it. Fortunately, installing clapboards or beveled siding isn't much harder than installing vinyl, and the end result can be well worth the effort.

Wood clapboard is the most common siding on existing homes and is probably the most desired siding treatment in the United States and Canada. The natural look and feel of wood is its most attractive quality, even though wood siding isn't as maintenance-free as manufactured siding.

Wood clapboard and beveled siding must be painted or varnished to seal out the weather. Some suppliers insist that clapboard and beveled siding

made from cedar or redwood doesn't require finishing, but after you shell out the big bucks, it would be wise to protect your investment from the weather. The siding boards should be finished on both sides so they will transfer moisture evenly. Some suppliers sell wood siding already primed on both sides.

Unlike vinyl siding, which comes in panels that mimic two or three siding courses, clapboard is installed one course at a time, as are clapboard-style hardboard and OSB clapboard sidings. These materials, like vinyl siding, are applied over sheathing that has been covered with a house wrap, such as Tyvek. Nails will be sunk through the sheathing and into studs to firmly anchor the siding.

At the corners, wood clapboard is butted up against wood corner boards, with two 1⅛-inch-thick boards attached to the outside corners, as shown in *Outside Corner Detail* on the right (top). The 4-inch-wide board overlaps the 3-inch-wide board to make each side of the corner appear uniform. Inside corners are finished with a single 1⅛-inch-square corner board, as shown in *Inside Corner Detail* on the right (bottom).

The layout of clapboard is crucial. Unlike vinyl siding, which has a predetermined exposure, clapboard's exposure can vary, giving you the flexibility to choose where the courses will fall. Instead of notching the boards to fit around window tops—a visual break in a typical wall—you can adjust how much of the width of the siding is exposed so the bottom of a course aligns exactly with the top of the window drip caps, as shown in *Window Top Trim Detail* on page 170 (top).

Begin laying out clapboard with the bottom course. Near one corner, measure down from the top of the top plate or, if the soffit is in place, from the soffit to establish the lower end of the siding; it should fall at least 1 inch below the sheathing's lower edge. (For more on wood soffits, see "Constructing a Wood Soffit" on pages 172–173.) Make a baseline mark on the foundation at that point and record the overall height measurement. Mark the foundation at the opposite corner, then snap a chalkline between the two marks.

To determine the number of courses the wall will require (and to coincide with the drip caps of the first-floor windows), first figure out the maximum exposure for your particular siding. Four- to 6-inch-wide siding requires a 1-inch overlap, and any siding over 6 inches

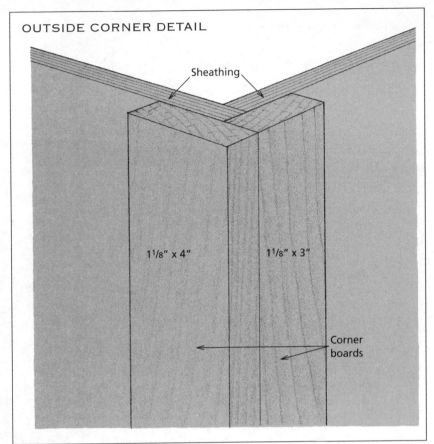

OUTSIDE CORNER DETAIL

Sheathing

1⅛" x 4"

1⅛" x 3"

Corner boards

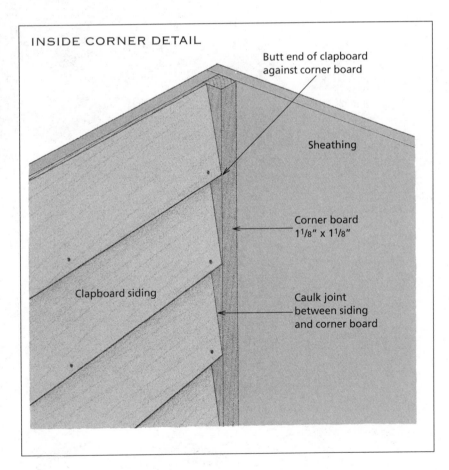

INSIDE CORNER DETAIL

Butt end of clapboard against corner board

Sheathing

Corner board 1⅛" x 1⅛"

Clapboard siding

Caulk joint between siding and corner board

WINDOW TOP TRIM DETAIL

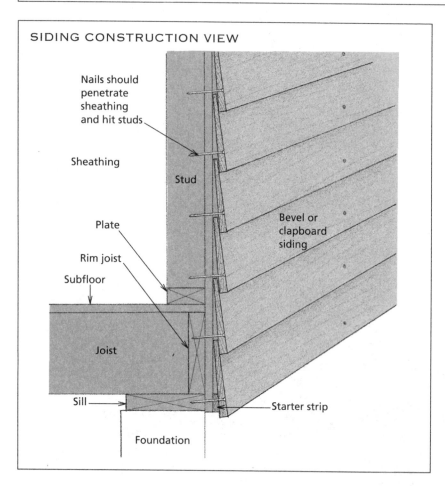

Frieze

House wrap

Sheathing

Clapboard siding

Flashing

Drip cap

SIDING CONSTRUCTION VIEW

Nails should penetrate sheathing and hit studs

Sheathing

Stud

Plate

Bevel or clapboard siding

Rim joist

Subfloor

Joist

Sill

Foundation

Starter strip

wide requires a 1½-inch overlap.

As with other lumber, wood siding is sold in nominal widths; 4-inch-wide siding is really only 3½ inches wide, 10-inch-wide siding measures 9¼ inches wide, and so on. So subtract the minimum overlap from the actual width of your siding to determine the siding's maximum exposure. For example, if you have siding with a nominal width of 8 inches, you would take the actual width of 7¼ inches minus a 1¼-inch minimum overlap and end up with a 6-inch exposure.

With a rule, mark off the maximum exposure for your siding from the first course line below the sheathing to the soffit. Lay out these first, tentative marks near a window so you can see how closely one of the courses comes to the top of the window. Then decrease the exposure of each siding board slightly, if necessary, to align a course above the window. Remember, you cannot increase the maximum exposure. When you have determined the exposure, lay out the exposure widths of each course on the corner boards at the ends of the run.

Before you begin nailing the clapboard in place, you need to attach a starter strip to the bottom edge of the sheath-ing, as illustrated in *Siding Construc-tion View* on the opposite page (bottom). The starter strip holds the first course of clapboard away from the wall at the same angle as the following courses. Cut the ends of the strip (and the clap-board) on a miter saw. Make the starter strip 1½ inches wide, and bevel its thickness from ⅜ inch at the top edge to ½ inch at the bottom edge. Nail the starter strip to the wall.

With the starter strip in place, nail the first course of clapboard to the wall with corrosion-resistant (aluminum or hot-dipped galvanized) 8d siding nails. The nails should be driven through the siding and sheathing and into the studs. As an aid to finding the studs, snap a vertical chalkline at the location of each stud. Predrill for nails at the ends of boards that might split, and, if you plan on painting the siding, set all of the nails and fill the holes with wood filler.

Cedar is especially prone to splitting, so you may need to predrill all of the holes. Start by butting the first strip of siding against a corner board and continuing the course across the wall toward the other corner. Adjoining boards in the same course should be butted together tightly. Stagger butt joints from course to course, making sure the joints

fall over studs. Nail through the siding face and starter strip and into the wall. As shown in *Siding Construction View,* align the nails with the studs; this low on the wall, the nails will hit the sill or rim joist, but all of the nails on the wall should align vertically.

▲▲▲▲▲▲▲▲▲▲

Picture yourself painting the exterior of the addition, and you're probably wobbling atop a ladder. That doesn't have to be. You can paint or stain the siding and trim *before* it is nailed up, then simply touch up the nail holes once it's installed.

▼▼▼▼▼▼▼▼▼▼

With the first course nailed snugly in place, snap a chalkline from corner to corner for the next course, using the exposure layout lines you drew earlier. Attach the second course and all that follow so that the nails just clear the top edge of the preceding course, as shown in *Siding Construction View.* All nails should pass through the siding and sheathing and hit studs.

Snap a new exposure layout line for each course. Cut the siding to butt up against the edges of door and window trim.

You may need to notch the siding to fit below the windows; the underside of most windowsills comes ready to accept the top edge of siding. Flashing is applied over the top of the windows and doors, as

shown in *Window Top Trim Detail* on the opposite page (top). Like the drip cap used with vinyl siding, flashing prevents water from seeping into the wall.

Most quality windows come with a piece of flashing that is shaped and ready to install. If flashing wasn't included with your window, bend metal flashing to conform to the top of it, then nail the flashing in place. Position the nails so that their heads will be protected behind the siding.

Instead of ripping a last course of siding to fit up under the eaves or soffit, finish off the siding with a frieze. A frieze is a piece of nominal 1-inch-thick stock that has a rabbet cut in its lower back edge to fit over the top siding course, as shown in *Window Top Trim Detail.* Using a table saw with a dado blade, cut a rabbet in the frieze stock to fit your siding. Then, rip the frieze stock on the table saw to fit between the last siding course and the soffit.

On the gable end of the addition, the siding must be cut to match the angle of the rake board. It is easiest to hold the siding in place and mark the top and bottom edges where they meet the rake board. Then draw a cut line between the two marks. If the angle is between 45 and 90 degrees, you can make the cut with a power miter saw, but if the angle is less than 45 degrees, use a trim saw (small circular saw) or backsaw. Butt the siding boards against the rake boards and nail them in place.

After installation, butt joints must be caulked end to end, end to corner, and end to window or door frame in order to keep water from penetrating.

CONSTRUCTING A WOOD SOFFIT

If you're siding your house with wood, you'll probably want to complete the eaves with wood *soffits.* Most commonly, a boxed cornice is constructed to support plywood soffit panels under the eaves. The elements of this type of cornice are shown in *Boxed Cornice Construction* below.

To construct a soffit, first temporarily attach a 1 x 4 *ledger* to the sheathing, even with the ends of the wall and tight against the bottom edges of the roof rafters. This is not the permanent position of the ledger boards, but serves to establish where they should go. Next, lay out the position of the lookouts by holding a straightedge against the left side of each rafter and drawing a line across the face of the ledger. The *lookouts* will give midpanel support to the soffit panels. Mark the nailing position of

the lookout to the left of your line with a pencil. Remove the ledger from the wall.

Lay out the position of the ledger on the wall. Its bottom edge should be level with the beveled bottom edges of the rafters, as shown in *Cornice Construction End View* on the opposite page. Use a level to transfer this point from the rafters to the wall, mark on the wall to indicate the bottom of the ledger, and snap a chalkline to connect these marks.

To determine the length of the lookouts, measure from the ledger layout line on the wall to the nearest edge of a rafter's horizontal end cut; again, refer to *Cornice Construction End View.* Subtract the width of the ledger from this measurement for the lookout length. When the lookouts have been cut to

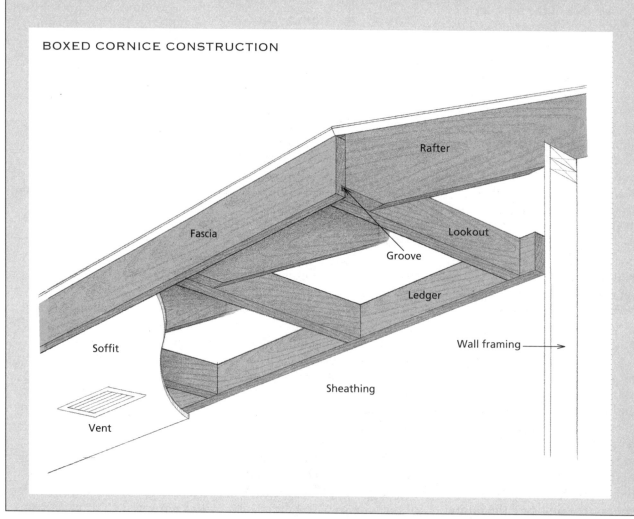

BOXED CORNICE CONSTRUCTION

Rafter

Fascia

Lookout

Groove

Ledger

Soffit

Wall framing

Sheathing

Vent

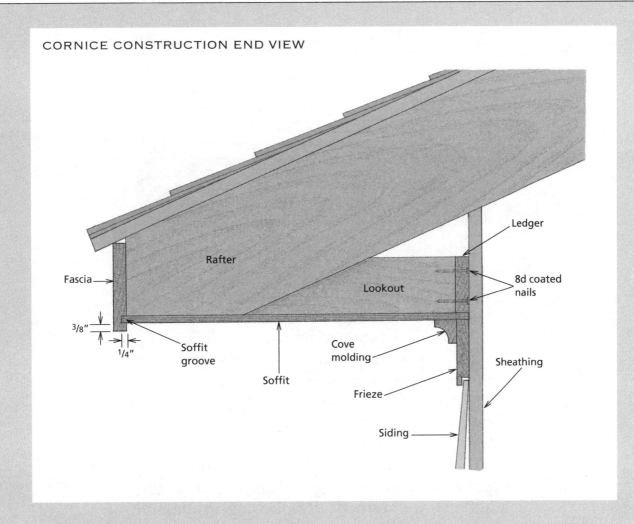

Ledger

Rafter

Fascia

8d coated
nails

Lookout

3/8"

Soffit
groove

1/4"

Cove
molding

Soffit

Sheathing

Frieze

Siding

length, position each along the layout lines on the ledger and nail them in place. Nail through the back of the ledger and into the ends of the lookouts with 8d coated nails. When the ledger and lookouts have been assembled, nail the assembly to the wall and rafters, as shown in *Boxed Cornice Construction.*

Next, rip the fascia to width and cut the groove to accept the soffit. The fascia should be wide enough to extend past the bottom edge of the rafter by the thickness of the soffit plus ³/₈ inch, as shown in *Cornice Construction End View.* Rip the fascia to width on a table saw, then lay out and cut a ¼-inch-deep groove to accept the soffit, using a dado blade in the saw. Position the groove so it aligns with the bottom beveled edge of the rafter, as shown in *Cornice Construction End View.*

Then, rip the soffit to width on the table saw or with a circular saw. The width of the soffit is determined by measuring from the wall to the end of the rafter and adding the depth of the soffit groove. Install vents in the soffit panels to allow air to circulate through the eaves and up through the ridge vents. To install each soffit panel, fit one long edge into the soffit groove in the fascia, and push the other edge up against the ledger. Nail the soffit panels to the ledger and lookouts with 4d coated nails. Vary the length of the soffit panels so that joints between them fall on the lookouts. Securely nail the end of each adjoining panel to the lookout.

To finish the soffit, add a frieze board and cove molding, as shown in *Cornice Construction End View.* Note how the frieze's lower edge is rabbeted to accept the top course of beveled siding.

THE SHAPES OF DREAMS

Every addition begins as a dream. Between conception and reality, a thousand bridges will be crossed, and many will involve compromise. No matter how grand or inspired your addition starts out in your mind's eye, it will probably end up more as a down-to-earth, livable place than a neighborhood landmark. And well that it should. But there are real benefits to dreaming big in the early stages. The following color pages are filled with 22 additions to inspire you. All of them are successful in the two ways that matter most: The owners got the new living space they wanted, and the additions are aesthetically pleasing inside and out, anchored solidly and gracefully—in some cases seamlessly—to the original homes.

The owners of this Dutch Colonial (LEFT) distinguished the rear of their home from surrounding houses. The answer lay in the sleek curves, metal railing, and walk-out decks of this 380-square-foot, California condo-style addition (BOTTOM). The new second floor contains a master bedroom suite (INSET) with a glass wall that lights an adjoining bathroom.

To separate this master bedroom addition from the noise and action of the main house, the architect designed the addition as a separate double-gable cottage. Four cascading windows light the stairway that connects the new suite to the old house. The subtle difference in siding materials on the addition and the covered stairway reinforces the transitional function the stairway serves.

The master bedroom's denlike sleeping alcove (ABOVE) features French doors that open onto a sitting deck. A sense of perfect symmetry has been achieved in the stairway passage (LEFT), where descending closet doors on the left mirror the window frames on the right.

This 1,200-square-foot addition was built over a garage (ABOVE), providing guest quarters without expanding the footprint of the house. The combination of gable, shed, and octagonal roofs over board-and-batten siding capture the New England vernacular style intended by the architect. Cathedral ceilings and exposed rafter ties make the space inside feel spacious and airy (RIGHT).

The attic space in this 1920s ranch (TOP) was too low to stand in, so the architects raised the hip roof and added dormers on each side to create a master bedroom suite. The whirlpool tub set into a raised platform (ABOVE LEFT) gives *the bathroom a feeling of greater height. Triangular windows on the walls of the bedroom dormer (ABOVE RIGHT) bring added facets of light, while built-in dressers and bookcases take advantage of precious space under the eaves.*

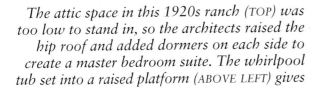

THE SHAPES OF DREAMS

The all-glass ceiling and walls of this 250-square-foot triangular addition seem to disappear against the house, but the cedar shingles extending from the house and deck around the lower walls of the addition visually anchor the new structure to both the house and the yard.

*Inside, the glass-wall addition is home to a gardening
workroom. Douglas fir pilasters and workbenches,
slate floors and counters, and sailcloth ceiling shades
make this an efficient and practical work center.*

Perched dramatically on a hill, the large rear addition to this Cape Cod home is firmly anchored by the stone steps and sweeping stone wall that flank the foundation. In time, the cedar shingles on the addition will match those on the original house as perfectly as the new windows match the old. Note how the short second-floor wall breaks rank with the original roof-line to accommodate the back window on the house.

On the main floor of the addition are an open kitchen with
recessed cabinetry and mammoth work island (ABOVE) and
a combination dining and sitting room (BELOW). Both
rooms share light and air from the bay window.

The 600-square-foot addition adjacent to the entranceway (LEFT) looks small here, but it dominates the back of a 1930s colonial (see the front cover for a full view). The main floor of the two-story project holds a country kitchen with a dining area (ABOVE AND BELOW LEFT). Downstairs is a new recreation room. The architect added the covered entranceway (LEFT) to the corner of the original house to act as a transitional element between new and old. It opens to a small mudroom and a stairway leading down to the rec room.

A 2¹/₂-story glass stair tower (VISIBLE IN THE BACKGROUND, TOP) ties this 400-square-foot addition to the original house by repeating the pattern in the gable-shaped box window.

The antique billiards table (ABOVE) served as inspiration for this game room addition, which opens onto a garden terrace. The trusses were site-built, then covered with drywall.

THE SHAPES OF DREAMS

The owners of this Victorian Gothic (circa 1850) were determined that an addition maintain the architectural character of the original house. Every detail on the 2½-story gabled wing was meticulously matched to the original house. The skylights and greenhouse offer the only suggestion that something new was added.

Bedeviled by a warren of small rooms on the second floor of the original house, the owners removed walls and ceilings to create spacious and bright bedrooms (LEFT). *The new library* (BELOW) *was set two steps lower than the original first floor so that the room could have a higher ceiling that would impart classical proportions. The columned cherry casework and antique chandelier recall the period in which the home was built.*

Building an addition often requires that you remove something first. A dilapidated 3-story dormitory once bridged the space between the 1860s farmhouse (LEFT IN TOP PHOTO) and the former barn (RIGHT IN TOP PHOTO). The owner demolished the eyesore, converted the barn to a guest house, and connected it to the main house with a covered porch. A new 200-square-foot screened porch on the left of the house opens onto the dining room (ABOVE).

The owners of this 1840s-era farmhouse considered building a new house farther from the road it sits on. But an enduring fondness for Robert Frost's poem "A House by the Side of the Road" led them to expand what they had. After stripping the 1,250-square-foot house down to its frame, they built additions on either side of the original house, tripling the overall size. The entire exterior was then sided with cedar (ABOVE). A huge stone fireplace anchors the new great room (LEFT), while the soaring wall of glass fills the space with a view of the adjacent woods.

THE SHAPES OF DREAMS

The new front entry to this 1970s ranch (ABOVE) crosses a 20-foot bridge that spans a stream and ends on a portico leading into a formal gallery/entertaining/dining room (BELOW). The elephant's eye window, parquet floors, and classical columns supporting a gable wall combine to give the room palatial character.

A rear addition was also added atop the home's existing garage (ABOVE). Again, classical symmetry is evident in the columns and paladian windows and is carried into the master bathroom suite with brass fixtures (BELOW). Note how the columns are split perfectly, with half on the outside of the window pane and half on the inside.

Originally the corner of this house contained small and poorly located windows. To open up the space, the owners added this 200-square-foot sunroom and entry foyer (BELOW). In contrast to the massive solid quality of the brick house, the addition was conceived with a light, transparent wood frame. Oak floors in the sunroom (RIGHT) reflect dappled light, and the built-in window seats make good use of the octagonal bay.

Modeled after a Nova Scotia lighthouse, this original tower house had only 1,000 square feet of living space. The owner/architect built a 1,500-square-foot addition onto the back and remodeled the tower at the same time (TOP), but the tower is still the focus of attention. A pair of ship's knees frame an opening between the addition and the tower (RIGHT).

THE SHAPES OF DREAMS

The modest 200-square-foot addition at the center of this home replaces a screened-in porch of the same size and provides space for a year-round eating area. The large windows and French doors of the addition give the house a focal point and cast more light into the adjoining kitchen, which had been dark and cramped.

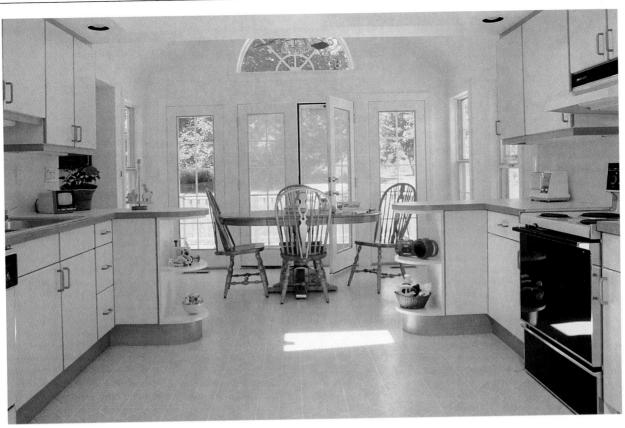

As part of this project, the architects also completely redesigned the kitchen to give it a more open and airy feel (ABOVE AND BELOW).

A combination of stock and custom cabinets frames a sleek work center and separates the kitchen from the eating area.

Structural problems required that roughly half of this sprawling Greek revival house (ABOVE) be rebuilt from scratch. This allowed the owners to redesign the old spaces to better relate the interior of the original house to an existing addition.

The principal change in the redesigned space involved adding vaulted ceilings to the kitchen and dining area. The soffit over the hardwood counter (FAR LEFT) divides the space while still allowing light from the arched window to reach the dining area and the old addition, shown through the doorway (LEFT).

Most additions grow from the inside out, wrought of the need for more space. This glass-wall rotunda (RIGHT) was designed to bring the outside in. No other shape would so fully capture this sweeping view of landscape and ocean (ABOVE). As part of the bargain, the top of the addition became a walk-out deck from the master bedroom.

Giving a building multiple facets reduces the broad surfaces where the wind can take hold. That was one of the design imperatives for this unique addition on a rocky Maine promontory (BELOW). The arched window in the stair tower faces the ocean (LEFT), giving the home the presence of a lighthouse.

THE SHAPES OF DREAMS

A classic American farmhouse exudes a welcoming warm light on a snowy night. Adding a meager 120-square-foot addition to the right side of the front entranceway enabled the owners to make dramatic alterations to interior rooms without changing the exterior greatly.

To open up what was once a cramped dining room inside the house,
the owners eliminated the room above, leaving them with high
ceilings and light from the windows in the old second-story room.

A Pennsylvania
schoolhouse built
in 1888 stands
proudly unchanged
(ABOVE)—and that's
how its owners
wanted to keep it.
By tucking the
1,500-square-foot
addition carefully
behind the school
and recessing the
connecting walls,
the architect let the
school retain its
distinctive presence.
It's not by accident
that the school's
bell tower can be
seen through a roof
window in the
second-floor
bedroom (RIGHT).

The home's new kitchen serves as the transitional space between the school and the addition. The warm look of solid cherry cabinetry and an antique butcher block contrast with new appliances and a stainless steel counter. Instead of conventional cabinets, open shelves were hung in front of windows to maximize light and space in the small 12 x 12-foot room.

Tired of sharing a small bathroom with their two young children, the owners of this Oregon Cape Cod built a 300-square-foot gabled suite with a small arched-top veranda. A second benefit was the covered section of terrace below the addition.

*A vaulted center hall divides the suite into two
functional spaces: an open vanity and bath area
(VISIBLE AT LEFT) and a private toilet and shower
room. The French doors and circle head window
direct light through the hall to the bedroom.*

A new sunroom with tall casement windows was added to this eighteenth-century Pennsylvania farmhouse (ABOVE PHOTOS). New stucco and roofing on the entire house helped unite the elements harmoniously.

Native flagstone and locally milled rough pine beams give the new space the feel of the old, while the full-height insulated windows allow a twentieth-century view of the outdoors (BELOW).

Architects and Designers

Page 175: Roderick Ashley Architect, Portland, Ore.

Pages 176–177: Frank J. Gravino Associates, Westport, Conn.

Page 178: Peter Wormser & Associates, Architects, New York, N.Y.

Page 179: Richard T. Donohoe Architects, Sherman, Conn.

Pages 180–181, 186–187: Peter Kurt Woerner, Architect, FAIA, New Haven, Conn.

Pages 182–183: Doug Williamson, Designer, Branford, Conn.

Page 184: Paul F. Hopper Associates, Greenwich, Conn.

Page 185: Wayne S. Garrick, AIA, Architects, New Haven, Conn.

Page 188: Perry Dean Rogers & Partners, Boston, Mass.

Page 189: Lester M. Stein, Architect, Bethlehem, Pa.

Pages 190–191: Johnn Kanastab, Design Principles, New York, N.Y.

Page 192: James Gauer Architect, New York, N.Y.

Page 193: Jane Davis Doggett, Architect, Young's Point, Maine

Pages 194–195: Jeff Bianco, Bianco Giolito Architects, Cromwell, Conn.

Pages 196–197: Nancy Hemenway, Designer, Joseph Barth, Jr., Builder, Alna, Maine

Page 198: Sam Van Dam, Van Dam & Renner Architects, Portland, Maine

Page 199: Tony DiGregorio Architects, Damariscotta, Maine

Pages 200–201: Bob Knight, Knight Associates, Blue Hill, Maine

Pages 202–203: Phil Kelly, Architect, Zionsville, Pa.

Pages 204–205: Jerry L. Ward, Ward Architecture PC, Portland, Ore.

Page 206: Ken Amey, Designer, Lower Gwynedd, Pa.

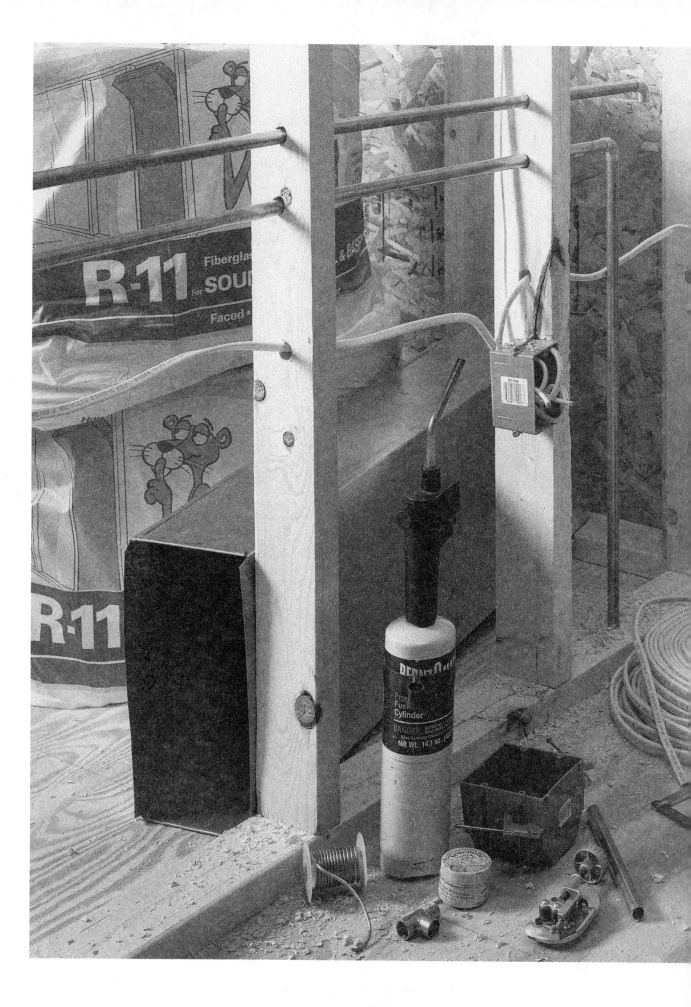

THREADING THE
UTILITIES

From your neighbors' vantage point, the addition looks complete. Never mind that the yard around it still resembles a moonscape of dirt and debris. But a glimpse inside reveals a small army of mechanics running pipe and wiring through the walls and floors and filling cavities with insulation to bring water, light, and relief from the weather. Warm rooms in winter, cool air in summer—these are the amenities that keep us comfortable when we're home and longing to be there when we're not.

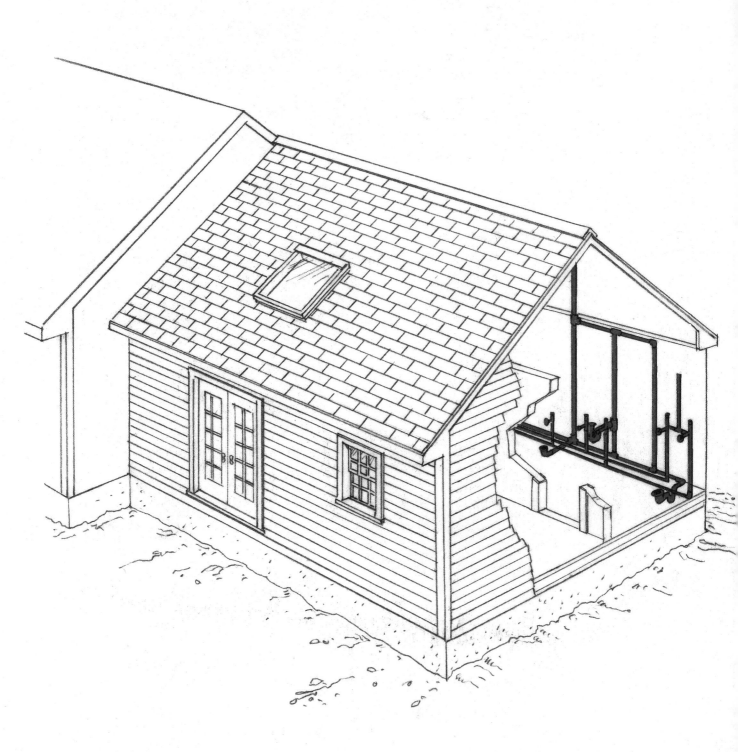

11
ROUGH PLUMBING

As with any project, plumbing requires careful planning if the job is to go smoothly. Even experienced plumbers like Kevin Carney and Bob Jenkins, who handled the Baileys' addition, took time to review the plans and map out the job before a single pipe was soldered. If you will be tackling this part of the addition yourself, consider hiring a plumber as a consultant—not to sweat pipe and such, but to guide you through planning the new system and connecting it with the existing plumbing.

When he first went to the Baileys, Kevin studied the floor plan with contractor Ted Currier to see what fixtures were required and where they should be placed. He marked these locations on his copy of the plans. Then he went down into the existing basement to see where the new pipes would tie into the old ones and

marked his plan accordingly. With these points mapped out, he drew a diagram of the new pipes, noting each bend and junction.

Later, back at his shop, Kevin referred to this diagram as he counted all the fittings needed. He also measured on the floor plan to estimate the length of the pipes as he prepared his bid for the job. As he made his calculations, he compiled a list of the necessary pieces that needed to be gathered from the warehouse.

DESIGNING THE DWV SYSTEM

This same approach to planning a drain, waste, and vent (DWV) system can work for you as an amateur plumber. As you're laying out your addition, mark the plumbing fixtures on the floor plan.

Choose the fixtures and check the manufacturers' spec sheets to make sure you've allowed enough space for everything. (While you have the spec sheets in hand, note the rough-in measurements. You'll need them later.)

Next, explore your house to figure out where the new system will tie into the old one. This might be in the basement—as it was at the Baileys—or it might be within a wall. Planning at this stage can save you a little money. The closer you locate new plumbing to the old, the less pipe you'll need. For example, by backing a new bathroom up to an existing one, you can connect the new pipes to the old through the connecting wall. Make sure that the old system is properly vented and that the pipes you're tying into are large enough in diameter to handle the increased amount of water.

If not, you'll have to update the system according to the code in your community.

Once you've determined where the new pipes must go, it's time to figure out what pieces you'll need to connect them. The surest way is to do what Kevin did—make a three-dimensional isometric drawing of the house and plumbing system.

As explained in Chapter 1, an isometric view involves two basic rules: All vertical lines are drawn vertically, and all horizontal lines are drawn at a given angle (say, 30 degrees) from horizontal. Before you break out your protractor, you can make things easier on yourself by going to an art- or office-supply store and buying isometric graph paper with ¼- or ⅜-inch spacing. This paper has the proper angles printed right on it; all you have to do is trace along the lines. Get a large tablet—at least 11 x 17 inches—so you'll have plenty of room to draw.

Start by laying out the floor plan of the room you're putting the fixtures in. Your drawing should look something like the one in *The Baileys' Floor Plan* on the right. Have each division on the graph paper equal 1 foot or, if you need to show more detail, 6 inches.

After you've drawn the floor layout, sketch in the drain, waste, and vent system, as shown in *The Baileys' DWV System* on the opposite page. Show all of the bends and connections so you'll know exactly what to buy. Each of these connections will be made with a fitting such as a *wye* or a *tee*, which are named for their shape.

Your DWV system drawing should start with the main drain. This is the largest-diameter pipe. In a bathroom, it

will be the line running to the toilet. In a kitchen, it will be the one running to the sink. Next, draw in the smaller drain lines as branches from the main line.

Although you'll show all pipes running either straight up and down or parallel to the floor, in reality the horizontal lines will drop ¼ inch for every

foot they travel. (A drop of ⅛ inch per foot is permissible if space below the floor is limited.) Hanging the horizontal pipes at this slight angle allows the water to drain steadily and carry away debris along with it.

The exact degree of pitch is important: If the pipe drops

THE BAILEYS' FLOOR PLAN

Tub/shower room

Dressing room

Closet

Existing kitchen

Master bedroom

Linen closet

Living room

DRAW BASIC FLOOR PLAN

Outline of first floor

Basement walls

ADD BASEMENT

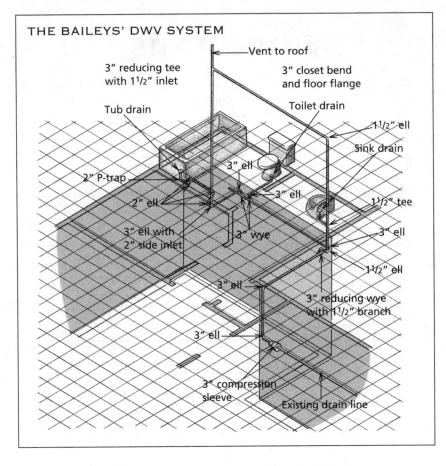

THE BAILEYS' DWV SYSTEM

Vent to roof

3" reducing tee
with 1½" inlet

3" closet bend
and floor flange

Tub drain

Toilet drain

1½" ell

Sink drain

3" ell

2" P-trap

3" ell

2" ell

1½" tee

3" ell with
2" side inlet

3" wye

3" ell

1½" ell

3" ell

3" reducing wye
with 1½" branch

3" ell

3" compression
sleeve

Existing drain line

too quickly, at an angle of 30 degrees, for example, it will allow the water to drain so fast that debris is left behind, causing clogs. However, if you run into an obstacle in the wall or don't have enough space to allow the required gradual pitch, it is permissible to hang pipes at an angle of 45 degrees or greater. This is close enough to vertical for gravity to carry along any debris in the pipes.

If possible, however, run your pipes either just slightly off horizontal, as mentioned, or vertically. Standard fittings are set up to join pipes at these angles. So if your pipes come together at some odd angle, you may have difficulty connecting them. Also, it's easier to run a line vertically down through a space between studs or horizontally under the floor.

As you sketch in the junctions between pipes, keep in mind that while branches can be attached with either 45 or 90 degree junctions to the main line, pipes with a 45 degree junction are less likely to clog because the bend isn't as abrupt.

CHOOSING DWV MATERIALS AND SIZES

When picking the materials for a drain system, you have two basic choices: metal or plastic. Traditionally, plumbers used cast iron, copper, or steel pipes for DWV lines, but plastic is becoming the most popular choice. It is light, inexpensive, and easy to install with ordinary tools. As a result, it's perfect for homeowners installing their own plumbing.

The disadvantages of plastic drainpipe are slight but worth mentioning. First, plastic is noisier; the rumble of water flowing from an upstairs toilet will carry through the walls. You can cut down on noise transmission by putting up a double layer of drywall or wrapping the plastic drainpipe in batts of fiberglass. (Note that the wall will have to be framed with 2 x 6s to allow room for both pipe and insulation.)

Second, plastic pipe crushes more easily than cast iron. If you run it underground, you'll have to be careful when you fill over it, especially if you're working with heavy equipment. And you should take care not to drive nails and screws into the pipes once they're hidden behind drywall. With these points in mind, plastic pipe can be every bit as good and as durable as metal.

The diameter of each drain line is determined by the fixtures it serves. Obviously, the more waste water a fixture produces, the larger its drainpipe should be. In determining drainpipe size, the term *fixture unit* is used to describe the peak rate of discharge through a drainpipe. A given diameter of pipe can handle up to an assigned number of fixture units. Work with the tables "Fixture Units" and "Drain and Vent Pipe Sizing" on page 214 to figure out the size of drain line for your household fixtures.

A typical bathroom requires a 3-inch main drain connecting to a toilet. Branching off that main line will be a 2-inch line for a shower and a 1½-inch line for a sink. ("Fixture Units" says a 1¼-inch line will work for a single wash basin, but for a few pennies more, the larger line offers insurance against blockages.) A kitchen sink also requires a 1½-inch line, although a 2-inch line is better if you plan to install a garbage disposal.

A drain system needs *traps* and *vents* to work safely and reliably. Together, they keep potentially poisonous and explosive sewer gases in the system from entering your house. These are probably the most misunderstood parts of plumbing (unless you're a three-year-old, in which case the most misunderstood part is what shouldn't be flushed down the toilet).

Traps are curved sections of pipe that hold water as a barrier to block gases from entering the house. The trap under a sink, shown in *Photo 11-1* on the opposite page, is the most visible example. Vents are also pipes. They provide a place for sewer fumes to escape. They also let air into the system, breaking the vacuum

FIXTURE UNITS

Fixture	Fixture Units	Minimum Drain Diameter
Bar sink	1	1½"
Bathtub	2	1½"
Bidet	2	1½"
Clothes washer	2	2"
Double wash basin	2	1½"
Floor drain	2	2"
Kitchen sink	2	1½"
Laundry tub	2	1½"
Shower stall	2	2"
Sink and dishwasher	3	1½"
Toilet	4	3"
Wash basin	1	1¼"

DRAIN AND VENT PIPE SIZING

Pipe Diameter	Drain Pipe				Vent Pipe	
	Vertical		Horizontal		Vertical and Horizontal	
	Maximum fixture units	Maximum length, feet	Maximum fixture units	Maximum length, feet	Maximum fixture units	Maximum length, feet
1¼"	1	45	1	no limit	1	45
1½"	2	65	1		8	60
2"	16*	85	8*		24	120
2½"	32*	148	14*		48	180
3"	48	212	35		84	212

* Excludes toilets, which require at least a 3" diameter drain.

214

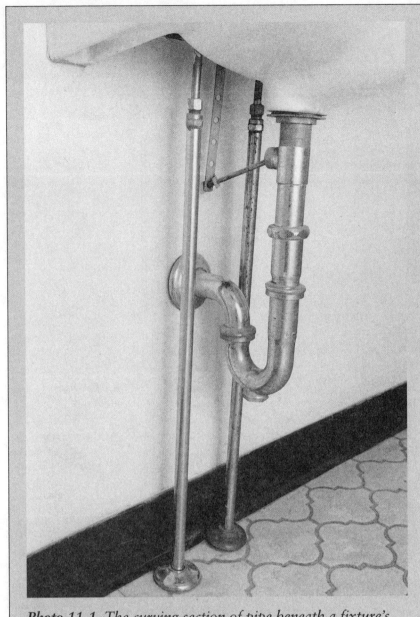

accommodate the maximum drainage from all fixtures served. A third alternative, a wet vent, is used when the drain for one trap must also be the vent for a lower trap. Both fixtures served must be on the same floor of a building. The size of the wet vent pipe should be one size larger than what the upper fixture requires and no smaller than 2 inches.

Once you know what size the pipes are, go back to your DWV system drawing and label all the parts. If you're not sure what fittings are available, look over the selection at your plumbing-supply house.

DESIGNING THE SUPPLY SYSTEM

For the most part, the supply system will follow the DWV system through the house, as shown in *The Baileys' New Plumbing*. Compared to designing a DWV system, designing a supply system is a snap.

Draw an isometric diagram on isometric graph paper just as you did for the drain. Your drawing should look something like the one in *The Baileys' Supply System* on page 217. You may want to use colored pencils to differentiate between the hot and cold lines. Note the fittings you'll need where the lines change direction (*ells*) or split (*tees*), as well as any special equipment like a shower *diverter*. A diverter is the valve that mixes hot and cold water for bathing and shifts the water between the tub spigot and the showerhead.

Plan to keep the two lines at least 6 inches apart as they run through the addition. This way, you'll be less likely to weaken any studs if you have to drill access holes for the pipes,

Photo 11-1. The curving section of pipe beneath a fixture's drain is known as a trap. The water it contains keeps sewer gases from escaping into the house.

that would otherwise form behind draining water. Without this added air, the draining water would siphon the water from the trap, allowing sewer gas to leak into the house.

Each trap (and therefore each fixture) needs a vent. But this doesn't mean that each vent has to poke through your roof. All the vents in a single bathroom may tie into a single *stack vent,* which extends through the

roof; see the illustration *The Baileys' New Plumbing* on page 216 (top).

The vents for the branch drains are connected to the stack in any of several ways, as shown in *Vent Types* on page 216 (bottom). With an individual vent, the drain line serving a given fixture is extended to serve as the vent. A common vent serves more than one fixture. It should be sized to

THE BAILEYS' NEW PLUMBING

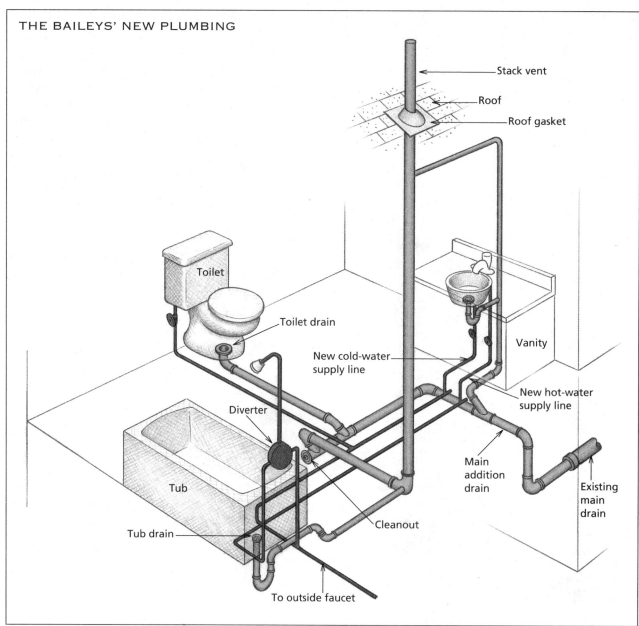

Stack vent

Roof

Roof gasket

Toilet

Toilet drain

New cold-water supply line

Vanity

New hot-water supply line

Diverter

Main addition drain

Existing main drain

Tub

Cleanout

Tub drain

To outside faucet

VENT TYPES

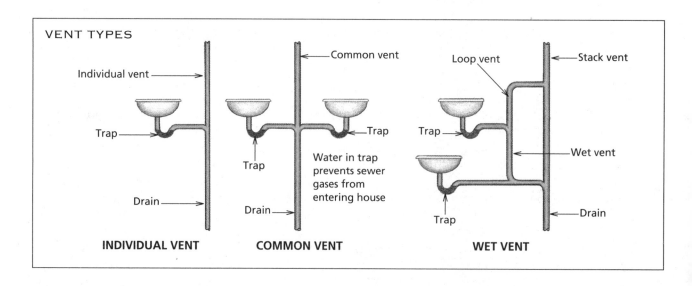

Individual vent

Common vent

Loop vent

Stack vent

Trap

Trap

Trap

Wet vent

Drain

Trap

Water in trap prevents sewer gases from entering house

Trap

Drain

Trap

Drain

INDIVIDUAL VENT

COMMON VENT

WET VENT

and the pipes will be far enough away from each other that the hot water won't warm the cold and vice versa. You can run your supply lines alongside the drain line as it runs from point to point, since the fixtures that require drains generally require a water supply, too. But don't feel compelled to do this if there is a closer source of water.

Keep in mind that you won't have to run hot water everywhere. Toilets and outdoor faucets only require cold. Also, remember to include lines for ice makers, dishwashers, and other appliances that require water. Check the information supplied with your appliances to see what fittings are necessary.

As you're planning where to run the lines, try to keep them toward the inside of the building if possible. Lines running through exterior walls are more susceptible to freezing. If you have to run pipe along an exterior wall, be sure to insulate the wall. For added insurance, you can insulate the pipes individually as well.

Choosing the pipe material for the supply system may not be as straightforward as it was for the DWV system. Plumbing codes vary from region to region as to what kinds of pipes are allowed. Some codes even differentiate between hot- and cold-water lines. For example, in the Baileys' area, the code allowed plastic cold-water supply lines but required copper for the hot. (Contractor Dennis Grim specified copper for both since it was simpler and matched the existing system.)

Advances in plastic technology have made plastic pipe more competitive, but copper tubing is still the material of choice with most

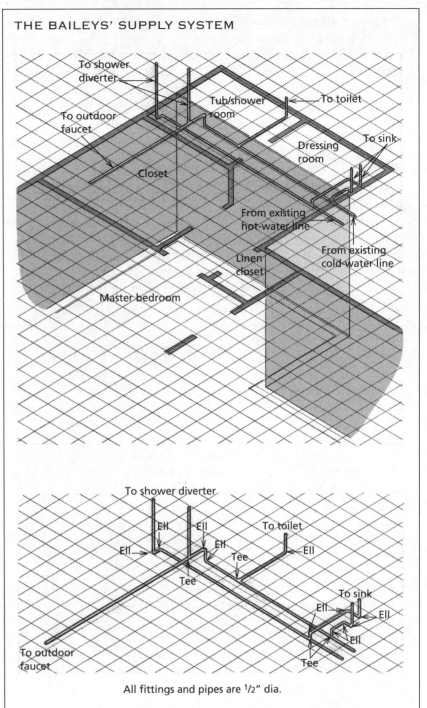

THE BAILEYS' SUPPLY SYSTEM

To shower diverter
Tub/shower room
To toilet
To outdoor faucet
Dressing room
To sink
Closet
From existing hot-water line
From existing cold-water line
Linen closet
Master bedroom

To shower diverter
Ell
Ell
To toilet
Ell
Ell
Tee
Ell
To sink
Tee
Ell
Ell
To outdoor faucet
Ell
Tee

All fittings and pipes are 1/2" dia.

home plumbers. Copper is relatively expensive, but it is also light, strong, noncorrosive, relatively easy to work with, and capable of withstanding high temperatures.

Copper tubing comes in two tempers, *drawn* and *annealed*. Drawn (hard) pipe is available in three wall thicknesses: Type M (thin wall), Type L (medium wall), and Type K (thick wall). Annealed (soft) pipe comes in coils and is available in Types K and L; it is rarely used for supply lines, however. Unless your local code calls for something different, drawn Type M is the standard for residential plumbing.

Copper tubing is specified by its approximate inside diameter (I.D.). The outside diameter (O.D.) is always ⅛ inch larger than this dimension. Thus, ½-inch copper tubing has a true O.D. of ⅝ inch; the true I.D. varies somewhat based on wall thickness.

If you opt for plastic supply lines, there are two types approved for both hot and cold water: chlorinated polyvinyl chloride (CPVC) and polybutylene (PB). CPVC pipe is joined with fittings similar to those available for copper, but it is is joined with solvent, not solder. PB tubing is flexible and requires fewer joints and fittings, but those joints can be difficult to make tight. If your local code allows plastic, either is a good choice if your original plumbing is iron pipe. Plastic pipe is easily joined to iron and is easier to install than copper.

As for the size of the pipes, the principal supply lines for an addition should be the same size as the lines you're tapping into. If you're lucky, the existing lines will be ¾ inch, which will provide better water pressure than anything smaller. Use this large-diameter pipe to create the main lines of your system. Use ½-inch pipe to branch off the main lines to feed the various fixtures. If you have to tap into a ½-inch line, use ½-inch pipe throughout.

Once you've labeled all of the supply lines and waste lines, you're ready to write up a shopping list, buy the parts, and then start the installation.

▶ INSTALLING A TUB

Putting in a tub is straightforward. First, cut a hole in the floor for the tub's drain. Make the hole somewhat oversize; the tub will cover it when you are finished, and you won't have to measure as carefully to get its position right. Set the unit in place. Check it for level along the top of the tub or, if you have a one-piece enclosure, along the top of the unit's walls. Adjust it if necessary by placing shims underneath or between the shower walls and the studs to bring it into plumb. Then anchor the fixture to the wall. Fiberglass tubs and shower/tub enclosures have a flange, or lip, along the top edge that you can nail through to fasten them to the studs. See the illustration *Tub/Shower Plumbing* on the right.

To help keep fiberglass tubs from cracking with use, many plumbers pour concrete underneath them for additional support. Get a couple of bags of gravel mix from a home center and prepare a fairly wet mix. After leveling the tub, pick it up so you have access to the floor underneath. Be sure not to disturb the shims, if you've used them. Shovel the wet concrete onto the floor where the tub is to sit, then set the tub in the concrete and push it down into place. (If necessary, build a scrap wood dam around the hole you cut for the drain to keep the concrete from dripping through the floor.) The concrete will conform to the shape of the tub.

TUB/SHOWER PLUMBING

Blocking

Shower arm fitting

Shower pipe

Diverter valve

Hot-water supply

Cold-water supply

Blocking

ROUGHING IN THE PIPES

The initial hands-on part of the plumbing job is known as roughing in. The DWV system and supply lines are installed first. The fittings—faucets, toilets, showers, and the like—come later and will be explained in Chapter 16. Because the pipes will be largely hidden by walls, roughing in takes place before the drywall goes up. Once the pipe is in place, you can put away your plumbing tools until the walls are complete and the fixtures can be installed.

An exception is installing a tub that will involve framing short walls. That was the case at the Baileys' house, where a single-piece, fiberglass tub/shower enclosure was ready to go in. Because its installation and framing were interconnected, the fixture was hooked up at this early stage. See "Installing a Tub" on the opposite page.

The drain lines generally are put in first because they are bigger and require more space. This system includes all the pipes leading away from fixtures as well as the open-air vents that extend through the roof. After the drainpipes are in, the supply lines can be installed.

Installing a DWV system doesn't require drilling many holes. Wherever possible, run pipe parallel to the joists; running them perpendicular would require large access holes in the joists, which would weaken the floor. You do need to drill *some* holes—through the decking, for example, as the pipes run from one floor to another.

At the Baileys, Bob also had to make a hole through the common foundation wall between the addition and house to tie into the existing plumbing. He cut the hole from both sides of the wall to reduce the chance that the pressure from his hammering would shatter the concrete block.

Despite its sturdy appearance, concrete block is not too difficult to punch through. Professionals often use a demolition hammer for the task. This powerful tool moves a punch with a reciprocal motion similar to the way a jackhammer works. It can save a lot of time and effort if you have many holes to punch in concrete or block and can be rented for the short time you'll be needing it. As an alternative, you can do the job by hand with a star drill and a 3-pound hand sledge, as shown in *Photo 11-2* below.

Cut the holes for the individual fixture drains according to the specs provided by the manufacturer. Remember to include the thickness of the drywall in your calculations if you are measuring out from a bare stud wall.

Most professional plumbers use large-diameter drill bits and hole saws to cut the holes for drain lines. These require powerful electric drills to drive them, but you can just as easily lay out the holes with a compass, then cut them out with a saber saw, a reciprocating saw, or even a keyhole saw.

The hole diameter for a toilet drain should be big enough to allow the *floor flange* to drop in place. The floor flange is the fitting that connects the toilet to

Photo 11-2. You can cut holes through concrete block with a star drill and a small sledgehammer. Be sure to wear goggles to protect your eyes from the flying debris. You'll be surprised how quickly this simple tool breaks through a block.

the drain line. If you're using plastic pipe, you'll notice that the opening in the floor flange is blocked by a thin wall of plastic; this barrier keeps debris from falling into the drain before the toilet is installed and should be left intact until just before you set the toilet permanently in place.

Drop the flange in the hole and check to make sure the mounting stud holes end up equidistant from the wall—otherwise, you won't be able to make the toilet perpendicular to the wall. Before you drive in screws to lock the flange in position, consider the finish flooring your bathroom will have. The toilet may not seal correctly over the flange if there's a thick ceramic or wood floor between the two.

To bring the flange up to the proper height, shim it before you screw it down. Use wood scraps to match the thickness of the finish flooring, as shown in *Photo 11-3* on the right, and use screws through the scraps to hold the flange in place. Then install the rest of the toilet drain line with the flange at its proper height. When you're ready to put in the finish floor, remove the scraps and slip the flooring under the flange.

Back at the Baileys, Bob finished the hole for the toilet drain, then moved to the narrow wall next to the shower that Barry had just framed. The hole for the tub drain was already cut, so Bob only had to install the drain fitting and the trap under the tub. He laid the main stack vent for the new plumbing in this narrow wall. The stack was going to be 3-inch plastic pipe, a standard size that just fits inside a 2 x 4 wall, provided the top and bottom plates can be cut away, as shown in *Photos 11-4*

and *11-5* on the opposite page. Here, this was no problem since the wall was nonbearing. Bob cut away the bottom plate with his reciprocating saw, then cut a square hole through the subfloor for the pipe.

Holes for the supply lines can be cut much faster since they can simply be bored with a drill bit. Self-feeding bits are often used for these holes. These bits have a threaded pilot that pulls them through the cut—a great advantage when boring holes where it is awkward to apply pressure to the drill.

If you have many large holes to bore (1-inch-diameter holes are common for supply lines), purchase or rent a heavy-duty ½-inch drill for the job. A small drill may not be up to the task. Be careful, however—if a powerful drill hits a knot or other defect in a board and the bit stops, the drill itself may start to rotate. This can twist your arm painfully or even pull you right off a stepladder. Brace yourself carefully and be ready to let go of the trigger at the first sign of trouble.

If you don't have a lot of experience installing toilets or sinks, refer to the spec sheets that cover those fixtures to find where the supply lines should be. Then drill away. If you're off by an inch or two, don't worry. The lines that will connect the fixtures to the supply lines are quite flexible and can be bent enough to make an acceptable connection. If you think you might need more adjustability, bore an oversize hole. This will allow you to shift the pipe slightly if necessary.

Photo 11-3. If the surface of the finish floor will be more than ⅛ inch or so above the subfloor, you'll have to make an allowance for it when you install the floor flange for the toilet. Prop up the flange on pieces of scrap wood to hold it at the desired elevation while you attach it to the drain system.

Photos 11-4 and 11-5. A 3-inch drainpipe or vent pipe will just fit inside a 2 x 4 wall (above), provided the plates can be completely cut away (below).

As Bob drilled holes for the pipes at the Baileys' house, he was creating the dots in a giant follow-the-dots puzzle. The task then was to connect them with the supply line and main drainpipe. While the resulting assemblies may not qualify as fine art, they do possess certain sculptural qualities, particularly if you believe that form follows function.

The DWV lines are generally installed first. Two types of plastic are used for these systems: Polyvinyl chloride (PVC) and acrylonitrile-butadiene-styrene (ABS). Both are worked in much the same way, but they are not interchangeable. Aside from aesthetics (ABS is black, PVC is white or something close), the choice between the two hinges on price (which varies from region to region), availability, and the dictates of the local code.

Joining the new drain system to the old may be one of the most challenging steps to installing plumbing for your addition, especially if you'll be joining dissimilar materials. Fortunately, manufacturers have devised ways to tie today's technology to yesterday's.

If your house is relatively new, the existing DWV system is apt to be plastic, and it will be a simple matter to cut out a section of pipe and splice in a new fitting. Just be sure to use the same type of plastic because PVC and ABS require different solvents.

In an older home, however, you're likely to come across metal pipe, cast iron in particular. Here's where the fun starts.

Cast iron pipe can be one of two types: bell and spigot or hubless. The difference is apparent when you look at how the pieces are joined together. In the bell-and-spigot system, the ends of the pipes and fittings are shaped so that they plug into one another, as shown in *Photo 11-6* on the right (top). The joints are made waterproof when caulked with oakum and lead. With the hubless system, the pieces simply butt into one another and are sealed with a neoprene rubber sleeve, as shown in *Photo 11-7* on the right (bottom). These neoprene sleeves are also the key to joining plastic pipe to metal. Luckily, plastic-pipe diameters match those of cast iron, so the two types of pipe are joined with these same rubber sleeves.

If you're not lucky enough to have a convenient place to tie into the existing drain line, like a cleanout plug, you'll have to make a place. This involves cutting into the line and splicing in a new fitting. It can be done on either a horizontal or a vertical section of pipe.

In most cases, you'll need a new plastic *tee* or a *tee-wye* fitting of the same diameter as the drain line. The difference between the two is in the angle of the junction. In a tee, the pipe entering from the side comes in at 90 degrees. In a tee-wye, the junction is at 45 degrees.

You'll also need two short lengths of plastic pipe to make the transition from the fitting to the old pipe. Then, if the old pipe is also plastic, you'll need coupler fittings to join the old to the new. If the old pipe is cast iron, the job requires two neoprene gaskets of the appropriate diameter to tie the disparate materials together.

Before you cut into the existing line, make sure to

Photo 11-6. *In bell-and-spigot systems, one end of each section of pipe is flared to receive the small end of the next pipe.*

Photo 11-7. *With hubless cast iron pipe, the joints are made with neoprene rubber gaskets.*

support it on either side of the cut. Most plumbing suppliers have an array of hangers designed to hold pipes in a variety of situations. Plastic pipe can easily be cut with a hacksaw. Cast iron is slightly tougher. Although it looks akin to armor, cast iron cuts quickly with a soil pipe cutter, shown in *Photo 11-8* on the left. This specialized device is available at most tool-rental centers. It works much like small tubing cutters used to cut smaller-diameter pipes.

After you've made the cuts, slip the new fitting in place and make the connections between the old and the new. *Photo 11-9* below shows a completed connection between cast iron and plastic pipe.

Although most older DWV systems are made of cast iron, copper or galvanized steel were used as well. The techniques for tying plastic into these metals are similar. Have your plumbing supplier help you choose the fittings.

Photo 11-8. A soil pipe cutter makes the job of cutting through cast iron pipes fairly easy.

Photo 11-9. To install a neoprene rubber connector, slide it on one pipe first, then bring the second pipe into position and slide the sleeves of the connector over the joints.

WORKING WITH PLASTIC PIPE

You need only a few tools to install plastic pipe. Use a tape measure to measure the pieces and a hacksaw to cut them to length. Then, as you install the pieces, use a hammer to attach the hangers to the framing and a small adjustable wrench to tighten the bolts on the hangers that lock the pipes in place. These tools, plus a knife, a file, and possibly a level, will take care of the job.

The first task you're likely to come up against is cutting the pipe to length. While you can buy or rent different styles of cutter, a hacksaw does the job effectively. The ends of the pipe must be cut square. If you have a good eye, you can cut freehand. Otherwise, use a miter box as a guide.

The cut leaves a slight bur around the rim of the pipe. A bur on the outside might prevent the pipe from seating properly in a fitting; on the inside of the pipe, the bur can cause an obstruction in the line. Remove burs with a knife or file.

By planning the pipe run so it will hug the basement wall just below the floor joists

you can keep it out of the way of passing heads. Start by measuring the horizontal distance from the far end of the run to the hole in the old foundation. With this figure in hand, calculate how much the pipe has to drop over its horizontal run. Ideally, you want the pipe to drop ¼ inch for every foot it travels.

At the Baileys, unfortunately, this was impossible. At that slope, the pipe would have hung too low and overlapped the doorway between the old and new basements. Bob decided to go with a ⅛-inch-per-foot drop to provide the necessary clearance.

Begin installing the various pieces of the new drain line at the end farthest from the tie-in to the old system. This is probably where the line turns to form the main stack vent. Install a cleanout at this point to make it easy to clean the drain should it ever prove necessary. Then locate the fittings where any branches from the main drain will tie in. Hold the fittings in position and measure between them to determine the lengths of the connecting pipes. Cut the pipes to length, then join them with the appropriate solvent. For

more on solvent welding, see "Solvent Welds: Joining Plastic Pipe" on pages 226–227.

As you piece the drain line together, suspend it from the joists with pipe hangers. One of the most common hangers is a narrow steel strap with a line of holes running down the middle, known in the trade as *plumber's tape*. Bend one end of the tape around the pipe to form a U-shape, then run a bolt through the two sides of the U and thread on a nut to fasten the strap around the pipe. Nail the tail of the strap to the floor joists to hold the pipe at the appropriate height.

To hang the pipe at the appropriate slope, simply measure down from the bottom of the floor joists at intervals. Since you know the length of the pipe, you should be able to calculate how much it should drop from one end to the other.

If you're working in an older home where you don't have a predictable surface from which to measure, you can also determine the pipe's slope with a level. Hold the level horizontally, with one end touching the pipe at the high side. Then measure the appropriate drop at the other

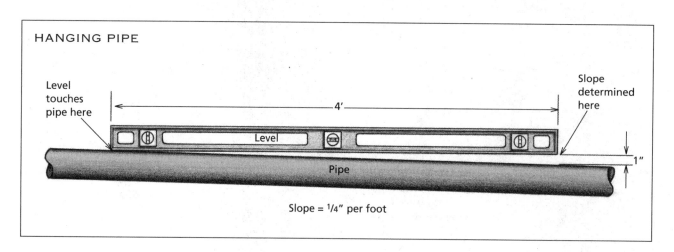

HANGING PIPE

Level touches pipe here

Slope determined here

4'

Level

Pipe

1"

Slope = ¼" per foot

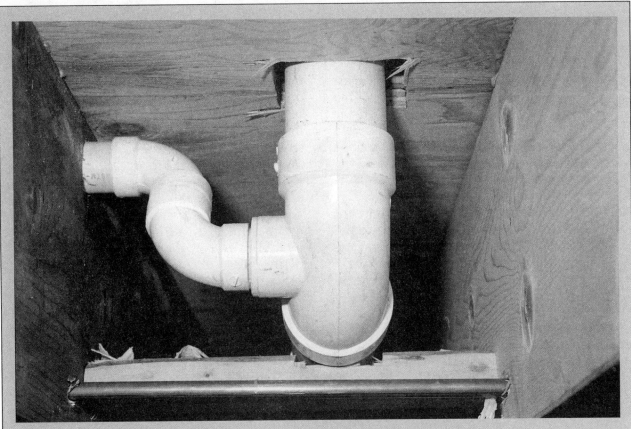

Photo 11-10. Having the shower drain join the main drain at the bottom of the stack vent helps to keep the main drain clear. The water from the shower washes away any debris that might accumulate at the bottom of the stack. Note the wooden brace that supports the stack from underneath.

end. For example, if you're using a 4-foot level, a drainpipe should drop 1 inch over the length of the level, as shown in *Hanging Pipe* on the opposite page.

Once the main drain is installed, add the various branches. These additional horizontal runs should also be sloped appropriately.

At the Baileys, the stack vent was actually located on a branch just beyond the place where Bob installed his initial cleanout. Not only did this branch connect to the stack but it also connected to the shower drain. Bob tied the smaller line from the shower into the branch with a 90 degree elbow having a side inlet, as shown in

Photo 11-10 above. The fitting took the place of an elbow and a tee-wye. And it had an additional advantage: "It will wash the heel," as Bob put it. The water from the shower will flush away any debris that might fall down the stack from above.

Once the branches are in place, hang and brace them as necessary. To support the elbow at the bottom of a stack, you can often use a 2 x 4 nailed between the studs or joists, as shown in *Photo 11-10*.

At the Baileys, Bob was particularly careful to place his braces properly. "You have to be really meticulous with your bracing," he explained. "The inspector around here is fussy about the spacing.

Besides, I don't want to have to come back later because something leaks." Even if your local code doesn't require a plumbing inspection, brace your pipes well. Improperly supported pipes can sag. If you're lucky, all that will result is a clogged drain. In the worst case, the entire stack vent can slip down, causing a leaky roof.

Most codes require plastic pipe to be supported with hangers at least every 4 feet along horizontal runs and with braces at each floor (or ceiling) vertically.

The wooden brace Bob installed on the Baileys' job was positioned advantageously. It supported the bottom of the

► SOLVENT WELDS: JOINING PLASTIC PIPE

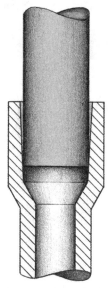

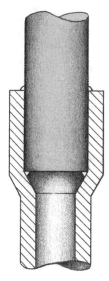

Plastic pipe is joined with a process called solvent welding. A solvent is wiped on both the pipe and the fitting, then the two parts are forced together. The solvent softens the plastic and allows the two parts to fuse. After the solvent evaporates, the plastic hardens again and the joint becomes permanent.

If you assemble a pipe and a fitting dry, the pipe will go only about halfway into the socket. This is intentional. The sockets in the fittings are tapered slightly so that after the plastic has been softened by the solvent, the socket molds to fit tightly around the

INTERFERENCE FIT

Before solvent welding   After solvent welding

end of the pipe. This is known as an interference fit and is critical to the success of a solvent weld; see *Interference Fit* above.

Both ABS and PVC pipes have their own solvents. Be sure to purchase the appropriate solvent for the type of pipe you're using. The two are not compatible. Several brands of "universal" solvent are supposed to work with either type of pipe, but they don't seem as reliable as the dedicated solvents.

Making a solvent weld is the same for both types of pipe, except that you have to prime PVC first. The primer cleans the pipe and removes its glaze coating. Primer and both kinds of solvent come in cans with swab applicators attached to the lids. Keep the lids closed as much as possible. Make sure there is plenty of ventilation in the area where you're working—the solvent fumes are toxic.

If you're using PVC pipe, begin by swabbing the primer around inside the fitting. Try not to allow any to puddle inside. Then prime the outside of the pipe for a distance equal to the depth of the fitting, as shown in the photo on the opposite page (top). (You can tell the primer is working because it will remove the lettering from the outside of the pipe.) Wait about 10 seconds, then swab the solvent on both pieces. For ABS, this is the first step. Apply a full, even coat. Be generous, but not sloppy. Again, you don't want a puddle inside the fitting. If you use too much solvent, you can create an obstruction inside the pipe; if you use too little, the joint may leak.

With both of the pieces swabbed, quickly assemble the joint before the solvent evaporates. Push the pieces together with a twisting motion and make sure the pipe bottoms out against the shoulder inside the fitting. If the alignment between the pipe and the fitting is critical (and it will be when you put the second fitting on a pipe), dry fit the pipes before you apply solvent and make an alignment mark with a pencil across both pieces, as shown in the photo on the opposite page (bottom).

As you push the pieces together, a bead of solvent should squeeze out all around the pipe. This is a sign that you've got a good joint. Wipe off the excess,

Coat the pipe with the appropriate solvent. Most cans of solvent come with a built-in applicator.

leaving a fillet of solvent all around the joint. If the squeeze-out looks spotty, the joint may leak. Correct this now, before you bury the pipe behind drywall. You may be able to slip the fitting off, apply more solvent, and try again. Move quickly—you only have a few seconds before the pieces fuse.

If the joint is satisfactory, hold the pieces together for about 10 seconds to let the plastic bond and to keep the taper in the fitting from pushing the pipe back out.

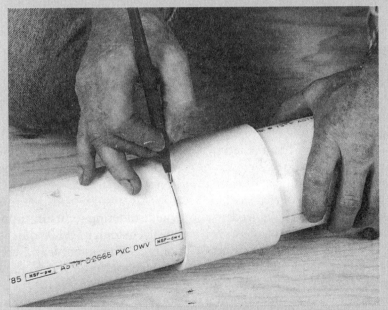

When alignment is critical, strike a pencil line between the pipe and fitting to mark their relative positions. Be careful not to remove the mark when applying the solvent.

vertical vent pipe as well as the horizontal branch leading to the vent.

Once you have the main drain and branches in place, continue running the pipes where they'll be needed for the various fixtures. For sinks, you can usually just leave a short bit of pipe protruding from the wall. The branch for a toilet ends at the floor flange. Continue the vents up and through the roof. You may want to join several vents together in the ceiling to avoid making more than one hole in the roof. Run pipe up from the end of the drain line to the attic and brace it where it comes through the ceiling. Then continue the pipe up and through the roof.

At first glance, figuring out where a stack is going to intersect a sloping roof looks tough. But it's actually easy. Just go up in the attic and hold a plumb bob to the underside of the roof. Move it until it dangles over the center of the vent stack, and you've got the point of intersection.

From there you'll have to lay out the shape of the hole— which will be elliptical because the roof is angled. This isn't hard either. Just take a scrap of pipe and cut it off at an angle equal to the slope of the roof. Then hold it against the sheathing and trace around it to make the layout. Cut the hole slightly oversize with a reciprocating saw.

Once you cut the hole in the roof, install the final section of the pipe and weld it to the rest of the stack to complete the DWV system. Go up on the roof and slip a roof gasket, a special rubber seal with metal flashing at its base, over the pipe to seal the hole in the roof from the weather.

INSTALLING SUPPLY LINES

With the drain in place, you can turn your attention to installing the supply lines. This task requires a slightly different set of tools than you used for installing the larger DWV pipes: a tubing cutter, a reamer, and a torch, among others. You can cut either hard or soft copper pipe with a hacksaw, but if you have more than one or two cuts to make, buy a tubing cutter. It is inexpensive and makes fast work of cutting pipe to length.

To make a cut, clamp the pipe between the tool's cutter and two rollers, as shown in *Photo 11-11* on the right, and rotate the tool around the pipe several times. After each rotation, tighten the tool's grasp. Cutting through the pipe will take several rotations. Once you've made a cut, remove the bur from the inside of the pipe with a reamer. Most tubing cutters have a reamer built in.

In the Baileys' basement, Bob proved his experience as he cut pieces of pipe to length. He measured and cut in one economical, fluid motion. After cutting all the pieces for one stage of the system, he soldered them together before moving on.

Soldering as you go is a good way to stay organized. It means you'll have fewer loose parts to keep track of.

WORKING WITH COPPER PIPE

Lengths of hard copper pipe are joined by fittings that are soldered in place. Most fittings are available in either copper or bronze. They cost about the same, so the choice is really a matter of availability and

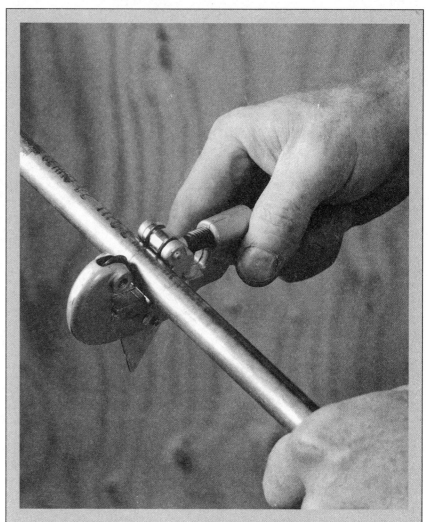

Photo 11-11. Copper tubing is easily cut with a tubing cutter.

personal preference. The bronze fittings often have flanges that you can use to attach them to the framing, but these can get in the way in a tight spot.

The pipes are attached by a process referred to as "sweating a joint" or "sweating a pipe." The job doesn't require too many tools. You'll need a torch to heat the joint, steel wool to clean the pipe and the fittings, solder, flux, and a small flux brush. If you're working in tight quarters (which is often the case when installing pipes) or in a place where a pipe is right up against a joist or stud, protect the framing with a fabric heat

shield, available at most plumbing-supply houses. Also have a fire extinguisher or a squirt bottle full of water close at hand so you can quickly put out a fire should things go amiss. For step-by-step directions on joining pipe with solder, see "Sweating Joints" on pages 230–231.

Always use lead-free solder when soldering joints in supply lines. The older 50/50 solder contains 50 percent lead, which can leach into the water, and its use has been banned for domestic water supplies because of this metal's toxic effects. (If the existing plumbing in your house has been assembled with lead solder, you can minimize lead levels by running the water for a minute or two before using it for drinking in the morning and for 30 seconds every time thereafter.)

There are a few rules to follow as you solder joints. If you are soldering several joints within a few inches of each other, treat them as an assembly. If you try to solder each joint individually, the heat from soldering the second joint usually unsolders the first. So prepare all of the joints, put the pieces together, and then heat the entire assembly at once. Before soldering a valve in place, disassemble it and remove the washers so your torch won't turn them into a sticky, molten mess.

A diverter, the valve that combines the hot and cold water in a shower, presents a special problem, and you should be very careful when installing one. Many models contain numerous plastic parts that can be damaged by heat.

▲▲▲▲▲▲▲▲▲▲▲▲

A short section of copper tubing makes a handy container for a used flux brush. Just slip the brush inside to keep the flux-covered bristles from making a mess.

▼▼▼▼▼▼▼▼▼▼▼▼

Some can be disassembled so you can solder them without problem; others should be installed using threaded fittings rather than solder. If you're in doubt, check with your plumbing supplier for details.

Since roughing in the plumbing doesn't involve any of the fixtures except the tub, the supply lines must be capped off before the water can be turned on. Here you have several choices. Some plumbers leave the pipes several inches too long and flatten the ends, as shown in *Photo 11-12* below. Fortified with a bit of solder, this is a quick, cheap seal. Other plumbers solder a cap in place. While these caps cost more than pounding the pipe flat, they don't have pointed corners waiting to slash passersby.

A more time-consuming solution is to solder a cutoff valve to the pipe end. Eventually, you'll probably want to install these anyway, as they allow you to cut off the water on the spot if you have to work on a fixture. Installing them during the rough plumbing phase involves a risk, however; if someone turns them on, accidentally or otherwise, the house can be flooded.

For a really top-notch supply system, you may want to consider adding air cushions to the lines. These combat *water hammer*, a knocking or pounding in the pipes caused by suddenly interrupting the flow of water—for example, by closing a valve quickly. Over time, this hammering can damage your pipes severely. For more on creating these cushions, see "Air Cushions" on page 232.

Running the pipes through a basement or under a floor is straightforward. These horizontal runs of pipe are called branches and connect the vertical pieces, or *risers*, that feed the fixtures to the supply lines in the existing house. They usually run through holes drilled in the floor joists. The joists then provide support for the pipes.

(continued on page 232)

Photo 11-12. When you're finished running the supply lines, they must be sealed before you can pressure test the system. Three options are shown from the left: crimping the end and soldering it closed, soldering a cap in place, and adding a cutoff valve.

229

◤ SWEATING JOINTS

Sweat soldering is really quite simple. Start by cleaning the outside of the pipe and the inside of the fitting thoroughly with a piece of steel wool (grade 00 or 000). You could use sandpaper, but steel wool lasts longer. Polish the dull brown copper to a shiny pink, as shown in the photo below (top). Then apply a little flux to the outside of the pipe and the inside of the fitting with a brush, as shown in the photo below (bottom). Most suppliers that sell flux also sell small metal *acid brushes* specifically for this purpose.

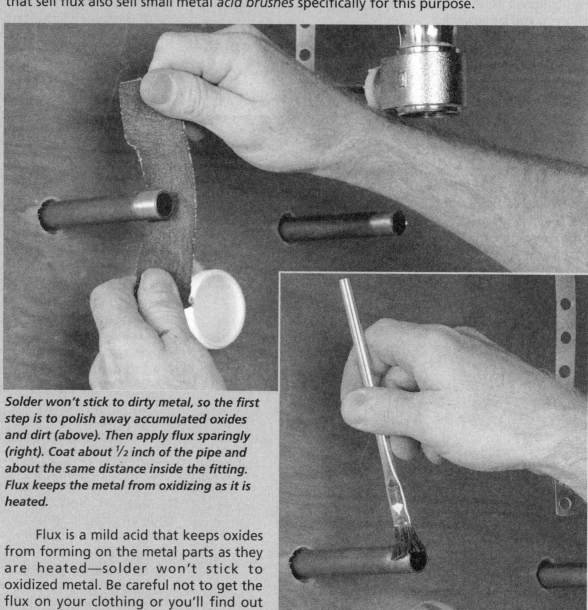

Solder won't stick to dirty metal, so the first step is to polish away accumulated oxides and dirt (above). Then apply flux sparingly (right). Coat about 1/2 inch of the pipe and about the same distance inside the fitting. Flux keeps the metal from oxidizing as it is heated.

Flux is a mild acid that keeps oxides from forming on the metal parts as they are heated—solder won't stick to oxidized metal. Be careful not to get the flux on your clothing or you'll find out exactly how effective an acid it is. As a precaution, you may want to wear leather work gloves throughout the operation to protect yourself from getting burned.

As you heat a joint, you'll see the flux bubble and melt. By applying the flux sparingly, you can prevent it from running out of the joint. This in turn will keep the solder in the joint where it belongs.

Slide the fitting onto the pipe until it bottoms out inside the fitting. Most fittings have a step inside that acts as a stop for the pipe. In the event that you come across a fitting without a step, slip the pipe in only about ½ inch. Apply heat to the joint, playing the flame over the fitting first, since it is thicker and will take longer to heat than the tubing.

Most plumbers work with an acetylene torch. Acetylene burns hotter than propane, the fuel common to the torches sold at most hardware stores. Working with acetylene saves time, but the required torch is expensive, so you would have to do a lot of plumbing to justify the purchase price. For the homeowner, a regular propane torch is adequate.

As the joint heats up, you'll see the flux bubble. Touch the solder where the fitting and pipe meet. Be careful not to melt the solder with the flame. Keep the solder on the side of the pipe that is *opposite* the flame, as shown in the photo below. The metal must be hot enough to melt the solder on its own. Capillary action will pull the solder into the joint. Run solder into the joint until you see a silver bead all around the pipe. If one part of the joint doesn't seem to be getting enough solder, try playing the flame over it. The heat will draw the solder around the pipe to fill in any gaps.

When you are finished, wipe around the joint with a coarse rag to remove any excess solder and flux. Once the pieces are cleaned up, don't move or jar them until they cool completely or you may fracture the solder interface in the joint and cause a leak. Likewise, resist the temptation to cool a freshly soldered joint with water. The sudden temperature change will cause the various pieces to contract quickly, possibly spoiling the joint.

Heat the joint with a torch. When you see the flux bubble, touch the solder to the joint at the side opposite the flame.

You can also run the pipes under the joists, supporting them with any of a number of pipe hangers. Copper pipe 1¼ inches and less in diameter should be supported every 6 feet.

When you drill holes through floor joists and wall studs, place the holes far enough in from the edge so that an errant nail or screw won't punch a hole in the tubing. In a 2 x 4 stud wall, center the holes in the studs. In wider lumber, locate the holes 1½ inches from the edge. This keeps the pipes out of harm's way, but doesn't put them so far into the wall that they're difficult to work on.

TYING THE NEW TO THE OLD

Once you have the branches run, the next step is to tie the new lines to the old ones. The first step is to find the shut-off valve and cut off the water. This valve is usually in the line that runs up from the water meter; if you have a private well, the valve might be attached to the water storage tank.

Next, drain the system. This eliminates two problems. First, unless the water is drained, you'll get drenched when you cut into the old lines. More important, it's virtually impossible to solder fittings onto water-filled pipes. The water absorbs much of the heat, so the pipes won't get hot enough to melt the solder. The water, however, may get hot enough to boil, creating a lot of pressure in the line. If this pressure builds high enough, it can rupture the pipes and send scalding water and steam flying.

To drain the pipes, open the lowest valves in the house. Also

Have you ever heard your pipes thump and clang in the walls when you turn the water off? This cacophony is caused by a phenomenon called *water hammer*. It happens when the water flowing through a pipe runs into a barrier, like a valve. The water stops, but the contained energy shakes and rattles the pipes as it disperses. Over time, this can be very destructive to your plumbing system.

The plumbing in the Baileys' addition is a good, sound system, but it makes no provision to control water hammer. Plumber Kevin Carney didn't feel it was a big enough problem to justify the added expense. But if you want to make your plumbing system that much better, consider including some sort of shock absorbers in the supply lines. While there are devices especially made for this purpose, you can save money by making them yourself from common fittings.

In the wall behind a fixture, simply add a capped 12- to 18-inch section of pipe to a tee in each supply line, as shown in *Making a Homemade Air Cushion* below. The air in the dead-end section of pipe will act as a cushion to absorb the energy in the water when a valve is suddenly closed. This air will gradually be absorbed into the water, diminishing the cushion's effectiveness. To trap a new supply of air in the cushion, drain the lines and then refill them.

MAKING A HOMEMADE AIR CUSHION

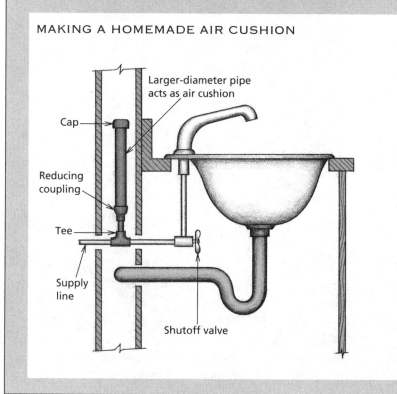

Larger-diameter pipe acts as air cushion

Cap

Reducing coupling

Tee

Supply line

Shutoff valve

232

open some higher valves or faucets to let air into the system. Gravity will then do most of the work for you. Your house may have a valve in the basement for the sole purpose of draining the system. Beware, however, if this is a valve that sees infrequent use. Seldom-used valves often leak once they're opened. You may need to replace the washer or even the entire valve as part of the job.

With the water cut off and drained from the lines, you can get to work. Remove a short section from both the hot- and cold-water lines at the point closest to the addition. Add tee fittings to connect the new pipes. You may also want to install cutoff valves into the connecting lines so the water supply to the addition can be shut off, if the need arises. A nice feature to look for in these valves is a built-in drain plug, which makes it easy to drain the lines.

At the Baileys, Bob simply installed the cutoff valves where they seemed to make sense. What he didn't know was that the heating contractor would come through a few days later and cover them up with ductwork, making them basically inaccessible.

This sort of problem happens often when a number of subcontractors work on the same job. Unless someone keeps a very careful eye on the proceedings, one sub may interfere with the work of another. If you're acting as your own contractor, you need to coordinate the work the subcontractors do and check their progress frequently to avoid problems.

Once the valves and new lines are soldered in place, make sure the valves are closed, then turn the water back on.

Check the splices for leaks, then check to be sure all the ends of the new plumbing are sealed. Open the valves to pressurize the new system. You'll have to open another valve in the addition to give the air in the lines a way to escape.

With the system under pressure, inspect your work for leaks. The telltale sign of a bad solder joint is a thin spray of water arcing across the room. Even the pros find an occasional leak.

If you find a leak in your plumbing work, shut off the water and drain the system. Then heat the bad joint and ease the pieces apart. Wipe both the pipe and the inside of the fitting with a rag until each has just a thin, shiny coating of solder. Apply flux and slip the joint together again. Heat and solder as before. You won't need as much solder since the pieces already have been *tinned,* or coated with solder from your first try.

A VISIT FROM THE INSPECTOR

Most municipalities require some kind of plumbing inspection before the pipes can be covered up with drywall. This can range from the casual "Yup, it looks alright to me," to the rigorous "Okay, put it under pressure and we'll see if it holds." When you apply for your building permits, ask what the plumbing inspector will expect to see.

At the Baileys, the inspector carefully checked the venting and the placement of the pipe supports. He even measured to check the slope of the drain line. During all this, Bob stood by, amicably answering questions.

When the inspector was ready, Bob set up to do a pressure test of the drain system.

A drain-system pressure test involves plugging up the openings in the drain line and pressurizing it. To pass, the pipes must hold the pressure for a certain length of time, usually 15 minutes. Pressure tests can be done on both supply and drain systems using either water or compressed air. The test at the Baileys was done with water.

Bob plugged the various drain openings with inflatable rubber plugs sold for the purpose; these devices look something like heavy-duty balloons. He also inserted a plug into the main addition drain line through a cleanout in the old basement. Once everything was plugged, Bob took a hose up on the roof and filled the system through the vent pipe. The system held the water for the required amount of time without any trouble, earning Bob's handiwork the plumbing inspector's approval.

The inspection of the supply system was far simpler. The inspector verified that the pipes were under pressure, then checked all the fittings for leaks.

If the code in your area requires an involved inspection, you may want to hire a plumber for a few hours on the big day. Plumbers have the expertise and the equipment necessary to perform pressure tests or any other tests the inspector requires. Otherwise, you may have to rent or purchase the items necessary for a pressure test; inspectors rarely provide them. And if you've hired a plumber to serve as a consultant as you planned, you'll be sure everything is up to standard before the inspector arrives.

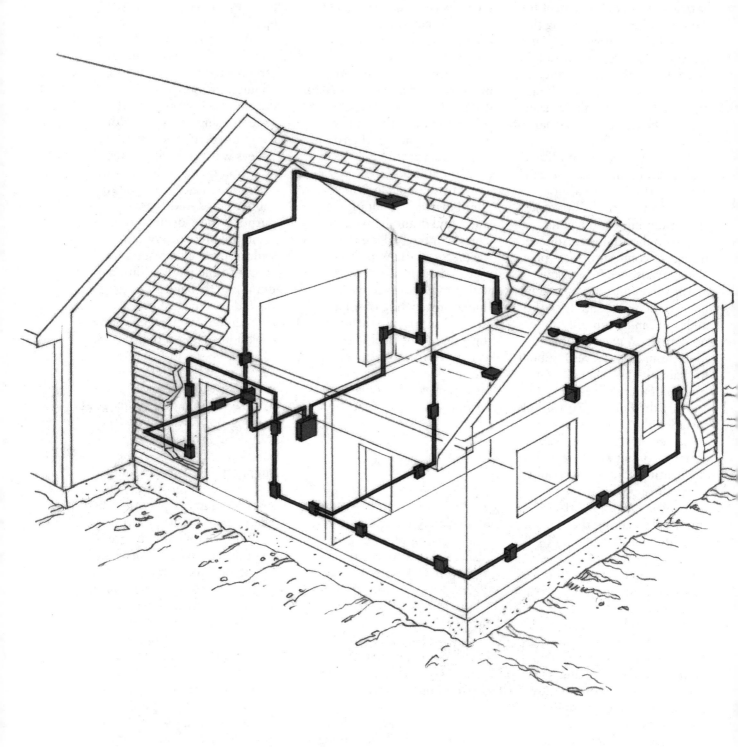

12
ROUGH WIRING

The electrical work involved in building an addition is, for good reason, not the most likely area for DIY involvement. There are some very real dangers. After all, lives—yours and your family's—are at stake. The risk of electrocution during installation is not great, since all that work is done with the power off; but in the years ahead, a fire or severe shock could be caused by improper evaluation and planning or by faulty wiring techniques. Personal injury, liability, and the possible effect on the eventual sale of your home are important issues to consider.

With this said, wiring can be one of the most gratifying ways to get involved in building an addition. The logic of wiring systems has its appeal, as does the well-thought-out hardware.

The demands on manual skills are slight, although it takes some dexterity to do the fine work of making attachments in tight electrical boxes. You must be willing to spend time to become familiar with wiring to code, and you should have an understanding of the theory behind all those wires and gadgets. See "To Learn More" on page 236.

Finally, you should be comfortable with having an inspector check your work closely, both before any wall coverings conceal the rough wiring and after everything is hooked up and current is coursing through the system. Wiring is not a DIY project that you can do on your own terms. Because of the potential hazards involved with wiring, your work must meet minimal local requirements, which are there

to ensure that installation is completely safe.

WHAT'S INVOLVED?

At the outset, someone has to draw the plans and write up the specifications (a list of all the fixtures such as lights, fans, and so on). But wiring to code alone won't ensure an adequate system for the particular needs of a family now or in the future. Most homeowners have never had to think about their home electrical system. It's there when they need it and tucked behind walls where it can't be seen.

Jim and Carol Bailey, along with the great majority of homeowners, were all but unaware of the wires running through the walls of their home. Electricity was something of a gentle giant—helpful yet with a potential for harm. The few times over the years that Jim had gone into the basement to reset a tripped breaker (these terms are discussed below), he felt in awe of the bundles of white cables disappearing up into the house.

When it came time to plan the wiring for the addition, the Baileys were happy to have as little involvement as possible. But the contractors, Dennis and Ted, asked that the couple sit down at the kitchen table one evening and talk over just what it would take, in time and money, to bring electrical power into the new rooms.

Jim and Carol learned that there was a strict set of regulations in force to guarantee safe and standard practice in the electrical trade. As the contractors went over the basic requirements, they had to take time to explain a dozen terms to the Baileys. "Right inside here," Ted said, rapping a kitchen wall, "you've got *cables*, which are the wires running around the room. The cables in here are part of a *circuit*, like a branch of your electrical system, and I'd guess it serves a half-dozen wall

switches and outlets. But over there," he said, pointing to the wall oven, "you've got an energy-hungry appliance that has its own circuit."

The four got up from the table and went down into the basement with a flashlight.

▲▲▲▲▲▲▲▲▲▲▲▲

Don't skimp on electrical outlets—they're fairly inexpensive and easy to add at the rough wiring stage. You should have at least one on every wall.

▼▼▼▼▼▼▼▼▼▼▼▼

Mounted to a wall was the inconspicuous gray box that Jim had occasionally visited, the *service panel* (also known as the service box, load center, circuit breaker box, or fuse box if fuses are used). This is the hub of the home's electrical system and its tie with the outside electrical world. The service panel distributes power through *breakers*. These are on-off switches, but they're not just a matter of convenience. "Each

one of these switches is a safety device," Ted explained, "like the fuses you used to see. They're designed to *trip*—shut off automatically—when a jolt of current is caused by a foul-up somewhere in the system."

Dennis held the flashlight so the Baileys could read the numbers printed on each breaker. Breakers are rated to carry certain amounts of current, expressed in *amperes* (or amps, abbreviated "A"). Those with the lowest capacity, typically 15 amps, can serve lighting fixtures, electrical receptacles (the fixtures you stick plugs into), and light-duty appliances. More amperage is needed for circuits that will power appliances with a greater demand.

As Dennis closed the door of the panel, he pointed out a particularly fat cable snaking off toward the laundry area. To explain what it was doing, he had to bring up another word used to describe electrical power, *volts* (abbreviated "V").

While standard household circuits carry 120 volts, some electrical appliances draw more power and are supplied by 240-volt (240V) circuits. The dryer in the basement was one of them. These high-voltage lines have receptacles with unusual-looking slots; only the plugs of 240V appliances will fit into them.

Back upstairs, the Baileys faced the task of imagining their life in the unbuilt addition so that the contractors could plan an adequate level of electrical service.

The electrical code will establish a certain minumum capacity. But each family has its own type and pattern of demands on the home's electrical system. At the minimum, you'll be adding new circuits to the service panel; you may also need to install a second, smaller panel, called a *subpanel*, as a center from which the addition's new circuits can branch. The added needs of the project may even mean that a complete upgrade of your electrical service is necessary.

The contractors ended their meeting with a quick description of what lay ahead. After the planning stage, the system would be *roughed in*. Electrical boxes and equipment such as fans and recessed lights wouldl be attached to the frame of the addition. Cables would be threaded to these spots, run through holes drilled in the framing members. Specially designed staples would be used to anchor the cables along their route.

Once the rough-in has been completed, the circuit wiring must be tested. One test confirms that there is no continuity (or electrical connection) between the black *hot wires* and either the white *grounded wires* or the bare *grounding wires*. Another ensures that all grounding wire connections are well made. Still another confirms that the circuit is complete when each

circuit's hot wire is connected to the white grounded wire. These tests need to be performed before the framing is covered with drywall or plaster so changes can be easily made.

Finish wiring (covered in Chapter 17) is perhaps the easiest part of the task, assuming that all wires were carefully labeled when roughing in. Nevertheless, wiring techniques and know-how are critical at this stage as well. For example, a switched light may work whether the switch is connected to the white grounded wire or black hot wire, but for safety, it's essential to switch the hot wire. Similarly, a receptacle will work with black and white wire connections reversed, but it, too, is dangerous and illegal.

Finally, there are more tests to ensure that all wiring connections have been made correctly. Since you would already know there were no problems with the rough-in wiring, any trouble that arises would clearly be related to finish wiring or to a short caused by a nail or screw that was driven into the wires when walls, cabinets, or trim were installed. Theoretically, of course, all the wires should have been positioned far enough away from the surface (or if not, protected with metal plates). But in practice, accidents happen.

DIY OPTIONS

At the least, you should get involved in planning your electrical system. In the process, you'll gain a valuable understanding of how it all works. And by taking an interest, there's a better chance that the

system will do what you want it to. Before you start, discuss the basic code requirements, such as the spacing of receptacles, with your electrical inspector, licensed electrician, or contractor. Plan for related in-wall wiring, too, for coaxial cable, telephones, intercom, security, speakers, doorbell, and thermostats.

Your level of involvement will depend on a few factors: the provisions of local restrictions, your confidence, and the cooperation from an electrician or the local electrical inspector. You might tackle everything yourself. Or you could hire an electrician to perform critical, well-defined tasks (such as the service panel work and circuit planning), then do the rest yourself. Another alternative would be to become, in effect, an electrician's helper by working under his or her supervision.

Obviously, doing all of the work yourself offers the greatest potential for savings, but this isn't always possible. Even if local laws allow you free reign, practically speaking you may not be able to do the work required. For one thing, some inspectors are known to be uncomfortable with the responsibility of checking DIY work; they are accustomed to taking for granted the professionalism and experience of licensed electricians. An inspector might be unwilling to okay your work unless a licensed electrician first signs off on it. That means you would have to find a local electrician to look over your shoulder as you do the crucial stages of the wiring.

Legal and liability issues aside, you still should not consider doing the work yourself unless you become thoroughly familiar with both basic and advanced wiring theory, as well as the body of code regulations related to such work. Invariably this involves considerable study. And remember, if you do the work yourself, it is very important to have the job inspected by a professional, even in rural areas that may not require it.

Perhaps the optimum approach for do-it-yourselfers is to hire an electrician to do the most demanding part of the work. Just what that includes will be determined by your abilities and knowledge and by the electrician's confidence in you. This arrangement ensures that the electrician will be available to answer your questions, keep an eye on your work as it progresses, and sign off on the completed job. For the sake of fairness and to avoid misunderstandings, you should very carefully detail (preferably in writing) who is responsible for what work, material purchases, and so on.

If you plan on working with an electrician, it is best to pay on a time-and-materials basis—you agree to pay an hourly rate for the electrician's labor and for any materials (with or without a markup above the electrician's discounted price, depending on your agreement). The work you contribute will reduce the amount of time spent by the electrician, saving you some money.

AN OVERVIEW OF THE WORK

Even if your involvement will be limited to making final connections to switches, receptacles, lights, and other fixtures, you'll need basic wiring skills. That means knowing how to strip cables and wires, connect wires to screw terminals, connect wires to each other, size wire nuts, and test for polarity and grounding. You should also have a knowledge of common wiring layouts. The minimum basic tool kit includes screwdrivers, long-nose pliers, an electrician's combination tool for stripping and cutting wire, a utility knife, a cable stripper, a circuit tester, and a receptacle analyzer. See the illustration *Basic Tool Kit* on the left.

The more involved your task, the more skills, knowhow, and tools are required. For a rough-in, you need a thorough understanding of the circuitry required for kitchens, baths, dining areas, family rooms, laundries, garages, basements, and outdoor fixtures. You must know how to read an electrical plan, size boxes according to the number of wires or fixtures involved, feed cables through framing, and make connections at the box.

Your addition may include high-voltage 240-volt circuits to serve appliances and baseboard

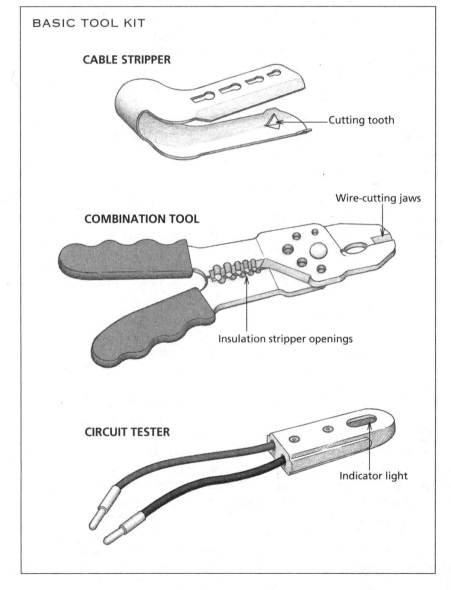

BASIC TOOL KIT

CABLE STRIPPER

Cutting tooth

COMBINATION TOOL

Wire-cutting jaws

Insulation stripper openings

CIRCUIT TESTER

Indicator light

heaters. If you'll be tangling with the wiring in the existing house as well, you'll need to know the tricks used to "fish" cables behind ceilings and through floors.

To take on adding a subpanel or installing a new main panel, you need to be still better grounded, so to speak, in how an electrical system works. When adding a subpanel or adding breakers to an existing panel, the main breaker will be shut off, but the power lines coming into the house from the street will remain hot, so there is some risk of accidental injury or electrocution to a novice. As for installing a new service panel or upgrading an existing one, a licensed electrician is usually called on to do that work.

AN ELECTRIFYING HOUSE TOUR

Begin the evaluation of your home's electrical system by walking around the house, starting outdoors. Notice the service wires that extend from the utility pole to a post on your house called a *service head*. Telephone and television cables may also be strung from the same pole, but they are not connected to the service head. Alternately, you may see no wires if they run underground.

From the service head, a heavy cable extends through the electric meter, which is used to monitor and display your electric consumption, then through the exterior wall to the service panel, as illustrated in *Service Entrance* on the right. The panel is typically located in the basement or, in homes without basements, the garage or kitchen. Nearby, you may see a heavy copper wire attached to

a copper rod driven into the earth, serving as the system's *ground*.

Take a look at the service panel. Open the panel door and you'll see the breakers (or fuses, in older installations). As explained previously, a breaker is a heavy-duty switch that

controls the flow of current in two ways. You can manually flick this switch to shut off power. And a sudden increase in the flow, caused by a surge of power outside the house or by a short circuit within it, will automatically trip the switch as a safety feature.

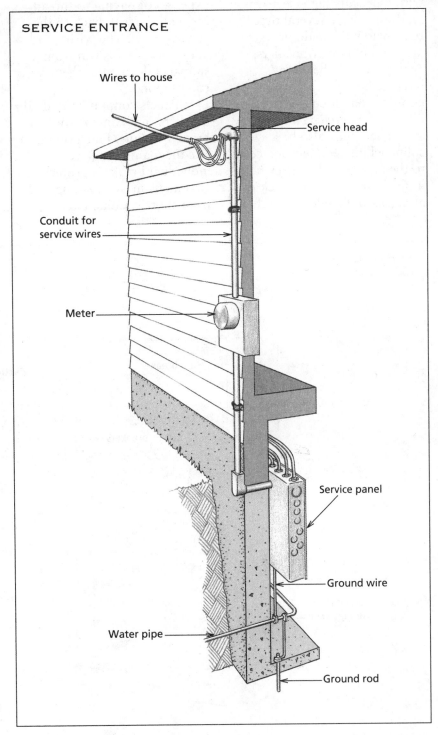

SERVICE ENTRANCE

Wires to house

Service head

Conduit for service wires

Meter

Service panel

Ground wire

Water pipe

Ground rod

The main breaker controls electricity from the service entrance. It is marked with an amperage (abbreviated "A") rating, which tells the size of the service to the house. In older houses you may find 60A service, but newer homes usually will have at least 100A service. Large homes and ones with especially high electrical loads may have several times that. Below the main breaker are rows of circuit breakers; again, each is labeled to indicate how much power is going to that circuit. See the illustration *Service Panel* below.

There may also be a subpanel immediately adjacent to the main panel or elsewhere in the home. You can track it along a stout feeder cable that runs from a breaker in the service panel, usually rated at least 30A, to the smaller subpanel box. A subpanel is added if the original service panel was not large enough to accommodate growing needs; it is also used as a remote center from which to run circuits, thereby avoiding the work (and expense) of having to thread them all the way back to the service panel. The wiring for additions often is run from a subpanel devoted to the new rooms alone.

Panels contain individual breakers that control power to branch circuits. Functioning like the main breakers, individual breakers protect circuits from overloading and from short circuits. Each breaker displays its amperage rating, ranging from 15A, for basic lighting and receptacle circuits, to 20A, for kitchen, dining, or family room "small appliance" circuits, to 30A, 40A, and 50A double breakers, for large appliances such as electric dryers, ranges, water heaters, and ovens that require 240V power.

Each circuit breaker should be clearly labeled with the area it serves (such as "kitchen outlets," "refrigerator," or "range"). If not, your first project will be to map the existing circuits of your house—a time-consuming but straightforward task that involves turning off one breaker at a time and checking lights and receptacles to see where the

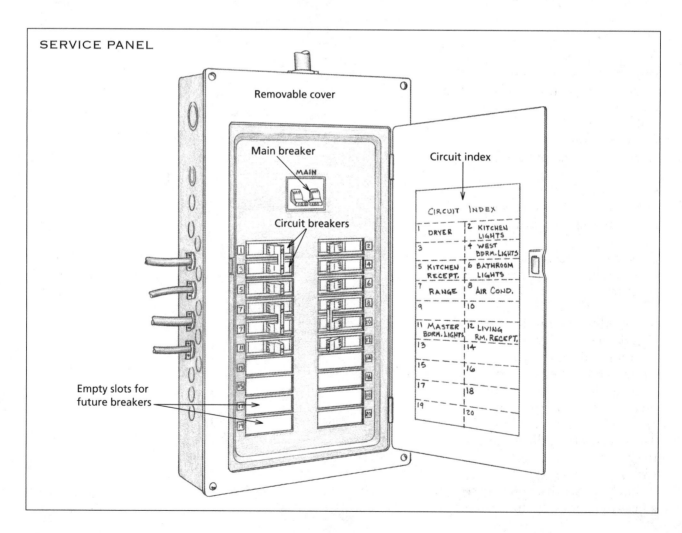

SERVICE PANEL

Removable cover

Main breaker

MAIN

Circuit breakers

Circuit index

CIRCUIT INDEX

1 DRYER	2 KITCHEN LIGHTS
3	4 WEST BDRM. LIGHTS
5 KITCHEN RECEPT.	6 BATHROOM LIGHTS
7 RANGE	8 AIR COND.
9	10
11 MASTER BDRM. LIGHTS	12 LIVING RM. RECEPT.
13	14
15	16
17	18
19	20

Empty slots for future breakers

circuit travels. Number the circuits. Then draw a simple floor plan showing what goes where. Write the results on self-sticking labels that can be affixed to the inside of the panel door. Label all of the individual circuits (serving such appliances as the water heater, range, and disposal) as well.

Your tour should extend into the heart of the electrical system, the service panel. Have a good flashlight in hand and sturdily soled shoes on your feet. You should be standing on a dry area of the floor. Shut off the main breaker (or pull the main fuse plug). Then carefully remove the panel cover to get a look inside. Remember, the power is still live upstream from the main breaker, so don't touch anything inside the box.

Review the illustration *Inside a Service Panel* on the right. Notice the three multi-strand, heavy wires coming from the meter. The two power lines, or hot service wires, are connected to a pair of metal bars, called hot bus bars or buses, to which circuit breakers or fuses are connected. The neutral service wire is connected to a neutral bus bar.

Power flows into the home via the hot wires and returns to the utility via the neutral wire. The neutral bus bar is, in turn, connected to a grounding conductor. The grounding conductor runs to a metal grounding rod driven deep into the ground and usually to a metal water pipe as well. It provides a path for electrical current in the event it seeks to return to the ground along a path other than the white grounded wire. This condition, called a *short circuit,* or short, would occur if a loose hot wire

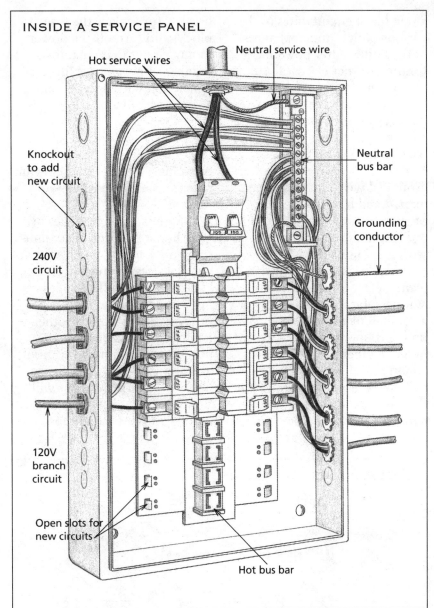

INSIDE A SERVICE PANEL

Hot service wires

Neutral service wire

Knockout to add new circuit

Neutral bus bar

Grounding conductor

240V circuit

120V branch circuit

Open slots for new circuits

Hot bus bar

were to contact the side of a metal fixture box, for example. (If there is an indoor water meter, a *jumper wire* serves to bypass the meter and ensures uninterrupted grounding.)

All of the black wires from the various branch circuits connect to the circuit breakers. All of the white grounded wires are connected to the neutral bus bar, as are the bare grounding wires, which are distinct from grounded wires. The capacity of the circuit cable is rated by its gauge; cables must be sized

according to the amperage of the breaker serving it to avoid an overload. Notice that some breakers are doubled. They have two 120V black wires connected to them and provide 240V power to appliances.

As you look at this maze of wires, you can think of electric current as a flow, something akin to water. Its force, termed voltage, flows from the service lines through the main breaker and along the hot bus bars to the individual circuit breakers. It continues along black circuit wires to the various outlets and appliances in the home. After powering a fixture or other electrical equipment, current returns (now without force, or at zero voltage) via the white grounded wires to the neutral bus bar and back to the utility via the neutral service wire. The white grounded wire must never be interrupted by a breaker, fuse, or switch.

Note that cables for circuit wiring are now almost exclusively plastic sheathed (called NM, for nonmetallic). Wiring subject to damage, such as on basement walls or underground, often is protected in metal pipes called rigid conduit.

To continue your tour, put the cover back on the service panel, then turn on the main breaker (or replace the fuse block) and turn off the power to any circuit that contains a number of *receptacles* (in which plugs are inserted) and switched lights (those operated with a wall switch). Most receptacles are called duplexes, meaning there are places for two plugs; a receptacle that can take four is a quadraplex or fourplex.

Unless the receptacles in your home were installed quite some time ago, you will see two parallel slots of unequal length. Each mates with the prongs on "polarized" plugs, and one prong is wider than the other. Polarization ensures that the hot wire will connect with tools and appliances as their design intends—that the current will flow a certain way through the unit. Chances are good that you'll also see a third, U-shaped grounding slot. Electric tools and appliances with three-prong plugs will be grounded when plugged into such receptacles.

Other receptacles are designed to deliver a certain amperage or voltage to specially arranged plugs. See the illustration *Receptacles on the Outside* below.

Before looking inside a receptacle, test to make sure it is off by plugging in something that you know is operating properly or by using an electrician's circuit tester. Remove the center screw to take off the cover plate and, if you wish, remove the two screws that secure the receptacle in its plastic or metal box. This box, and boxes like it, is the only place in which electrical transactions are allowed to take

---

RECEPTACLES ON THE OUTSIDE

NORMAL VOLTAGE

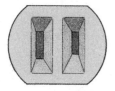

Earlier receptacles did not provide slot for grounding

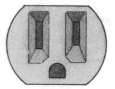

Receptacles now must have U-shaped grounding slot, as on this standard 15A receptacle

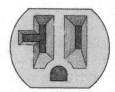

Receptacle with T-shaped slot provides 20A current

HIGH VOLTAGE

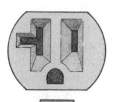

Ground-fault circuit interrupter receptacle

RESET
TEST

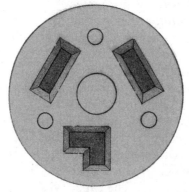

Receptacle used for clothes dryer

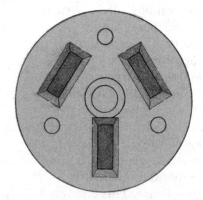

Receptacle used for range

place, according to code. See the illustration *Receptacle on the Inside* on the right.

If this receptacle is at the end of a cable, you'll find just one cable running to it. The one illustrated is within the circuit, as indicated by two cables—one running in and one running out. The bare grounding wire is attached to the green screw terminal on the bottom of the receptacle. If the circuit continues through this fixture, the grounding wires from both cables are connected to each other and a third bare wire, called a *pigtail*, that runs to the terminal.

The black hot wire bringing power to the outlet is either connected to one of the brass screws or anchored with a push-in fitting; the white grounded wire is connected to one of the silver-colored screws on the opposite side or is housed in its own push-in fitting. (Connections to screws may be obscured if the receptacle has been wrapped with electrical tape.) Any additional wires that may be present are probably there to take power to another location.

Now, go to a switch you are certain is on the same powerless circuit and remove the cover plate. To make sure there is no power running to the switch, touch the leads of a circuit tester to the silver and brass terminals. If this switch is the only one controlling the fixture, there will be two wires (and possibly a bare grounding wire) attached to it. You'll see another insulated wire on a three-way switch, which is used in tandem with another switch to control a common light.

This concludes the tour. Put the cover plates back in place and restore current to the circuit.

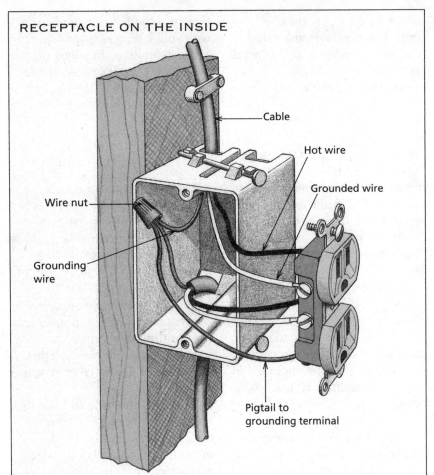

RECEPTACLE ON THE INSIDE

Cable

Hot wire

Grounded wire

Wire nut

Grounding wire

Pigtail to grounding terminal

EVALUATING YOUR ELECTRICAL SYSTEM

If you have an older fused system, it probably should be replaced with a modern breaker system as you wire for your addition. If you have less than 100A service, you will almost certainly be required to upgrade to that capacity or more, depending on the total demand for power of your new, expanded house.

You can estimate just how much power you'll need by anticipating the fixtures and appliances you'll have in the addition; for your final calculation, however, consult your electrical inspector for guidelines. To determine the gross *load,* or the home and addition's total demand for power, compute the following:

• Multiply the square footage of living area (including the planned addition) by 3 watts (or 3W) to find the basic lighting and receptacle load.

• Add 1,500W for each of the kitchen's small-appliance circuit and for a laundry circuit.

• Add the specific watt ratings (they also may be labeled volts-amps) found on product nameplates for all permanently wired appliances, such as a range, garbage disposal, dishwasher, water heater, freezer, and electric clothes dryer.

• Add actual W ratings for any outdoor fixtures, taking them off of products or packaging.

• Multiply the number of outdoor lights and receptacles by 180W, then add that to your total.

• Add 65 percent of a central heating system's rated load or 100 percent of a central air conditioner's load, whichever is greater.

The grand sum you'll come up with is an inflated figure. Since you'll never use every light and appliance at the same time, a "demand factor" is used to make this sum an approximate real-life situation. One approach usually approved by inspectors is to calculate the first 10,000 watts at 100 percent and the remaining load at 40 percent. Add these figures to get the total load, then divide by 240V to arrive at the required ampere rating.

If this projected load exceeds the main breaker rating, your service must be upgraded to handle the addition. If not, you'll be able to add circuits needed for your addition. That may be as simple as snapping in new circuit breakers, if there are open spaces; alternately, you can replace some full-size breakers with split breakers (sometimes called "slim line" breakers or "skinnies"), which take half the space in the panel. But if there won't be enough room in the existing panel, you should install a subpanel.

DRAWING AN ELECTRICAL PLAN

To plot the electrical system of the addition, begin by tracing over or redrawing a floor plan of the proposed layout. See *Electrical Symbols* below for conventional ways of indicating the positions of receptacles, switches, wall and ceiling lights, and other direct-wired electrical equipment.

This is the time to become familiar with the minimum code requirements, such as installing receptacles every so many feet, running three-way wiring for stairway lighting, and using GFCI-protected outlets (GFCI stands for ground-fault circuit interrupter) wherever dampness or water would increase the chance of electrical shock, such as in the kitchen, bathrooms, garage, and basement. Then add any convenience outlets for special needs, such as an isolated-ground circuit for a computer, a four-outlet receptacle for a spaghetti-like network of stereo power cords, and convenient central lighting controls. See the illustration *Electrical Plan* on the opposite page.

Once you've mapped the addition, you can determine the number and amp capacity (and thus cable sizes) of the new circuits. It's important to plan an even distribution of outlets; if two floors are involved, make sure the lighting and receptacles on each floor are served by more

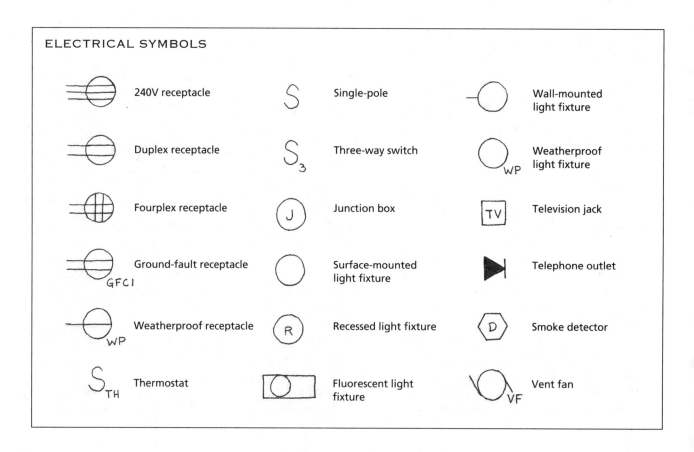

ELECTRICAL SYMBOLS

240V receptacle	Single-pole	Wall-mounted light fixture
Duplex receptacle	Three-way switch	Weatherproof light fixture
Fourplex receptacle	Junction box	Television jack
Ground-fault receptacle (GFCI)	Surface-mounted light fixture	Telephone outlet
Weatherproof receptacle (WP)	Recessed light fixture	Smoke detector
Thermostat	Fluorescent light fixture	Vent fan

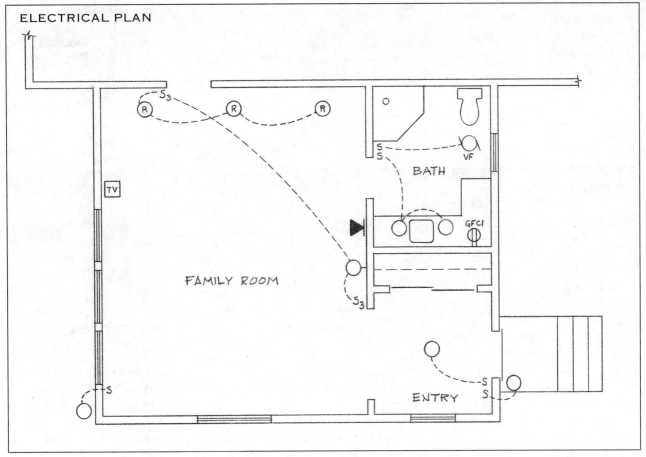

FAMILY ROOM

BATH

VF

GFCI

TV

ENTRY

than one circuit. This means a whole floor won't be without power if a single circuit breaker trips. Careful planning will also minimize waste when routing cables.

Don't forget to include direct-wired smoke alarms wherever they are required, preferably on a circuit with an often-used light, such as in a bathroom, so that you'll know if the circuit breaker has tripped.

Once you've reached this stage, all that remains to be done before you begin installation is to complete a shopping list, room by room and circuit by circuit, based on a plan you've run by the inspector or an electrician. Include every box, device, or piece of electrical equipment, together with such specifications as size, model number, and manufacturer. For tips on where

to find what you need, see "Buying Electrical Supplies" on page 246.

ROUGHING IN

Wires shouldn't be strung through the addition until after all framing is in place and it has been inspected and approved by the building inspector. And now is not too early to remind yourself of the most basic rule of working with electricity: Turn off the power to the area in which you are working, then confirm that the power is off by checking the lines with a circuit tester. To be sure that no one turns the power back on while you're working, post an obvious warning on the service panel. And never connect new

work to power until you've completed a low-voltage test (explained later).

For roughing in an addition, you'll need boxes and cable, as well as the rough-in portions of recessed light fixtures, bathroom fans, and similar equipment, which are best installed while walls and ceilings are open. And of course you'll need related supplies such as cable staples, wire nuts, and electrician's tape. You may also need materials for service panel work, but most homeowners will leave that job to an electrician.

All wire splices and wiring connections to devices must be made within UL-approved electrical boxes. (UL stands for Underwriters Laboratory, an industry group that sets standards for electrical hardware.) You must install a box unless there's a UL-approved box on the equipment itself. The rough-in portion of that equipment (recessed light fixtures, fans, and the like) must be installed while framing is exposed. (Incidentally, only those light fixtures marked "IC" [insulation contact] can be used in contact with insulation in ceilings and roofs.)

Use plastic boxes wherever they are allowed by local code; generally, that means all indoor applications where the box is to be covered with a finished wall. Plastic boxes are cheaper than metal ones, and you don't need to ground them. Those with preattached mounting nails are easier to install. See the illustration *Receptacle on the Inside* on page 243. For outdoor wiring, use either rigid metal conduit and cast aluminum boxes or PVC (polyvinyl chloride) conduit and weatherproof PVC boxes.

Boxes come in several sizes. The code sets the minimum box size allowed for a given number of wires and devices being installed inside. (Keep that in mind when making your materials list.) Consider using an oversize box wherever you intend to install dimmers, GFCI receptacles,

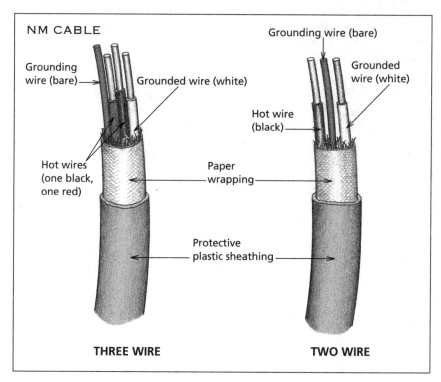

NM CABLE

Grounding wire (bare)

Grounded wire (white)

Hot wires (one black, one red)

Paper wrapping

Protective plastic sheathing

THREE WIRE

Grounding wire (bare)

Grounded wire (white)

Hot wire (black)

Paper wrapping

Protective plastic sheathing

TWO WIRE

timers, or other bulky devices that will take up much of the space inside a box; it's dangerous and counter to code to cram wires into a box by shortening their in-box length to less than 8 inches or by bending them sharply.

Electrical boxes must be installed at consistent heights. Measured to the center of the box from the floor, receptacles are usually 12 inches high and switches 48 inches high. Switches can be lowered for children and for people in wheelchairs.

The most common wiring used today is NM-sheathed cable, sold in boxes of 25 to 250 feet. It comes with either two or three insulated wires and, usually, a bare grounding wire. (Note that so-called "two-wire" cable typically has *three* wires, including the grounding wire). See the illustration *NM Cable* above. Cable with three insulated wires is used to provide power to 240V devices; it also is used for 120V circuits that include both receptacles and switches, for split-circuit receptacles, and for lights

▶ BUYING ELECTRICAL SUPPLIES

When you shop for boxes, cables, and other electrical materials, let the supplier know you're wiring an entire addition—you may qualify for a discount. Note that there are real differences in quality in certain product lines. Manufacturers may offer grades ranked good, better, and best; another scale is consumer, contractor, and commercial-industrial. In most cases, consumer-grade products will be adequate. But a bargain receptacle, for example, may not be as reliable or as long-lasting as one that grips the plug prongs securely, and a better product would be appropriate for a busy workshop or kitchen small-appliance center. An upgrade may cost a little more.

controlled from two or more locations.

A wire's gauge, or diameter, determines its capacity in amps and also determines the rating of the circuit breaker protecting a circuit with that gauge of wire. Generally, a 15A breaker is used with 14-gauge wire, 20A for 12 gauge, 30A for 10 gauge, 40A for 8 gauge, and 55A for 6 gauge. Most home wiring is done with copper wire, which this chapter assumes you will be using.

Keep cables running perpendicular or parallel to framing; avoid making diagonal runs. The point is to have cables following a predictable course behind walls. Cables within walls should run about 20 inches above the floor. Install cables through the center of studs or a minimum of 1¼ inches from the faces of the studs to prevent chance

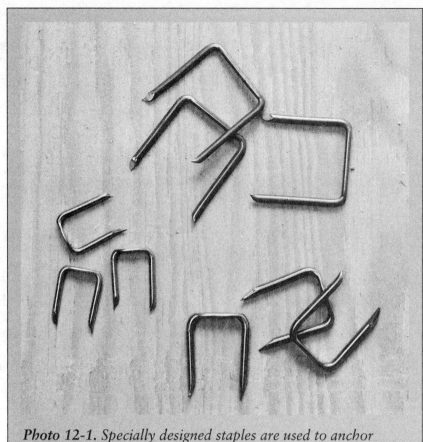

Photo 12-1. Specially designed staples are used to anchor several cables at once.

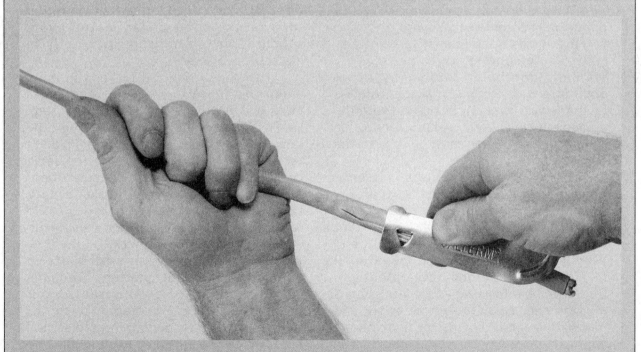

Photo 12-2. Use a cable stripper to slice sheathing. This special tool makes the risk of slicing through the wire insulation minimal.

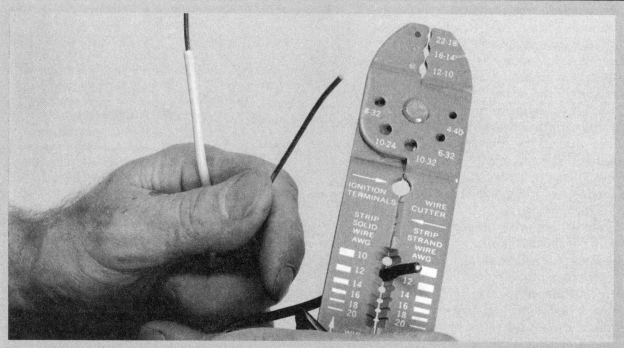

Photo 12-3. A combination tool has a graduated series of openings. Each opening pinches through the insulation of a given wire gauge, allowing you to then slide the insulation off easily.

 # RELATED WIRING

With the walls open, you have the opportunity to hide other types of wiring for thermostats, speakers, low-voltage controls, telephone, TV cable, security systems, doorbells, and many other applications. These wires can be installed by the service company associated with the equipment (telephone, security, and cable companies), by electricians, or by you, the homeowner.

These are low-voltage systems, powered by transformers that typically produce no more than 30V. That means they present little of the hazard inherent in standard (or "line voltage") 120V and 240V lines. The voltage is too low to even give a shock, let alone develop enough resistance heat to cause a fire. Insulation is much thinner, boxes are not necessary, and most other requirements for line-voltage wiring do not apply. But it still makes sense to protect the wires from possible damage or failed connections by running wires through holes drilled in the framing rather than on the edge surfaces. And avoid splicing wire in midrun, especially in inaccessible places.

The key safety rule to keep in mind when installing this wiring is to avoid mixing it with the line-voltage system. Don't run low-voltage wiring through the same holes in framing, and, above all, don't terminate low-voltage wires in the same box as line voltage. If uninsulated portions of the two systems were to make contact, the overload to the thinner wires could cause a short or a fire, damage equipment, or give someone a nasty shock.

Always use the transformer specified by the equipment manufacturer. The line-voltage connection to the transformer must—like all line-voltage splices or connections—be made within an electrical box. This can be a new or existing junction box in an accessible area, such as basement or unfinished attic.

penetration with nails and screws. Where this is not feasible, protect cables with metal plates designed for that purpose. As you run wire and begin to think of the probable functions of each framed-out room, consider other electrical lines that might be threaded through the walls. See "Related Wiring" on the opposite page.

Use staples to anchor cables to framing within 8 inches of each box and every 4 feet where cables run along studs or other framing members. Staples are sized according to the number and gauge of wires they'll hold, up to as many as four cables at once; see *Photo 12-1* on page 247 (top).

In cases where surface-mounted equipment, such as a baseboard heater or fluorescent light, is to be installed after finish walls are in place, run cables to the location, staple them to the side of a stud, and leave an adequate coil of extra within the framing. Mark the subfloor so this spot can be located later if it is accidentally covered with drywall.

At a box, at least 8 inches of wire should be left extending beyond its face. Use a cable stripper to slice through the outer sheathing, as shown in *Photo 12-2* on page 247 (bottom), then cut the insulation off the individual wires with a combination tool, as shown in *Photo 12-3* on the opposite page. It's a good idea to label all wires, identifying the circuit number and what you intend to place there. Information that seems obvious when walls are open can be baffling weeks later, when you return to complete the wiring and you're staring at brand new drywall.

Metal boxes conduct electricity, and the bare ground wire of NM cable must be connected to a grounding screw in the box and the grounding terminal on the device or receptacle. When more than one wire is to be secured to any terminal, connect the wires to a single pigtail that runs to the terminal. (The metal sheathing of armored cable is bonded to the box and grounded at the service panel, thus providing the necessary ground.)

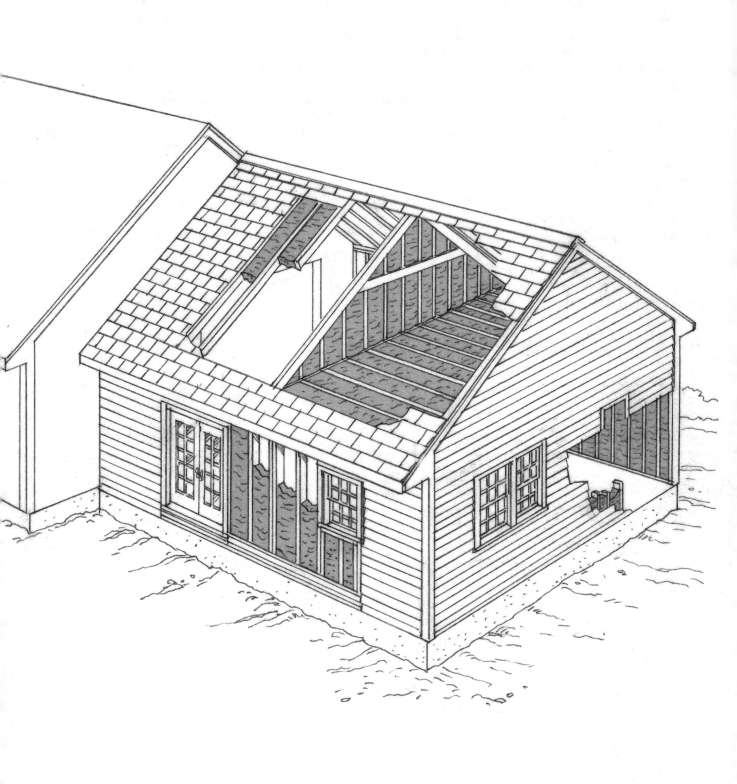

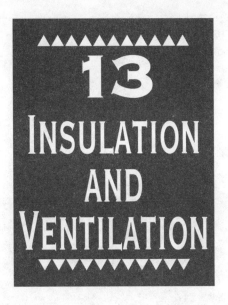

13

INSULATION AND VENTILATION

An addition can do more than increase your living space. It can increase your comfort—if you give some thought to insulation and ventilation and make use of technologies that may not have been available when your house was built.

Insulation is the system that creates a thermal envelope around a living space. The resistance of this envelope to the transmission of heat is expressed as its *R-value*. The higher the R-value, the better your living areas will retain heat in winter and exclude it in the summer.

Insulative materials are installed in floors, walls, and ceilings to slow the flow of heat through the home's perimeter. They work by trapping air or other gases to resist heat transfer. These materials must be coupled with sealing materials to envelope the home, slowing the *infiltration* of air. A house, being a complex assembly of hundreds of parts, tends to be leaky. There may be all sorts of opportunities for inside and outside air to sneak through walls. Some exchange is necessary; otherwise, we'd all die of suffocation or at least find rooms to be stuffy. But wise use of sealing materials, such as vapor barriers and caulk, along with careful construction will make a tighter, more comfortable addition and one that is cheaper to heat and cool.

The subject of insulation tends to suffer from the out-of-sight, out-of-mind syndrome. There are more-interesting, more-visible ways to allocate your construction budget. But a well-insulated living space will pay back the money invested over time; and a certain level of insulation in walls and windows may be required by code as well. Check into these regulations as you explore other areas of the building code.

Insulation is often planned along with another important aspect of the home environment—*ventilation*. This involves encouraging the movement of air to and from the appropriate places. An addition's ventilation system may include vents (in the crawl space, basement, soffits, gable ends, and ridge) and fans vented to the outside.

The goal of the ventilation system is to remove cool, damp air or hot air from enclosed but uninhabited areas of the addition. Dampness can condense to cause water damage to framing, sheathing, and, in severe conditions,

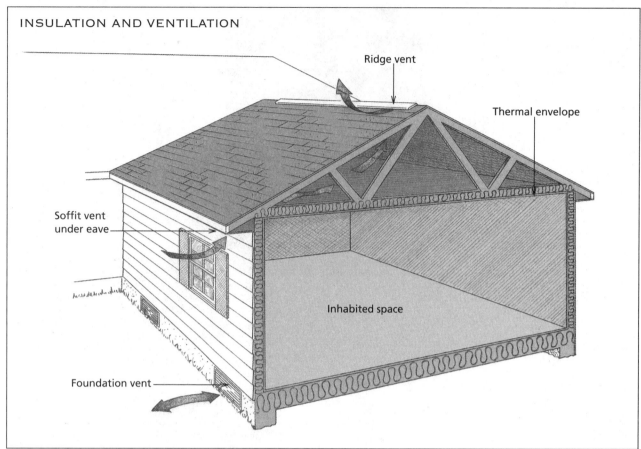

INSULATION AND VENTILATION

Ridge vent

Thermal envelope

Soffit vent under eave

Inhabited space

Foundation vent

Photo 13-1. Wrestling with fiberglass batts isn't for everybody. But the work goes quickly, and the long-term comfort and the energy savings make the job worthwhile.

finished interior areas. Unvented hot air in an area bordering the living space, such as an attic, can radiate heat into the house, forcing the cooling system to work harder or making you uncomfortable.

Some ventilation systems are passive, relying on breezes or the convection of warm air. Others add fans to keep air moving. Beyond these needs, the entire living area, kitchens and bathrooms in particular, must have a regular exchange of inside air.

Insulation and Ventilation above shows the location of the thermal envelope in a one-story, gable-end addition and notes air flow through ventilated, uninhabited areas.

Is insulating and ventilating your addition a job you can handle? For starters, consider that nearly 90 percent of the insulation sold in the United States is fiberglass—the material used in the Baileys' addition—so odds are you'd be involved with this material.

Some people find fiberglass very unpleasant. They seem to get itchy just looking at it. And the extremely fine fibers can find their way into your lungs and skin, so precautions must be taken when working with fiberglass, as described in "Dressed to Fill" on page 258. On the positive side, most insulation work is relatively easy and requires few tools.

Also, you can put extra care into doing the work just right, while a contractor's hired hands might not. The work in progress at the Baileys is shown in *Photo 13-1* on the opposite page.

Keep in mind that this is a time-sensitive job—insulation is sandwiched in between closing in the exterior and applying drywall or other interior surfaces. Add to this the involvement of plumbers and electricians, who will be working intensively on the same wall cavities in which insulation will go. To avoid gumming up the construction process, the team responsible for insulation should be prepared to get in and out fairly quickly.

Ventilation is a more difficult matter. To get involved with this system, you have to deal with other areas of construction. Vents are installed as parts of the foundation, roofing, and siding. Wall, ceiling, and whole-house fans involve electrical and perhaps framing work.

TYPES OF INSULATION

Form	Material	R-Value	Where Applied	Other Information
Blankets and batts	Fiberglass	Between R-11 and R-38, depending on the thickness and density	Floors, walls, and ceilings	Fiberglass is the most-used do-it-yourself insulation. Blankets are easily cut to size with a utility knife; batts come in precut lengths. Blankets and batts are available with or without facing, sometimes called a vapor barrier (though not a good one). The materials can be irritating to work with.
Loose fill	Vermiculite Perlite Cellulose fiber	R-2.0 per inch R-2.7 per inch R-3.7 per inch	As fill in odd-shaped and hard-to-reach areas	Vermiculite and perlite are often used in cavities of concrete blocks; cellulose is often used as fill between attic joists. Cellulose is highly flammable unless chemically treated.
Blown in	Cellulose fiber Urethane foam	R-3.7 per inch R-5.3 per inch	Floors, walls, and ceilings	These are most often blown in by professionals, though homeowners can apply small amounts of urethane foam from spray cans. Urethane cures to create its own vapor barrier; in a fire, it emits harmful fumes. Cellulose is highly flammable unless chemically treated.
Rigid boards	Polystyrene Polyurethane Isocyanurate	R-3.45 per inch R-5.3 per inch R-7.0 per inch	Basement masonry walls, exterior walls, or under siding	These materials have high R-values for relatively little thickness. They are highly flammable and easy to dent; create a vapor barrier once they're in place. The materials are easy to cut to size and are often used below grade.

CHOOSING INSULATION MATERIALS

Although fiberglass has much of the insulation market, there are other materials that may work better in certain applications. Most types of insulation fit into one of four categories: blankets or batts, loose fill, blown-in foam, and rigid boards. See the table "Types of Insulation" on page 253.

The first step in deciding what type of insulation you need is to figure out the R-values you're after. Begin by learning the levels required by code and the levels typically used in new construction in your region. General insulation zones are suggested by the illustration *R-Value Map* below. The U.S. Department of Energy

recommends higher R-values in ceilings of homes with electric resistance heat because this system is more expensive to run.

Don't accept conventional or code-mandated levels of insulation as givens. You might want to go beyond them to make your addition more comfortable, to lower heating bills, or to conserve energy. An exceptionally well-insulated addition may even spare you the expense of having to upgrade your existing heating system if it doesn't now have much excess capacity.

INSTALLING INSULATION

Although fiberglass insulation is a near-universal choice in home

construction, it isn't quite a generic product. First, you have a choice of R-values, thicknesses, and forms. *Batts,* shown in *Photo 13-2* on the opposite page (top), are lengths that have been precut for convenience; a *blanket* is a single rolled-up strip that must be cut to length on site. The width of most batts and blankets is sized to fit snugly between standard 16-inch on-center framing members. You also can buy 23-inch-wide insulation to go between rafters.

Fiberglass can be had with or without *facing,* a thin layer that serves as a vapor barrier and typically extends beyond the insulative material to provide a border for stapling to framing members. The barrier must be on the side of the living

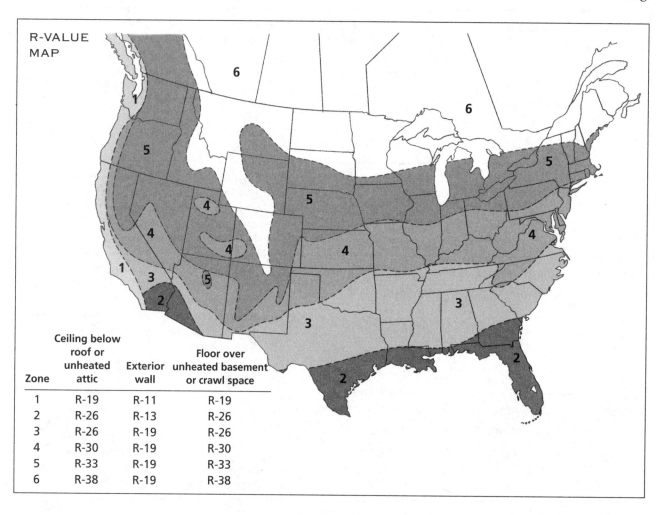

R-VALUE MAP

Zone	Ceiling below roof or unheated attic	Exterior wall	Floor over unheated basement or crawl space
1	R-19	R-11	R-19
2	R-26	R-13	R-26
3	R-26	R-19	R-26
4	R-30	R-19	R-30
5	R-33	R-19	R-33
6	R-38	R-19	R-38

space. In walls and between roof rafters, the barrier should face *toward* the living space to keep the moist air in the home from settling in the cavity within the framing. Between floor joists of an unfinished, unheated attic or between joists spanning an unheated basement, the barrier must be *away* from you, so you can access the framing for wiring and the like.

To cut blankets to length, use a utility knife and a metal straightedge or scrap wood to guide it, as shown in *Photo 13-3* on the right (bottom).

Drive staples with a staple gun or a staple hammer, spacing them every 6 inches. See the sequence of steps in *Photos 13-4 through 13-6* on page 256.

When installing batts face up in a basement ceiling, the stapling strips aren't accessible to you. You can keep the insulation in place with wire supports, which are sold already cut or which you can clip from coat hangers. For joists on 16-inch centers, cut straight 15-inch-lengths of wire. As you lift the batt in place, push wire every 16 inches or so, as shown in the illustration *Wire Braces* on page 257 (top).

In a basement or crawl space that is prone to wetness, especially if it has an earth or gravel floor, you should add the protection of a 4-mil polyethylene barrier. Lay the barrier on the floor, overlapping the sheets about 6 inches, and use duct tape to secure them to the walls at the end of each course. Secure the seams with bricks or stones.

Note that unfaced batts are used as a top layer when adding a second layer of insulation, above faced insulation, on the unfinished floor of an attic; they also can be stuffed into less-than-

Photo 13-2. You can buy fiberglass insulation precut into 8-foot lengths for easier installation between studs.

Photo 13-3. Cut blankets to length with a utility knife. A piece of scrap wood or a metal straightedge serves to both guide the blade and compress the bulky material for easier cutting.

Photo 13-4. Position the batt so that the fiberglass is contained within the framing cavity.

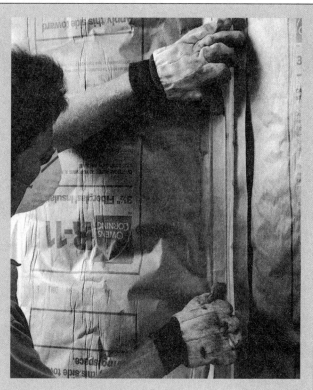

Photo 13-5. Fold out the flaps on either edge of the batt so they overlap the framing.

Photo 13-6. Attach the batt with staples spaced every 6 inches.

standard openings wherever they occur. If unfaced batts will be used in place of the faced product, include a polyethylene vapor barrier on the side where the facing would normally be.

At the Baileys' addition, most of the insulative value was invested in the ceilings. This is as it should be. Heat rises, and a home will tend to lose most of its warmth through ceilings and the roof. The Baileys' ceilings were cloaked with 9½-inch-thick fiberglass batts for an R-value of 30.

If you have an unfinished attic floor, you can achieve an R-value over 40 by using batts of this thickness between joists, then running 3½-inch-thick batts perpendicular over them. Arranging the top layer in this way ensures that the joists, and not the drywall ceiling, carry the added weight.

If you intend for the attic of the addition to be a comfortable living space, then the insulative perimeter follows the roof rafters. If there will be knee walls, this space can be insulated by continuing the insulation down the rafters to the eaves. Or you can insulate the knee wall and place batts face down between the floor joists behind these low walls, as shown in *Insulating an Attic Room* below. For more on insulating top floors, see Chapter 7.

Remember, the goal is to create a thermal envelope around the perimeter of the living areas. So, just as you shouldn't insulate an interior partition wall (a wall dividing the living space into rooms), neither should you insulate the finished floor shown in the illustration. You're also spared having to insulate the

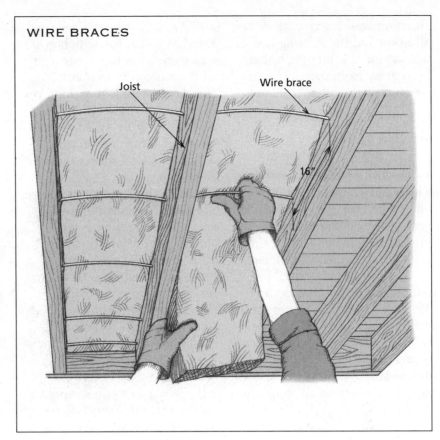

WIRE BRACES

Joist

Wire brace

16"

INSULATING AN ATTIC ROOM

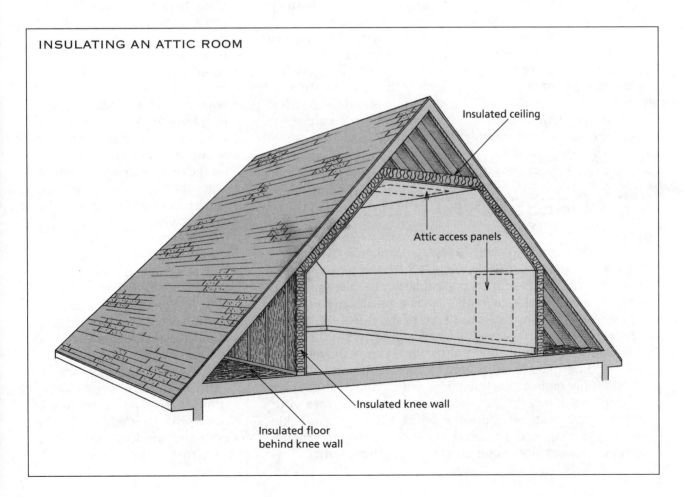

Insulated ceiling

Attic access panels

Insulated knee wall

Insulated floor behind knee wall

common wall between an addition and the existing house, unless you're insulating to help keep noise from traveling from one side to the other.

ACHIEVING HIGHER R-VALUES

The standard insulation job once called for 3½-inch batts between 2 x 4 studs, yielding a modest R-value of 11. But the standard may not be sufficient to satisfy either your needs or the prevailing building code. R-19 is often given as an optimum wall rating, and there are a few ways to coax that performance from a framed wall, as shown in *Insulating Walls to Achieve an R-19 Rating* on the opposite page (top).

The first option is to frame a wall with 2 x 6s, a technique many builders have adopted. Although 2 x 6 framing is more costly, using 6-inch fiberglass batts means saving the time and expense of a two-step alternative.

Another alternative is to use conventional 2 x 4 framing and 3½-inch fiberglass batts rated at R-15, for which you pay somewhat more per unit of R-value; coupled with standard ½-inch sheathing on the exterior (at an R of 0.625) and 1-inch polystyrene board over the sheathing (adding 3.45), this wall meets the R-19 goal.

The third option is to use urethane foam, which is sprayed in place by a professional contractor. Rated at R-18.55 for a 3½-inch cavity, urethane allows you to use 2 x 4 framing with only a ½-inch skin of sheathing needed to complete the R-19 requirement. (Note that in a fire, urethane foam emits harmful gases.)

Why can't you simply stuff a thicker fiberglass batt into a 2 x 4 wall? Fiberglass loses much of its insulating ability if compressed. Remember, dead air does the real work, not the pink scratchy stuff; fiberglass is simply the structure that keeps that air motionless. Mash it down, and the R-value plummets.

The energy crunch of the 1970s helped to inspire builders and homeowners to go beyond ordinary framing in exploring better ways to conserve a home's heat, as explained in "Superinsulation" on page 261.

TIGHTENING UP

Although the lion's share of the insulating job involves dealing with large areas, don't neglect the little ones. As a window is installed in its rough opening, for instance, there is a gap (see Chapter 9) that needs to be filled and sealed.

For sealing the gaps between rough framing and the jambs of windows, doors, and skylights, use unbacked fiberglass. Sprayed urethane foam can also be used, but it should be a special low-expansion type to avoid pushing against frames enough to interfere with the operation of doors and windows. Temporarily bracing the jambs with scrap wood will prevent this from happening, as shown in *Foaming a Window* on the opposite page (bottom). Once the foam is dry and has hardened, trim it flush with a utility knife.

Weather stripping is a standard item that helps to ensure a home is well sealed. It comes in a variety of forms: rolls of self-adhesive foam strips; springy metal strips that compress as doors and windows close; thick felt, which gets tacked in place; and vinyl and rubber gaskets. If weather stripping doesn't come with your addition's new door and window units, you'll have to look into these options.

DRESSED TO FILL

Before working with fiberglass insulation, be sure to get a dust mask specifically designed for this type of work. Check product labeling on the insulation to make sure you buy the right type of mask. Fit the mask to your face carefully so the tiny fibers can't get past the seal. Be sure to protect your skin as well. Wear long pants and a long-sleeved shirt, goggles, and tightly woven work gloves.

If fiberglass finds its way to your skin, don't scratch. You'll only embed the fibers into your skin. When you've finished the job (or can't stand it anymore), rinse your skin in cold water to close the pores, then blot your skin gently to remove the fibers. Be sure to launder the towels and your work clothes separately from other wash.

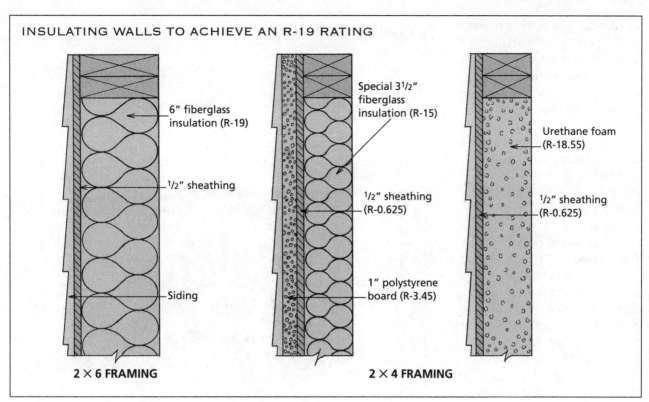

INSULATING WALLS TO ACHIEVE AN R-19 RATING

6" fiberglass insulation (R-19)

1/2" sheathing

Siding

2 × 6 FRAMING

Special 31/2" fiberglass insulation (R-15)

1/2" sheathing (R-0.625)

1" polystyrene board (R-3.45)

2 × 4 FRAMING

Urethane foam (R-18.55)

1/2" sheathing (R-0.625)

WRAPPING UP WITH A VAPOR BARRIER

The perimeter of the house may have two paper-thin layers that are important elements of the insulation and ventilation. *House wrap,* discussed in Chapter 19, is used on the outside of the walls as an aid to blocking wind penetration. It is permeable to water vapor (the gaseous form of water), however, so that moisture is not trapped within walls. A *vapor barrier* is intended to be nearly impermeable to water vapor, and it is used on the inside surface of walls to protect them from the ill effects of condensing water vapor.

While the facing on fiberglass insulation serves as a partial vapor barrier, it is best to include another barrier over the batts for better resistance to moisture damage. A family

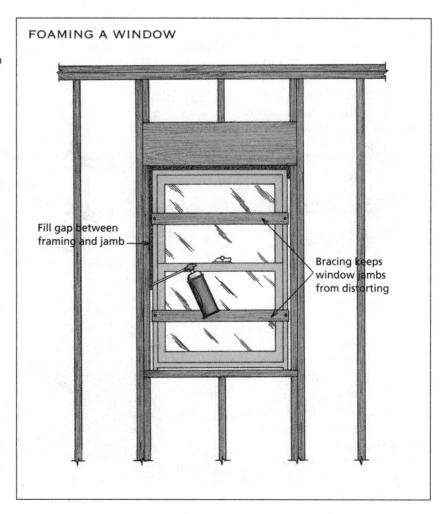

FOAMING A WINDOW

Fill gap between framing and jamb

Bracing keeps window jambs from distorting

creates a good deal of moisture in the process of cooking, cleaning, washing and drying clothes, and bathing. Once water vapor gets into exterior walls, it can condense into water on insulation, framing, and sheathing. Wet insulation conducts heat flow. And condensed moisture can contribute to the decay of framing and sheathing materials.

Use 4-mil polyethylene for a vapor barrier. It comes in 3-foot-wide rolls that unfold to widths ranging up to 20 feet. Lengths can be cut as needed. Overlap these widths by one stud cavity as you staple the plastic to the framing. Around window and door framing, however, trim back the vapor barrier so that it overlaps the last rough framing member—jack studs, header, or sill—around the opening. Then run a continuous bead of silicone caulk on the framing under the plastic and staple through both the plastic and caulk to create a good seal.

Silicone caulk is also a good choice for sealing electrical boxes and other fixtures. *Cutting around a Small Opening* on the right (top) shows how to begin.

Using the fixture itself as a guide, cut the barrier around its inside edge. Work carefully, so the opening you make closely matches the fixture's shape. Then, embed the plastic in a continuous bead of silicone caulk around the outside of the fixture.

Run the vapor barrier 3 or 4 inches onto the floor and ceiling to make a good seal. Staple the barrier tightly into floor and ceiling corners, to avoid causing problems when installing drywall.

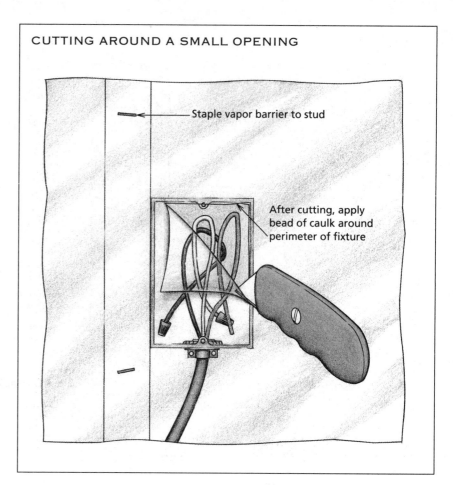

CUTTING AROUND A SMALL OPENING

Staple vapor barrier to stud

After cutting, apply bead of caulk around perimeter of fixture

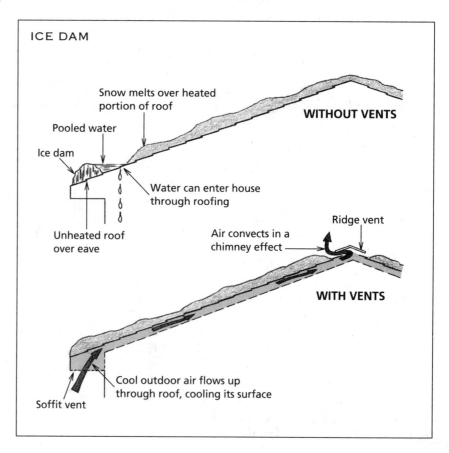

ICE DAM

Snow melts over heated portion of roof

Pooled water

Ice dam

WITHOUT VENTS

Water can enter house through roofing

Unheated roof over eave

Air convects in a chimney effect

Ridge vent

WITH VENTS

Cool outdoor air flows up through roof, cooling its surface

Soffit vent

▶ SUPERINSULATION

The energy crunch of the mid-1970s triggered wide interest in heating and cooling homes more efficiently. "Superinsulation" was a term coined to describe houses with lots of extra insulation, and the construction details needed to accommodate it. Super-insulating usually meant building two frames for exterior walls, blocking the outer frame away from the inner one so insulation could be used between the two, and then insulating the outer frame as well.

In the enthusiasm of overinsulating and stopping air infiltration, some builders used plastic sheets over the sheathing as air barriers. This had the effect of trapping moisture in the wall, damaging framing. And inside the house, homeowners reported feeling lethargic or sickened because the interior air was so efficiently trapped.

Superinsulation technology has experienced quite an evolution since then. Thin, papery layers called house wraps are now used to arrest air while allowing moisture to pass harmlessly through exterior walls. Chapter 10 covers the use of house wrap.

VENTILATING WITH VENTS AND FANS

The potential problems caused by moisture from inside the home are at the heart of ventilation theory and practice. Much of the job of ventilating an addition can be done with simple vents—screened or slotted openings in basement and crawl space walls, soffits (the ledges under a roof's overhang), and ridges (the uppermost part, or peak, of a gable roof). Installing vents is discussed in Chapters 8 and 10.

Attics require ventilation for cooling and to carry off water vapor. In summer, soaring attic temperatures can radiate heat into adjacent living spaces unless the attic is well vented. Hot air under the roof will convect up through the ridge vent in a continuous stream; soffit venting below promotes this flow.

This flow of air is also an asset in winter since it can help to prevent ice dams. Ice dams form in a simple but insidious process. Warmed by escaping heat from the house, snow on the roof melts; it runs down to the eaves, which are cooler because they aren't above an enclosed, heated space; this water then turns to ice. Water backed up behind this ice dam can penetrate the roofing material and enter the house, as illustrated in *Ice Dam* on the opposite page (bottom).

If you do a very good job of providing a vapor barrier for the addition, a side effect is that you create a need to vent noxious fumes and vapors given off within the living area—indoor pollution, in other words. Most traditionally built homes are leaky enough for this not to be a problem, and omitting the vapor barrier from ceilings usually permits enough air exchanges to counteract this effect. Still, if you're chemically sensitive, additional fresh air may be needed. The solution is an air-to-air heat exchanger. This device replaces stale indoor air with fresh outside air. The incoming air is heated by the outgoing air, helping to conserve energy.

Exhaust fans for kitchens and bathrooms are not only sensible but are also required by most building codes. Kitchen fans vent to the outside, or clean the air through change-able filters; bathroom fans may vent to the outside or to the attic. The wiring of these fans should be done as part of the rough electrical work for your addition, as explained in Chapter 12. Also see the illustration *Whole-House Fan* on page 269.

A fan may also be needed to encourage evaporation of moisture from an extremely damp crawl space. First, however, try installing a vapor barrier over the floor.

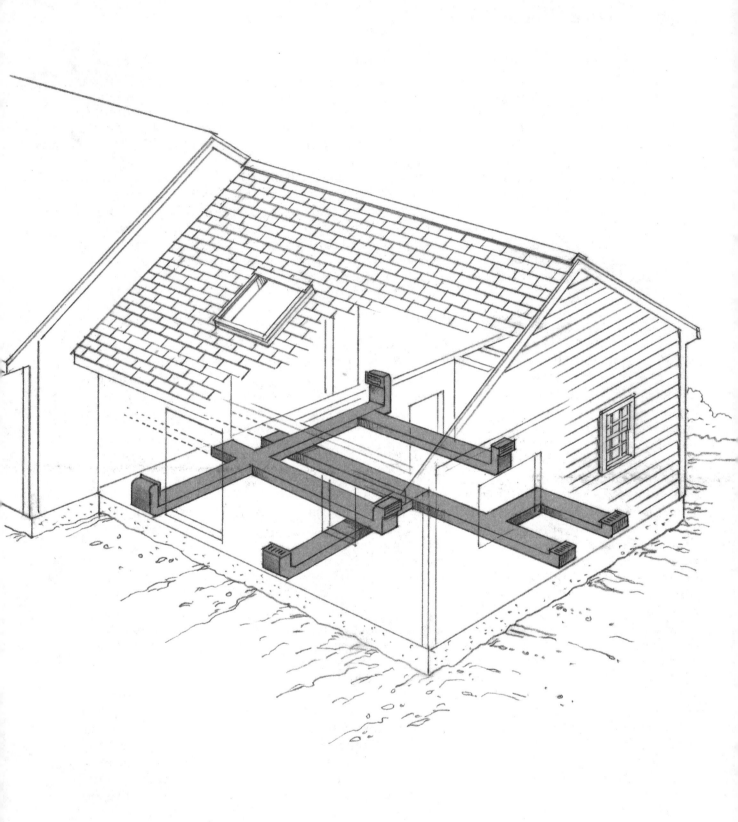

14
HEATING AND COOLING

Years ago, heating a house was simple. You didn't have a lot of choices—you burned whatever fuel was around. If a family lived near the woods, they burned wood. If they lived near coal, they burned coal. Then as trains, tankers, and pipelines began transporting fuel, the options proliferated.

Over the past 25 years, the technology of heating and cooling has really taken off, in part because of dramatic rises in the price of fuel. Choosing a heating system has become something of an ordeal. You have to choose not only the fuel but also the product that will convert that fuel into heat or cool air. (Even fireplaces have come a long way; see "Are Fireplaces Thermal Disasters" on page 266). As a result, it's up to you to learn a bit about fuel efficiency, heating zones,

and heat load calculations even if you don't have to buy a new system to handle the load of the addition.

The simplest scenario is to have a small addition that is only partly walled off from the house and will be comfortable without having to introduce any heating or cooling at all. However, chances are good that you, like the Baileys, will have to do more than that to moderate temperatures in the new living space. (The Baileys were able to extend ducts from their existing system to do the job.)

Another option is to add a new, independent system to serve the addition only. Or, as you investigate the capacity and efficiency of your home's unit, you may decide that now would be a good time to replace the existing unit with a more recent model or change to another fuel altogether.

HEATING WITH HOT WATER

Heating systems can be broken down into those that heat water and those that heat air.

Units that heat water are called *hydronic*. (Steam heat is also hydronic, but its use has declined over the past few decades.) Water is heated in a boiler, fired most often by natural gas, oil, or coal. Although this is regular household tap water, it doesn't share the home plumbing system. Instead, it travels in pipes of its own system.

As the heated water circulates through the house, it is encouraged to give up its heat in radiators or pipes that course through floors and ceilings; see the illustration *Hydronic System* on page 264. It then circulates back to the boiler to be heated again. A home may

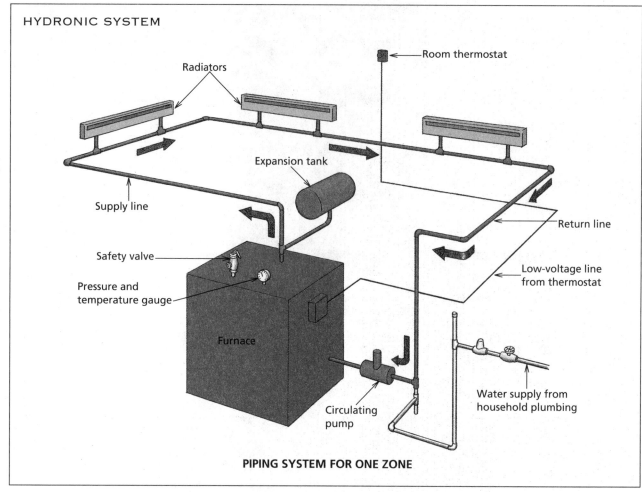

HYDRONIC SYSTEM

Radiators

Room thermostat

Expansion tank

Supply line

Return line

Safety valve

Low-voltage line
from thermostat

Pressure and
temperature gauge

Furnace

Water supply from
household plumbing

Circulating
pump

PIPING SYSTEM FOR ONE ZONE

have one or more of these loops, called *zones,* each with its own circulating pump to propel the water and a thermostat to turn the pump on and off as necessary to maintain the air temperature within the range you've set.

You may be able to heat a very modest-sized addition by extending an existing zone, if that zone has spare capacity; this is the least-expensive alternative. But you probably will want to be able to control heat in the new living space. If the addition has two or more major rooms or more than one level, consider having two new zones.

There are all sorts of radiators. The traditional material is cast iron, but you

don't have to settle for the clunky behemoths of old.

▲▲▲▲▲▲▲▲▲▲

To see whether your old system can handle the increased demands of heating and cooling an addition, have your utility company or an HVAC contractor run an efficiency and capacity check on the system.

▼▼▼▼▼▼▼▼▼▼

You now can buy slim-profile, wall-mounted radiators in a wide range of colors; rather than slouch along the floor, these radiators are hung like

works of art, and their relatively high cost reflects that.

Today's conventional systems have baseboard radiators consisting of aluminum fins soldered to sections of copper pipes; the finned tubes are delicate and protected within a metal casing. But whatever kind of radiator you use, its function is to speed the transfer of heat from the water to your rooms.

If you don't have the space for a baseboard radiator in an area that needs the heat, investigate fan-assisted kick-space radiators. These incorporate a small, relatively quiet electric fan that pushes air through the fins, dramatically increasing the transfer of heat. The fan is automatically controlled by a thermostat in the heating unit itself so that it will come on only when hot water is being pumped through the zone. When the wall thermostat dictates that no hot water is circulating through that zone, the heater fan stays off automatically.

The plumbing pipes themselves can transfer heat to the living space, if they are long enough. By passing them back and forth within floors, the floor becomes a radiator. The pipes can be embedded in a poured slab, or tubes with fins can be attached to the underside of a wooden floor.

Hydronic systems have many advantages. First, they don't push volumes of warm air around in the manner of a forced hot-air system (see "Heating with Forced Air" below). They require minimal maintenance. Best of all, the delivery pipes are not bulky (as are hot-air ducts) and can be placed easily within walls. The disadvantages are that you can't cool with a hydronic system and you can't clean the air with in-line filters as you can with a forced-air system.

HEATING WITH FORCED AIR

Forced-air systems have electric fans that drive air through ductwork within the framework of the house and into the living space. Planning for the ductwork is tricky. You not only have to install delivery ducts to carry hot air to in-wall *registers* but you also have to install return ducts and floor *grills* to take air back to the furnace, as shown in the illustration *Forced-Air System* on the right. To run

▶ WOOD OR COAL HEATING

Wood and coal stoves are probably best suited as secondary heating sources that you don't have to depend on all the time. Before deciding to heat your addition solely with wood or coal, take a hard look at what this would entail.

One of the hassles is storing and transporting the fuel. Wood and coal are bulky, and wood litters the floor wherever it is handled. There are also ashes. Ashes are light and easily become airborne, which means they probably will be distributed as a fine dust all over the addition. And you have to dispose of ashes regularly, throughout the heating season.

Finally, you face the challenge of keeping the stove stoked. Some people enjoy this; others don't. If you burn coal, you might be able to get away with fueling the stove only twice daily. But wood burns faster than coal, and you have to be willing to stoke the fire throughout the day.

If you decide to heat with a stove, get good advice on sizing the unit. Any stove has a temperature at which it works most efficiently, and that temperature should correspond with keeping your addition comfortable—neither too hot nor too cold.

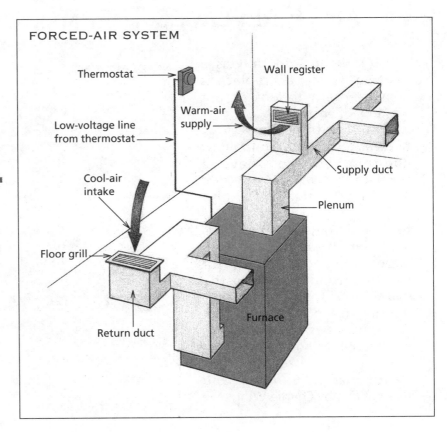

FORCED-AIR SYSTEM

Thermostat

Wall register

Low-voltage line from thermostat

Warm-air supply

Supply duct

Cool-air intake

Plenum

Floor grill

Return duct

Furnace

ducts to your addition, you will probably need to tap into an existing branch after you figure how much more fan power you'll need to drive the air all the way to the new area.

If your addition is built on a slab, rather than over a basement or crawl space, you may have trouble accommodating ducts. They will have to be run in the ceiling or through fattened walls, and this has to be taken into consideration when you plan the framing of the addition.

There are a couple of advantages to this type of heat distribution—you get warmth more quickly than with a hydronic system, and the air can be cleaned with filters. And some of these systems can also double as air conditioners. A disadvantage is that the room quickly cools after the thermostat shuts off the warm air; you don't have radiators or adjacent room surfaces and furnishings to continue radiating heat.

HEATING WITH ELECTRICITY

Rooms can be heated in the same way that a toaster heats bread—by running electricity through special wires that are intended to glow red-hot. Electric baseboards are inexpensive and easy enough to install for a reasonably adept do-it-yourselfer. If you choose units that come with thermostats, you don't even have to route wire to a wall-mounted thermostat. Each room—even each side of a large room—can be its own zone. There are no supply pipes or ducts needed, just wires within walls. If your addition is on a slab, this would be a system to consider.

All of these advantages sound great. But there is a big drawback that has kept electric baseboards from rendering other heating systems obsolete. They are relatively expensive to run; just how expensive will depend on local rates for electricity.

Electric baseboards find their best application as back-up heat sources for other less-expensive types of heat. In particular, you can use them to supplement single-source heaters; see "Wood or Coal Heating" on page 265. Electric baseboards are more attractive in warmer climates, where homeowners don't need heat all winter long.

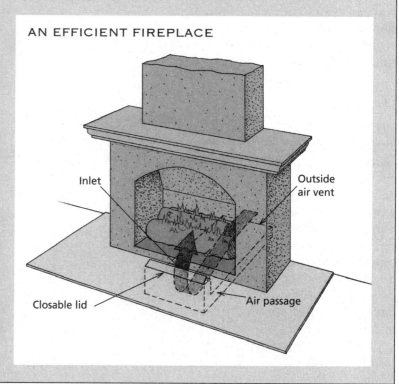

▶ ARE FIREPLACES THERMAL DISASTERS?

It's often said that as a heating device, a fireplace is archaic—pretty to look at, but wasteful of energy.

But with some extra planning as you build your addition, you can have a fireplace that will not only give you cheerful flames but also heat. By adding a passageway to bring in outside air to burn, as shown in *An Efficient Fireplace* on the right, you prevent the fire from consuming the warm interior air and thereby drawing in the cold air through doors, windows, and cracks. For information on how to design an efficient fireplace, see *The Visual Handbook of Building and Remodeling* by Charlie Wing.

AN EFFICIENT FIREPLACE

Inlet

Outside air vent

Closable lid

Air passage

HEATING AND COOLING WITH A HEAT PUMP

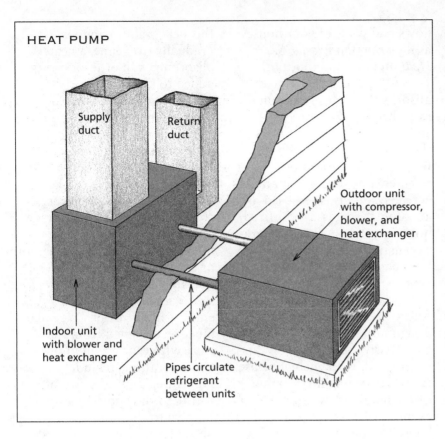

HEAT PUMP

Supply duct

Return duct

Outdoor unit with compressor, blower, and heat exchanger

Indoor unit with blower and heat exchanger

Pipes circulate refrigerant between units

Heat pumps are often discussed as a revolutionary method of getting free heat. This isn't quite accurate. Heat pumps are simply appliances that work like backward air conditioners. Imagine turning a window air conditioner around so that it pumped hot air into your home. In cool weather, a heat pump does just that by using a refrigerant to absorb heat from outside the house and pumping it inside for distribution as forced hot air. Like an air conditioner, a pump also can be run in reverse, taking heat from within the home and exhausting it outdoors. See the illustration *Heat Pump* on the left.

You don't often find heat

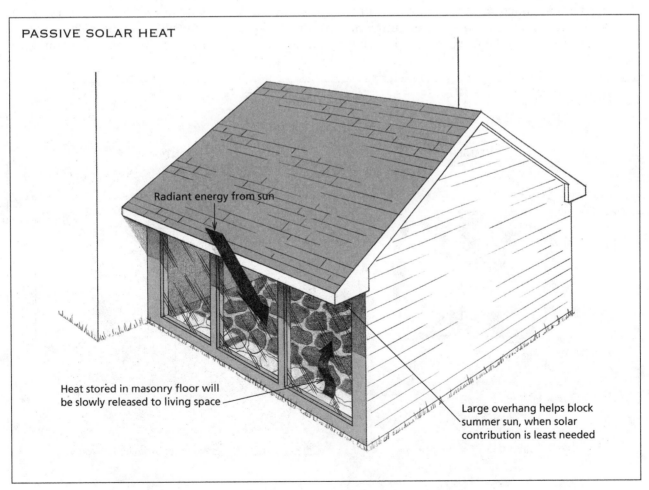

PASSIVE SOLAR HEAT

Radiant energy from sun

Heat stored in masonry floor will be slowly released to living space

Large overhang helps block summer sun, when solar contribution is least needed

pumps in very cold climates for a good reason: They can't take much heat from frigid outside air. So only people who live in more-moderate climates will find heat pumps economical; and these people will be the ones who benefit more from the heat pump as an air conditioner.

MAKING USE OF SOLAR HEAT

Solar energy has one big plus and one big minus as a heat source. The heat is free. But this is a very diffuse energy source, and it's only around part of every 24-hour cycle. As a result, you have to gather it with big collectors, store it up for cloudy or nighttime use, and conserve it with excellent insulation.

Solar-energy collection is described as either active, relying on dedicated collectors, or passive, relying on the win-dows and walls of your house, as illustrated in *Passive Solar Heat* on page 267 (bottom).

A typical active system absorbs the heat of the sun's rays through rooftop collectors or large windows; it then stores the heat as hot water or hot air and dis-tributes it as forced hot air. An active system is often used as an adjunct to gas- or oil-fired hot-air systems. This system is expensive to install and has a long *payback period* (the time it takes to earn back your investment in energy savings). And you need a specialist to design and install it.

Passive solar heat, on the other hand, is an energy we use every day. Sunlight streaming through a window is an example of passive solar heat. A house can be designed to take greater advantage of the sun by orienting most of its windows to face roughly south. To store this heat and distribute it gradually over time, a heat-absorbing wall or floor can be added to the design.

Passive systems are rarely the sole energy source, but they are excellent as a supplemental companion to fuel-based systems. A built-in problem with passive solar applications is that the very collectors that take advantage of the sun are difficult to insulate well; you can lose a lot of energy through them when the sun isn't shining.

An addition that will employ active or passive solar must be designed from the start with that use in mind. Considerations include everything from the size of the soffits to the addition's site, relative to the sun and obstacles that will cast shade. Consult with an architect who is well versed on solar design at an early stage of planning.

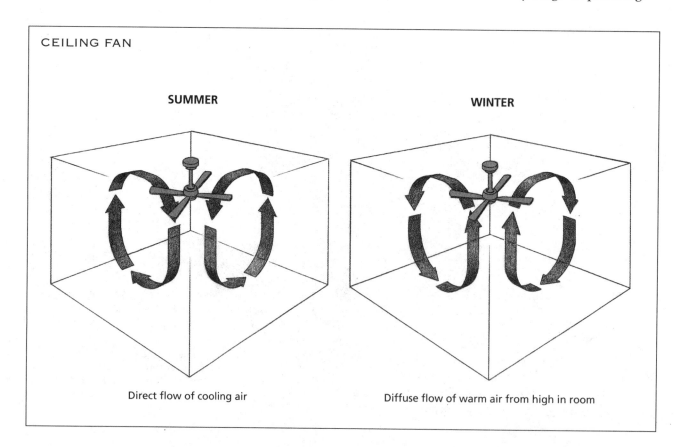

CEILING FAN

SUMMER

WINTER

Direct flow of cooling air

Diffuse flow of warm air from high in room

KEEPING COOL

There are three ways to cool an addition. You can install in-window air conditioners, you can blow cool air through ducts from a central air-conditioning unit, or you can suck naturally cool air from beneath your house up into the living space.

In-window air conditioners are simple enough to install, and they spare you the trouble and expense of running ductwork through the addition. The big question is how big the air conditioner should be. A dealer should be able to project your needs, based on rough estimates of square feet.

A whole-house unit is considerably larger. The conserver unit is installed outside the home on a concrete pad. Inside, there is an evaporator and blower. Cool air is distributed by fans through ductwork. As you plan an addition, you might decide that this is the time to install the whole-house system you've been living without.

If you've already been cooling your home with a whole-house forced-air air-conditioning system, you can connect it to the addition with ducts and perhaps upgrade it by increasing the capacity of the system's supply fans. If your forced-air system delivers heat only, then the cooling function will require an evaporator coil in the furnace and a condensing unit somewhere outside the building. Refrigeration piping connects these two. Ask an HVAC (heat, ventilation, and air conditioning) contractor to tell you what your system is capable of. You may be able to adapt it for cooling, while at the same time upgrading it to heat the addition.

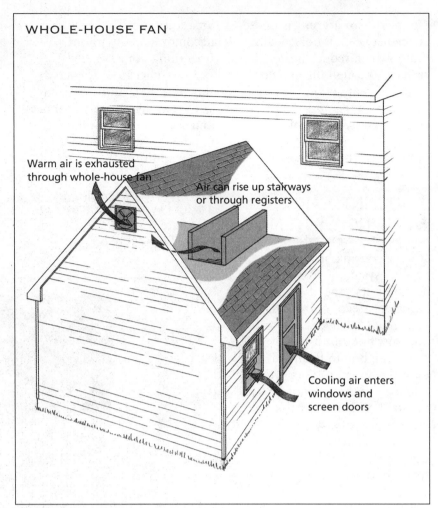

Warm air is exhausted through whole-house fan

Air can rise up stairways or through registers

Cooling air enters windows and screen doors

USING FANS FOR MORE COMFORT

Fans don't heat or cool air (beyond the negligible heat produced by the motors), but if they are reversible, they can make an addition feel more comfortable in any season.

A ceiling fan circulates air in a primarily vertical path. In summer, it can be used to send a cooling breeze down on the people below; in winter, it can distribute warm air that collects at the ceiling. In this way, a ceiling fan may save you money by allowing you to rely less on a heating or cooling system. See the illustration *Ceiling Fan* on the opposite page.

A whole-house fan draws cooler outside air up through the house and is especially valuable for moderating summer temperatures on the top floor. See the illustration *Whole-House Fan* above. Even an operable skylight will help by serving as a warm-air chimney; warm air is lighter than cooler air and tends to rise out the skylight, bringing in cooler air from below.

Windows can contribute their share to keeping the addition comfortable. Windows with glazing termed low-E are coated to reduce heat transfer. Windows with this glazing cost more, but they help to retain heat in winter and reduce the sun's influence on indoor temperatures in summer.

Coupled with argon gas in the space between double glazing, a window can reduce heat transfer through the glass by up to 65 percent. Though the payback on the added cost of these windows may take a few years, the windows will add to your comfort in the meantime.

TYING INTO AN EXISTING SYSTEM

If your existing heating-and-cooling system is to serve an addition, its capacity must be sufficient. Second, there must be a way to deliver the warm or cool air; find out if pipes or ducts can be run from the existing system to your addition. If these conditions are satisfied, you may be able to tie into the existing system.

The Baileys were able to use their existing hot-air furnace to heat the new living area, so ducts were run through holes in the common foundation wall between the house and addition. The addition had a full basement, and a passageway was chipped through (see *Photo 14-1* on the right). This made installing the ductwork easier—the HVAC workers were spared many trips up and down cellar stairs of both parts of the house.

Often, furnaces and boilers are oversize for the job of heating or cooling the existing home. HVAC contractors may do this intentionally, ensuring that the system can handle any unusually extreme needs. And it could be that the contractor who worked on your existing house found that there was no unit that matched your heating and cooling demand and therefore chose a model with excess capacity—meaning that

an addition might be accommodated without upgrading your system.

So, check the capacity of the unit, then subtract what your existing house consumes and see if the remainder will handle the anticipated demands of the addition. To figure out how much heat and cool air you will need for your addition, ask an HVAC contractor to calculate heating-and-cooling loads. Don't rely on

guesswork—and don't hire a contractor who relies on it, either.

The calculation is often done on a computer after the contractor collects information about the existing house and planned addition. The load figure is compared to the capacity of your supply system and to the ability of the system to deliver the hot water or warm or cool air. At the same time, separate heating and

Photo 14-1. This isn't a very dramatic part of the job—even with sunglasses standing in for a pair of safety glasses. A passageway is knocked through the Baileys' foundation once the addition has been enclosed.

Photo 14-2. At the Baileys', a supply duct is brought through a hole made in the cement wall of the original foundation. This difficult job may be best left to a professional installer.

cooling load calculations should be done for the addition to aid in sizing the delivery system to the new rooms.

How are the numbers generated? A heating or cooling load is figured using a *load form,* on which the HVAC contractor enters data about your house and addition to determine the amount of heat the structure loses and gains through the year. Factors include wall area, the area occupied by windows and doors, the number of people who will regularly be in the house or addition, the influence of appliances that might add heat to the rooms, and leakiness (the frequency with which the air within the structure changes). Another factor is

what you consider to be the ideal indoor temperatures.

With all of these variables entered on the load form, the HVAC contractor will figure out the heat lost or gained in BTUs and recommend a supply-and-delivery system to accommodate worst-case scenarios.

HVAC DIY

Is there room in this highly technical area for you to get involved? Probably not, unless you have unusual skills.

Unlike drywalling or painting, HVAC installation is not something you can easily contribute to without substantial skill and training. Typically, a contractor will bid the entire job:

calculating loads, upgrading the system, and installation. Since the work is specialized and each part of the system is so integral to the others, there is little opportunity for you to save money by helping or doing part of it yourself.

For instance, the furnace or boiler obviously has to be installed by experts. You may be able to help with plumbing or ductwork—if your copper sweating or tin-knocking skills are up to snuff. See *Photo 14-2* above. But perhaps a better role for you would be to streamline installation by making provisions for ducts or pipes when planning the addition. This involves only pencil lines on paper, but a real contribution nonetheless.

MAKING ROOMS

Stud walls have only hinted at what the addition might feel like. Now, brittle sheets of drywall suddenly define rooms, frame views, and suggest traffic patterns (there's no more stepping through a wall, ghostlike, to get from here to there). Plumbing and electrical fixtures are hooked up to the systems that service them. The place is beginning to seem livable.

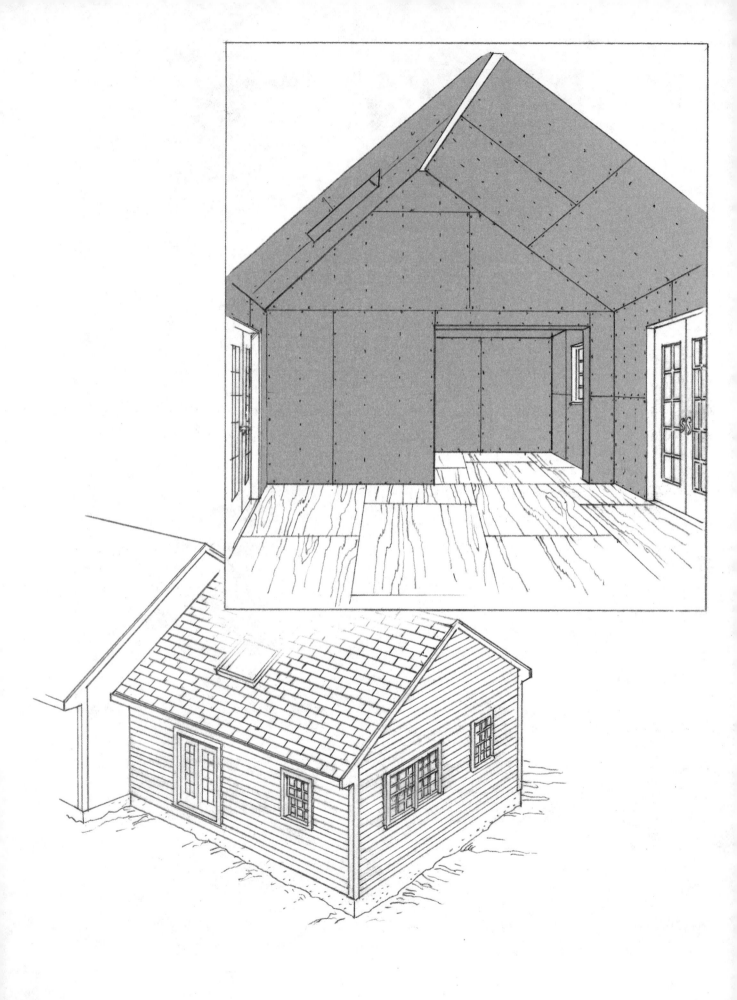

15
INSTALLING DRYWALL

Drywall is odd stuff. The heavy, floppy sheets seem too fragile to sheath the interior walls of a house. They have to be handled and installed with some delicacy.

But drywall is inexpensive, goes up quickly, and can produce the seamless, machine-made perfection most of us expect in a wall. Or something approaching perfection, if you know how to tape and spackle the joints and nail holes. There is a knack to this job that comes more quickly to some people than to others.

Although homeowners can hang drywall themselves, even some highly competent do-it-yourselfers prefer to sub this job out to specialists. Before deciding whether or not to get involved, watch an experienced person at work or, better yet, try a small patch-up drywall job around the house.

GETTING TO KNOW THE MATERIAL

Standard drywall has white paper on one side and gray paper on the other. Versions are made for special applications, as explained in "Drywall for Special Uses" on page 276. The paper skin on either side keeps the sheets together. Under the paper is a core of gypsum, a crumbly and chalky mineral also used to make the plaster of traditional plaster-and-lath walls. Plaster walls take longer to put up than drywall because a few coats are needed, and each must be allowed to dry; in the meantime, the interior of the house becomes very humid.

Drywall (also known by the brand name Sheetrock) is fairly easy to cut and attach, but there remains the task of smoothing over corners and joints between sheets by spreading a few coats of a special compound and waiting for each coat to dry.

Common drywall thicknesses for residential use are ½ and ⅝ inch. The thicker sheet is a little heavier to handle, but it stands up better over time and transmits less sound between rooms. Widths are a standard 4 feet, while lengths run from 6 to 16 feet. The longer a sheet, the more difficulty you'll have getting it off the truck, into the addition, and onto a wall or ceiling. (A ½-inch-thick 12-footer runs about 90 pounds.) But big sheets can save you time—there will be fewer joints to conceal, and fewer joints mean a smoother job.

Covering joints is a two-stage process. First, you apply paper or fiberglass *joint tape* over the seams, then you cover the tape with three or more layers of *joint compound*, a creamy water-based mixture called "mud" in the trade. Paper tape requires a layer of compound underneath it, while self-adhesive fiberglass mesh tape goes up dry.

The long edges of drywall sheets are tapered, making it easier to conceal taped joints. This allows you to build up layers of joint compound without it rising above the sheets' surface. The short edges are full thickness; with the panels run vertically on a wall of conventional height, these edges will be concealed under baseboard molding at the bottom edge and along the ceiling at the top edge. If sheets are run horizontally, you'll have to butt the ends, but taping and finishing are easier when the job is done this way, as explained later. Edges are unavoidable on ceilings of rooms of any size.

Calculate how many sheets you'll need by going around each room wall by wall and making diagrams showing how panels will run. You want to make the most efficient use of the sheet sizes available to you.

▲▲▲▲▲▲▲▲▲▲▲▲

Drywall provides little support, so if you will be installing wall-hung fixtures that need special support, such as towel racks and cabinets, check that blocking is in place. Then screw through the drywall and into the blocking.

▼▼▼▼▼▼▼▼▼▼▼▼

Beyond that, the sheets should meet at tapered edges whenever possible.

USING NAILS, SCREWS, OR BOTH

Because it is brittle and not very strong, drywall is attached rather gingerly. The head of the fastener, whether it be a nail or a screw, should be set just below the paper surface, leaving a slight hollow to be filled with joint compound.

The best nails for the task are those with annular rings; buy 1¼-inch nails to put up ½-inch drywall and 1⅜-inch nails for ⅝-inch sheets. The rings help keep the nails from pulling out as the addition's frame dries and shrinks away from the shanks. For good results, use a drywall hammer; its slightly rounded head dimples the sheets with less chance of tearing the paper.

If nails do pull away from the frame, they are apt to push through the drywall surface if you press on the walls. The resulting tell-tale bulges are known as nail pops, and they necessitate reattaching the wall, making another couple of passes with joint compound over the new dimples, and then repainting.

 DRYWALL FOR SPECIAL USES

Not all drywall is alike. Standard drywall has some inherent resistance to fire due in part to the chemically bound water found in all gypsum products. You can increase the fire rating of a wall by using thicker drywall or by applying more than a single layer. (In the latter case, use less-expensive gypsum *backing board* for all but the face sheet.)

Applying multiple layers is time-consuming. An alternative is to use fire-rated sheets, known as *Type X*, intended for garage walls and the ceiling of a room with a furnace. These sheets are strengthened with fibers and treated with chemical additives to retard fire. Before purchasing drywall, check building codes for locally mandated fire ratings.

Moisture-resistant drywall, sometimes called *greenboard*, is color coded to distinguish it from the standard stuff. Use it in bathrooms and laundry rooms or in any area subject to high humidity. It is also a good choice where walls and ceilings may be subjected to condensation from windows and skylights.

Another option for moisture resistance is foil-backed drywall. Use this on any exterior wall where an added vapor barrier is desired. To drywall a foundation wall, use foil-backed sheets over furring strips. When faced against a ¾-inch air space, the foil layer acts an insulator, increasing the wall's R-value.

Screws have a few advantages over nails. They anchor more soundly in the framing members, so drywall sheets aren't apt to move and spoil the job. Screws are less likely to tear the surface paper or break the fragile gypsum core, and they leave a smaller, easier-to-finish dimple.

Driving hundreds of screws does require a specialized tool. You can buy or rent an electric screw gun with its variable-speed control and clutch to disengage the bit when the screw reaches the proper depth. Or you can buy an inexpensive countersink adapter for a standard drill. The best screws to use are 1¼-inch-long type W drywall screws. With their widely spaced threads, they are quick to drive.

Whichever type of fastener you use, you can make certain you have a good bond between drywall and framing by applying a general construction adhesive or a specialized drywall adhesive along every stud and ceiling joist. A cartridge gun should be used to squeeze an unbroken ⅜-inch bead. Wherever two sheets will meet, zigzag back and forth to catch both. Don't worry about putting the sticky stuff on plates at the top and bottom.

Apply glue to as many framing members as you can comfortably expect to cover with panels before the adhesive begins to lose its tack (about 15 to 20 minutes). If you aren't sure that a sheet is the right size, test fit it before applying adhesive. Place nails or screws following the illustration *Nail and Screw Spacing* above; note that there are two patterns for placing nails.

At the Baileys, the drywalling was done by a father-and-son team, Jim Terra and Jim

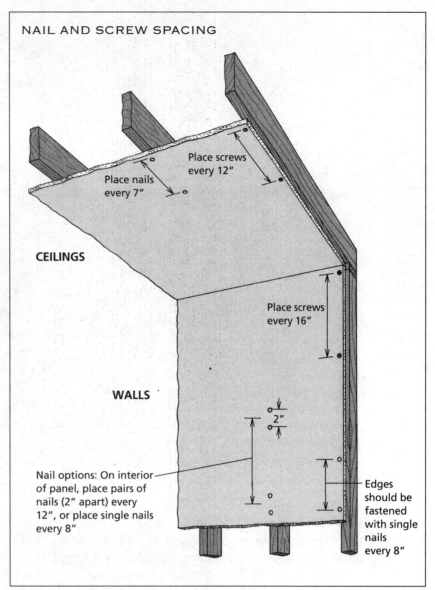

CEILINGS

Place nails every 7"

Place screws every 12"

Place screws every 16"

WALLS

2"

Nail options: On interior of panel, place pairs of nails (2" apart) every 12", or place single nails every 8"

Edges should be fastened with single nails every 8"

Jr. They knocked out the job in a day and didn't even skip lunch.

▲▲▲▲▲▲▲▲▲▲

Hang the biggest sheets of drywall first. This creates scraps you can use to fill the smaller puzzle pieces needed to complete the walls and ceiling.

▼▼▼▼▼▼▼▼▼▼

They didn't need to. The men started at 9 a.m. and were

packing up their materials by 1 p.m. The Terras used 12- and 14-footers as much as possible. This reduced the number of untapered butt joints that would need to be taped.

If you're hanging drywall yourself, begin the job at the top—the ceilings come first.

Rig up simple staging to give you the couple of feet you need to comfortably reach overhead. Pros may be able to get by with two-person crews (see *Photo 15-1* on page 278), but you should plan on two people to hold the sheets in place while a third drives screws or nails.

Photo 15-1. It takes strength, know-how, and a little desperation to drywall a ceiling with just two people. Try to recruit a third to make the job manageable.

Take care to stagger butt joints in the ceilings. This way, if a joist eventually shifts, it won't make a crack clear across the room. Also, the eye is less likely to notice these hard-to-finish butt joints if they are staggered.

The panels you put on the walls will help to support the edges of the drywalled ceiling. Place the wall sheets snugly against the ceiling. The usual practice is to install drywall horizontally around the room. Although this leaves butt joints where they'll show, a couple of advantages outweigh this.

There will be fewer running feet of joints to tape than if sheets were arranged vertically; also, it's easier to walk around a room taping and "mudding" a 4-foot-high horizontal seam than to finish a floor-to-ceiling seam every few feet.

Arrange the sheets so the untapered butt joints fall near corners, making the joints less conspicuous than if they fell toward the center of the room. Another tip is to work on these edges before installation, using a rasp or utility knife to make a slight bevel that will be filled with joint compound.

At the Baileys, the Terras hung first and cut later—that is, they installed the sheets right over window and door openings and electrical boxes, even though window frames and boxes protrude slightly beyond the studs. Then they cut out the openings, as shown in *Photo 15-2* on the opposite page, using the tools illustrated in *Drywall Knife and Saw* on the opposite page.

The knife is a standard utility model with a retractable

blade. To cut a window opening, as shown in *Photo 15-2,* begin by sawing up the vertical edges of the opening, guided by the framing. Next, reach outside the opening and score the back of the drywall along the top line with the knife. You aren't trying to hack your way through the dense material; you're simply preparing the sheet for the next step. Snap the cutout along the scored line by pulling it toward you, then run the knife along the paper hinge to free the piece. See the illustration *Sawing and Snapping an Opening* on page 280 (top).

To make cuts on drywall before installing it, you'll have to carefully transfer measurements from the wall to the sheet. Extra-long metal T-

Photo 15-2. *Spare yourself the trouble and potential errors of transferring cutouts for wall openings to the drywall by installing the material right over windows, doors, and electrical boxes. Then make the cuts, which will be accurate.*

squares will assist you in laying out lines on drywall. Use a saw to cut lines that can't be snapped and a knife to score those that can, as shown in *Sawing and Snapping a Corner* on page 280 (bottom). To snap along a line, stand the sheet on the floor; or support the larger portion of the sheet on a steady horizontal surface, just shy of the line. Carefully apply pressure on the shorter portion to make a clean break, as shown in *Photo 15-3* on page 281 (top). Turn the sheet over and use the knife to cut this face for a clean edge.

After the top row of drywall goes up, the lower row is cut to fit between it and the floor. You can get away with a somewhat ragged bottom edge because the baseboard will conceal it. To snug these sheets

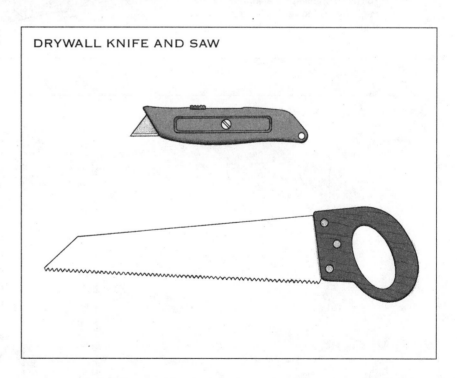

DRYWALL KNIFE AND SAW

up against the bottom of the top row, lever them by putting your foot on a flat pry bar with a scrap of wood as a fulcrum.

Use a level to establish the location of electrical boxes lurking behind these lower sheets of drywall. Make a mark

SAWING AND SNAPPING AN OPENING

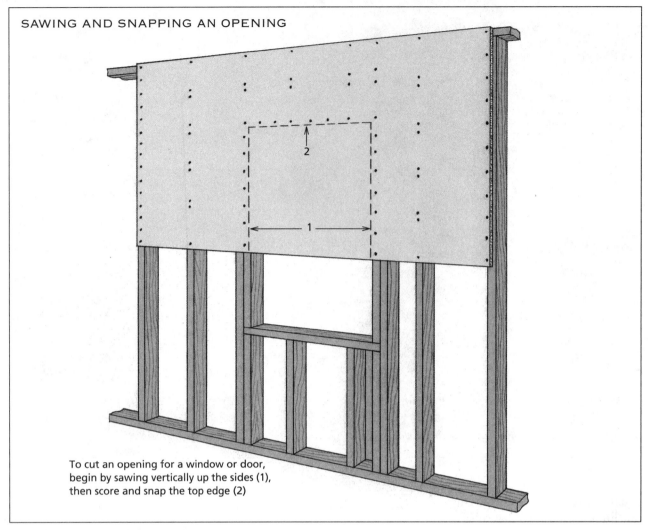

To cut an opening for a window or door, begin by sawing vertically up the sides (1), then score and snap the top edge (2)

SAWING AND SNAPPING A CORNER

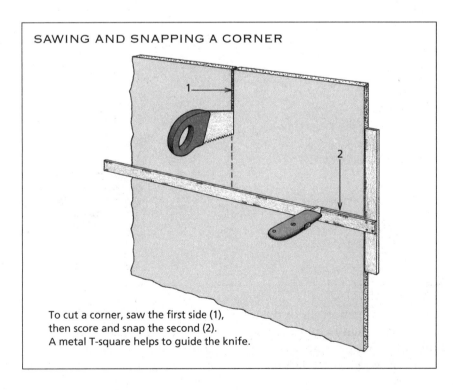

To cut a corner, saw the first side (1), then score and snap the second (2). A metal T-square helps to guide the knife.

directly above the center of the box on the installed upper sheet. Make another mark level with the center of the box on a stud or sheet to the left or right that will remain visible. Put the lower sheet in place, then transfer these marks to find the location of the box. Poke through to the box with a screwdriver or old chisel, and cut around its perimeter with a utility knife or drywall saw.

Outside corners and door and window openings that won't be covered with trim are reinforced with strips of metal corner bead, shown disappearing under a coat of compound in *Photo 15-4* on the opposite page (bottom).

Photo 15-3. *It doesn't take much force to snap a sheet of drywall. Once you have scored the paper on one side, turn the sheet over and cut the paper hinge on the underside.*

Corner bead comes with perforations to anchor the compound and for nailing into studs and headers. Cut it to length with metal snips. Take care when nailing corner bead in place; if pushed very firmly onto the corner, the bead can't function as it should. If it is sunk too low, it won't guide the knife distributing the relatively generous layer of compound needed to conceal the metal flanges on either side. To see this clearly for yourself, try pressing a piece of this metal strip against a corner before nailing it in place.

Begin nailing each length of bead at the middle, then work toward the top and bottom to make sure it lays flat. Use a pair of drywall nails, one hammered into each flange, at least every foot. With the corner bead installed, you're ready to conceal all of the seams.

Photo 15-4. *Metal corner bead reinforces vulnerable outside corners. It gets covered with joint compound in the same multistep process used for concealing joints.*

TAPING

Paper tape or fiberglass mesh? That's the choice you face at this stage. Paper tape is cheaper than mesh, but it must be embedded in a thin coat of compound and then smoothed over. This added step takes more time than simply unwinding mesh and sticking it in place. Curiously, paper tape is stronger than fiberglass mesh. And it is the better option for inside corners between walls and between walls and the ceiling. Because it comes with a slight indentation down the center, paper tape is easily folded in half and tucked into place.

Whatever your choice, tape covers the joints, and joint compound covers the tape. For years, drywallers mixed powdered compound with water, using drill-powered paddles and even potato mashers to arrive at a smooth consistency. But most people now use premixed compound, sold in little tubs for touch-up jobs and arm-straining 5-gallon buckets for addition-sized projects.

Freezing and drying can ruin the creamy consistency of the stuff, and lumpy compound is all but worthless. Take care to keep compound from freezing on the job site. Once you open a bucket, guard against it drying out. Keep the top on whenever possible. As you work, scrape down the inside walls of the bucket so that scraps don't dry and fall into the compound. If the product comes with an inner seal of plastic, save this disk and place it atop the compound before putting the lid back on. You can cut your own disk from a scrap of vapor barrier plastic.

Apply compound with a broad-bladed taping knife or trowel, taking the compound from a supply held in a pan or on top of a *hawk,* a square platform supported by a vertical handle. Taping knives have a very slight concave edge to leave a crowned seam of compound. This is useful in depositing a little extra mud over seams where sheets of full-thickness drywall meet.

Knives come in a range of widths. Equip yourself with blades of 4 or 6 inches, 8 inches, and 10 or 12 inches to take you through the three stages of applying compound over joints. A corner trowel may help you pave smoother corners than you could manage with two passes of a standard knife, but some experienced hands say that the tool isn't worth the cost. See the illustration *Taping Knife and Trowels* below.

The goal in drywalling is to produce near-perfect seams without having to sand away at mistakes forever. Drywall compound spreads on far more easily than it comes off. With some experience, do-it-yourselfers can get by with very little sanding; the trick is to carefully feather the compound out to near invisibility at the edges. Plan on applying three or four coats of compound—it's a novice's mistake to try to achieve a perfect joint on the first or even second coat.

"The first thing I was taught was 'Put on the mud and walk away,'" said Dennis Grim as he surveyed the Terras' work on the Bailey job. "Don't try to get great results

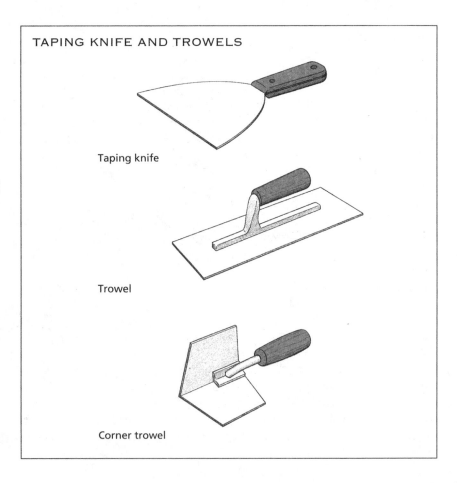

TAPING KNIFE AND TROWELS

Taping knife

Trowel

Corner trowel

all in one shot. If you don't like the way the coat looks, sand it later." Any ridges left on the first or second coat get sanded off, and depressions that remain get filled by the third coat.

When Dennis works with compound, he likes to apply it to the vertical joints first, "because they are the butt joints," he said. "It's easier to blend the tapered joints into the butt joints rather than the other way around."

Tapered joints are easier to finish because you just fill the hollow so that it is flush with the drywall surface. Butt joints, on the other hand, will never be flat. There must be a slight mound of compound along the seam. This imperceptible hill should be thick enough at the center to prevent cracking and taper very gradually to the surface of the drywall. The barely concave blade of a taping knife is a big help in mastering this delicate touch.

If you're using paper tape, lay down a bed of compound that fills the taper, then press the tape into place with a 4- or 6-inch-wide knife, as shown in *Photo 15-5* below. If you're using mesh tape, simply unroll it and press it firmly in place over the seams, then apply a coat of compound. As you go along, swipe compound over all the screws or nails that won't be covered by trim. Allow the joints and other areas to dry.

FINISHING THE JOB

Before beginning the second coat of compound, it is a good idea to go over the first dry coat with the drywall knife, removing any exceptionally high points. This reduces the chance that you'll add to any errors as you apply the next coat.

Use a medium-width knife to apply a second coat, feathering the edges. Give the fastener heads another hit, as well. Let this application dry. Then go over the compound with sandpaper, 150-grit or finer, or use the abrasive screen sheets sold for this purpose; they're less likely to clog than sandpaper. Wear a dust mask to avoid inhaling the dust.

Spread a thin finish coat over the joints and fastener heads, using the widest knife to feather the compound beyond the edges of the second pass. Once this last coat is dry, lightly sand again. A few passes with a damp sponge may work just as well as sanding, and you'll spare yourself the nuisance of cleaning up plaster dust.

Examine your work under the hard glare of a bright work light. A poor job will look just fine if the illumination is dim. If necessary, make a fourth pass with compound and touch up again with sandpaper or a sponge. Once you're satisfied, it's ready for paint.

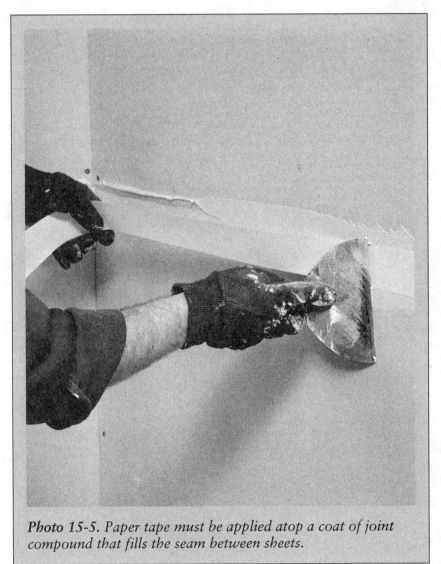

Photo 15-5. Paper tape must be applied atop a coat of joint compound that fills the seam between sheets.

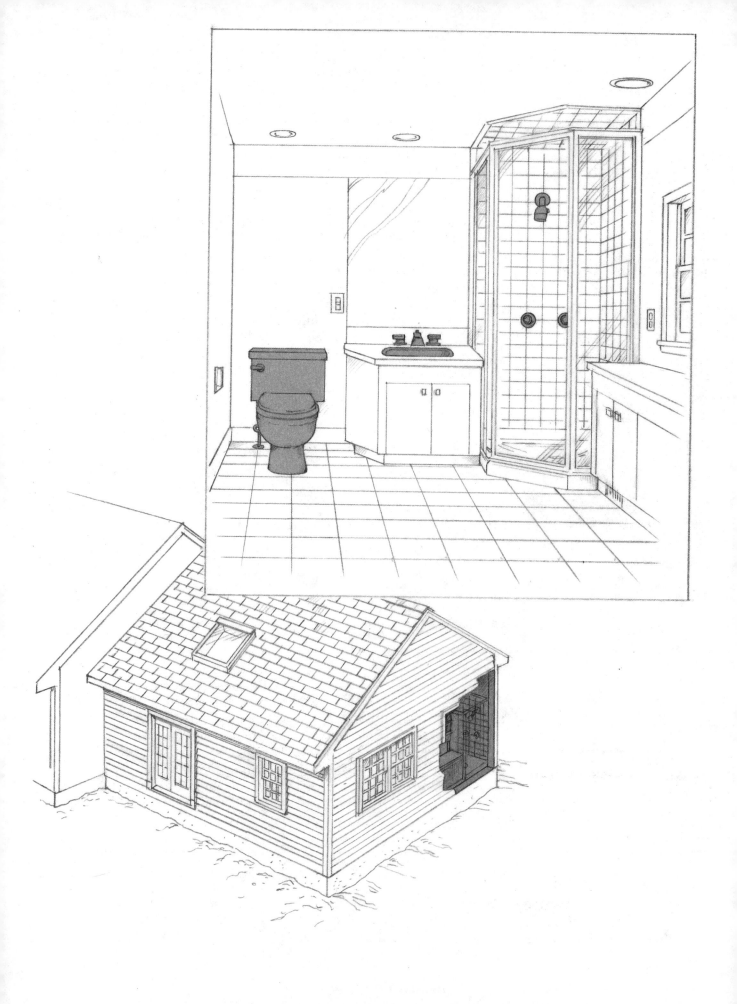

16 PLUMBING FIXTURES

Compared to rough plumbing (Chapter 11), doing the finish work of installing fixtures is a snap. The pipe has already been routed, so all you need to do is hook into the supply and waste line *stubouts* protruding from walls and floors. Their positions determine where you will locate the fixtures. Just how accurately you have to locate them depends on the type of connectors you choose.

Rigid joints, like soldered copper fittings and solvent-welded PVC, require that you hold to close tolerances. But if you're less than comfortable sweating a joint, you can purchase compression fittings, pliable copper tubing, and flexible PVC hoses that allow you to be less than dead on with your fixture location; and, for most hookups, you'll need nothing more than an adjustable wrench. You can also combine rigid and flexible materials by using *adaptors*, also called *transition fittings*; see "Fittings for Fixtures" on pages 288–289.

FIXTURE HOOKUPS SIMPLIFIED

If you haven't done finish plumbing work before, you can get a good idea of what's involved by taking a close look under a bathroom sink. (With hookups for a garbage disposal and/or dishwasher, kitchen sinks tend to be more complicated.) You'll see something similar to what's shown in the illustration *Typical Sink Plumbing* on page 286.

Slender rise tubes (cold on the right and hot on the left, according to plumbing convention) run to the faucets, and a heftier *drainpipe* leads away from the low point of the sink's basin. On better installations, *shutoff valves* (also called stop valves) will connect the hot and cold supply lines to the *riser tubes,* which head up to the *faucet assembly* above; these valves are not necessary, but for little added expense, they make it far easier to turn off the water when making future repairs. Because valves are typically attached directly to the stubouts, they should either be compatible with your supply lines or be connected with adaptors.

The drainpipe, or *tail piece,* drops from the sink drain and is connected to a *P-trap*. The trap may be metal or PVC. It always contains water, working in conjunction with the vent system to prevent waste gases from backing up into the house. It also traps debris that could block water flow. A *cleanout plug* lets you remove this debris, as well

TYPICAL SINK PLUMBING

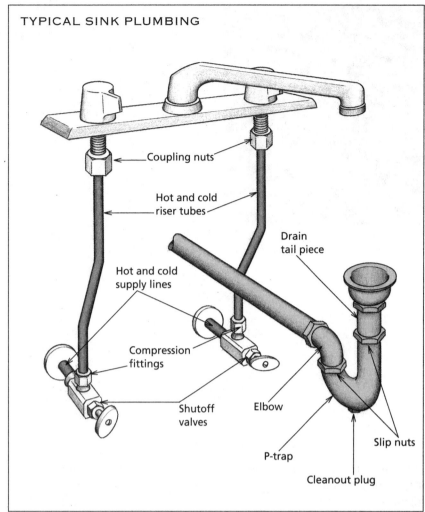

Coupling nuts

Hot and cold riser tubes

Drain tail piece

Hot and cold supply lines

Compression fittings

Shutoff valves

Elbow

Slip nuts

P-trap

Cleanout plug

as the occasional wedding ring that might disappear down the drain. The other end of the P-trap is connected to the waste line stubout.

This is about as complicated as it gets. There are other kinds of hookups to contend with, but each is a variation on one of these simple connections.

The first step in doing the finish plumbing is to select the fixtures. They determine the type and quantity of fittings you'll need. Kitchen and bath design centers provide the widest selection of toilets, sinks, tubs, showers, and faucets. Your local home center probably carries a basic line of fixtures. Plumbing-supply companies have access to a good variety, but they generally

sell only to plumbers. They may sell to you as well, but you can expect a smaller discount than the pros get.

If you've hired a contractor for the rough plumbing, consider having this person purchase fixtures as part of the job; you might get a better price.

As Archie Bunker might have said, a "terlet" is a "terlet" is a "terlet." But when you shop for fixtures, you'll find everything from run-of-the-mill toilets and faucets to high-end sinks and tubs meant to be the centerpieces of kitchens and bathrooms. As with other consumer goods, the best values may be found between the extremes. If you'll be hiring a plumber, ask about the reliabil-

ity of several brands. Knowledgeable salespeople at the retail center may be able to help.

It is also wise to check whether the models you choose use exotic parts that might be hard to replace in the future.

Another part of your background research is to learn if local regulations require water-saving fixtures in new construction. If so, there are several options available, including units that use a combination of water and compressed air to carry away waste.

BATHROOM FIXTURES

The first consideration when installing bathroom fixtures is whether the fixtures should go in before or after the flooring. Since the floor flange and the toilet base rest directly on the finish floor, ideally the floor should be installed before this fixture. Vanity cabinets, which house the sink, are liable to be replaced in years to come, so they, too, should sit on the finished floor. Tub and shower enclosures are more permanently embedded into the room. They can be installed before or after the floor. In either case, the joints at the floor should be well caulked.

The Baileys' new bathroom included a sink, shower enclosure, and toilet. Because this part of the plumbing job was straightforward, Barry and Dave installed the fixtures themselves, in between other parts of the construction process. (You might also contract the carpenters working on your addition to do this final stage of the plumbing as well, relieving you of the need to hire another subcontractor.)

The men started with the toilet, perhaps the easiest fixture to install. The waste hook-up was first, but not with a connection to a pipe. Instead, the base of the toilet was attached to a *floor flange*, which was installed during rough plumbing. (An alternate term is *closet flange*, derived from "water closet," a once-common term for a toilet.) The flange had two mounting bolts for anchoring the toilet to the waste line and the floor at the same time; see the illustration *Installing a Toilet* below.

Before attaching the toilet, Barry flipped it upside down onto a piece of cardboard to protect the fixture. Then he set a *wax gasket* over the *horn* on the base of the toilet. This is where the water exits into the drainpipe. The pliable wax conforms to the contour of the drain flange, preventing leaks. Barry also applied a bead of plumber's putty onto the rim of the base. In addition to containing a leak, this serves as a cushion between the toilet base and the floor. Then he set the bowl carefully onto the bolts, checked that it was level, and snugged down the nuts.

▲▲▲▲▲▲▲▲▲▲▲

Since stubouts have to be capped off anyway to protect the lines from debris during construction, consider installing shutoff valves instead of plain caps. That way, when you hook up your fixtures, there'll be one less joint you'll have to make.

▼▼▼▼▼▼▼▼▼▼▼

"You don't want to overtighten these," Barry commented, "or you could crack the base."

The Baileys chose a contemporary, single-piece toilet, in which the bowl and tank are all one unit. With a conventional two-piece set, the tank is bolted to the back of the seat with a gasket in between. Some tanks can also be attached to the wall for an extra-sturdy installation. If you choose this approach, you'll need to be more precise when locating the floor flange in the rough plumbing stage. The flange must be installed so the back of the tank will rest snugly against the wall. Be sure to get specific instructions with the toilet you buy.

The last step is to hook up the water supply to the tank. First, decide if you want a shutoff valve. Shutoff valves let you work on a single fixture without turning off the main supply line.

Shutoff valves are simple devices. Water enters through one fitting, the *inlet*, and goes out another to a riser tube. In between, a handle opens and closes the valve to regulate water flow. Shutoff valves are either straight or angled, depending on the orientation of

(continued on page 290)

287

INSTALLING A TOILET

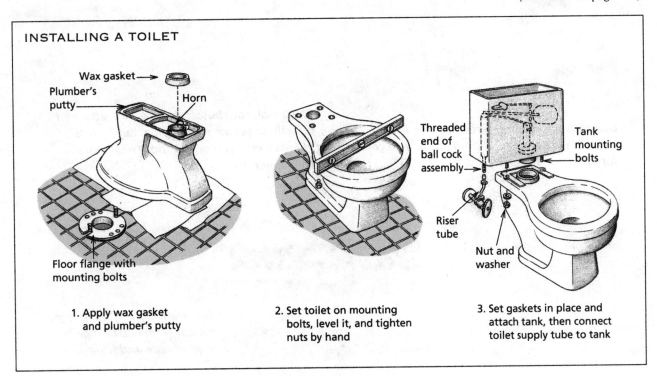

1. Apply wax gasket and plumber's putty

2. Set toilet on mounting bolts, level it, and tighten nuts by hand

3. Set gaskets in place and attach tank, then connect toilet supply tube to tank

FITTINGS FOR FIXTURES

Plumbers refer to anything that joins one piece of pipe to the next as a *fitting*, regardless of the material it's made from or how the connection is made. As shown in the photo below (top left), a union connects two lengths of straight pipe; an *elbow* makes a 90 degree turn; and a tee creates a perpendicular intersection.

Fittings can be made of copper, bronze, or even plastic. Connections between fittings and pipe are made in many ways. The two most common ways to install plumbing fixtures are with soldered joints and compression fittings. If this is your first shot at plumbing, consider using compression fittings wherever possible. Instead of solder and a torch, you'll only need an adjustable wrench.

Plastic supply pipe is inexpensive and easy to work with. But compared to copper, there are a limited number of fittings that work directly with plastic. The photo below (top right) shows a *shutoff valve* that can be attached directly to plastic pipe. (A valve is a fitting that connects pieces of pipe and lets you regulate the flow of water.) Another option with plastic supply pipes is to use a transition fitting like the one shown in the photo below (bottom). This lets you convert from plastic to copper when you hook up the fixtures.

If you're hooking up your own fixtures, you might as well install shutoff valves at every supply line; see the photo on the opposite page (top). That way, if you have to work on a fixture, you can shut off the supply to that one fixture and leave

Unions (top), elbows (left), and tees (right) come in various sizes in both plastic and copper for joining lengths of pipe.

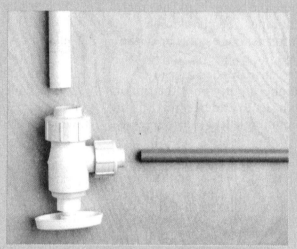

This all-plastic shutoff valve can be attached directly to plastic supply pipe, but it costs almost twice as much as those designed for copper.

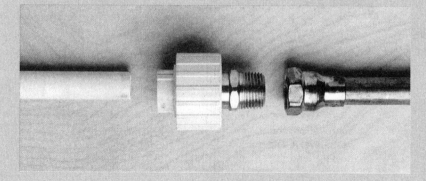

This transition fitting lets you switch from plastic pipe to copper pipe and fittings.

the rest of the system operating. Shutoff valves are inexpensive, considering the convenience they provide.

Riser tubes are available in many forms; most are flexible and designated for a specific fixture, such as a vanity sink or toilet. One end connects to a shutoff valve

straight *tail piece* mounts to the sink strainer assembly; depending on the location of the waste stubout, you'll need to either cut the tail piece or add an extension. A *P-trap* gets connected to the tail piece. This is the heart of the waste hookup. Finally, an elbow or *J-bend*

Shutoff valves can be joined to copper pipe with soldered joints or compression fittings. Here, a soldered joint is used between the shutoff valve and supply line (right), and a ³⁄₈-inch riser tube (left) is connected to the valve with a compression fitting.

and the other feeds the fixture. If your system doesn't use a shutoff valve, attach the supply tube directly to the supply stubout; here again, compression fittings will work best. The photo below (left) shows several supply lines.

As for the drain lines, there are four components in sink drain systems. A

connects the P-trap to the waste stubout; see the photo below (right).

Chrome-plated brass P-traps and waste pipes are still commonly available. These may look better and can be used even if the rest of your waste lines are plastic, but they're also more expensive than plastic. Because it's so simple to work with, 1½-inch plastic is fast becoming the standard for residential use. The photo below (right) shows typical assemblies in each material. For both assemblies, the parts slip together with washers and locking nuts.

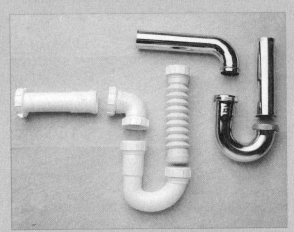

Three types of faucet riser tubes are commonly used: a braided-steel version (left) that has a soft rubber tube inside, ½-inch copper tubing (center), which can be joined with compression fittings, and a tube made of polybutylene, a flexible plastic (right).

The chrome-plated brass P-trap assembly (right) and the PVC version (left) are designed the same, but the PVC assembly has a flexible straight section that can connect a P-trap and tail piece that are slightly out of line.

the supply pipe to the fixture, as shown in the illustration *Shutoff Valves* below.

Water enters the toilet tank through the threaded end of the *ball cock assembly.* This is the valve inside the toilet tank that opens when the toilet is flushed, refilling the tank. If you forego a shutoff valve, you'll need just a *riser tube* (also sold as a toilet supply tube). Riser tubes come in flexible plastic, copper, and rubber covered with braided steel; see the photo on the bottom (left) on page 289.

One end of a toilet riser tube has a standard fitting to match the threaded end of the ball cock, which fits through a hole in the bottom of the tank. If you're using plain copper tubing elsewhere, it would make sense to use a short piece here, but you'll still need to add the fitting at the toilet end. The ready-made

riser tubes are inexpensive and convenient.

At the Baileys, Barry used a chrome-plated brass shutoff valve for the toilet supply tube. It had compression fittings on both the inlet and supply sides of the valve. Compression fittings can be used with copper pipe, flexible copper, or flexible plastic tubing; see the illustration *Compression Fitting* on the opposite page.

To use a compression fitting, first make a clean cut on the end of the supply tube or pipe; use a tubing cutter for copper and a hacksaw or razor knife for plastic. Next, slide the compression nut over the tube, with the threads facing the end. Then slide the tapered compression ring about $1/2$ inch over the tube. Insert the tube into the threaded fitting so the tapered ring sits squarely in the rim. Finally, slide the nut back down and tighten it.

Barry first attached the

valve to the $1/2$-inch supply pipe that protruded from the wall. Next, he connected a standard $3/8$-inch flexible riser tube to the other side of the valve. Finally, the other end of the riser tube was mounted to the tank.

Bathroom sinks, also called lavatories (or lavies by plumbing-supply countermen), may be hung on a wall, supported by their own bases, or installed in vanity cabinets. The first two types of sinks rely on added framing, or "blocking," within the walls for support, so it's important that you shop for a sink before the drywall goes up. If you use a cabinet, supply and waste lines must be routed through its back or bottom, but otherwise the hookups are no different than for sinks that mount to the wall. If you buy the sink and cabinet separately, you'll need to make a cutout in the countertop. See Chapter 20 for instructions on cabinet installation and for a step-by-step guide to cutting in a sink.

Before securing the sink to a countertop, check that you'll have sufficient access to make the plumbing connections. Mount the faucet assembly to the sink before installing the sink in the counter.

Once the sink is attached, you're ready to head underneath the sink for the hookups. First, cut the ends off the capped supply pipes, as shown in *Photo 16-1* on the opposite page (left). Then install the shutoff valves.

Some bathroom and kitchen faucets come with riser tubes in place. If yours don't, buy two *sink supply tubes.* These have a standard fitting on the faucet end and varying fittings on the other end to match your shutoff valve. They

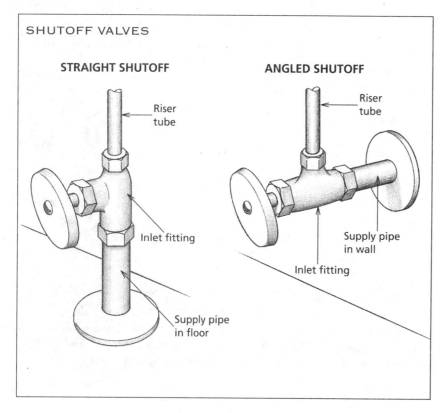

SHUTOFF VALVES

STRAIGHT SHUTOFF — Riser tube, Inlet fitting, Supply pipe in floor

ANGLED SHUTOFF — Riser tube, Supply pipe in wall, Inlet fitting

290

COMPRESSION FITTING

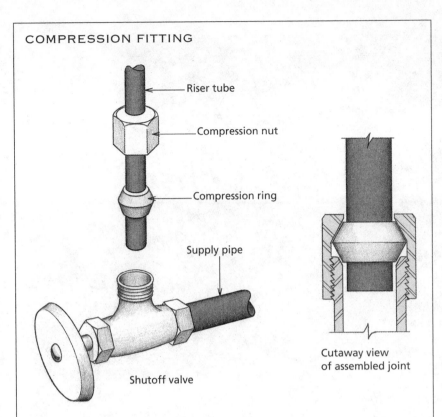

Riser tube

Compression nut

Compression ring

Supply pipe

Shutoff valve

Cutaway view
of assembled joint

come in two lengths—shorter for bathroom sinks and longer for kitchen sinks. If you have to cut the riser tube to length, measure all the way to the base of the valve threads, as shown in *Photo 16-2* below (right).

Attach the riser tube first to the valve with a compression fitting, as shown in *Photo 16-3* on page 292 (top left), and then to the threaded end of the faucet inlets. You'll need a *basin wrench* for this, as shown in *Photo 16-4* on page 292 (top right).

The drainpipe assembly with its P-trap is shown in *Typical Sink Plumbing* on page 286. Use PVC or stainless steel; both are joined with compression fittings that use rubber or plastic washers. To cut the drainpipe for the P-trap, hold a straight-edge parallel to the

291

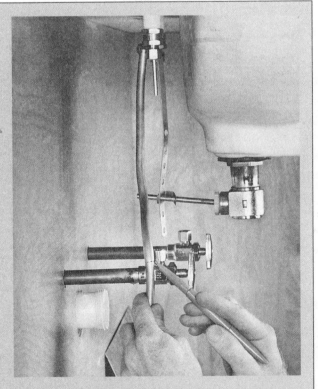

Photo 16-1. Cutting copper under a sink takes some dexterity, but a small tubing cutter makes the job easier.

Photo 16-2. When measuring to cut riser tubes, be sure to go all the way to the base of the fitting.

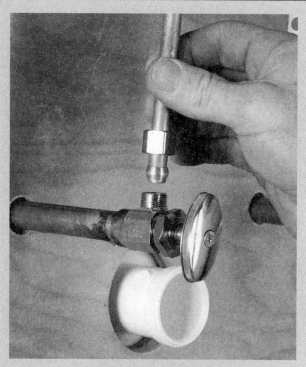

Photo 16-3. *A compression nut connects the riser tube to the valve. You'll know the compression sleeve is seated when the resistance increases noticeably. Then give the nut just one more complete turn.*

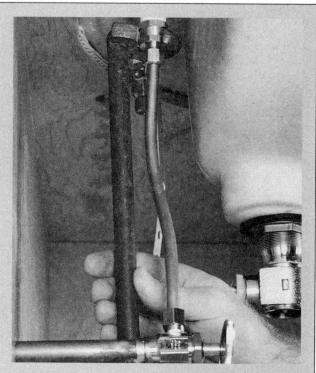

Photo 16-4. *A basin wrench is indispensable for connecting riser tubes to the faucet inlet shank. But before you buy a wrench, check your sinks; some come with supply tubes already connected to the inlet.*

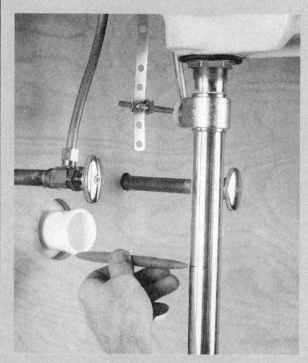

Photo 16-5. *The tail piece should extend until its end aligns with the lower edge of the stubout. Cut the tail piece with a hacksaw.*

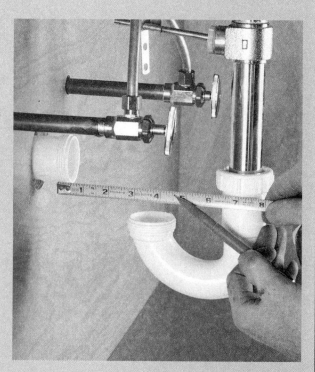

Photo 16-6. *Measure for the J-bend, as shown, then connect the P-trap to the stubout. Open the valves and check all connections.*

base of the stubout, as shown in *Photo 16-5* on the opposite page (bottom left), and mark the pipe. As with the riser tube, measure and mark at the base of the fitting, allowing about ½ inch of the pipe to enter the fitting. After cutting the drainpipe, attach the P-trap. Next, measure for the *elbow;* see *Photo 16-6* on the opposite page (bottom right).

Installing a bathtub or shower stall involves the same basic skills as putting in a sink, but there's the added element of having to create a waterproof enclosure around your plumbing. There are a number of ways to accomplish

this short of a conventionally tiled bath and shower. You could buy a cast iron or fiberglass tub, for example, and get a kit of interlocking fiberglass panels for the surrounding walls. The panels are nailed to the wall studs, then holes are cut for the faucets and shower head.

For a separate shower stall, you might start with a three-sided framed enclosure, install a molded fiberglass base, then tile the walls in conventional fashion. A three-piece stall kit, with or without a door, is another option. Or, least difficult of all, you can purchase a one-piece shower

surround; see the illustration *Shower Surround Kits* below. Whichever approach you take, it's obviously best to have the fixtures on site before installing the plumbing lines and, in some cases, before doing the framing.

KITCHEN PLUMBING

Once upon a time, kitchen plumbing meant a sink. Nowadays, that sink typically includes a spray hose, garbage disposal, and perhaps a water filter. Then there's the dishwasher—a standard issue in most kitchens—and

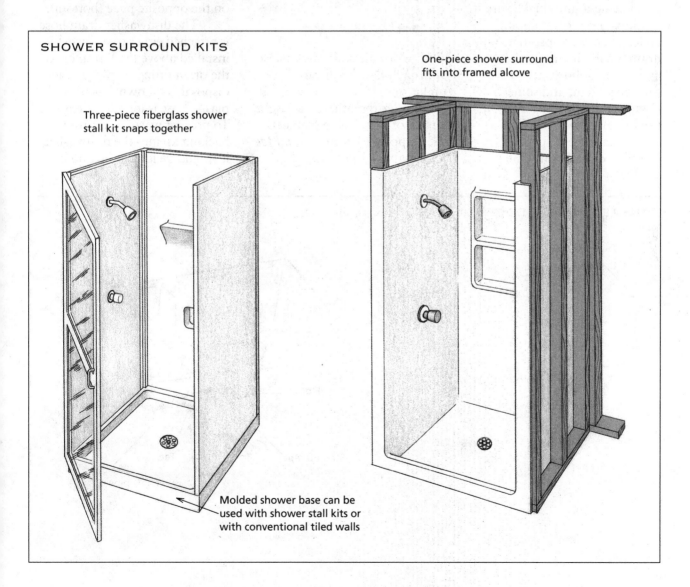

SHOWER SURROUND KITS

One-piece shower surround fits into framed alcove

Three-piece fiberglass shower stall kit snaps together

Molded shower base can be used with shower stall kits or with conventional tiled walls refrigerators that offer tap water and ice. These conveniences mean more connections to the water supply and waste lines.

There are numerous variations on the basic kitchen sink, depending on the added features you choose. A double sink, for instance, requires one of the waste line arrangements shown in *Waste Line for Double Sinks* below. The configuration on the right might seem better, but the other one requires fewer pieces of pipe and fittings, and it works just as well.

Garbage disposals are a real convenience, but before purchasing a unit, make sure it is allowed by the plumbing code. Their widespread use dramatically increases the amount of solid waste in a sewage system, and some communities have banned their use in new construction.

A garbage disposal is installed directly onto the base of the sink drain, in place of the straight drain tail piece. The P-trap is then attached to the disposal drain, as shown in *Garbage Disposal Hookups* on the opposite page (top).

▲▲▲▲▲▲▲▲▲▲▲

Standard dishwashers take up a chunk of cabinet space. Consider a dishwasher that fits under the sink. It is slightly smaller than a standard unit and requires a shallow sink. But it works just as well and occupies wasted space.

▼▼▼▼▼▼▼▼▼▼▼

With a double sink, the easiest approach has the disposal under one drain and a single P-trap under the other; a straight length of waste pipe connects the disposal to a *directional tee* fitting above the P-trap. But

some plumbing codes require separate P-traps for each drain when a disposal is used.

A dishwasher needs only a hot-water supply. There are two ways to make the supply connection. First, you could install a tee fitting in the hot-water supply line that runs to the sink and run a length of 3/8-inch flexible copper tube from the tee to the dishwasher supply inlet. A shutoff valve, though optional, could be installed in this line. Or, instead of a tee fitting, you could install a double shutoff valve at the hot-water supply stubout, with one line going to the sink and the other to the dishwasher; see the illustration *Dishwasher Hookups* on the opposite page (bottom).

The dishwasher drain hose is attached either to a waste tee installed above the P-trap or to the drain fitting on the garbage disposal, as shown. The flexible plastic hose is long for a reason. To prevent waste water from backing up into the dishwasher, it should be looped up and hung

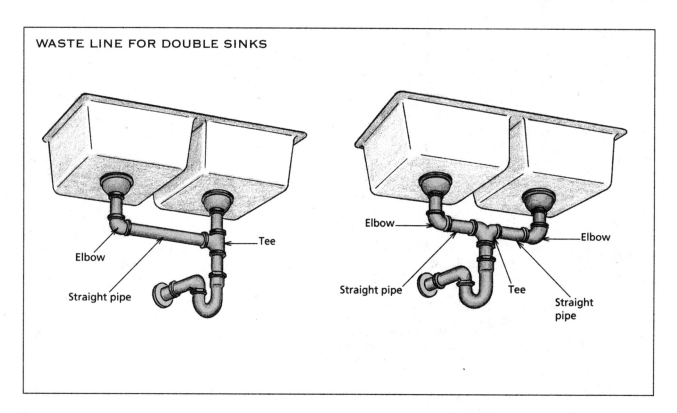

WASTE LINE FOR DOUBLE SINKS

Elbow

Tee

Straight pipe

Elbow

Elbow

Straight pipe

Tee

Straight pipe

GARBAGE DISPOSAL HOOKUPS

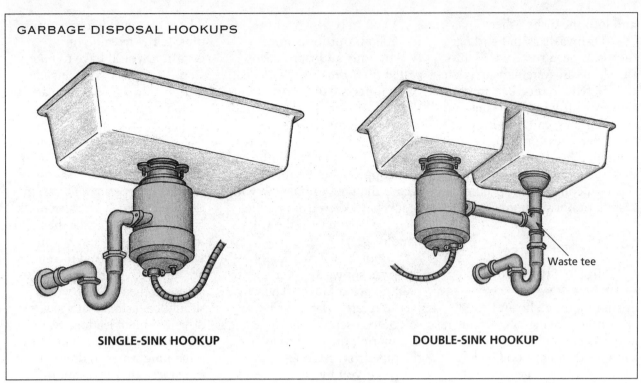

SINGLE-SINK HOOKUP

DOUBLE-SINK HOOKUP

Waste tee

DISHWASHER HOOKUPS

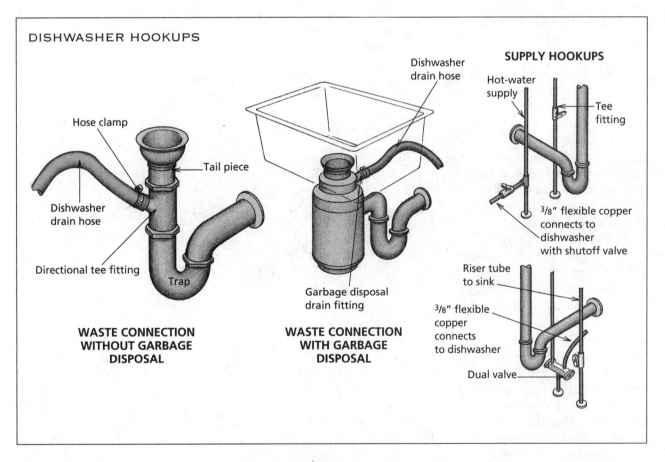

Dishwasher drain hose

SUPPLY HOOKUPS

Hot-water supply

Tee fitting

Hose clamp

Tail piece

Dishwasher drain hose

Directional tee fitting

Trap

³/8" flexible copper connects to dishwasher with shutoff valve

WASTE CONNECTION WITHOUT GARBAGE DISPOSAL

Garbage disposal drain fitting

WASTE CONNECTION WITH GARBAGE DISPOSAL

Riser tube to sink

³/8" flexible copper connects to dishwasher

Dual valve

from a strap on the underside of the countertop.

Additionally, some dishwashers and some local plumbing codes require that an *air gap* assembly be installed in the waste line. This fitting mounts in one of the auxiliary holes in the sink rim. It further ensures that water from a clogged sink won't be siphoned back through the waste tube and into the dishwasher.

Dishwashers and garbage disposals need to be wired into the electrical system, usually on designated circuits; be sure the power is off when working on the plumbing end of things. Note that these are typical plumbing hookups; every dishwasher and garbage disposal comes with specific installation instructions.

OTHER PLUMBING CONNECTIONS

A sink-mounted hot-water dispenser provides a convenient way to get a quick cup of tea without having to boil water. The typical arrangement involves a small, electric storage tank under the sink that keeps water at about 200°F. A flexible hose taps into the cold-water supply with a tee fitting and shutoff valve, and hot water is fed to a faucet next to the main faucet assembly.

Water filters can be installed at the sink in the same way. Some sit on the counter and may get in the way of a busy cook; others can be mounted underneath the counter.

A clothes-washing machine arrives with standard rubber supply hoses. These require male threaded shutoff valves on both hot and cold supply lines. Additionally, this is a good place to install air cushions, which absorb sharp vibrations that result when the valves are closed abruptly (see Chapter 11 for more on air cushions). The illustration *Clothes-Washer Hookup* on the right shows a typical arrangement for both supply and waste lines. A *stand pipe* with a built-in trap can be purchased as a single piece.

You may also want to include an outdoor faucet or two in your addition. Also called *hose bibs* or *sill cocks,* these faucets can be fitted onto the end of a cold-water supply pipe in a number of ways.

One of the simplest is to solder the valve right to the end of a copper pipe. Be sure to secure the pipe to the wall with brackets to keep from racking the pipe as you turn the valve's handle.

Photo 16-7 on the opposite page shows another way to mount such a faucet. The valve pictured has a flange at its base so you can screw it to the wall, eliminating the need to protect the pipe from racking.

If you live in an area where the outside temperature dips below freezing on occasion, you'll have to take steps to protect your outside faucets. Otherwise, the water in them can freeze and cause damage. There are a number of ways to do this, as illustrated in *Outdoor Faucets* on the opposite page. One of the easiest is to install a *frost-free faucet.* In this style fitting, the valve mechanism is located inside the building, where it will stay warm, while the handle and the outlet are outside, where you have access to them. These valves should be installed at a slight downhill pitch leading away from the building to allow any remaining water to drain out of the faucet after it is shut off.

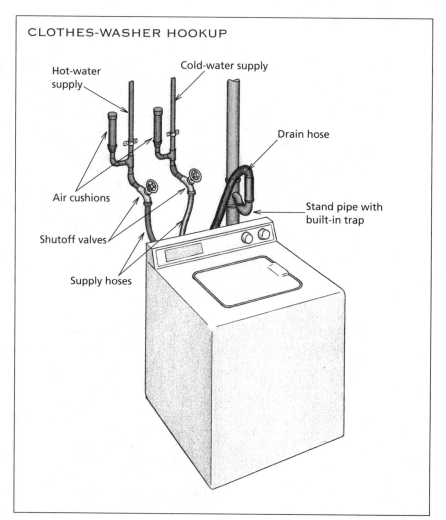

CLOTHES-WASHER HOOKUP

Hot-water supply

Cold-water supply

Drain hose

Air cushions

Shutoff valves

Stand pipe with built-in trap

Supply hoses

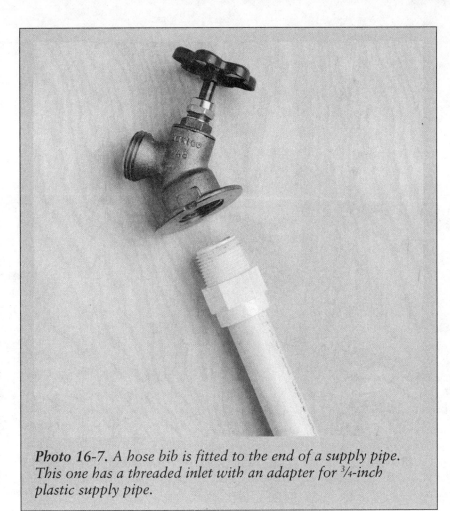

Photo 16-7. A hose bib is fitted to the end of a supply pipe. This one has a threaded inlet with an adapter for ¾-inch plastic supply pipe.

Frost-free faucets are convenient because they can be used year-round. It is a good idea, however, *not* to leave a hose attached to one in freezing weather. The hose can prevent water from draining away from the valve. If it gets cold enough, that water can freeze and cause the entire valve mechanism to burst.

If you opt for a regular faucet outside, you should install a cutoff valve for it inside. This cutoff valve should be of a *stop-and-waste* type. This kind of valve has a removable drain plug built into it, allowing you to easily drain the pipe on the downstream side of the valve. The pipe leading from the shutoff valve to the faucet should be pitched at a slight uphill angle away from the valve, as shown. This will facilitate drainage when you turn the valve off and drain the line in preparation for winter.

OUTDOOR FAUCETS

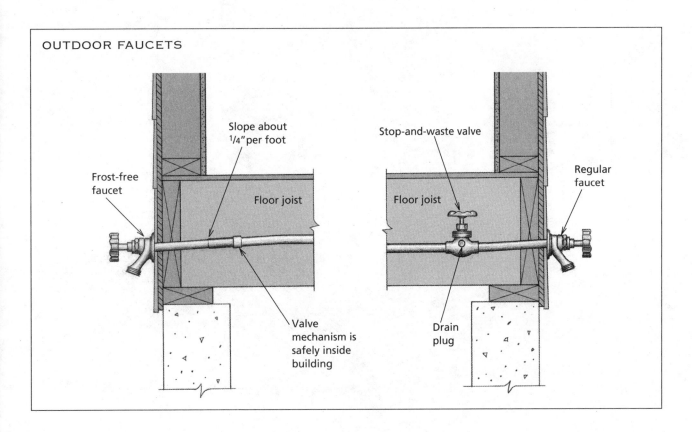

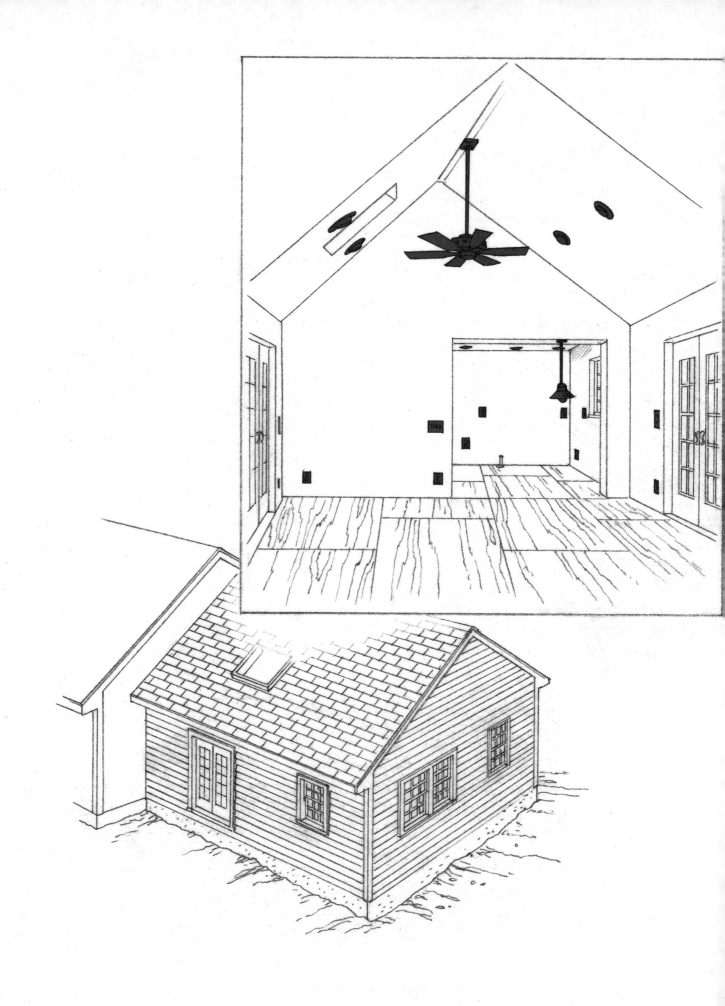

17
ELECTRICAL FIXTURES

Making connections. That's what the finish stage of wiring is all about. You also attach cover plates, hang lighting fixtures, and install fan grills. But the hard work has already been done.

It bears repeating, however, that all wiring should be done with the power off. If you have any doubt that a circuit is dead, use a circuit tester to confirm that you really did flick the breaker on the service panel. And don't forget to place a note on the panel, alerting anyone who might want to restore power that the circuit is off intentionally. This clear communication is especially important if there are other workers on the site, who may find that a saw has gone dead

and assume that an overload tripped the breaker.

There are basic skills involved in making connections. You have to know how to strip insulation from wires, how to bend and attach wire to screw terminals, and how to secure wires to each other. What connects to what has already been determined. Appliances usually come with wiring diagrams. Consult the sources cited in Chapter 12 for wiring diagrams and explanations of the code. Chapter 12 also covers many terms used in this chapter.

Although steps like hooking up the black wire to the brass-colored screw may sound simple, this end of the job is finicky. You are dealing with rather stiff and stubborn

wires in the cramped space of an electrical box. Fingertips not used to such work soon get sore; patience frays, as a tangle of wires refuses to cooperate.

Most homeowners will do as the Baileys did and let the electricians see the project through right to screwing in the bulbs. "I'm happy to look over this guy's shoulder," Jim Bailey said of Gus Trayner, the electrician who was wiring the house. "I like having a rough idea of what wire goes where, but I'm not about to make a hobby out of wiring."

Gus said that looking over shoulders is time well spent. "That way, you pick up an idea of what this maze of wires is all about. You'll be less likely to accidentally stick a nail into a cable. And when an outlet goes dead, you'll have at least a clue about what's going on."

Another way to participate without so much as twisting on a wire nut is to shop for the fixtures yourself, rather than rely on the taste and price consciousness of the contractor or electrician. See "Buying Lighting Fixtures" on the opposite page.

If you decide to tackle the final hook-ups yourself, make sure you have the connections checked by a pro or your local building inspector. A faulty connection can cause a shock or start a fire, and most insurance companies won't cover damages that result from electrical work done by an unlicensed homeowner.

ATTACHING WIRES

Insulation must be stripped from the ends of wires before making a connection. This job is best accomplished with an electrician's combination tool, as shown in *Photo 17-1* on the right. Simply insert the wire into the correct opening, identified according to the wire gauge on the tool (14, 12, and 10, most commonly); then squeeze to cut the insulation and pull to slide the plastic jacket from the metal core. Avoid using a knife or standard pliers to cut through the insulation—you risk nicking the wire, which may cause it to snap.

Performing these fine-tuned manipulations is made all the more challenging in small confines, such as when wiring a fixture like a fan to a ceiling box. In this case, you'll have to use a wire safety harness to loosely connect the fixture so it won't fall.

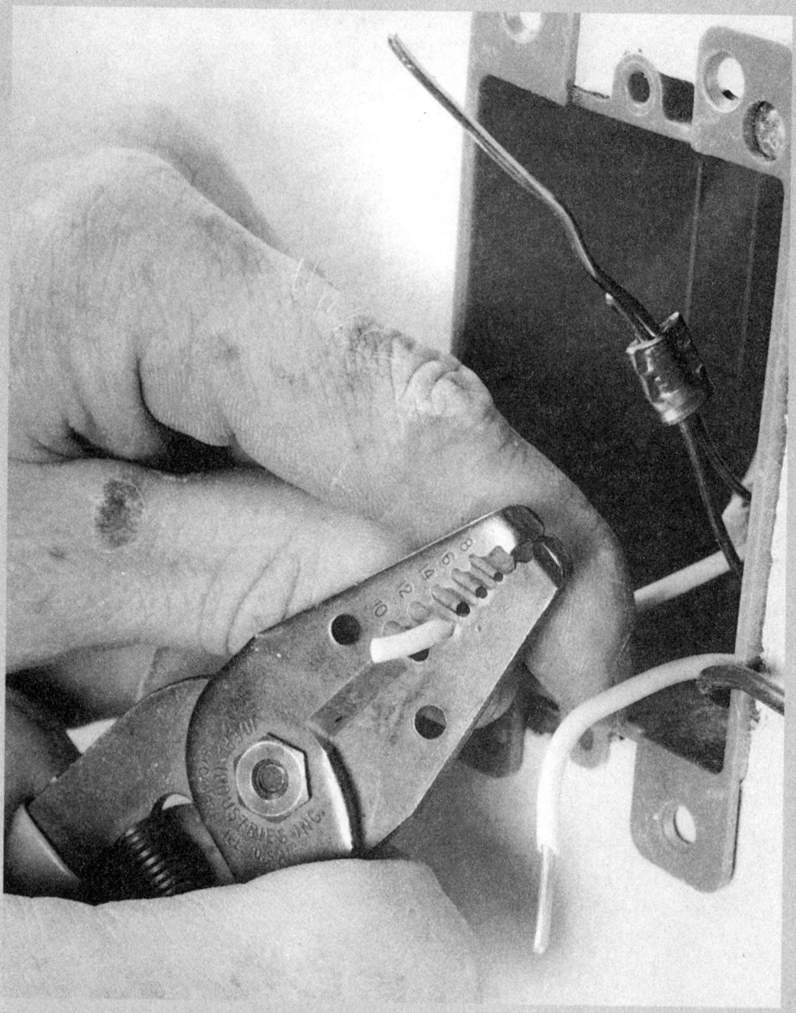

Photo 17-1. An electrician's combination tool is the only tool to use for stripping insulation from wires. Any other method risks damaging the metal core and causing a short circuit.

▲▲▲▲▲▲▲▲▲▲

Motion detectors switch outdoor lights on, providing security and energy savings at the same time. Similar devices can turn your indoor lights on as you enter or shut them off when a room has been unoccupied for a specified time period.

▼▼▼▼▼▼▼▼▼▼

Then work around the fixture's *cowling* to install the wires. The cowling is the bell-shaped cover that conceals the ceiling box and the wiring. Gently arrange the wires so they extend out from the fixture, not down into the cowling; see *Photo 17-2* on the opposite page. This gives you a better view of things and more room to work at the same time.

With a screwdriver, back out the terminal screws on the fixture until they resist further movement. Use long-nose pliers to bend a C-shape in the end of the stripped wire; this

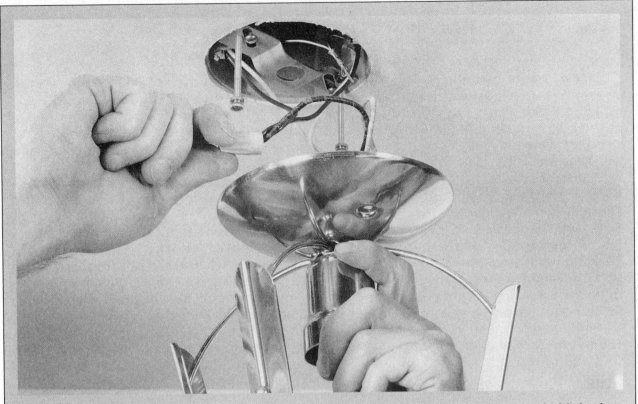

Photo 17-2. *Wiring ceiling fixtures requires either a third hand or a safety harness to hold the fixture in place while the wires are connected. Only very lightweight fixtures, like the one shown here, can be supported by the wire connections alone.*

 # BUYING LIGHTING FIXTURES

You can shop for lighting fixtures at lighting showrooms and electrical-supply houses with lighting showrooms. Discounts depend on the quantity ordered. You should expect a discount for purchases of five or more fixtures. Even if your electrical contractor makes the purchases for you, a discount may be passed on to you, but don't assume this is the case. Some contractors depend on a markup above discounted cost for part of their income.

Lighting showrooms generally have the broadest product range, especially in high-end fixtures and controls. They often are the best or only source for design services, which can range from free over-the-counter consultations to in-home visits. Although there's usually a fee for design help, all or part of it may be credited toward product purchases. Few homeowners consider bringing in a professional to help plan the lighting for a new room, but this option is worth investigating if you won't be satisfied with standard fixtures and effects.

It's easy to overlook the bulb within a handsome fixture, but this all-important part is worth a thought. It may be difficult to find replacement bulbs for idiosyncratic fixtures and impossible to find them for foreign-made models if discontinued by the importer. Ask about the availability and current cost of bulbs if the socket size is other than standard.

Finally, before going to a showroom, check out the latest in lighting design by perusing home-decorating and architectural magazines. *Architectural Lighting* (available from Miller Freeman Inc., 1515 Broadway, New York, NY 10036) specializes in new lighting technology as well as innovative ways to use traditional lighting sources.

▶ Choosing the Right Light

The quality of lighting is commonly overlooked, even by architects, when an addition is being built. Sure, you know some kind of light will be used in each room and roughly where the light sources will be located. But too often the final lighting decisions are made more to complete the electrical plan than out of careful consideration for how light will affect the room and the people who use it.

To get an idea of the importance of good lighting, think about how the quality of natural light influences the feel of a room during the day. Bright light pouring through large windows can give a room a feel of warmth, openness, and vitality, while darker rooms can feel smaller, somber, and even uninviting. Obviously, the kind of lights you choose will have the same effect on a space after the sun goes down, so your lighting deserves a thoughtful plan of its own.

The first step in developing a lighting plan is to identify the various functions a room will serve. Are you lighting a dining area, where the ability to dim the lights would give the room atmosphere? Will the space serve as a family room, where you'll need general room lighting for the TV and task lighting to read by? Once you know the function, you can choose the category of lighting.

There are three categories that will meet most household needs. General lighting is diffused over the whole room. Task lighting focuses light on a single area used for a specific job, like preparing food or studying. Accent lighting highlights a specific object or small area, such as a painting or a shelf of books. Since few rooms are reserved for just a single use, the best approach often involves combining two or three kinds of lighting.

Now you must consider which type of bulb (or lamp in the lighting trade) will best meet your needs. There are two main types: common incandescent light bulbs and fluorescent light tubes. The practical differences between these two kinds of lighting are rather simple. Incandescent lamps produce a type of intense light that is pleasant for most interior uses, since it can be easily directed and dimmed. It's commonly regarded as a warm light. However, the bulbs tend to burn out faster than fluorescents, and incandescents are more expensive to run. (Reflector bulbs, including spot lights and floodlights, are incandescent.)

Fluorescent fixtures are two to three times more energy efficient than incandescent fixtures. Also, they cast light over a broader area, making them good for general lighting. But common fluorescent lamps give off light that is much cooler and whiter than the light that is produced by incandescent bulbs. (Fluorescent bulbs with a warmer cast are available at a higher cost.) The way fluorescent light seems to "vibrate" can be disturbing to some people, and many fixtures give off a slight hum. Fluorescent lights can't be dimmed or directed as can incandescent lights. Still, fluorescents are a smart choice wherever the bulb can be concealed—under cabinets, above soffits, or behind panels that diffuse and soften the light.

There are dozens of new variations on these two types of lighting. Low-voltage incandescent bulbs, including halogens, consume a fraction of the energy that standard bulbs do. They're used widely for task lighting and spot lighting. Miniature fluorescent lights combine convenient size with energy efficiency. High-pressure sodium lamps have brought more subtle and natural coloring to outdoor lighting.

As you get away from the common everyday incandescent light bulb, prices can soar. In most cases, however, the higher cost of fixtures and bulbs is paid back in lower electric costs and longer bulb life.

Finally, choose and locate your lighting switches for optimum convenience. Use dimmer switches freely, and locate at least one light switch at every room entry. There are few things as needlessly frustrating as groping around a dark room in search of a light.

should be a clockwise turn, as illustrated in *Bending a Loop* on the right (top). In this way, tightening the screw will close the loop, not open it. The bare wire should extend almost all the way around the screw, without overlapping itself.

Some switches and receptacles permit you to simply insert bare wires into push-in fittings in the back. Once the wire is inserted, jaws inside the device work to keep it in place. A *strip gauge* molded right into the device will tell you how much insulation to strip off to make a good push-in connection. If you need to remove wire connected this way, insert a very small screwdriver into a slot provided for this function, immediately adjacent to the hole; apply pressure as your pull the wire free, as illustrated in *Push-In Fittings* on the right (center).

A solderless wire connector called a *wire nut* is used to make wire-to-wire connections. It looks something like a toothpaste cap and is twisted on over the bare ends of two or more wires. These connectors are color coded by size, but the coding varies according to manufacturer. Each size is suited to connecting a minimum and maximum number of wires of a particular gauge.

Wires are first twisted together with lineman's pliers in a clockwise direction; the connector is twisted on over them in the same direction, just as you would twist on a toothpaste cap. Make sure no bare wire is exposed at the open end of the wire nut. See the illustration *Wire Nut Connection* on the right (bottom).

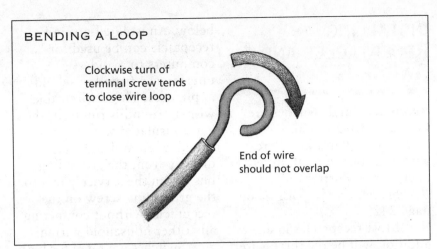

BENDING A LOOP

Clockwise turn of terminal screw tends to close wire loop

End of wire should not overlap

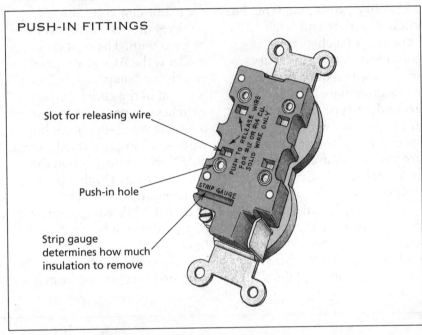

PUSH-IN FITTINGS

Slot for releasing wire

Push-in hole

Strip gauge determines how much insulation to remove

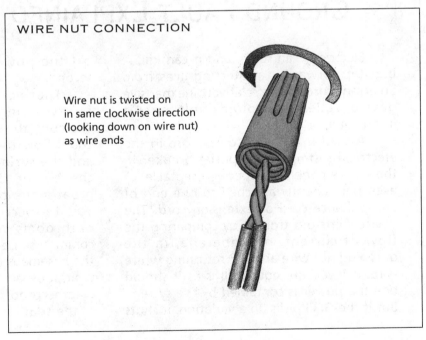

WIRE NUT CONNECTION

Wire nut is twisted on in same clockwise direction (looking down on wire nut) as wire ends

ELECTRICAL FIXTURES

INSTALLING RECEPTACLES AND SWITCHES

Receptacles and switches are familiar parts of home electrical systems, but there are variations of each. Refer back to the illustration *Receptacles on the Outside* on page 242.

Most receptacles in an addition will be the three-wire, 15A/120V grounding type. For kitchen outlets and large 120V appliances (such as air conditioners or heavy-duty power tools requiring 20A), use a three-wire 20A/120V grounding-type receptacle. For appliances drawing 240V, special plugs and receptacles are made. Inquire at an electrical-supply firm for the proper receptacle.

GFCI (ground-fault circuit interrupter) receptacles are required in wet locations such as baths or kitchens. See "Ground Fault Explained"

below. An isolated-ground receptacle can be used for computers to avoid interference from household appliances. Three-wire cable with a ground is run to it; the extra insulated wire (red) is coded green and connected directly from the grounding bus bar in the service panel to the grounding screw on the receptacle, without contacting any other household wiring.

Switches are rated for both the maximum volts and amperes they are designed to be used with. The standard model is the AC-only toggle switch (or "snap switch," as it is called in the code). Most switches are designed to control only one wire—the black hot wire—and so are termed "single pole"; see *Photo 17-3* on the opposite page. Double-pole switches are required for switched 240V equipment, such as a motor on a heavy-duty table saw.

To control a light (or switched receptacle) from a

single point, use a single-pole switch identified as such by its two terminals and the words "on" and "off" embossed on the switch. To control a light from two locations, use two three-way switches (confusingly named for the three terminals on the switch and not because they control a light from three locations).

To control a light from three or more locations, use a three-way switch at the point nearest the light and nearest the source of power and a four-way switch at any other location. Three- and four-way switches are identified by the three and four terminals on the switches, respectively, and the lack of any "on" or "off" indication. (The light can be on or off regardless of the position of a particular switch.)

You might also want to investigate the following types of switches: those with pilot lights to control fixtures not visible from where the switch

---

▶ GROUND FAULT EXPLAINED

Electricity can serve, and it can kill. A big step forward in protecting lives from an errant current is a relatively inexpensive device called a ground-fault circuit interrupter, or GFCI.

A GFCI is installed somewhere in the electrical system—as a special breaker in the service panel, as a special receptacle, or even permanently attached to one end of an appliance cord or extension cord. The device sniffs out trouble by comparing the flow of current, or amperage, in the outgoing hot wire and the returning white wire. If levels are equal, all is as it should be—the power is contained by the system. But if the GFCI picks up a variation, it shuts

off the power within a fraction of a second.

That variation may be caused by faulty wiring within a hair dryer, for example; the current, seeking a ground, could flow through you. The wetter you and the surface you're standing on are, the better the conductivity and the greater the chance of injury or death. You'd expect to see GFCI repectacles in bathrooms and kitchens. Codes—and common sense—also dictate using them in the basement and garage, around a spa or whirlpool, and outside. Plan on adding a weatherproof GFCI outlet to the exterior of the addition.

---

is located; switch/receptacle combinations; dimmer switches, which allow variable control of light intensity; time-delay switches, which delay shutting off power for 45 seconds or so to allow you to leave an area before the light goes off; and manual timer switches, which shut off power after a set time period (often used to control bathroom exhaust fans). Line-voltage thermostats, such as those used for 240V baseboard heaters, are also considered switches.

TESTING THE SYSTEM

After all wiring has been completed, turn on the power for the ultimate test. If a breaker trips immediately, the cause is probably a faulty wire connection at one of the outlets, which is easy to track down. Or a nail or screw might have penetrated a cable somewhere, causing a short between wires. That's much harder to trace and may require the experience of an electrician.

But even if no breakers trip when the power is turned on, it's important to test each receptacle to ensure that it has been properly wired; make certain receptacles are not only operational but also polarized and grounded correctly. You can buy a simple testing device that plugs into a receptacle, as illustrated in *Receptacle Analyzer* on the right. Inspectors use such a device to check your finish wiring rather than remove cover plates to verify proper connections. If there is a problem, indicator lights tell you exactly what it is.

To test a receptacle on a

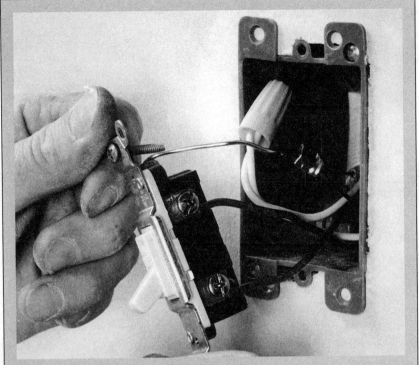

Photo 17-3. A simple single-pole switch will control a light or receptacle from one point. For safety, always install it so it breaks the power on the circuit's hot, or black, leg.

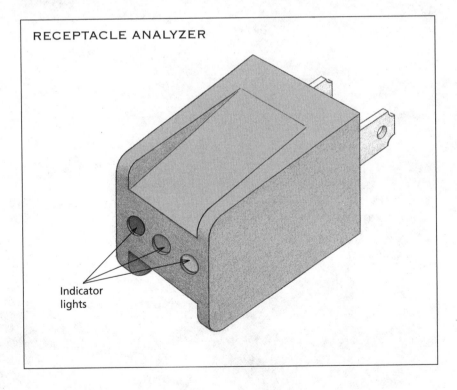

RECEPTACLE ANALYZER

Indicator lights

240V circuit, you need a specialized tool called a bar-meter voltage tester. Once the rest of the system is working smoothly, you can call in the electrical inspector for a last visit and have any 240V receptacles tested at that time.

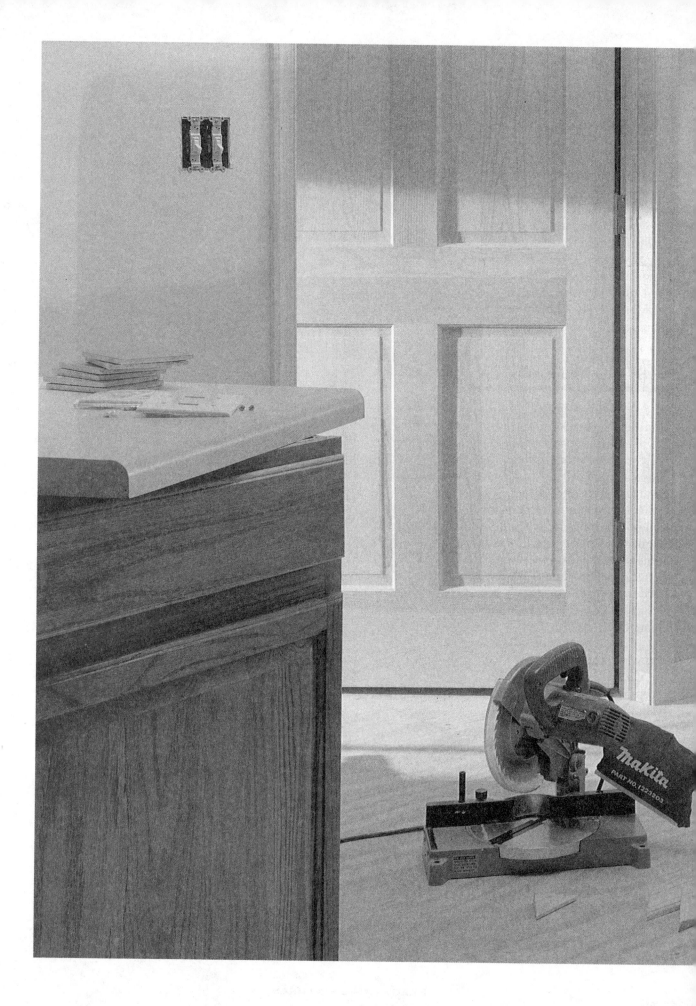

FINISHING UP

You could say that the addition is now 99 percent finished. But that lone remaining percent represents hundreds of tricky saw cuts, thousands of deft paint strokes, and a good deal of old-fashioned woodworking. One by one, each room and each surface must be wrestled to completion. And slowly, the raw, bright smell of construction will be nudged aside by the cozy, well-rounded ambience of home.

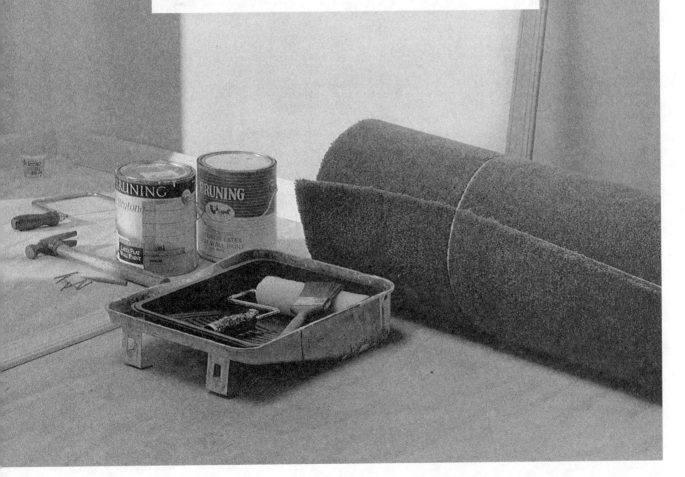

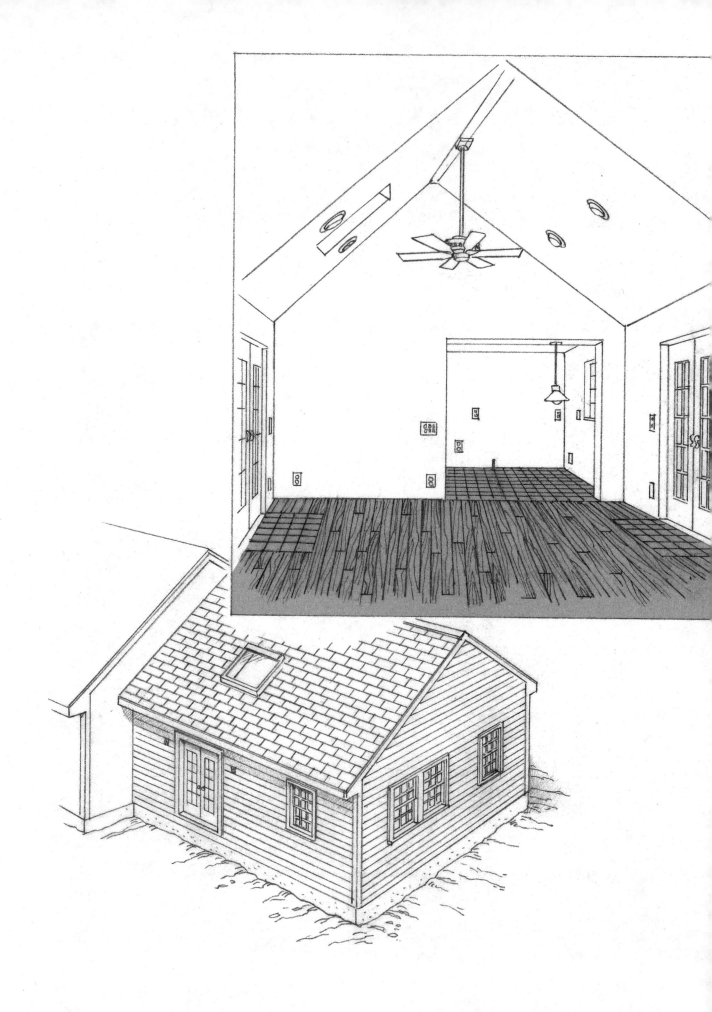

18
FLOOR COVERINGS

Floors take abuse. Shoes track in dirt, and gravity dictates that this surface is the eventual destination of every spill, from flowerpots to fruit juice. Another natural law dictates that a dropped slice of pizza will always land face down.

Since the rooms of the addition will have different functions, you'll want to consider various flooring materials. Each is designed to stand up to a different kind of use. Rooms in an addition often serve multiple functions, in which case thought should be given to a floor that's versatile as well as comfortable. Plush carpet would be a foolish choice for a kitchen, and tile might be too cold and hard a surface to use in a bedroom.

All flooring materials require a sound structural base. If the floor is framed, it will consist of joists and a subfloor. Tongue-and-groove boards were once the most common choice for subfloors, but plywood is the standard material used today. As discussed in Chapter 3, the subfloor helps to tie the joists together, and it provides a smooth, continuous surface for the finish flooring. This base must be especially level and free of gaps and ridges if it is to serve as an underlayment for wall-to-wall carpet. In this case, you probably will want to install thin sheets of lauan mahogany plywood over the subfloor and attach them with construction glue and screws to create a smooth surface. See "Wall-to-Wall Carpet" on page 310.

Applying floors over a concrete slab requires a different approach. Because it's porous, a slab can wick up moisture from the ground, which can wreak havoc with certain materials and adhesives. Proper drainage around the foundation reduces the likelihood of problems. A simple test can help determine if you have excessive moisture. Tape a 2-foot-square piece of clear plastic to the floor for 24 to 48 hours. If there is a lot of condensation when you remove the plastic, consider a material that is less affected by moisture.

Because it is porous, tile can be installed directly on concrete. However, extra care should be taken to screed the slab level when it's poured, and you should use a thicker adhesive, which will help level out any bumps or depressions. Carpet can also be glued on concrete.

Wood parquet tiles can be laid directly on concrete in a setting adhesive, but even a small amount of moisture may cause the adhesive to fail. To

▶ WALL-TO-WALL CARPET

Wall-to-wall carpet looks gracious, and it can be used atop a rough subfloor, sparing the expense of finished flooring. Relatively low initial cost and ease of installation make this an economically attractive choice. And many people have come to expect the quiet comfort of well-padded carpet in certain rooms of the house. Consider using it on stairs, both to deaden the sounds of traffic going up and down and to cushion the falls of young people.

Once woven from wool, almost all residential carpet is now made from synthetic fibers that resist stains and wear well. Most wall-to-wall carpet has a life span of only ten years on average. It may not be coincidental that homeowners tend to remodel with that frequency. Since carpet is laid right on the subfloor, replacing it with an alternate material, like wood or tile, is always an option.

Wall-to-wall carpet is usually installed by the retailer. For moderately expensive carpet, the cost of professional installation may only add 10 or 15 percent to the cost. And if the carpet is installed by the homeowner, stretched improperly, and starts to wear prematurely as a result, the warranty may not cover the damage.

help dissipate moisture and provide a nailing surface for a wood floor, rows of *sleepers* are attached to the slab. This mimics a floor frame, but is easier to construct.

To create this surface, first, lay down a moisture barrier of plastic or roofing paper, overlapping the seams 6 inches. Next, snap lines 16 inches O.C. and perpendicular to the direction the flooring will run. Then lay out strips of 1-bys or 2-bys, wide side down and centered on the lines. Pressure-treated lumber will stand up to moisture better than conventional lumber. Leave a ½-inch space between the ends of successive strips to allow air to circulate. Shim where necessary to create a level plane.

You can anchor the sleeper strips with concrete screws after predrilling with a hammer drill, or you can use a power nailer. In either case, construction adhesive applied first will make a stronger connection; apply the adhesive on the underside of each sleeper before attaching it.

Standard practice is to install a plywood subfloor over the sleepers, as explained in Chapter 4. Since plywood is more likely to expand over a slab because of higher humidity, you should leave ⅛-inch gaps at the seams and a ½-inch gap at the walls.

A full 2 x 6 floor frame may help counter very high levels of moisture, but it must be planned well in advance, taking into account doors, windows, and other features of the room. In a particularly dry area, you may be able to attach hardwood flooring directly to the sleepers without a subfloor.

WOOD FLOORING

The warm character of a wood floor has yet to be duplicated by synthetic materials. The wide range of grain patterns and colors combine to make every floor distinct. Wood ages naturally, even gracefully, and unlike other flooring materials, it can be periodically refurbished to its original beauty.

Plywood is the best choice for a subfloor under wood flooring. Oriented-strand board (OSB) costs less, but it responds more severely to moisture—a leak might prove disastrous, and the material may not perform well even in regions with moderate changes in humidity.

Chapter 4 describes laying down 4 x 8 sheets of plywood subfloor; the 8-foot dimension runs perpendicular to the direction of the joists, and the joints of the sheets are staggered. You should take other measures to help stiffen the subfloor if there will be a finish floor of wood: Use construction adhesive to bond the panels to the joists permanently, add bridging between the joists to prevent them from twisting, and run blocking supports along the 4-foot seams where the plywood isn't backed by joists.

A wood floor that gives under normal weight will squeak and may show open joints. So don't skimp on your subfloor.

Nearly any milled wood can be used for flooring, but

certain species have a reputation for beauty and durability. Hardwoods are the preferred choice because they're generally heavier, stiffer, and more resistant to surface wear than softwoods. Among the hardwoods, red oak, white oak, and maple are common choices. Other woods to consider are ash, elm, beech, and walnut. Yellow pine is an exception among softwoods; it's as hard as many hardwoods, generally less expensive, and attractive in its own way.

Every wood has a distinctive combination of color, grain, and texture. Wood floors can be stained or bleached to add even more color options. You can approach the color of walnut, for example, by staining maple, a less-expensive wood. Note, however, that stained floors will show wear more dramatically and may be more difficult to refinish.

To choose a wood species, don't rely on a single small scrap as a sample. You'll get a clearer impression if you borrow several strips of finished sample woods—1 foot long at least—from a flooring contractor or a retail flooring supplier. You might also inspect finished floors in your friends' and relatives' homes.

A home center is probably not the best source for hardwood flooring. The selection of woods is apt to be small and the mark-up substantial. Instead, check the Yellow Pages under "millwork" or look for custom millwork under "lumber." Specialty millwork companies advertise wood flooring in popular woodworking and builder's magazines, and you may be able to find a few sources in your region.

The most common size for wood flooring today is ³⁄₄ inch thick by 2¼ inches wide, called *strip flooring*. Random lengths typically run between 1½ and 8½ feet, ensuring that end joints can be staggered randomly. The flooring is milled with tongue-and-groove joints along all edges; ideally, the ends of each piece will also be milled, as shown in *Milled Wood Flooring* below. End-milled flooring speeds installation and will mean less movement at the butt joints.

Wider boards are available, as are random widths within an order; both create a less formal look. To deter wider boards from cupping, they are usually attached with counterbored screws, and the holes are filled with matching or contrasting wood plugs.

A parquet floor is made up of small strips of wood oriented into a repeating pattern. Parquet tiles, a preassembled mosaic of wood strips, are installed with adhesive backing or mastic rather than with nails.

They're thinner—³⁄₈ inch typically—and made of laminated solid wood, making them suitable for installing on a concrete floor. (See "Hard Tile Floors" on page 317 for instructions on laying out a tile floor.)

At flooring-design stores, you can buy most varieties of wood flooring already finished. This reduces the likelihood of movement due to moisture and eliminates the most onerous part of a flooring job. Some finishes on prefinishing flooring are better than those you would apply. Installing prefinished wood flooring is more demanding, though, since any minor height discrepancies can't be sanded flush. For this reason, many prefinished floors have small V-grooves at the joints to disguise imperfections.

Wood flooring is sold by the board foot, but 1 board foot of flooring will cover slightly less than 1 square foot of floor. How much less depends on the width of the stock. You should also add a per-

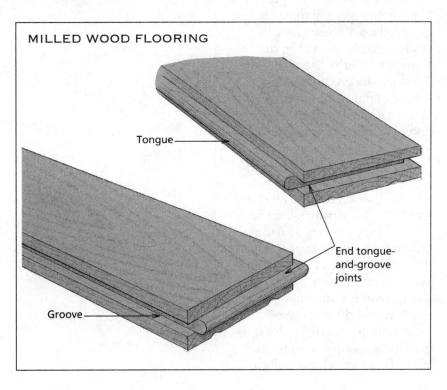

MILLED WOOD FLOORING

Tongue

End tongue-and-groove joints

Groove

centage for waste—5 percent for a *clear* grade of flooring and 10 percent or more for a lower grade. "Estimating Hardwood Strip Flooring" on page 316 provides a convenient chart for calculating exactly how much to order.

Moisture is the enemy of a wood floor installer because it can cause the flooring to buckle or twist. Assuming your material has been properly kiln dried, it's important to prevent moisture from being absorbed back into the wood before or during installation.

The room should be completely closed in, and doors and windows should be in place before you start installation. Wet work, like plastering or tiling, should be finished before you take delivery of the flooring, since the wood can absorb excess moisture these jobs produce.

To allow the wood to acclimate to the humidity of the room in which it will be installed, open the bundles and let air circulate between the strips for at least two or three days before getting to work.

When moisture is at its highest, typically during the summer months, wood will have expanded to its fullest extent. That means that the drying heat of winter is more likely to cause noticeable gaps to appear between boards. If you really want the floor to look seamless, you might put off installation until a return to cooler, dryer weather. On the other hand, be wary of nailing down wider floor boards when both temperatures and humidity are at annual lows; the boards later could expand enough to buckle, and there is some argument for leaving at least a hairline space between them.

There are a lot of nails to be pounded, and they have to be driven just right—at an angle, entering above the tongue at the edge of each board.

Rent a hammer-activated flooring nailer or an air-powered model (costing about twice as much). Either will prevent you from mashing the edges of the flooring (and fingers) with misdirected hammer blows. You'll also need a hammer and nail set, framing square, handsaw and miter box (or power miter saw), drill for pilot holes, block plane, and chalkline. A table saw will help you rip flooring into narrower widths and cut notches to go around obstacles.

On a plywood subfloor, strip flooring is best laid perpendicular to the joists. Aesthetically, rooms look better when the flooring runs in the longer direction. But if you want the floor to run with the joists, the subfloor should be 1⅛-inch tongue-and-groove sheets or two layers of ⅝-inch square-edged sheets. This makes it unnecessary to drive

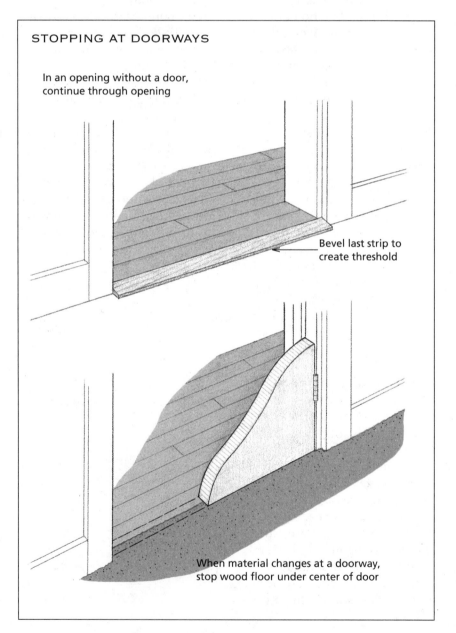

STOPPING AT DOORWAYS

In an opening without a door, continue through opening

Bevel last strip to create threshold

When material changes at a doorway, stop wood floor under center of door flooring nails into the joists and may be a convenience even if the flooring will be run perpendicular to the joists.

Once you know the running direction of the flooring, determine how transitional areas like doorways, closets, and stairways will be handled. Trim out stairways and floor grills first, and fit the running floor to these trim pieces. For the sake of appearance, you might want to use wider stock for these trim pieces rather than flooring strips.

When a wood floor terminates between rooms separated by a door, locate the joint under the center of the door. Install a metal threshold strip to bridge changes in flooring material if the height between the two materials is the same. If the wood floor will stop under an open passageway, continue it until it is flush with the wall of the adjoining room, as illustrated in *Stopping at Doorways* on the opposite page. Use a beveled wood sill for transitions where the flooring height changes.

If there is a closet along the starting wall or a doorway into another room that will receive flooring, reverse the direction of the tongue and groove on the first flooring strip, so the groove faces the closet or doorway. Cut a spline to fit between the groove in this piece and the one it will join, as shown in the illustration *Reversing Direction* on the right (top). Set aside short or flawed pieces for closets.

To install a wood floor, begin by cleaning debris from the subfloor. Transfer the locations of floor joists onto the lower walls; although the nails may barely reach the joists, that's where the subfloor is most sturdy. To keep moisture

from the underside of the wood, spread building paper over the subfloor, overlapping it 4 inches. Once the paper is down, snap chalklines at the marks.

Start the flooring along the longest wall that is parallel with the direction the flooring will run. Don't align the flooring with the wall; it may not be straight. Instead, snap a chalkline several inches out from that wall. Position the first strip of flooring by measuring from this line,

allowing an expansion gap of about ½ inch from both walls; the gap will be covered with base molding.

Use long and especially straight pieces for this course, placing them with the tongue facing into the room. Predrill and face-nail every 8 inches along the edge closest to the wall. If you install shoe molding with the baseboard, it will cover these nail holes; see *Installing the First Strip* below (bottom). If you don't, recess

313

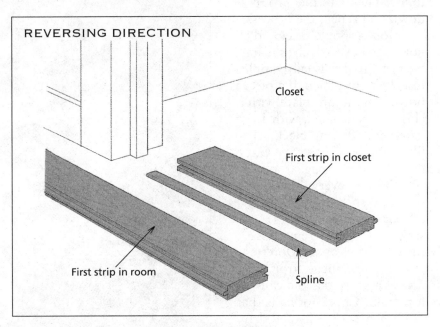

REVERSING DIRECTION

Closet

First strip in closet

First strip in room

Spline

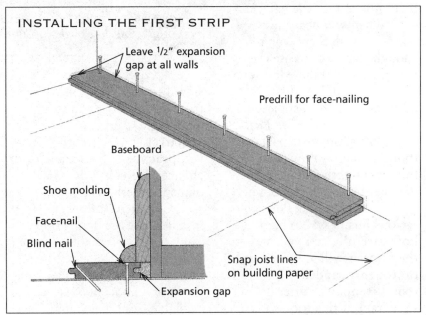

INSTALLING THE FIRST STRIP

Leave ½" expansion gap at all walls

Predrill for face-nailing

Baseboard

Shoe molding

Face-nail

Blind nail

Expansion gap

Snap joist lines on building paper

the nail heads with a nail set and fill the holes with wood filler.

Once you've installed enough strips, reorient your position so that you're on top of the laid floor, working with your back to the wall. This is the most comfortable way to proceed. Press your foot on the new strip to help engage the tongue and groove, as shown in *Photo 18-1* on the right. Lay down a half-dozen rows of strips at a time, arranging them loosely and staggering the joints. Then nail that group down and repeat the process.

Joints should be closed but not forced excessively; the impact of a nailer usually supplies just the right punch. If a piece is bowed, pry it into place with a chisel or persuade it with a hammer and scrap block, as illustrated in *Closing the Gaps* on the opposite page (top).

Be sure every other nail is over a joist. Butt joints on adjacent pieces should be staggered so they're no less than 6 inches apart. Don't nail closer than 2 inches from the end of a strip to avoid causing it to split. Check for nails that don't penetrate fully and drive them home with the nail set.

When you near the opposite wall, there won't be enough clearance to use the nailer. Face-nail these last few rows as you did the first. If necessary, rip the last piece to fit. The illustration *The Last Strip* on the opposite page (bottom) shows how to wedge this strip tightly in place. Remember to leave a ½-inch gap.

Sanding a new floor is serious business. No matter how carefully you've installed the floor, it will still need to be thoroughly sanded. Most tool-rental companies offer drum sanders, but this tool is more

Photo 18-1. Nailing flooring is tough on the back. Allow enough time to do the job without inviting discomfort.

suited to stripping the finish from an old floor than sanding a new one. And using it effectively takes practice. If you practice on your new floor, chances are you'll do some damage—perhaps a lot.

Commercial flooring installers use oscillating floor sanders, which resemble huge hand-held pad sanders. They can be used without fear of gouging the floor, but may be less readily available from rental companies.

If you can't find one, consider hiring a pro to do the sanding.

If you choose to sand, start with 60- or 80-grit paper, which does most of the work. Then switch to 100-grit and finally to 120- or 150-grit. Always sand with the grain of the wood. A hand-held belt sander or random-orbit sander will be better suited for getting close to walls than the heavy-duty disc sanders commonly rented for this purpose.

CLOSING THE GAPS

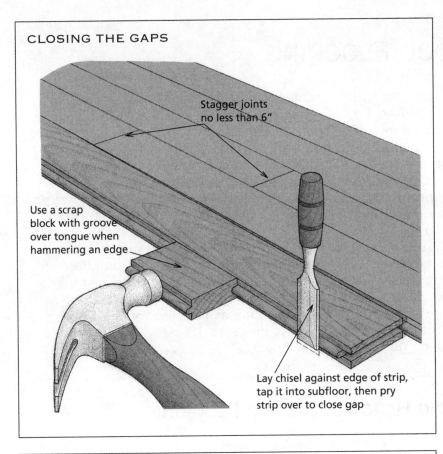

Stagger joints no less than 6"

Use a scrap block with groove over tongue when hammering an edge

Lay chisel against edge of strip, tap it into subfloor, then pry strip over to close gap

THE LAST STRIP

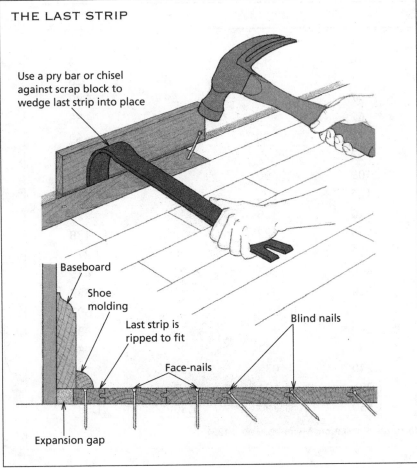

Use a pry bar or chisel against scrap block to wedge last strip into place

Baseboard

Shoe molding

Last strip is ripped to fit

Blind nails

Face-nails

Expansion gap

Compared to sanding, finishing a wood floor presents more manageable challenges. Varnish and polyurethane each provide a clear, hard finish, but there are some notable differences. In general, varnishes allow the wood to change color over time more than polyurethane. They also dry and cure more slowly and are typically more expensive.

Water-based polyurethane is another alternative. It imparts very little color change to the wood, emits far less solvent vapors, and is easier to apply and clean up after. But it's not as durable or resistant to water stains, heat, and chemicals as varnish and solvent-based polyurethane. Water-based polyurethane will also raise the grain more, so you'll need to sand more carefully between coats.

Start the finishing process by vacuuming the floor thoroughly; any dust that's left will interfere with adhesion and mar the surface. Then wipe the entire floor with a tack cloth. This type of cloth is sold at paint stores, but you can make your own by dampening a rag with an equal mixture of mineral spirits and varnish. Wrap it around a sponge mop so you can work standing up.

Once you've thoroughly cleaned the floor, use a low-nap roller or a lamb's-wool pad to apply the finish. Avoid working on very humid days, as this inhibits drying. Start in a corner and work with the grain. Only thin, even coats will dry and cure properly; plan on a minimum of three coats. Between each, sand the entire floor lightly with 220-grit paper, vacuum, then mop up the dust.

315

FLOOR COVERINGS

▶ BUYING WOOD FLOORING

Tongue-and-groove strip wood flooring comes in a variety of widths. It's sold by the board foot, but a board foot of flooring is not equivalent to a square foot of coverage; instead, it refers to the amount of rough lumber it took to make the finished stock. (This is one of those trade mysteries that can make purchasing materials a real adventure.) So if you ask for 100 board feet of ¾ x 2¼ stock, it will only cover about 70 square feet of floor.

The chart below converts square feet of floor space into board feet of flooring required for each of the most common strip flooring widths. Note that a waste factor of 5 percent is included. This is a minimum. If your rooms have an irregular shape or if you're installing the flooring diagonally to the walls, add another 5 percent. Note also that it takes less wide stock than narrow stock to cover the same square footage of floor space.

Strip flooring is delivered in tightly wrapped bundles averaging 100 board feet, with random lengths in each bundle. Plan on having help available to unload the bundles intact. Once the bundles are in the room where they'll be installed, break them, but leave them stacked. Allow as much time as possible for the flooring to acclimate to its new home before installing it.

ESTIMATING HARDWOOD STRIP FLOORING

Floor Area (square feet)	Board Feet Required, Including 5% Waste				
	¾" x 2¼"	¾" x 1½"	¾" x 3¼"	½" x 2"	⅜" x 1½"
5	7	8	6	7	7
10	14	16	13	13	14
20	28	31	26	26	28
30	42	47	39	39	42
40	55	62	52	52	55
50	69	78	65	65	69
60	83	93	77	78	83
70	97	109	90	91	97
80	111	124	103	104	111
90	125	140	116	117	125
100	138	155	129	130	138
200	277	310	258	260	277
300	415	465	387	390	415
400	553	620	516	420	553
500	692	775	645	650	692
600	830	930	774	780	830
700	968	1,085	903	910	968
800	1,107	1,240	1,032	1,040	1,107
900	1,245	1,395	1,161	1,170	1,245
1,000	1,383	1,550	1,290	1,300	1,383

Source: National Oak Flooring Manufacturers Association, Memphis, Tenn., 1991

HARD TILE FLOORS

For long-term durability, tile floors can't be beat. The surface glaze on ceramic and quarry tile determines durability; be sure to use tile intended for floors and not walls. Marble, slate, and other stones are also available in tile form. Hard tiles come in various sizes, from 3 to 12 inches square. Mosaic tiles, as tiny as 1 inch square, come preglued onto sheets of mesh backing. Special tiles are available for base molding, capping, and corners.

In new construction, either exterior-grade plywood or concrete provide an acceptable base. (Wall tile, in contrast, requires *masonry board,* a drywall-like panel that stands up to moisture and ensures a stronger bond.) Of any flooring, hard tiles are the least forgiving of flaws in the subfloor. Raised nail heads or shifting joints between sheets of plywood underlayment will lead to cracks, either in the grout joints or in the tiles themselves.

Tile is installed with a *thin-set* adhesive. Be sure the adhesive you use is compatible with both the subfloor material and the tile.

Few tools are needed to lay tile. A framing square, straight-edged board, notched trowel, chalkline, and rubber mallet comprise the basic kit. You'll need a tile saw for making straight cuts. You can rent this saw, or you can mark all the tiles to be cut and let your tile supplier make the cuts for you. Tile nippers let you trim tiles around odd-shaped obstacles like door jambs and pipes. A rubber float, some heavy rags, a large sponge, and a bucket of water are needed to apply and clean off the grout.

Start laying tile by first finding the center point of the room. Measure along each of the four walls at the floor and mark the centers.

▲▲▲▲▲▲▲▲▲▲▲▲

A tiled floor is an ideal choice in a room designed for passive solar heat gain. Choose a dark tile and grout, and the floor will absorb heat during the day and release it gradually throughout the night.

▼▼▼▼▼▼▼▼▼▼▼▼

Then snap lines across the room connecting these center points. Use a framing square to double-check that the lines are perpendicular. This step divides the room into four quadrants; you'll work one at a time.

A dry layout will preview how the perimeter tiles fit, as shown in *Laying Out Quadrants* below. If you're lucky, you won't need to cut the tiles. But this is not likely. Assuming the tiles need to be cut, the object is to have the perimeter tiles equal on opposite sides of the room. Additionally, you'll want to avoid cutting perimeter tiles to less than one-half their width.

Starting from the center, lay out a row of tiles along the shorter axis. Determine the spacing you want between tiles. Tiles may have self-spacing nibs on their edges. If yours don't, tile suppliers can provide nylon spacer tabs for this purpose. If the rows along the perimeter will be wider than a half tile, you can proceed. Otherwise, snap a new line a half-tile width away from the first line in either direction, ensuring that the end tiles will be wide

---

LAYING OUT QUADRANTS

Use a framing square or 3-4-5 triangle method to ensure layout lines are perpendicular

5
4   3

enough. Repeat this process on the other axis.

Here's a tip that may reduce the number of tiles you need to cut. If the perimeter tiles are close to full width, it may look fine to cut only one row, leaving the opposite ones full width. This depends on both the layout of the room and the size of the tiles. Also, if one side of a room is concealed somewhat by furniture or if the floor ends under a cabinet kickplate, you may choose to locate cut tiles along that wall only.

With your layout lines established, mix the adhesive material according to the instructions provided. Trowel out enough adhesive for roughly 10 square feet of tile, but don't cover the layout lines. The first series of tiles will establish the pattern for the rest of the floor, so be sure the tiles are laid straight and square.

Be aware of how long a batch of adhesive can be used before losing its holding power. In general, the ridges left by the trowel should remain distinct; if they get mushy or collapse, you probably need to mix another batch.

Set the first tile carefully and check that it's right on the lines. Press each tile firmly into the adhesive. Once you've laid a few tiles, lay a straight-edged board along one edge to check that they are forming a straight line. You can also use this board to level the tiles and press them more firmly into the adhesive. Alternately, lay the board flat and diagonally across the tiles and pound it moderately with a rubber mallet while sliding it across the tiled area, as shown in *Leveling Tiles* on the right (top). If your tiles are

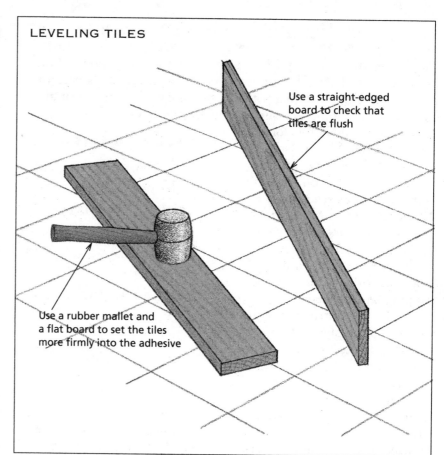

LEVELING TILES

Use a straight-edged board to check that tiles are flush

Use a rubber mallet and a flat board to set the tiles more firmly into the adhesive

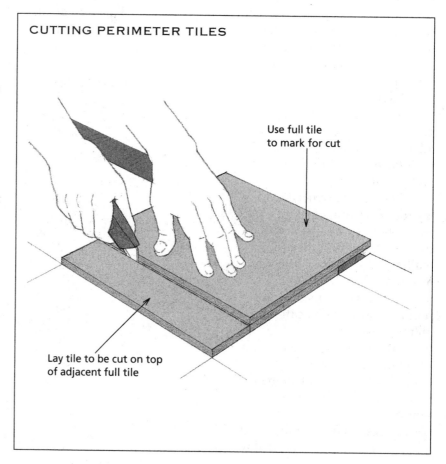

CUTTING PERIMETER TILES

Use full tile to mark for cut

Lay tile to be cut on top of adjacent full tile

particularly brittle, make a padded board using a scrap of carpet.

Work one quadrant of the room at a time. If you must kneel or walk on the newly laid tiles, lay down plywood pads to spread your weight and keep the tiles from shifting. Be sure the quadrant that includes the doorway is your last one.

Don't assume the perimeter tiles will all be identical. If the walls are out of square, the perimeter tiles will vary in size. If you're cutting the perimeter tiles yourself, scribe the line of the wall for each tile, as shown in the illustration *Cutting Perimeter Tiles* on the opposite page (bottom). If your tile supplier will be cutting the tiles, measure and mark all of the perimeter tiles when the rest of the floor is done. If they deviate ¼ inch or less, take the average and have them all cut to the same dimension. The wall joint will hide these minor differences. Where the wall has serious bumps or hollows, mark each tile and its location, then cut it to fit.

Cutting tiles to fit around obstructions takes a little more effort. If the portion to be cut out is square to the tile edges, butt the tile against the obstruction and transfer the marks with a try square. However, if the cut is more complicated, use the template method shown in *Fitting Tiles around Obstacles* below; this method lets you make an error without wasting a good tile.

Cut a piece of cardboard to the exact size of a tile. Fit the template by gradually cutting away the cardboard until it fits snugly against the obstruction. Allow a gap for grout. Then trace the template pattern onto a tile. Use tile nippers to cut irregular shapes. Just nibble away small pieces until you're satisfied with the fit. For notches that are square to the edges, the cuts can be started with a tile saw and finished up with the nippers.

Allow the adhesive to cure for the required time, then proceed to the grouting. Again, be sure to use the grout recommended for your tile. Trowel the grout onto the floor and use the rubber float to press it into the joints,

---

FITTING TILES AROUND OBSTACLES

Scribe lines on cardboard template, then transfer lines to tile

Chip away at tile with tile nippers to make cutout

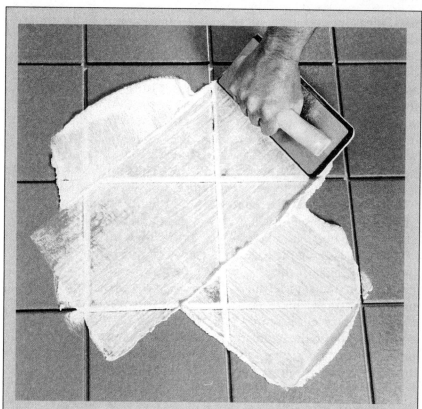

Photo 18-2. With a rubber float, apply grout over the tiles using long, diagonal strokes.

Photo 18-3. Using a wet towel, wipe the grout off the surface of tiles in a circular motion.

moving diagonally across the tiles, as shown in *Photo 18-2* on the left (top). Fill the joints flush with the tile surface.

After a specified time, usually 15 minutes, the grouted area can be wiped down with a coarse rag and water. Rinse the excess grout from the rag frequently, but don't saturate the tile. You want to remove the grout from the surface of the tiles without dragging it out of the joints. Move in a circular motion for the best results, as shown in *Photo 18-3* on the left (bottom).

After the entire surface appears dry, wipe it down with clean water and a sponge. Further instructions may be included with either the grout or tile for cleaning off grout residue.

RESILIENT FLOORING

Resilient flooring withstands heavy traffic with little sign of wear, is impermeable to spills and stains, and is slightly flexible under foot. This combination makes it an ideal choice for high-traffic areas like kitchens, baths, hallways, entry foyers, and recreation rooms.

Linoleum, the original resilient flooring material, has largely been displaced by vinyl-based products. Solid rubber, once found only in commercial settings, is also now available for residential use.

Your first choice will be between tile and sheet forms. Tiles are 12 inches square and typically backed with self-stick adhesive; you can mix different patterns to create decorative borders. Joints between tiles eventually attract dirt, making resilient tiles more difficult to keep clean than resilient sheet floors.

Resilient sheet flooring comes in 6- or 12-foot-wide rolls and in two very distinct types. In a nutshell, one type is flexible and easy to install, while the other is brittle and not recommended for do-it-yourself installation. Most flexible products are glued at the perimeter only, while the heavier versions are glued throughout. Each manufacturer supplies a particular glue that must be used with its flooring. If it is necessary to use more than one sheet, a liquid seam filler is applied at the seams. Both glue and fillers bond chemically with the vinyl, and the different brands are not interchangeable.

The subfloor under resilient flooring must be smooth, and the seams must be very stable and tight. Use a subfloor product that doubles as underlayment—a separate, thin layer used on top of a subfloor and under the finish floor; or apply a separate layer of ¼ inch plywood with the joints staggered relative to the joints in the subfloor. Particleboard can also be used. It's cheaper but needs to be thicker—½ or ⅝ inch—and is harder to nail or screw down.

If the subfloor material shifts, even a little bit, a sharp line will telegraph through the vinyl. This raised area will wear unevenly. Problems due to faulty subfloor or underlayment won't be covered by the manufacturer's warranty, so take extra care with this step. In any case, use countersunk screws and glue or construction adhesive at the seams. You can trowel on floor leveler, sold in powdered form, to ensure smooth joints and to cover uneven areas and nail holes.

In a room with very few cutouts, you could unroll the flooring and then cut it to fit the corners.

▲▲▲▲▲▲▲▲▲▲▲▲

Under resilient flooring, even tiny pieces of debris can telegraph through the surface. After sanding uneven joints and sweeping the floor, give the floor a thorough going over with a shop vacuum.

▼▼▼▼▼▼▼▼▼▼▼▼

But the safest way to fit a piece of resilient flooring involves first making a template. Some manufacturers sell a template kit. Or you can use pieces of kraft paper taped together to get the size pattern you need. (You may be able to use the paper that comes wrapped around the flooring.)

Roll the paper out in the longest direction, letting it overlap the walls by a few inches. Overlap and tape individual sheets together as needed until the paper covers the entire floor. Then carefully cut the paper into the corner along the longest wall. Vinyl expands and contracts slightly, so leave about a ⅛-inch gap at all walls. Tape the first edge in place, as shown in *Photo 18-4* below. Continue the process, first cutting the pattern to fit the opposite wall and then the remaining two walls.

Unroll the flooring face up in an area larger than the room template. If that means going outdoors, be sure the area is free of sharp stones or glass. Once the flooring is flat, unroll the template onto it. Tape or weight the template down so it can't move once

Photo 18-4. Before laying down sheet flooring, fit a paper template on the subfloor. Tape pieces into corners and cut small windows through the template to tape it to the floor.

Photo 18-5. After resilient flooring is marked to size from the paper template, it can be cut easily with scissors.

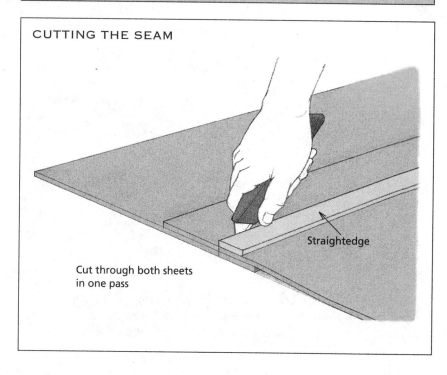

CUTTING THE SEAM

Cut through both sheets
in one pass

Straightedge

you start transferring the cut lines. Use a marker and straightedge to trace around the template. Finally, cut along the lines you've traced with a sharp utility knife or shears, as shown in *Photo 18-5* on the left.

Roll the flooring up so the longest wall edge is at the outside of the roll. Then lay the flooring in the room and unroll it. Be careful around projecting alcoves or closets—a tear can spread with surprising ease. Check the starting edge as you unroll the floor, repositioning it against the wall if necessary.

If there is a seam, overlap and tape the two pieces. Be sure the pattern lines coincide. Then, using a straightedge, carefully cut through both layers of flooring, as shown in *Cutting the Seam* on the left. Keep the knife vertical as you cut.

Tile glues are expensive, but don't be tempted to use a cheaper all-purpose substitute. The products are designed according to the floor's composition. Fortunately, most flexible resilient flooring is glued down only at the perimeter and seams, so you won't need much adhesive.

Glue any seams first. Roll back both pieces of flooring and apply the adhesive according to the manufacturer's instructions. Then lay the pieces down carefully. With a rolling pin, apply pressure along the entire seam.

To keep the seams closed and tight to the floor, apply the seam sealer recommended by the manufacturer. Again, make sure it's the one that is appropriate to your floor. The sealer fills any gap between the two pieces and forms a welded seam that should be nearly invisible if made properly. Finally, glue down the perimeter, one section at a time, as you did the seam.

Originally the Baileys had planned to use ceramic tile in their kitchen and new bath. But with money (and patience) running low, they opted for the lower cost and easier installation of resilent flooring. And since both rooms were small and had few jogs to deal with, Barry and Dave were able to install the flooring without making a pattern.

Barry ordered the materials 6 inches larger than the overall room dimensions, leaving a 3-inch overlap at each wall. First he unrolled the flooring and gently pressed it out toward the walls. Then he cut out for the corner column, as shown in the illustration *Relief Cuts in Resilient Flooring* on the right.

After pressing the material gently into the corners, he made the vertical relief cuts in the inside and outside corners.

"The important thing here," he noted, "is to make the cut from the outside in, working from the edge of the excess flap toward the finished corner. This allows the material to define the corner, instead of you trying to guess where it will fall."

Once all of the vertical corner cuts were made, Barry pressed the vinyl into the corners with a length of scrap wood. Finally, he used a metal straightedge as a guide and cut the material with a utility knife. He left about a 1/8-inch gap because vinyl expands and contracts a little bit.

323

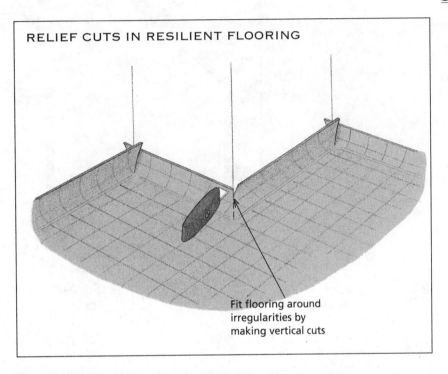

RELIEF CUTS IN RESILIENT FLOORING

Fit flooring around irregularities by making vertical cuts

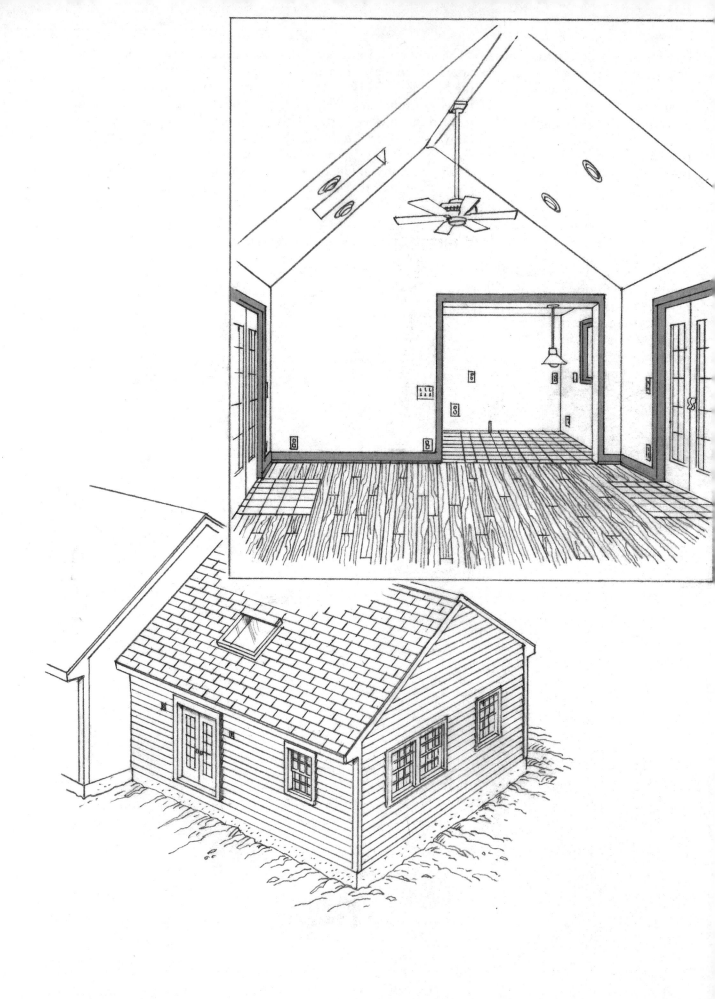

19
INTERIOR DOORS AND TRIM

We tend to take doors for granted. As long as they open and close, they get little attention. And trim really can blend into the woodwork. But these humble elements of an interior can call attention to themselves—if they're either shoddily installed or done with extra care.

Working with doors may seem a little intimidating, but prehung units cut the job down to size. You probably already have all the necessary tools needed. Even if you are relatively inexperienced, this can be a satisfying job.

SELECTING INTERIOR DOORS

Although solid wood frame-and-panel doors were once used almost universally inside the home, vinyl clad and fiberglass doors are also widely available now. They're generally made from lightweight, rigid foam core with wood-grain vinyl or fiberglass cladding. A border of solid wood provides the necessary anchor for attaching hardware. These doors look presentable (though they won't fool a true wood lover), and they're easy to keep clean. But they're a lot harder to repair in the event of damage. Painting is not recommended, so you're stuck with the color you buy.

There are two basic techniques for hanging a door: swing it on a hinge or slide it on a track. (Refer to Chapter 9 for instructions on installing a prehung door unit.) But interior doors offer numerous variations on these arrangements. What's more, you can either buy prehung units or buy the doors and hardware separately. In either case, make your purchases before framing in order to make the correct-sized openings in the walls.

A *pocket door* slides in a track, disappearing into the wall when opened. Sliding doors use less floor space than swinging doors, leaving more room for furniture and traffic. They're often used in pairs between two rooms to create one living space when the doors are opened. The Baileys chose a single-width pocket door for their walk-in closet. A hinged door would have obstructed the narrow passage between their bathroom and bedroom.

Pocket doors can be bought as a complete kit; see the illustration *Framing a Pocket Door* on page 326. Or you can purchase the door and hardware separately and build the pocket frame yourself. Hardware kits vary slightly, so purchase the kit before framing

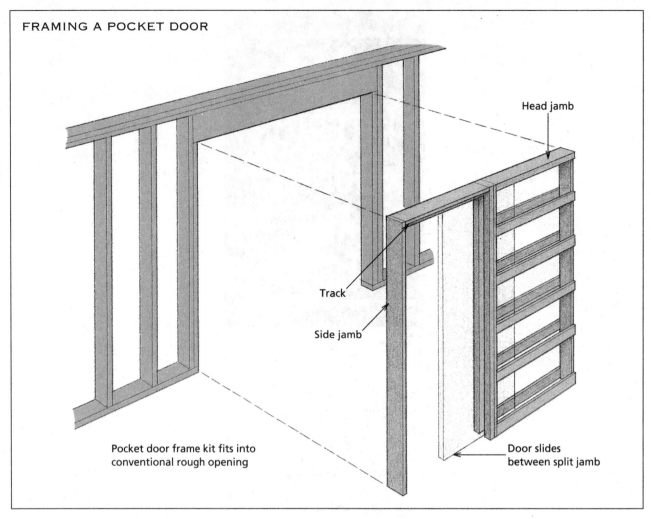

Head jamb

Track

Side jamb

Pocket door frame kit fits into
conventional rough opening

Door slides
between split jamb

and follow the manufacturer's instructions. Be sure the door operates properly before you apply the drywall, since adjusting the concealed part of the track later would require opening a hole in the wall—not a pleasant thought.

Sliding doors don't always disappear into pockets. Fully exposed bypass doors are used in multiples of two or more and slide past each other on a track mounted to the head jamb; these doors are commonly used on closets.

Bi-fold doors—two doors that are hinged together—combine hinges and a sliding mechanism. One door has top and bottom rotating pivots that are inserted in brackets, while the

top edge of the other door has a roller that rides in an overhead track. When opened, the doors fold back to back and extend into the room only half as far as a full door would. Bi-folds work well for closets and other storage areas. See the illustration *Bi-fold and Bypass Doors* on the opposite page (top).

HANGING A DOOR FROM SCRATCH

You don't have to settle for doors sold by stores and home centers. Architectural salvage companies are a great source of unusual doors, as well as mantels, stained-glass windows, and light fixtures. The character

of an old specimen may transform your new space from run of the mill to something very special.

Recycled doors are not likely to still be attached to their frames, and they may not be a standard size that can be hung in a store-bought frame. That means building a door frame and hanging the door will be part of the cost of salvaging an old door. (You may also have to frame and hang a door yourself if you use custom-made doors or have walls that are thicker than normal.)

A door frame, also called a jamb, is built from three pieces of wood—in carpentry parlance, two sides and a head.

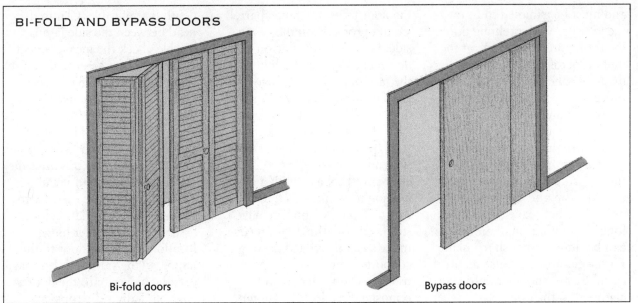

Bi-fold doors

Bypass doors

As shown in *Assembled Door Frame* on the right, the head can be attached to the side jamb with a dado, rabbet, or butt joint. A dado or rabbet joint makes the frame stronger, and assembly will be more precise. Either of these joints can be cut with a router and a straight bit or on a table saw with a dado head. A butt joint reinforced with screws will also suffice.

No matter which joint you choose, be sure to add braces, as shown. Use wood that's flat and has straight edges. A finished jamb thickness of ¾ inch is adequate for lightweight doors, but heavier doors require beefier jambs of ⅞ or 1 inch.

The other component of a door frame is the *stop,* the ledge that the door swings shut against. The frame and the stop are sometimes milled from a single piece of wood, but when building your own frame, it's much easier to add separate stops, nailing them in place *after* the door is hung.

In general, door frames are made to standard-sized openings. Doors that are not prehung are made to the same standard sizes

ASSEMBLED DOOR FRAME

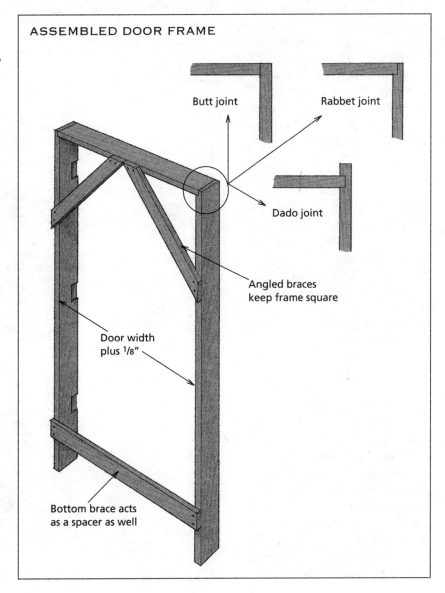

Butt joint

Rabbet joint

Dado joint

Angled braces keep frame square

Door width plus ⅛"

Bottom brace acts as a spacer as well

and must be trimmed to fit on the job site. With prehung doors, the fitting process is done at the mill or factory. With custom-made or salvaged doors, the process is reversed: the frame is made to match the door.

Before building the frame, make sure the door is square by measuring the two diagonals. If the measurements don't match, trim the top and edges as necessary, but leave the bottom long. Trimming small amounts can be done with a sharp plane. For larger amounts, use a circular saw and a straightedge clamped to the door.

The hinge and lock edges on doors are typically beveled slightly toward the back or stop side; this keeps the hinge edge from binding and allows a close fit at the lock edge. You can cut the bevel with a saw at the same time you trim the edges, or you can plane the bevel with a block plane after making the saw cut. Allow a bevel of $1/16$ inch per inch of door thickness; that is, a $1\frac{1}{2}$-inch-thick door should have a bevel of $3/32$ inch.

Next, locate the hinges for the door. For interior doors of standard height and weight, two hinges may suffice; heavier doors should get a third in the center. The exact location of top and bottom hinges is not critical, but there are guidelines. "Five and ten"—5 inches from the top edge and 10 inches from the bottom edge—is the rule of thumb.

On frame-and-panel or French doors, the edge of the hinge is often aligned with the top and bottom rails; see the illustration *Locating Door Hinges* on the right. When adding a third hinge, always center it between the top and bottom hinges.

To lay out a hinge mortise, first determine the orientation of the door faces; the hinge barrel should protrude on the swing side. Next, scribe a line on the door edge $3/16$ to $1/4$ inch in from the face opposite the hinge barrel. Then trace the two shorter lines directly from the hinge.

To cut the hinge mortises, start by scoring the layout lines with a utility knife. Carefully chop out the waste with a chisel, as shown in *Cutting Hinge Mortises* on the opposite page (top). To hold the door on edge, make a set of wedged door supports from 2 x 4 scraps, or use pipe clamps facing in opposite directions, as shown.

Next, cut the head jamb to length so the door opening will be $1/8$ inch wider than the door. Account for the dado or rabbet

depth if applicable. Clamp the head between the side jambs, double-check the measurement, and predrill for screws. If you're using a butt joint, mark where the inner face of the head jamb intersects with the side jambs.

Once the head is cut, lay out and mortise the jamb for the hinges. You can do this after the frame is in place, but it can be accomplished more easily with the side jamb laid flat, before assembly. To transfer hinge locations from the door to the jamb, lay the side jamb leg that gets the hinges onto the door edge, and align the tops, as shown in *Marking the Jamb for Hinges* on the opposite page (bottom). Now slide the side jamb piece *up* toward the top

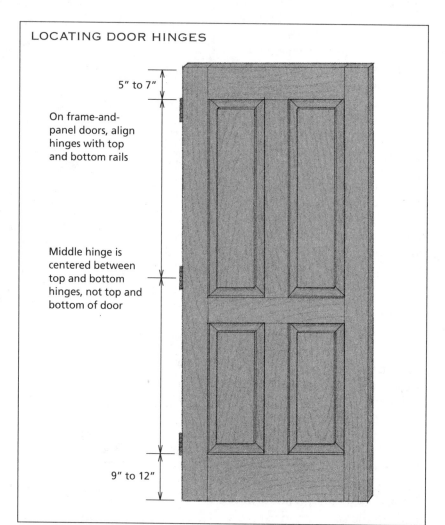

LOCATING DOOR HINGES

5" to 7"

On frame-and-panel doors, align hinges with top and bottom rails

Middle hinge is centered between top and bottom hinges, not top and bottom of door

9" to 12"

328

CUTTING HINGE MORTISES

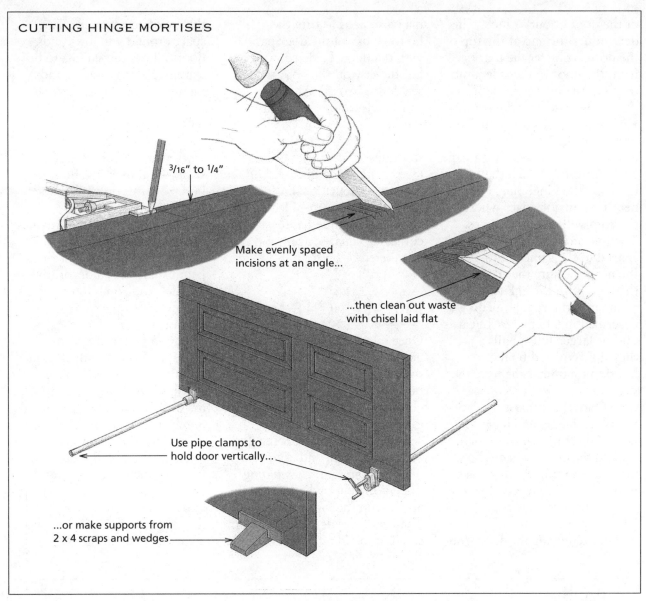

3/16" to 1/4"

Make evenly spaced
incisions at an angle...

...then clean out waste
with chisel laid flat

Use pipe clamps to
hold door vertically...

...or make supports from
2 x 4 scraps and wedges

MARKING THE JAMB FOR HINGES

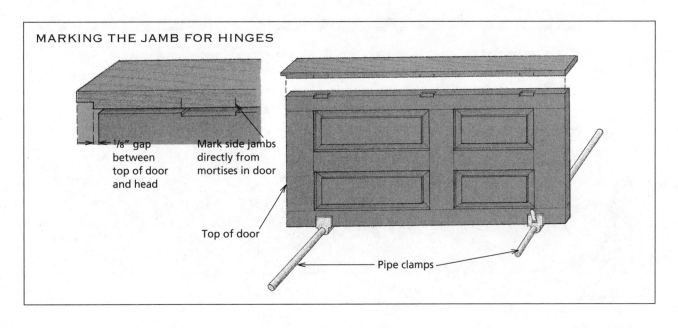

1/8" gap
between
top of door
and head

Mark side jambs
directly from
mortises in door

Top of door

Pipe clamps

of the door about ⅛ inch. This determines the gap at the top of the door. Transfer the marks from the door to the side jamb, then cut the mortises.

Now assemble the frame. Square the jambs and add the braces, as illustrated in *Assembled Door Frame* on page 327 (bottom). Attach the braces opposite the hinge side, and nail near the outside edges where the trim will cover the holes. The bottom brace keeps the legs spaced to the same width as at the head. Be sure the edges of the jambs are flush. Fit the frame into the rough opening as described in Chapter 9. Locate 10d or larger finish nails so they'll be covered by the stop, but don't hammer them all the way home.

Once the frame is in place, install the hinges and hang the door. Adjust the shims so the gap around the door is even. You may have to trim the lock edge of the door slightly, but this is easier if the edge has been beveled and can often be done without removing the door. You may also need to trim the bottom edge of the door parallel with the floor. To do so, scribe a line directly off the floor when the door is closed. Allow about ¼-inch clearance above the finished floor height.

Before nailing in the door stops, install the lock and catch. (See "Installing a Lockset" on pages 150–151.) Finally, install the door stops. A profiled stop needs to be mitered at the corners; a square-edged stop can be mitered or butted.

Installing Trim

Once interior doors are installed, you're ready to trim out the rooms of the addition. The main purpose of trim is to conceal the gaps and irregularities where different parts of a room converge. *Casing* covers the gap between drywall and door and window frames. *Base molding* bridges the joint where drywall and the finished floor meet. These gaps result inevitably from standard building practices, and they're often necessary. The space around windows and doors allows those units to be shimmed perfectly level and plumb. Wood floors must be kept back from walls a tad to allow for expansion. Trim also helps conceal flaws in workmanship and materials, such as a gully in the floor or a bump along a drywalled door frame.

Trim can be decorative as well. Although plain, square stock conceals gaps just fine, trim usually has a decorative profile. And some forms of trim are almost exclusively decorative.

Crown molding, for example, provides an elegant transition between walls and ceilings, even though a taped drywall joint works fine here. Similarly, a chair rail, which ostensibly keeps chairs from damaging the wall, adds a formal touch to a room and usually makes a room's ceiling appear higher and the room more spacious. Traditionally, chair rail capped off

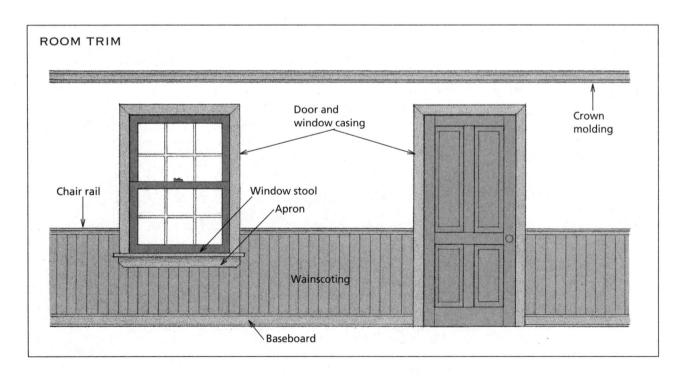

ROOM TRIM

Door and window casing

Crown molding

Chair rail

Window stool

Apron

Wainscoting

Baseboard

wainscoting, as shown in *Room Trim* on the opposite page, but it can also be used by itself.

You can purchase wood trim at any lumberyard or home center. Windows and doors require specific lengths of casing. Purchase lengths of trim that will produce the least waste. Standard 6-foot, 8-inch doors require two pieces of vertical casing just under 7 feet long. Buy a 14-footer for each door instead of two 8-footers, and you'll save 2 feet of casing per door.

Base, chair, and crown moldings, on the other hand, often need more than one length of material to trim any single length of wall. These lengths are called *running trim,* and the best approach is to tally the total running length needed and buy the longest lengths available. Always buy a little extra in case of mistakes.

Most retail sources buy stock from large regional manufacturers, making it easy to buy moldings to match existing trim.

▲▲▲▲▲▲▲▲▲▲▲▲

To save time masking around trim, paint it after cutting it, but before nailing it in place. You'll have to be conscious of working with clean hands and careful hammer blows as you install the painted trim, or you'll risk spoiling the look of the job.

▼▼▼▼▼▼▼▼▼▼▼▼

If the trim you want to match is very old or unusual, inquire about custom milling. Local lumber suppliers may be able to get you what you want; or check the Yellow Pages for custom-millwork or cabinet shops.

The most commonly available molding material is clear pine, which can be painted, stained, or left natural with a clear finish.

Oak molding has also become widely available. It costs about twice as much as pine, but its hardness and attractive grain make it an ideal choice for trim.

Consider priming or sealing trim stock before installing it; sealing the back will reduce shrinkage, which will keep joints from opening up. You can also buy trim prefinished with wood-grain vinyl or paint—all you'll need to do is fill the nail holes once the trim has been installed.

The best tool for cutting trim is a power miter saw. The one shown in *Photo 19-1* below *(continued on page 334)*

331

Photo 19-1. Barry uses a standard 10-inch power miter saw to handle all the trim work on the Bailey addition. Consider renting one to save time and to make crisp, accurate cuts.

INSTALLING CROWN MOLDING

Few things can transform a plain room more easily than crown molding. As its name suggest, this molding adds distinction. Unlike baseboard, which seems to recede into the floor, even a small (and inexpensive) crown molding catches the eye.

Installing crown is more difficult than other trim because it's oriented at an angle to both the wall and the ceiling. This makes cutting the joints a bit more complicated.

Unless your room is exceptionally

they would open up as the wood shrank during the winter when the air is heated.

The most efficient sequence of installing this molding is to start with the longest wall. Square-cut the first piece (or pieces) so it fits tight to the corners. Intersecting pieces are coped where they meet this first piece and square-cut at the other end where they meet the opposite wall. The last piece is then coped on both ends; see *Crowning Sequence* below (bottom).

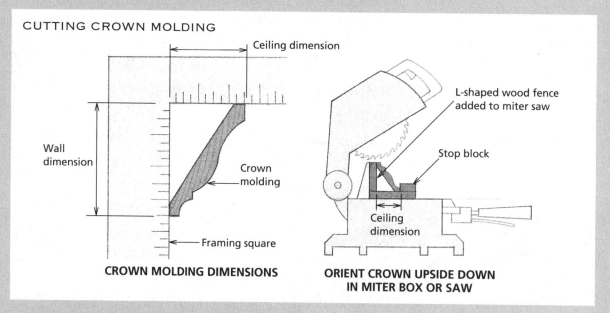

CUTTING CROWN MOLDING

Ceiling dimension

Wall dimension

Crown molding

Framing square

CROWN MOLDING DIMENSIONS

L-shaped wood fence added to miter saw

Stop block

Ceiling dimension

ORIENT CROWN UPSIDE DOWN IN MITER BOX OR SAW

large, a 3- or 4-inch crown will be wide enough. The photos and illustrations show a typical cove-and-ogee profile that you'll find at any good lumber store.

The first step, as shown in *Cutting Crown Molding* above, is to determine where the crown will meet the wall and ceiling. The miters are cut with the crown set at the same angle against the miter fence, only upside down, as shown. Attach an auxiliary base to your miter saw, then nail a stop block to the base to ensure that this angle remains constant for all cuts. You might also need an auxiliary fence if yours is not high enough to support the crown.

Inside corners of crown receive a coped joint, while outside corners are mitered. You *could* miter inside corners, but it is likely

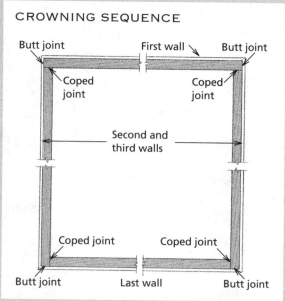

CROWNING SEQUENCE

Butt joint | First wall | Butt joint

Coped joint | Coped joint

Second and third walls

Coped joint | Coped joint

Butt joint | Last wall | Butt joint

A coping saw is held at an angle while following the contour revealed by the inside miter cut.

Only the leading edge of the coped piece contacts its mate, creating a crisp fit.

Outside corners are mitered. Cut them last since they're easiest to fit.

There are only four possible miter cuts—a left inside and outside and a right inside and outside. To prevent errors, use two pieces of scrap molding to make a sample of each cut. A coped cut should be started as if it were an inside miter. Then a series of cuts that follow the contour of the profile should be made with a coping saw. The cuts should be angled toward the back so that the leading edge is as thin as possible; see the photos above (left and center). Cut outside miters last; start the cut heavy of the mark slightly, then trim back for a tight fit; see the photo above (right).

If you'll be joining pieces end to end, use a *scarf* joint (shown in the photo below). First, cut and fit the corner joints on each piece. Then cut one of the scarfed ends with an inside 45 degree miter. After securing that piece in place, mark and cut the mating scarf with an outside miter. Make each cut with the saw set at the same angle, but with the stock on opposite sides of the blade.

Crown molding is more demanding to attach than flat molding. You may be able to nail smaller crown into the top plate anywhere along the wall. Larger crown requires that you locate studs and joists for nailing. Finish-trim screws are a worthy alternative to nails. As shown in *Attaching Crown Molding* below, you can drive the screws at an angle into the top plate to pull the crown tight to both the ceiling and the wall. Even with small heads, these screws still leave a large hole to fill.

Thin crown molding may conform to ripples in walls and ceilings. With larger crown molding, you'll have to caulk the gaps or feather in a swath of joint compound.

Use a scarf joint when two pieces meet end to end.

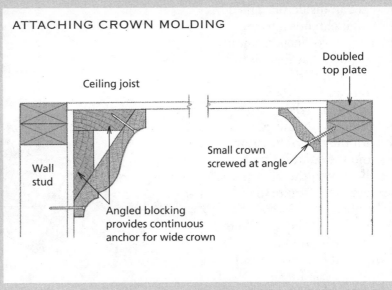

ATTACHING CROWN MOLDING

Ceiling joist

Doubled top plate

Wall stud

Angled blocking provides continuous anchor for wide crown

Small crown screwed at angle

INTERIOR DOORS AND TRIM

is a 10-inch model capable of cutting a full 4 x 4. It is an excellent addition to any carpentry tool arsenal. When setting up to use a power miter saw, attach an L-shaped fence made from scrap wood. It provides a longer platform to support the work and keeps small cutoffs from being thrown by the blade. If your trim work is limited or you don't want to spend the cash to buy or rent a power saw, you can trim out an addition with the time-tested miter box and backsaw.

▲▲▲▲▲▲▲▲▲▲▲

If a bump in the drywall interferes with a good miter joint, don't keep cutting the joint. Instead, remove a patch of drywall by scoring the outline with a razor knife.

▼▼▼▼▼▼▼▼▼▼▼

When trimming a room, start with the windows. Some windows are trimmed like a picture frame, with the casing mitered at all four corners. Others get an inside sill, called a *stool*, that extends into the room a couple of inches. The casing is mitered at the top but meets the stool with a butt joint. You can buy stool stock along with your other trim. On some windows, the sill edge is flush with the rest of the frame edges, and the stool is simply nailed directly to the sill edge. Other windows require that the stool be notched at its ends to meet the sill. In either case, the stool extends beyond the window opening, forming *ears*, as shown in *Installing a Window Stool* on the right.

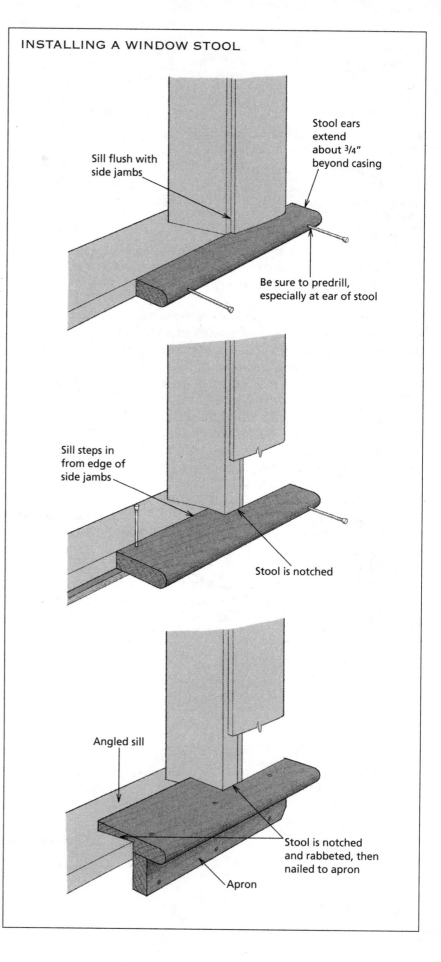

INSTALLING A WINDOW STOOL

Sill flush with side jambs

Stool ears extend about ³/4″ beyond casing

Be sure to predrill, especially at ear of stool

Sill steps in from edge of side jambs

Stool is notched

Angled sill

Stool is notched and rabbeted, then nailed to apron

Apron

Photo 19-2. Using a square as a guide, Barry marks the notch that will form the sill ear.

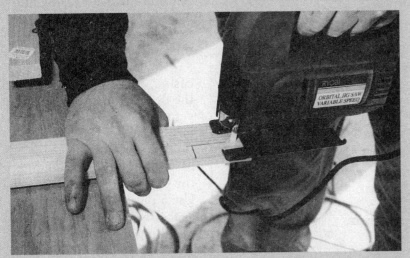

Photo 19-3. Barry cut the notch with a jigsaw, but you can also use a handsaw or a table saw.

Photo 19-4. After Barry attached the stool, he finished trimming the window by attaching the casing.

Photos 19-2 through 19-4 on the left show how Barry cut and fit a window stool in the Baileys' new family room.

With the stool in place, proceed with the casing, starting with the head piece. The casing covers all but a small strip of the window or door frame. This *reveal*, as it's called, is typically between ⅛ and ¼ inch wide. Mark the reveal right on the window or door head jamb where it intersects with the side jamb, as shown in *Window and Door Casing* on page 336. After cutting the first miter, set the piece in place, with the inside corner of the miter on the reveal mark. Then mark where the other reveal falls on the opposite inside edge. Strike the 45 degree line and make the cut.

▲▲▲▲▲▲▲▲▲▲

Instead of using a drill bit to predrill trim at the edges and ends, chuck one of the nails you're using to attach the trim into your drill. By using that size nail, all of the holes will match perfectly.

▼▼▼▼▼▼▼▼▼▼

Only rarely do miters come together perfectly on the first try. To adjust the angle of cut, try slipping a wedge between the saw fence and the stock instead of adjusting the blade angle. This way you avoid the risk of forgetting to reset the angle and inadvertently cutting a modified angle when you want a true 45 degree cut. Always make the cut a bit "heavy" so

WINDOW AND DOOR CASING

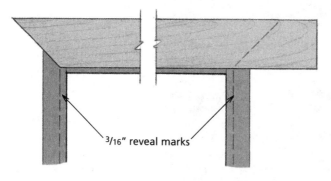

Typical door or window frame →

3/16" reveal marks

1. Mark reveals at inside corners of frame

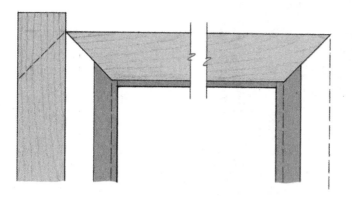

3/16" reveal marks

2. Cut a miter, set piece in place, and mark opposite miter

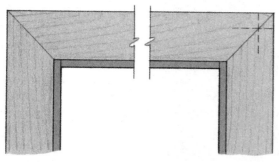

3. With head casing nailed in place, make square or scribed cut at floor or stool first, then flip piece around and use tip of miter to mark for the final cut

4. Nail casing legs to trimmer studs, keeping reveal even, and glue and lock nail miter to keep joint closed

you can adjust the angle if necessary, then trim as necessary until the piece fits snugly.

Nail the head casing to the frame using 3d or 4d finish nails. Once it's in place, add 6d or 8d finish nails along the outside edge into the studs. Next, make the square cut where the casing meets the floor or sill. Adjust the angle of cut if necessary. With that done, you can mark for the miter cuts. Flip the piece around so the outside edge rests against the point of the miter in the head casing and mark that point. Be sure the vertical casing is parallel with the jamb.

When installing door casing, be sure to account for the flooring material if it's not yet in place. Generally, it is best to leave space for the flooring to slide under the casing rather than trimming the flooring around the casing. Use a piece of the flooring as a spacer when measuring and installing the casing.

Apply white or yellow wood glue to miter joints to help keep them closed. Nail the jamb casing at the miter first. Then predrill and *lock nail* the miter itself, as shown in *Window and Door Casing* on the left. Finally, nail the rest of the casing in place, first along the reveal, then along the outside edge.

The window stool is finished off with a piece of casing underneath, known as an *apron*. The ends of the apron should line up with the outside edges of the vertical casing. There are two ways to finish off the ends of the apron or any piece of molding that ends without butting into another piece of trim.

The traditional approach is to cut a *return* piece back to the wall. With returns, the profile makes a true 90 degree turn and keeps end grain from showing. To cut the returns, first miter the ends of the apron. Then cut miters on both ends of a scrap piece that's at least 1 foot long. With the inside edge of the miter facing up, cut the returns off, as shown in *Cutting Window Aprons* on the right. Set the returns in place with some glue and a few seconds of firm hand pressure. See *Photo 19-5* below.

If fitting apron returns is too finicky for your taste, there is an easier method. Cut the apron to length with square cuts on the ends. Then nip off a portion of the thinner, bottom profile at 45 degrees, so a line in the profile meets the corner, as illustrated. This method works fine, especially with flatter profiles and when the trim will be painted. Casing with curves or beads, like the one in the photo, are best returned in the traditional manner.

Nail holes need to be set below the surface of the wood and then filled. Use a filler that matches the finish being used—colored if you're staining or plain white spackle if you're painting.

There are other ways to trim windows and doors. *Casing Alternatives* on page 338 illustrates some of them. Most home centers sell the decorative corner and plinth blocks that let you customize window and door trim. These variations eliminate the need to cut miter joints.

You can also buy crown molding and fireplace surrounds in preassembled components to reduce the need to make finicky cuts.

CUTTING WINDOW APRONS

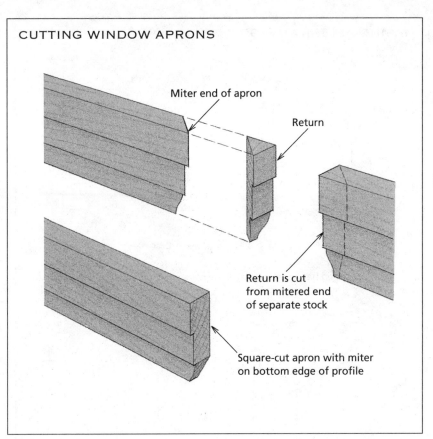

Miter end of apron

Return

Return is cut from mitered end of separate stock

Square-cut apron with miter on bottom edge of profile

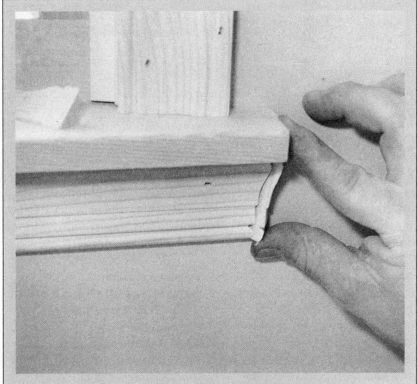

Photo 19-5. Apron returns are too small to nail, so apply a coating of glue on each piece and a few seconds of firm hand pressure to keep them in place.

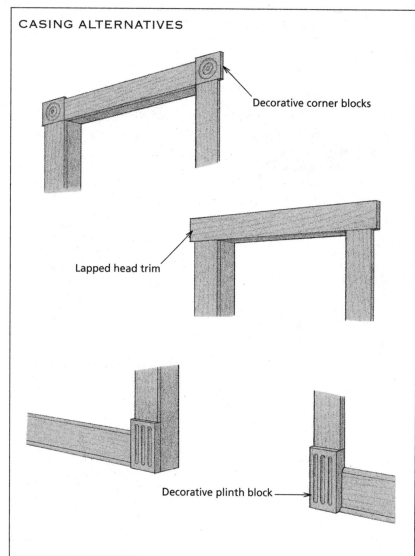

CASING ALTERNATIVES

Decorative corner blocks

Lapped head trim

Decorative plinth block

INSTALLING BASEBOARD

Baseboard (also called *base molding*) is installed after the door casings. Three varieties are shown in *Types of Baseboard* on the opposite page (left). Traditional baseboard is composed of three pieces. For the main piece, use a standard 1 x 4 or 1 x 6. Then add a profiled *base cap* and *shoe molding*, which conform to unevenness in the wall or floor and add a decorative element at the same time. A three-piece base gives you more design options but takes longer to install than simpler alternatives.

Contemporary baseboard is a single piece with a slight profile across the face. It's the least expensive and the easiest to install. Because the stock is rather thin, this product can be bent somewhat to follow floor and wall irregularities.

A cross between these two varieties is a standard piece of 1-by stock, into which a profile is milled to serve the same decorative purpose as a base cap—without having to add a separate piece. Although it has more visual weight than contemporary baseboard, it won't conform as easily to any bumps and bows in floors and walls.

Begin installing baseboard by locating and marking the stud locations on the floor or wall. If both surfaces are finished, use strips of masking tape on the floor. Next, lay the longest pieces around the walls where they're destined to go. Cutoffs from these can be used for shorter wall sections.

▲▲▲▲▲▲▲▲▲▲▲

When installing baseboard, consider working around the room clockwise if you're left-handed and counterclockwise if you're a righty. You may find it's easier to nail the parts in place.

▼▼▼▼▼▼▼▼▼▼▼

Three joints are used to install baseboard. Inside corners can either be mitered or *coped*. A coped joint is achieved by butting one of the pieces into the corner with a square cut on its end and then cutting the profile of the other piece into the end of the mating piece, as shown in *Coped Joint in Baseboard* on the opposite page (top right). It requires a coping saw and is difficult to execute accurately, especially on small moldings.

You can use a plain miter, but a coped joint is less likely to show a gap if the walls or floors move slightly after settling. It also works better when the corner is out of square. For inside corners in three-piece molding, use a butt joint for the square stock, a coped joint for the cap, and a miter joint for the shoe.

Outside corners should always be mitered. You can set the piece in place and mark the

TYPES OF BASEBOARD

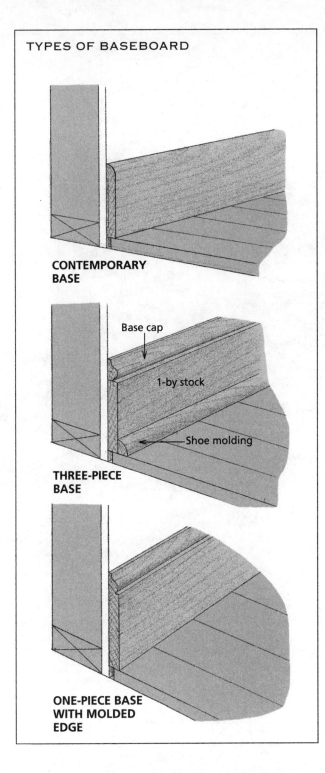

CONTEMPORARY BASE

Base cap

1-by stock

Shoe molding

THREE-PIECE BASE

ONE-PIECE BASE WITH MOLDED EDGE

COPED JOINT IN BASEBOARD

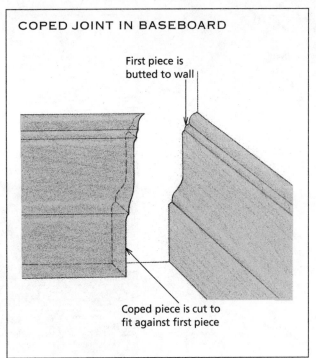

First piece is butted to wall

Coped piece is cut to fit against first piece

MARKING OUTSIDE MITERS

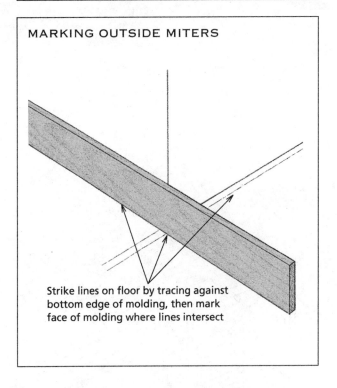

Strike lines on floor by tracing against bottom edge of molding, then mark face of molding where lines intersect

top edge where the back of the molding intersects with the corner. But cutting to this mark is difficult. A more accurate approach is to extend lines that cross where the faces will intersect, as shown in *Marking Outside Miters* above (bottom right). This allows you to mark

the face at the bottom edge and set the mark on the kerf in the base of the saw.

If wood or tile floors are somewhat irregular, baseboard may have to be scribed for a close fit. Set the piece in place after completing any joinery at the ends. With a compass,

scribe along the floor to mark the high spots that need to be removed from the edge of the base. Trim to the line with a block plane or jigsaw. Note that if one piece needs to be scribed at a corner, the mating piece will probably need attention as well.

20 INSTALLING CABINETS

With drywalled partitions ready for paint, the Baileys' new living space was ready for a bathroom vanity and kitchen cabinets and countertops. As a permanent part of the home, built-ins deserve special attention. When you move, the cabinets stay—something has to hold up the kitchen sink, after all.

Even if you're on a tight budget, give some thought to selecting cabinets and countertops that work for the way you live. Are your tastes utilitarian or fancy, colorful or subdued? Do you entertain often or is it just you and the kids? Will basic cabinets fit your needs, or do you want the latest in storage technology?

No matter what you buy, consider installing the cabinets yourself. This is among the most owner-friendly tasks that building an addition offers.

You'll need only a few basic tools—a drill, screw gun, level, and a few clamps—for a no-frills job. Add a jigsaw and block plane if you need to shape a cabinet edge to fit snugly against the dips or humps of a wall.

MANUFACTURED CABINETS

Most homeowners choose manufactured kitchen and vanity cabinets, sold directly by distributors or through most home centers. They are available in a dizzying array of styles, woods, and finishes, and with enough bells and whistles to rival a toy store. Most manufacturers divide their cabinets between stock and custom lines.

Stock cabinets are made in huge volumes, but only in certain standard sizes. Base and upper cabinet widths range from 9 to 48 inches, in 3-inch increments. The standard base cabinet height is 34½ inches; the standard depth is 24 inches. The standard heights for uppers are 12, 18, and 24 inches for use over sinks, refrigerators, and stoves; 30-, 36-, and 42-inch heights are for above-counter use. The standard depth of upper cabinets is 12 inches.

Custom manufactured cabinets are usually more expensive but are made with the same processes used for stock cabinets. But because custom cabinets are made *after* you order them, all sorts of size and shape modifications can be introduced. They are made in smaller batches—often one kitchen at a time. This ensures greater consistency in the quality of materials and finishing. Additionally, custom cabinet lines generally feature better grades of materials, higher standards of construction, and more styles and accessories than are available in stock lines. While nearly every home center carries a display of stock cabinets, you may need to visit a kitchen-design store to see custom cabinets.

You may be able to get kitchen design help for no charge if you order custom cabinets from companies specializing in kitchens. A staff kitchen designer will help you arrange everything in this complicated room, right down to the layout of the silverware drawer.

Standard and optional dimensions for kitchen and vanity cabinets are illustrated in

Stock and Custom Cabinet Dimensions below.

▲▲▲▲▲▲▲▲▲▲▲▲

To increase storage space in a small kitchen, consider installing tall, custom-made wall cabinets that extend into the space normally occupied by the soffit.

▼▼▼▼▼▼▼▼▼▼▼

To judge the quality of cabinets—stock or custom—you'll want to look closely at the details. Plywood cabinets

are sturdier than flakeboard cabinets. They're also lighter in weight. (You'll appreciate this if you're installing them yourself.) Check the top or bottom edges of the sides to determine which material is used. Most stock cabinets are made from flakeboard products covered with vinyl or wood veneer.

Consider joinery, too. Better cabinets are put together with structural joints, in which the edges of parts are machined to lock into one another; cabinets of lesser quality are held together with butt joints and staples. You can't tell which joinery is used from the face of a cabinet, so look at the sides, top, bottom, and back.

Cabinet drawers are subject to far more wear and tear than the cases themselves. Most drawers are built as a box, with an added front that matches the doors. Better drawers are made from solid wood or plywood, not flakeboard. Dovetail joints in solid wood are found on the best drawers, but rabbet-and-dado joints in plywood form an adequate combination. In quality drawers, the bottoms are made from plywood and locked in grooves.

Almost all drawers are mounted on ball-bearing or nylon wheel slides, which take the stress of continuous opening and closing. Slides should be *full extension*, allowing you access to the entire drawer interior, and the drawers should operate smoothly, with little side-to-side racking, and close snugly to the cabinet face. Stapled drawers on plastic slides are a sure sign of an inferior product.

Doors are the most visible part of cabinets. Solid wood *frame-and-panel* doors are the

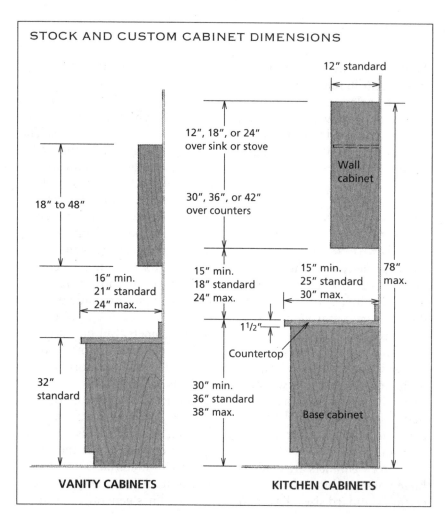

STOCK AND CUSTOM CABINET DIMENSIONS

12" standard

12", 18", or 24" over sink or stove

30", 36", or 42" over counters

Wall cabinet

18" to 48"

16" min. 21" standard 24" max.

15" min. 18" standard 24" max.

15" min. 25" standard 30" max.

78" max.

1½"

Countertop

32" standard

30" min. 36" standard 38" max.

Base cabinet

VANITY CABINETS

KITCHEN CABINETS

traditional choice. Panels are either flat or raised, as shown in *Cabinet Doors* on the right. Flat panels are usually made from plywood; raised panels are either solid wood or veneered fiberboard. In any case, joints should be perfectly tight.

The parts of doors and drawers should be uniform in color and grain. Beware of wood doors that are deeply stained; the coloring may not be intended to conceal anything, but dark stains can be used to hide defects or poorly selected wood. In painted cabinets and doors, the same rules apply. Since you can't see the material, ask for a description of it and the joinery. The paint may conceal molded plastic or fiberboard, neither of which will provide the long service of a well-made wood door.

An alternative to the frame-and-panel style is *flush* doors. These are made from plywood or veneered particleboard, also illustrated. To hide the material, the edges are banded with veneer or solid wood. Solid wood edging will better handle the bumps and bruises of normal wear and tear. If particleboard is used, be aware that screws don't hold as well as they do in solid wood, so hinges on these doors often become loose after a few years.

Flush doors provide a more contemporary look than frame-and-panel doors, and they're easier to keep clean. Whether you choose frame-and-panel or flush doors, they should all be dead flat so they lay against the cabinet face, without any of the edges lifting up.

You'll encounter two kinds of fronts, or faces, on cabinets, as shown in *Frameless and Face Frame*

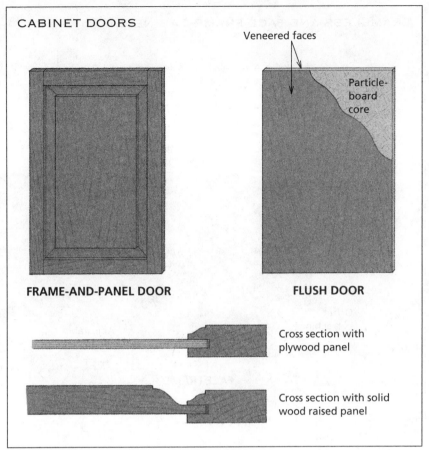

CABINET DOORS

Veneered faces

Particle-board core

FRAME-AND-PANEL DOOR

FLUSH DOOR

Cross section with plywood panel

Cross section with solid wood raised panel

343

Cabinets on page 344. In recent years, *frameless* cabinet designs have secured their place next to the more traditional *face frame* style. The differences are more a matter of appearance and manufacturing techniques than of quality. In general, doors on frameless cabinets are tightly spaced, creating a continuous flush surface. Face frame cabinet doors have wider spaces, called *reveals*, between them. And while face frame doors are usually hung with a pivot or barrel-type hinge, frameless cabinets typically have concealed, adjustable cup hinges.

Ready-to-assemble, or *knock-down,* cabinets have become popular with do-it-yourselfers. They are exclusively the frameless style because packaging and

assembly are easier without a face frame. Choosing this type of cabinet is somewhat involved because it is sold in modular form. This means you'll select shelves, doors, and even handles individually, then put it all together at home. The hardware used is intelligent and sturdy, and the instructions are straightforward.

But even a small kitchen starts out as a pile of parts, which can test anyone's patience. The payoff is price: Self-assembled cabinets cost roughly half as much as conventional ones of comparable quality.

ONE-OF-A-KIND CABINETS

The only way to get exactly the cabinets you want in any room of the house is to have them

FRAMELESS AND FACE FRAME CABINETS

Cabinet side

Solid wood face frame

Cabinet side

Thin edgeband

Flakeboard or plywood case

Flakeboard or plywood case

Offset barrel hinge

Adjustable cup hinge

FACE FRAME

FRAMELESS

custom-made by a cabinetmaker. (See *Photo 20-1* on the opposite page.) Function comes first, so know what you want to store in the cabinet and how you expect to use it. Design and style come next. If you're discerning about the furnishings you choose to live with, this is a chance to participate in the design of an important part of your addition. Look for photos from books or magazines to help convey the style you want to the cabinetmaker.

Some cabinetmakers charge a separate design fee, while others include this in the cost of the job. Either way, request a *working drawing* of the project. This shows both the materials and the construction techniques that will be used. Never rely on a verbal description as the basis for a custom cabinetry project.

If the cost of custom cabinetry seems prohibitive now, consider having it done later. Include the necessary space and framing in the plans for the addition, and postpone having the cabinets made until your budget has recovered.

PLANNING A KITCHEN

A well-planned kitchen is a cook's dream. But many kitchens are not only used by cooks but also serve as the main family gathering place. If this is the case for your kitchen, the room's design must consider more than just food prep and storage.

The kitchen should be planned early on—before plumbing, electrical, and gas lines are roughed in. Try to

anticipate how your new kitchen will be used. Kitchen design can be broken down into the juxtaposition of three basic functions and the appliances that serve them: food storage (refrigerator), food preparation (range and oven), and cleanup (sink and dishwasher). The best layout for a kitchen is one in which these functional areas form a compact *work triangle,* requiring as few steps as possible without being cramped. If the room will be a living area as well, consider how this added role will affect the efficiency of the work area.

Many cabinet suppliers offer design assistance, and even home centers now provide computer-aided design (CAD) as a sales tool. Take advantage of this help when planning your kitchen. In just minutes, you

Photo 20-1. *Choosing custom-made cabinetry lets you design exactly what you want. This window seat provides concealed storage as well as a cozy nook for reading.*

can have clear perspective drawings of cabinet options based on your room conditions. The illustration *CAD Kitchen Layout* on the right shows the work triangle in a typical L-shaped kitchen.

As Carol Bailey reflected back on the process of building the addition, she pointed out that problems with the cabinetry had been caused by a lack of planning, aggravated by poor communication with the contractor. The Baileys tried to save money by not having an architect draw up working plans.

The result was that less-than-accurate drawings of the bathroom showed a two-sink vanity where it could not fit. One solution would have been to steal space from a walk-in closet. But Carol wouldn't hear of this. She ended up settling

CAD KITCHEN LAYOUT

Courtesy of Channel Home Centers, Inc.

for a single sink instead.

Then, as the kitchen cabinets were being installed, it became clear that the corner space would be inaccessible, thus completely wasted. Under pressure to get a working kitchen in order, Carol let the base cabinet stay. But she insisted that the contractor order a new wall cabinet because the one that was delivered proved too narrow to hold the dinner plates she intended to store in it. Again, better planning could have prevented both of these glitches.

HANGING WALL CABINETS

In preparation for installing cabinets, clear the room as much as possible and sweep the floor. Remove doors and drawers from the cabinets to reduce their weight and allow you full access to the interiors. Be sure to label all parts; a strip of masking tape makes a convenient and removable tag.

The sequence to installing kitchen cabinets is a matter of preference. If you install base cabinets first, they become a work platform for assembling the uppers. But reaching over the base cabinets to install uppers is tough on the back. Your best best is to start with the uppers.

Cabinets must be installed level and plumb. Otherwise, doors and drawers look shoddy and operate poorly; and, of course, eggs tend to roll off slanted countertops.

The first step in any installation is to create reference marks and lines on the walls that show where the cabinets are to go. Take your references from the floor. (If the floor slopes, locate the highest spot and measure up from there.) Establish two horizontal lines—one representing the bottom of the upper cabinets and the other indicating the top of the lower cabinets. (See *Layout Lines for Installing Cabinets* below.)

Extend these lines around the walls, adjusting them for cabinets of different heights. Locate and mark the studs along these lines, unless you planned for this moment by adding *blocking* to the frame; see Chapter 5 for more on blocking. (To protect walls that have already been painted, use masking tape as your mark.) If the wall cabinets mount flush against a soffit, locate those studs as well.

The first step in mounting wall cabinets is to nail or screw a temporary ledger strip to the wall. The ledger will support the cabinets until you screw them to the wall studs. Next, connect individual cabinets that can be lifted as one unit. Face frame cabinets are screwed together through their frames; frameless cabinets are screwed through their sides or bolted with threaded inserts. (Be sure to

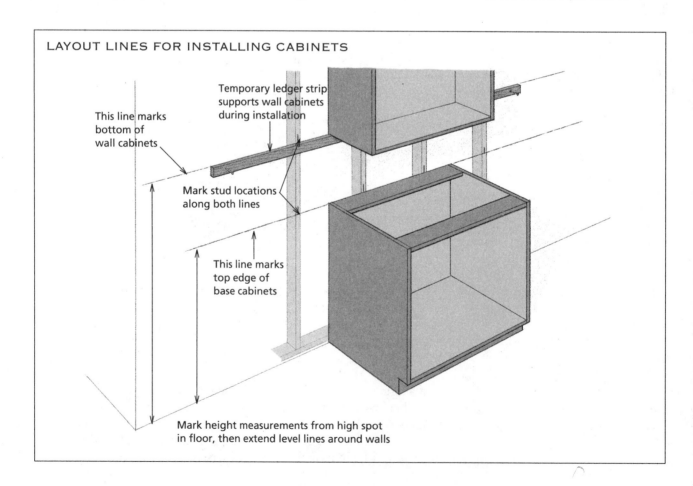

LAYOUT LINES FOR INSTALLING CABINETS

This line marks bottom of wall cabinets

Temporary ledger strip supports wall cabinets during installation

Mark stud locations along both lines

This line marks top edge of base cabinets

Mark height measurements from high spot in floor, then extend level lines around walls predrill for the holes.) Now check the backs of the cabinets. If they are flush—that is, not recessed—you're ready to go. If they are recessed, you'll have to add strips of wood or plywood equal in thickness to the recess at the studs with screws.

If there are too few studs to support the cabinet, add drywall inserts or toggle bolts. These require you to locate the cabinet, mark the holes, remove the cabinet to set the inserts, and then install the cabinet. Use toggle bolts or masonry inserts and the same procedure to hang cabinets on a masonry wall.

Hanging cabinets is a two-person job. With a helper, lift the cabinets onto the ledger strip, then transfer the stud locations to the inside of the cabinet backs. Predrill through the top hanging strip. You'll need long screws—2 to 3 inches, depending on the combined thickness of the back and the drywall.

Now check the cabinet for plumb; slide tapered shims (cedar shingles are best) from above or below if necessary. Then add screws to the bottom hanging rail on the underside of the cabinet (if there is no rail, drive screws through the back of the cabinet). Be sure you are right on the stud, or you could break the back panel.

INSTALLING BASE CABINETS

Follow the same sequence to install base cabinets: Connect banks of cabinets where possible, shim until they're level and plumb, and attach securely to studs with screws.

Photos 20-2 through 20-4 on the right show Dave installing the Baileys' base cabinets. When turning corners,

Photo 20-2. Dave assembles the base cabinets with screws through the face frames. Frameless cabinets are assembled with screws right through the sides.

Photo 20-3. After he connects cabinets into units, Dave uses a level to make sure the cabinets are plumb.

Photo 20-4. Dave attaches the cabinets to the wall by driving screws through the solid rail in back. If your base cabinet doesn't have a rail, run screws directly through the back, but be sure the back is tight to the wall or a spacer strip.

Dave had to make sure the cabinets were square to each other since the walls were not perfectly square. He used a framing square against the cabinet faces as a guide.

The installation of the sink cabinet took more trouble. With the plumbing and stud locations clearly marked, Barry set out to drill holes in the back of the cabinet for the pipes. He set the cabinet on the floor lines, pushed it back against the protruding supply pipes, and traced lines around the two pipes.

The waste pipe was cut closer to the wall and didn't touch the back. (Plumbers aren't necessarily thinking about cabinet installers when they rough in lines.) So Barry laid his pencil flat against the waste pipe and rotated it to scribe a line on the cabinet back. See *Marking for Plumbing Holes* below.

Barry drilled the supply pipe holes slightly oversize; this allowed him to slide the cabinet over the pipes and adjust its position slightly without straining the plumbing. He used spade bits, which are the least expensive type for drilling large-diameter holes. The hole was started from the outside until just the point of the bit broke through. Then Barry worked from the inside to prevent the material from splintering on its visible surface. (The waste pipe hole could also have been cut with a saber saw.)

Wherever a cabinet butts against a wall, you'll be reminded of the nature of drywall—it's rarely perfectly flat. Even if the walls are plumb, the straight edge of a cabinet side may reveal a bump or two on the adjacent drywall. For this reason, you may need to rely on a *scribe edge,* a piece of trim intended to be cut to fit against walls that are uneven or out of plumb.

Face frame cabinets usually come with a scribe edge at both front edges. Other cabinet styles require that you add a separate scribe strip or piece of molding where gaps occur, as shown in *Scribing Cabinets to Walls* on the opposite page.

You may also need to fit the finished side of an end cabinet to the wall. To do this, set a compass a little wider than the gap at its widest point. Run a strip of tape along the edge to show the line better and to prevent the material from chipping when cut with a saber saw. Then slide the compass from top to bottom, transferring the contour of the wall to the cabinet, as illustrated. Saw along the line. To trim smaller amounts, use a block plane.

INSTALLING COUNTERTOPS

If you've never glued up a plastic laminate countertop, this is probably not the best time to try. It's a messy job, requires special tools, and involves materials that are hard to handle. What's more, you can buy ready-made counters at very competitive prices from most home centers. They're supplied with various edge treatments and even with the backsplash already attached. If you can't find a stock item that meets your needs, most suppliers should be able to get you what you want with a custom order. Failing that, locate a cabinet shop that handles laminate work. In any case, be sure to provide an accurate drawing based on the cabinet layout. See "Countertop Options" on page 351 for a look at the wide range of choices in countertop materials.

L-shaped counters may be

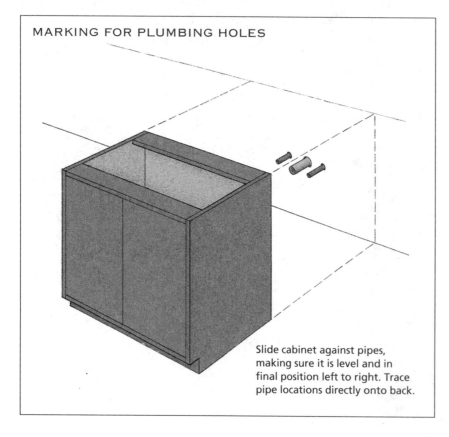

MARKING FOR PLUMBING HOLES

Slide cabinet against pipes, making sure it is level and in final position left to right. Trace pipe locations directly onto back.

SCRIBING CABINETS TO WALLS

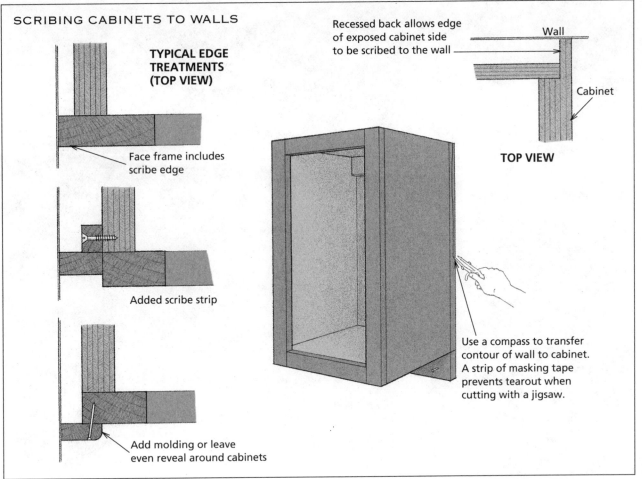

TYPICAL EDGE TREATMENTS (TOP VIEW)

Face frame includes scribe edge

Added scribe strip

Add molding or leave even reveal around cabinets

Recessed back allows edge of exposed cabinet side to be scribed to the wall

Wall

Cabinet

TOP VIEW

Use a compass to transfer contour of wall to cabinet. A strip of masking tape prevents tearout when cutting with a jigsaw.

supplied in two sections that will be connected from underneath with hardware. This is not a structural joint, though, so be careful when moving an assembled counter.

Scribe counter ends that butt into walls as previously described for cabinet sides. Apply a bead of caulk where countertops or backsplashes meet the wall. Complete the countertop installation by screwing up through the cabinets into the underside of the counter. Be sure to predrill, using a depth stop on the bit so it doesn't go all the way through the countertop. Also, select screws that are not so long that they go all the way through.

Once the countertop is in place, but before you attach it to the cabinets, make the cutout for

the sink. You may need to pull the counter away from the wall to make the cut.

Since Dave and Barry were building and laminating the Baileys' countertop in place, they cut out for the sink before applying the laminate.

Dave started by transferring the centerline of the base cabinet onto the countertop. Centering the sink left to right and front to back on the countertop, he then traced around the sink's flange. (Some sink manufacturers supply a cardboard template of the cutout; others have you use the sink flange as the template, which involves scribing a cut line a specific distance inside the flange line.) With a compass and pencil, Dave then scribed the cut line ¾ inch inside the flange line.

To start the cut, Barry

drilled a ½-inch-diameter hole at the four corners. Then he made the cut with a saber saw. Dave wedged a screwdriver into the saw kerf to keep the piece of flakeboard from crashing onto the cabinet floor. This is safer than trying to catch it from underneath. *Photos 20-5 through 20-7 on page 350 show* Barry and Dave cutting out for the sink.

Before attaching a sink, you should make sure your faucet assembly fits properly and that the plumbing supply and waste lines can be connected without obstruction. Most sinks are mounted to the countertop with metal clip anchors. Use the recommended sealant, typically silicone, under the sink flange.

You'll need some kind of molding to conceal any gaps

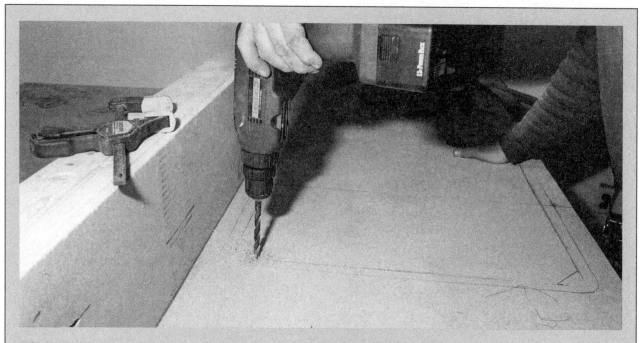

Photo 20-5. Dave drills holes in corners to start the sink cutout with a jigsaw.

Photo 20-6. A screwdriver is wedged into the saw cut so Barry doesn't have to risk reaching underneath while Dave makes the cut.

Photo 20-7. Barry lifts the cutout from the countertop. The sink is then attached to the counter with metal clips.

between the floor and the base cabinets. Vinyl cove molding is the least expensive choice and the most simple to install and easy to clean, making it a good option for kitchens and baths. It's commonly sold in 3-foot lengths that butt end to end and in 12-foot-long rolls.

Wrap vinyl cove around outside corners after scoring the back slightly with a utility knife; cut a small notch in the back of the material to help it turn inside corners. You can also butt inside corners and miter just the bottom cove. Use an adhesive sold specifically for vinyl cove, and apply it to the back of the molding with a toothed trowel.

COUNTERTOP OPTIONS

If the new kitchen is a room where the family will spend a lot of time, then countertop choice deserves extra thought.

Plastic laminate is the economical first choice for countertops. It's sturdy, long-lasting, easy to clean, and resists stains almost completely. It stands up to moderate heat, but it will be damaged by hot pots and pans resting on it.

Standard plastic laminate is made by sandwiching layers of pressure-glued kraft paper with a very thin layer of color on top. See *Stock Plastic Laminate Countertop* below. Where perpendicular edges meet, the brown core is exposed as a brown line. A recently developed version is solid color, which eliminates the brown line at edges; however, solid-color laminate costs two to three times as much as the standard form. All laminates are glued with contact cement to a platform of flakeboard or plywood.

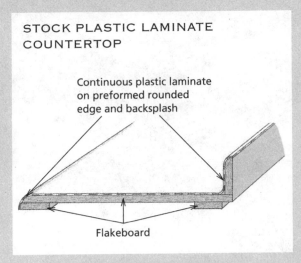

STOCK PLASTIC LAMINATE
COUNTERTOP

Continuous plastic laminate
on preformed rounded
edge and backsplash

Flakeboard

Ceramic tile makes a highly serviceable countertop. It goes virtually unscathed under normal use, resisting scratches and scalding pot bottoms. And it costs only marginally more than plastic laminate. Individual tiles are held in place by grout, but conventional grout is not a good material for use in countertops. It stains, cracks, and disintegrates over time. Recently, epoxy grouts have eliminated most of these problems. Exterior-grade plywood should be used as underlayment. Before the tile is applied, underlayment and any wood edging should be sealed against moisture with a coat or two of polyurethane.

Wood has largely been displaced by the array of manufactured countertop products, but butcher block has again become popular. It usually is made from edge-glued maple for stability and durability. Wood needs to be sealed, especially around sinks. Only certain finishes are safe for countertop use; check labels carefully. Wood requires some maintenance—oiling and perhaps resurfacing in the future. And you can expect to pay twice as much for wood as for plastic laminate.

Solid-surface materials were developed specifically for countertop use. Plastic is cast from liquid into sheet form. The result is a product that can be bonded to itself using the liquid form as an adhesive. Seams are invisible—if the bonding is done properly. The process is exacting, however.

Sinks made of the same plastic can be joined to countertops with no visible seams. Multiple pieces can be joined in place, eliminating joints that in many materials become traps for water and dirt. Should you need to repair a solid-surface countertop, scratches can be sanded out and the whole surface repolished. The cost is three to five times higher than that of plastic laminate.

Stainless steel has long been the choice in institutional kitchens. It won't scratch, chip, stain, or burn. It does have a somewhat cold and sterile appearance, although this can be offset by using warmer colors throughout the rest of the room. Fabrication is quite exacting and suppliers may be limited. For this alternative, you'll have to budget about four times as much as for plastic laminate.

Marble, slate, granite, and other types of *stone* make an outstanding countertop material. Marble is somewhat porous and soft; slate is dark and rather brittle; and granite is extremely expensive—five or six times the cost of plastic laminate. Every slab of stone is unique, so plan on a trip to a stone yard to pick out your pieces. Many types of stone are also available as tiles.

21

FINISHING, INDOORS AND OUT

If you've made it this far without getting your hands dirty, you've just run out of excuses. Anyone can do the jobs outlined in this chapter, and almost every homeowner has tried at least once.

There's no good reason not to do the painting yourself. Approached with patience, this can be a relaxing part of the job, unlike the occasionally stressful construction work that has gone before. Wallpapering isn't quite as meditative, but you get results fast and always have the option of peeling off the first try and having another go; see "Wallpapering" on page 358.

GETTING STARTED

Paint covers a multitude of minor sins, such as dings and scratches. "Paint'll cover that!" was heard more than once as the drywall and trim went up at the

Baileys. That's why prep work, the first stage of painting, is so important to doing a good job.

This being a brand new addition to your home, there won't be arduous scraping to prepare surfaces for paint. But the person who accepts the responsibility of painting can expect to spend time filling imperfections and nail holes and sanding lightly.

At the Baileys, this responsibility fell to Carol and Jim Bailey. "Fell" is not quite the right word, in that the couple insisted on doing all the painting and finishing themselves. They expected to save money; and as it turns out, they enjoyed the job as well. "Painting new work is a lot different than painting over old," said Carol. "It takes more coats. And along the way you appreciate the walls more—I'll never complain again about having too little space, now

that I've been over every inch of these walls a couple of times."

Painting is the final step in blending the new space with the old. At the Baileys, the existing kitchen opens into the new family room. An island counter provides a functional bridge between the two rooms. Painting both rooms the same color smoothed the transition and created a feeling of unity, as shown in *Photo 21-1* on page 354.

Primers are specialized paints used to seal new surfaces before putting on the finish coats. A sealed wall or ceiling will soak up less paint. Still, many painters dispense with primer on new drywall, opting to use an extra top coat instead.

Selecting the type of paint for the top coat is simpler than the aisles of your local paint store might lead you to believe. There are only two kinds of interior paint for walls—*latex* and *alkyd*. Water-based latex goes on easily and can be recoated in a couple of hours. It emits very low levels of unpleasant vapors and is cleaned from tools (and hands and anything else you've slopped it on) with warm water. Oil-based alkyd paint is more difficult to apply, though it may cover better, thus requiring fewer coats. It gives off harmful fumes and should be used only with plenty of ventilation.

354

Some localities regulate the use of alkyds due to concern over volatile organic compounds (VOCs) they emit. Unused cans of leftover paint pose a disposal problem as well. If you use oil-based paint, you'll have to subject yourself further to paint thinner or mineral spirits when cleaning rollers and brushes. So, for interior walls, stick with latex.

Some paint companies offer as many as four levels of sheen to choose from—flat, eggshell, satin, and gloss, in ascending order of shininess. Flat latex flows out smoothly, reflects light softly, and conceals minor imperfections in a wall's surface. You'll have to pay for these benefits in scuffs and dirt, which show up readily and are relatively difficult to clean. But a fresh coat of flat latex will blend in so seamlessly that repainting high-traffic areas is not much harder than cleaning them. In rooms likely to get scraped and smudged regularly, choose semigloss latex; the smoother surface can be wiped clean.

Paint stores are stocked with many gizmos to make painting easier. You can do without most of them. Spend your money instead on better roller covers, which do make a difference. You'll get what you pay for when shopping for this

Photo 21-1. *A view through the Baileys' new family room into the old kitchen shows a smooth transition created by both of the rooms having been painted the same color.*

product. Cheap covers hold little paint, aren't durable, and may leave a pattern created by the cardboard tube liner. Buy better quality, unless you're touching up an unimportant area.

Roller covers offer you different options of how thick and high the material is on the cover. Low-nap covers give a smoother surface, if that is what you're after, but they hold less paint than thicker ones.

Standard-issue metal roller pans work fine. To spare the time of rinsing out a pan, you can buy disposable plastic liners. (These liners are too flimsy to serve as roller pans themselves.) You can also buy plastic roller pans, which are easy to clean and won't rust like the metal ones.

A 5-foot roller extension handle allows you to work with both feet on the ground, but requires a two-handed stroke.

With a shorter extension, you can work one-handed from the first or second step of a ladder and get a closer look at how the paint is rolling on. Position work lights at an angle to the wall surface to help gauge paint coverage. Clamp-on type lights mounted on a ladder work well. See the illustration *Painter's Tools* on the opposite page (top).

Spraying systems are sold for homeowners' use; now, as you face the prospect of painting your new addition, is a good time to investigate these. Sprayers apply thinner layers than rollers, so you'll need to lay on more coats. Power rollers can also make the job easier. The typical system uses a plastic roller arm with a 1-gallon pot attached, runs on four D-size batteries, and has two flow rates.

Both sprayers and power rollers eliminate constantly reloading a roller with paint.

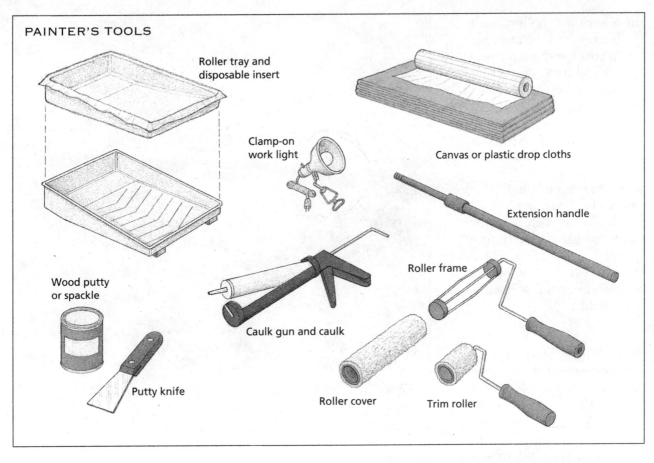

PAINTER'S TOOLS

Roller tray and disposable insert

Clamp-on work light

Canvas or plastic drop cloths

Extension handle

Wood putty or spackle

Caulk gun and caulk

Roller frame

Putty knife

Roller cover

Trim roller

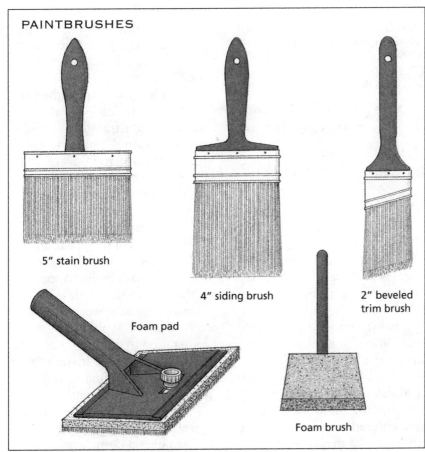

PAINTBRUSHES

5" stain brush

4" siding brush

2" beveled trim brush

Foam pad

Foam brush

But keep in mind that there is a trade-off between time saved by using these systems and time spent learning to operate the equipment. Both also require meticulous cleaning after use in order to get optimum results the next time you paint.

You'll also need brushes (like those illustrated in *Paintbrushes* on the left) to *cut in* around trim and to paint inside corners that rollers can't reach.

As with roller covers, price is closely related to quality. If you will take the time to carefully rinse out brushes, then consider buying those close to the top in price. There are no strict formulas as to brush width. Buy a small selection, and you'll soon have your own favorites for specific jobs. As you gain confidence with your painting, you may find that you naturally progress to wider brushes. The wider the brush, the fewer dips you'll make in the bucket, and the more area you'll cover with each stroke.

Wood trim is usually painted a different color or sheen to stand out from the walls. Use a latex or alkyd bare-wood primer, then a top coat of enamel paint. A 3-inch angled brush is the best single choice for trim; use a brush with nylon bristles for latex, natural bristles for oil. Before painting, caulk any gaps between trim and drywall; see *Photo 21-2* on the right. Make sure the caulk is paintable; paint won't stick to some kinds.

INTERIOR PAINTING

Which to do first, the walls or the trim? This is a matter of preference. Some pros do the trim first, especially if they're spraying it. Then they mask off the trim when painting the walls. A drawback with this approach is that the trim paint has to be very dry, or the tape may pull it off. If you instead paint the walls and ceilings first, you'll have to cut in all the trim against the walls, but this allows you to finish the trim at a more leisurely pace, one window or door at a time, even after you've moved in. Another option is to paint the trim before you nail it in place, then install it over painted walls.

However you decide to do it, completely cover finish flooring with heavy plastic or canvas drop cloths before you start. Always work from the ceiling down. If the ceiling is to be a different color than the walls, paint it first, then allow it to dry thoroughly. Next, mask off the ceiling from the walls with painter's tape. Unlike standard masking tape, this has relatively weak adhesive applied

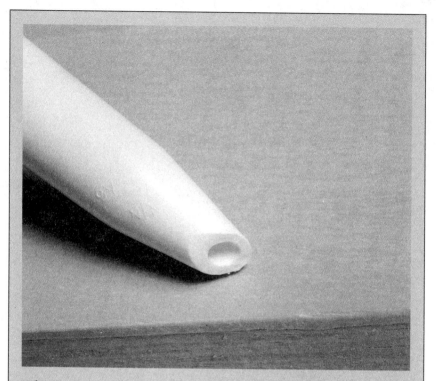

Photo 21-2. Cut the tip of the caulk tube at an angle, and use the tip to spread the caulk as you apply it.

only along one edge, so there's less chance of pulling off paint when the tape is removed.

▲▲▲▲▲▲▲▲▲▲▲

Doors are easier to paint if you remove them and lay them flat on sawhorses or a bench to do the job.

▼▼▼▼▼▼▼▼▼▼▼

Use a brush to paint wall corners and around trim. Then roll out the rest of the wall. There's no single right way to roll paint, but here are some guidelines. To minimize runs and make lap marks less noticeable, roll vertically. Start a fresh roller load of paint by overlapping the wet edge of the just-painted area and creating an M- or W-shaped pattern, as

shown in *Photo 21-3* on the opposite page. Then repeat the pattern, overlapping the first by half a roller width. Never stop the roller in midstroke; instead, gently lift it away from the wall at the top of each vertical stroke, as illustrated in *Roller Technique* on the opposite page. Or for better coverage with fewer coats, roll the paint on horizontally first, and then roll it out vertically.

Lap marks are inevitable—they often seem to appear after you've moved on to the next section. What's really happened is that your angle of view has changed, causing wet paint to appear shiny. Avoid the temptation to go back over paint that's begun to dry. If you use flat latex, the lap marks will fade completely as the paint dries.

Outside corners require a careful touch. As the roller passes over a corner, paint is

Photo 21-3. Roll paint out in overlapping M- or W-shapes to minimize runs and lap marks. Finish each section with light vertical strokes, feathering the edges.

condensed into bands around the roller and then dumped onto the wall as heavy lap marks. To avoid this, start applying paint with strokes at a sharper angle toward the corner. The last stroke should be vertical and very light.

Before cutting in the trim, be sure the walls are thoroughly dry, which will make it easier to wipe off any stray trim paint. Use a good-quality angled sash brush or tapered trim brush, and load the bristles no more than halfway with paint. Work out of a smaller paint can or bucket, one that you can hold comfortably in your hand.

Try painting a piece of trim freehand; it's easier than you might think, and overall takes about the same time as with masking. If you decide to mask off the walls, try a metal

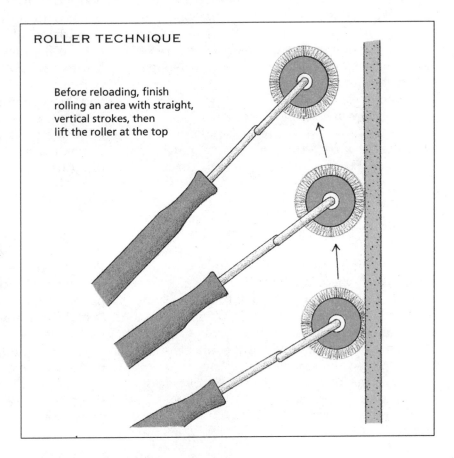

ROLLER TECHNIQUE

Before reloading, finish rolling an area with straight, vertical strokes, then lift the roller at the top masking edge, as shown in *Photo 21-4* on the opposite page.

If you want to see the grain of wood trim, apply two coats of polyurethane; it comes clear and with stain already mixed in. A natural finish requires more thorough sanding. Use 120-grit paper, followed by 180-grit. You can save some time and do a better job if you sand *and* finish the trim before installing it. After installation, fill the nail holes and apply a final coat of finish.

EXTERIOR FINISHING

Finishing indoors is primarily an aesthetic affair. Wood trim and drywall might last just as long if left unpainted. In contrast, finishing outdoors is necessary to protect wood against water, sunlight, and wind.

The popularity of both aluminum and vinyl siding speaks loudly of the desire to drop exterior painting from the long list of homeowner chores. In many new homes, nary a stick of wood can be found exposed to the elements. So why do people continue to use wood? It looks good, and it is the standard that manufacturers of vinyl and aluminum siding try to match. When properly cared for, it can last well over a century. And it can be finished in several ways—with any color of paint you can dream up, as well as with clear or pigmented stain.

WALLPAPERING

Wallpapering is one of those skills that doesn't look tricky. To the uninitiated, it seems like kindergarten cutting and pasting. But if you talk to homeowners who have gotten involved, you'll probably get a tour of the mistakes they made—a bubble here, a misaligned edge there.

Call in a pro, and the job will be done quickly and well. But although wallpapering may be more demanding of skill and patience than painting, it is within the reach of most of us. If possible, find a wallpaper store that will help guide you through techniques and tools. Here are some tips to help any wallpapering job go smoother.

• At the joint where the last piece meets the first, a pattern is unlikely to match up cleanly. Start in an inconspicuous corner or over a door.

• Inside corners are rarely perfectly plumb. Always measure both at the top and bottom of the wall when fitting a piece into a corner.

• With vinyl wall covering, use a vinyl adhesive where inside corners overlap.

• Seams should butt together, not overlap. To help ensure that seams don't open, press them together until both pieces start to lift slightly where they meet. After hanging the next piece, go back and roll down the previous joint. Don't overdo it; excessive rolling can leave marks and squeeze out the adhesive.

• Where a length of paper lays partially over a window or door, fit paper at the seam as usual. Then cut out all but 2 inches of the excess paper with scissors. Finally, trim paper with a razor blade against the trim or corner.

• Mark outlets and switches with a pencil or tab of masking tape. After all the paper is up, turn off the power supply. Then score diagonal lines across the opening and cut the flaps away with scissors. To conceal outlet and switch covers, cut a piece of paper 1 inch larger than the plate after aligning it both horizontally and vertically with the surrounding pattern. Use spray adhesive or contact cement to bond the paper to the face of the cover. Make a diagonal cut in from the corners of the overlapping material, then fold back the four flaps. Cut out the holes for the switch or outlet with a razor.

• If you notice a bubble *after* you thought you were done and you think there is still wet glue under it, prick a pin hole in it to let the air escape, and press the paper down with a smooth wood block. If it has been more than an hour since the paper went up, make a clean slice with a new razor blade, following a line in the pattern if possible. Gently lift the paper, one side at a time, insert some glue, and spread it with a small brush. Then press the paper down.

A few woods, including cedar, redwood, and cypress, age nicely without a protective coat; if you prefer to retain the wood's new look, apply a penetrating wood preservative. Other woods used for siding and trim—pine, spruce, and fir are among the most common—need to be painted.

Paint has been protecting wood for at least a thousand years. It's still not perfect—"repainting" will probably always be a part of our vocabulary—but it keeps getting better. Oil-based alkyds were once the sole product used on exteriors. But water-based latex paints have taken much of the market. In addition to the advantages pointed out for interior latex, exterior latex paints are flexible, retain their color, and bond to most surfaces.

Finishing a wood exterior is more demanding than painting indoors. Using a roller is impractical, unless you are painting plywood sheets. And operating a brush takes more stamina and more time. Consider spraying. The self-contained sprayers sold at paint stores and home centers are easy to operate and suitable for small jobs.

In addition to ladders, you may want to set up scaffolding as a convenient platform for prepping and painting. Have a caulk gun handy, and seal seams around windows, doors, and soffits with a paintable exterior caulk. Your schedule will have to revolve around the weather. Don't paint if there's a good chance it will rain that day; and postpone getting started on a wall until any dew has evaporated from it.

When siding and trim are getting the same treatment,

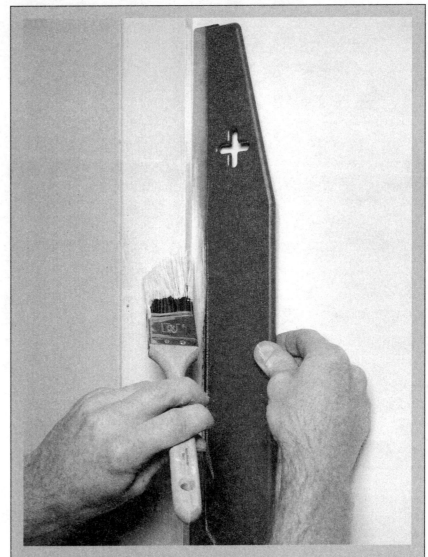

Photo 21-4. An alternative to using tape to mask off walls is this metal masking strip. It's especially useful when finishing baseboard against carpet.

you'll need to make only one trip around the addition. If the trim will be highlighted, finish the siding and then do the trim, starting at the top and working down. You can eliminate this step by finishing trim pieces before installing them; see *Photo 21-5* on page 360.

GUTTERS AND DOWNSPOUTS

Rain gutters and downspouts are the first defense against water damage to exterior siding and trim. If rainwater is allowed to run freely off the edge of the roof, it will splash against the siding and erode soil around the foundation.

Of the many materials that have been used for gutters, copper and wood last especially long and age nicely. But they're stocked by few companies and cost a lot of money. Galvanized steel gutters are stronger than aluminum, but joints need to be soldered or riveted and bare steel needs to be painted to

Photo 21-5. *Save time by painting exterior trim stock before nailing it up. For extra resistance to decay, paint the back of the trim as well as the front.*

prevent rust and to improve appearance.

Aluminum and vinyl gutters are the most practical. They're readily available at home centers in modular form; see the illustration *Gutter Systems* on the opposite page. The various joints are assembled easily, and the gutters don't need painting.

Gutter sizes generally refer to the width across the *mouth*. Select a gutter size according to the roof area it will serve. As a rule of thumb, 4-inch gutters can handle up to 750 square feet of roof; step up to 5 inches for between 750 and 1,500 square feet; and use 6-inch gutters for anything over 1,500 square feet.

Gutters are attached either to the fascia board with clips or spikes or to the roof sheathing with metal hanger strips, as shown in the illustration. Roof mounting may be slightly stronger, but it can be less convenient, especially if you need to replace a hanger. Use 8d hot-dipped galvanized nails, and locate the hangers at rafters, but space them no more than every 3 feet—less in areas with heavy snows.

Start by locating downspouts; inconspicuous corners are generally the best place for them. Be sure the area that receives the runoff is adequately sloped away from the house. A gravel bed or concrete splash block can help here. (If you anticipate drainage problems, consider digging a *dry well,* a hole filled with course gravel located 8 or 10 feet away from the house and connected to the downspout with an underground length of plastic pipe.) Spouts from a second-story roof can be routed straight to the ground or to the system serving a lower roof, whichever works and looks better. Or rout a new lower roof spout into one on the main part of the house. Note that spouts must be assembled from the roof down so runoff won't leak from the joints.

Next, lay out lengths of gutter on the ground under their eventual locations along the roof. Allow an extra ½ inch or so beyond each edge of the roof. Do whatever assembly you can at this point, so you don't have to carry out these steps on a ladder or scaffolding.

Attach hangers, starting at the end opposite the downspout. To carry runoff efficiently, gutters should drop about 1 inch per 16-foot run. Snap a line from the first

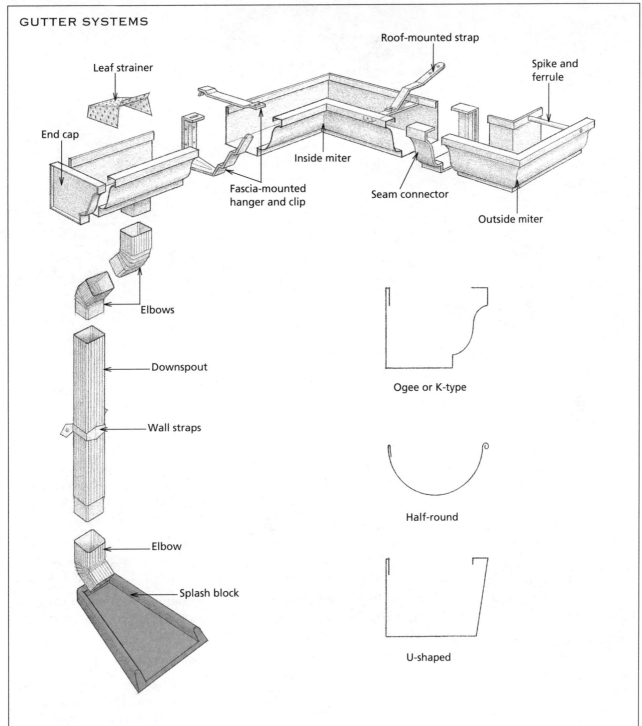

Roof-mounted strap

Leaf strainer

Spike and ferrule

End cap

Inside miter

361

Fascia-mounted hanger and clip

Seam connector

Outside miter

Elbows

Downspout

Ogee or K-type

Wall straps

Half-round

Elbow

Splash block

U-shaped

hanger out to the other end, then install the remaining hangers. Gutters much over 20 feet can be started at the center, then dropped to downspouts at either end.

Hauling up gutters is a two-person task—one on the ladder and another handing up lengths from the ground. Get everything in place before securing the hanger clips. Double-check downspout locations, then attach mounting brackets for them to the wall. Finally, attach the hangers to the gutters and connect the downspouts. Sheet metal screws are usually required to reinforce all the joints of aluminum spouts. Apply a generous bead of exterior latex caulk on the inside of all gutter seams and downspout outlets. If broad-leaf trees will be littering the area each fall, install leaf strainers to keep downspouts wide open.

Note: Italicized terms within definitions are defined elsewhere in the glossary.

Air gap. Plumbing fitting that vents the dishwasher waste line.

Allowances. Projected costs for specific parts of a job, or the materials used in completing those parts.

Amperes, amps. Standard unit for measuring the rate at which electrical current flows. *Circuit breakers,* for example, are rated to handle a specific amperage. See also *Volts.*

Apron. Horizontal piece of window trim nailed to the wall just below the *stool.*

Backfill. To replace earth around the outside of a basement *foundation.*

Ball cock assembly. Mechanism inside a toilet that controls the flow of water.

Baseboard, baseboard molding. *Molding* that runs along the joint between the floor and wall.

Batter boards. Pair of short, narrow boards nailed to a post, used to locate the corners of a building or its *foundation.*

Batts. Preformed blankets of fiberglass insulation sized to fit between framing members; sold in rolls and precut lengths.

Bearing wall. Any wall that supports a vertical load as well as its own weight.

Bevel. Any angle other than 90 degrees; an edge that is other than 90 degrees to the sides.

Bird's-mouth. Notch made in *rafters* to allow them to sit squarely on the top plate of a wall.

Blind nail. To nail in such a way that the nail head will be covered by a piece applied later.

Board. Piece of solid wood milled to a *nominal* thickness of less than 2 inches; see also *Lumber* and *Timber.*

Board foot. Unit of lumber equal to a 1-inch-thick piece measuring 12 x 12 inches.

Bridging. Diagonal bracing added between floor *joists* for strength.

Building paper. See *Roofing felt.*

Building permit. Release issued by the local government allowing construction or renovation to begin.

Cable. Multiwire electrical line that is run through the home. Two-wire cable includes two insulated wires to carry current and a third grounding wire (usually uninsulated) for safety.

Casing. Trim around a door or window.

Chair rail. *Molding* that runs along a wall roughly 3 feet above the floor; it may cap the upper edge of *wainscoting*.

Chalkline. Straight reference line for laying out framing and courses of roofing and siding made by snapping a string dusted with chalk.

Change order. Document between homeowner and contractor in which an aspect of the contracted job is altered.

Circuit. Branch of the home's electrical system.

Circuit breaker. Switch in a *service panel* governing the flow of electricity through a *circuit*.

Clapboard. Siding of horizontal boards.

Clear. Term used in wood grading systems to describe the best grade of material; see also *Select* and *Common*.

Code, building code. Used to regulate the practices and materials of construction.

Common. Term used in wood grading systems to describe a grade of material that contains visual flaws that don't impair structural integrity.

Common rafter, common stud. Rafter or stud that runs full length.

Comprehensive service. Most complete level of service offered by an architect in a building project. Includes all aspects, from preliminary design consultation to overseeing the building process; see also *Limited service*.

Concrete. Mixture of cement, gravel, sand, and water that hardens to form foundations and slabs.

Contractor. Person with whom you sign a contract to build an addition or other project. A contractor may do the work himself or contract with others and manage their work; see also *Subcontractor*.

Cope. To cut one member to fit the shape of another. Also, the type of joint created by coping.

Cornice. Roof *overhang*, often closed in with trim, including *fascia* and *soffit*.

Cowling. Bell-shaped cover on a ceiling-mounted electrical fixture that conceals the wire connections.

Cripple stud. Short stud used to frame spaces above and below window or door openings.

Dado. Groove in the surface of a piece of lumber at a right angle to the grain; see also *Rabbet*.

Dead load. Fixed loads placed on the structure of a building, as opposed to a *live load*. An interior wall is an example of a dead load.

Dimensional lumber. Softwood lumber for framing, milled to standard sizes of 1½-inch thicknesses and 2½- to 11¼-inch widths. See also *Board* and *Timber*.

Directional tee. Plumbing fitting that connects a dishwasher waste line to the sink waste line and prevents sink drainage from entering the dishwasher.

Diverter. In rough plumbing, the valve that switches water flow between the tub spigot and the showerhead.

Dormer. Raised section of roof, increasing headroom and admitting light through one or more windows.

Downspout. Vertical pipe that carries rainwater from the *gutter* to the ground.

Draws. Partial payments a contractor receives over the course of a project, as stipulated in the contract.

Drip cap. Piece of vinyl molding used over a door or window opening to divert water away from the opening.

Drip edge. Metal lip that protects the edge of a roof from water.

Drywall. Sheet material with gypsum core and paper covering used on interior walls and ceilings; also called plasterboard, Sheetrock, and gypsum board.

Eave. Lower edge of a roof that projects over the walls.

Ell. An L-shaped plumbing fitting with two openings at 90 degrees to each other.

Exposure. Surface area of a board, shingle, or roofing tile or slate that will be seen after installation.

Face frame. Traditional style of cabinetry in which a solid wood frame is attached to the front of each cabinet. See also *Frameless*.

Face-nail. To nail at a right angle to a surface, with nail heads exposed; see also *Toenail* and *Blind nail*.

Fascia. Horizontal board capping the lower ends of a roof's rafters, sometimes forming part of a *cornice*.

F-channel. Strip of vinyl molding, shaped like the letter F, that is used around the perimeter of *soffit* panels.

Fixed-price bid. Bid from a *contractor* that covers all costs: materials, labor, and management of the project.

Flashing. Water-resistant material used to protect exterior joints around doors, windows, and skylights.

Float. Tool used to smooth poured concrete.

Floor flange. Plumbing fitting that anchors a toilet to the floor and connects it to the waste line. Sometimes called a closet flange.

Flush. Describes adjacent surfaces that are in the same plane.

Flush doors. Doors made from a flat veneered surface applied over built-up core stock.

Fly rafter. End *rafter* on a roof that overhangs the *gable* wall.

Footer, footing. A masonry structure set in the ground that is wider than the *foundation* it supports.

Foundation. The part of a building, usually made of masonry, that supports the entire structure by transmitting loads directly to the ground.

Frame, framing. Skeletal structure of a building; also, the members surrounding a window or door opening.

Frame and panel. Traditional style of door made of a solid wood frame surrounding one or more panels.

Frameless. Style of cabinet constructed without a solid wood frame attached to the front of each cabinet; also called Euro-style. See also *Face frame*.

Frost-free faucet. Faucet in which the handle and spout are mounted outside of the house while the valve mechanism is located inside to prevent water from freezing.

Gable. Type of roof having two sloping sides meet at a *ridge*;

the triangular section of wall at either end of a gable roof.

Girder. Heavy beam used to support floor *joists*.

Grade. A level of quality used in classifying wood construction products including lumber, plywood, and shingles.

Ground. Part of an electrical system that makes a connection to the earth.

Grout. Fine cement used to fill the spaces between tiles.

Gutter. Trough along the roof eave that collects rainwater and diverts it to a *downspout*.

Hand, as in right- or left-handed. Side to which a door is designed to open.

Hardwood. Wood from a deciduous tree (one that sheds its leaves).

Hawk. Square, flat wooden platform with a handle used to hold a supply of joint compound.

Header. Structural member spanning the top of a window, doorway, or other wall opening.

Head jamb. Top of a window or door frame.

Hose bib. Valve with external threads for attaching a flexible garden hose; also called a sill cock.

House wrap. Thin, paperlike air barrier attached to the *sheathing* of a house. Unlike other wraps, it is permeable to water vapor.

HVAC. Abbreviation for a building's heating, ventilation, and air conditioning systems.

Hydronic. System of heating that uses water (as opposed to air) as the medium for transferring heat, such as steam and hot-water radiators.

Jack stud. See *Trimmer*.

Jamb. Sides of a window or door frame.

J-channel. Strip of vinyl molding, shaped like the letter J, that is used around window and door openings.

Joist. Framing member that supports flooring or ceilings.

Keyway. Slot formed in the top surface of a poured concrete *footing* that helps to hold the *foundation* wall in place.

King stud. Full-height stud nailed to a *trimmer* stud at a window or door opening.

Knee wall. Short wall under the low *eave* of a top floor.

Lally column. Trade name for a steel post that is often adjustable and used to support a beam or *girder*.

Ledger. Framing member fastened to a vertical surface that is used to support the ends of *joists* or *rafters*.

Lien. Legal claim placed on a property in order to get payment for a debt.

Light. Individual pane of glass in a *sash*.

Limited service. Arrangement by which an architect is hired to handle only selected parts of a project, such as design consultation or drawings; see also *Comprehensive service*.

Live load. Moving and variable loads placed on the structure of a building, as opposed to a *dead load*. Furniture and the occupants of a room are examples of a live load.

Load form. Method of analyzing the heating and cooling needs of a house and the capacity of existing heating and cooling systems. Used in determining the needs that an addition will place on those systems.

Low-E. Abbreviated form of low emisivity, describing window glazing that is treated to reduce the transfer of heat from one side to the other.

Lumber. Wood milled for use in construction; see also *Board* and *Timber*; *dimensional lumber* is sawed to a *nominal* thickness of 2 to 4 inches.

Masonry board. Waterproof sheet material used on walls instead of drywall as a base for tile.

Mil. Unit of thickness equal to $1/1000$ inch.

Molding. Thin, often decorative strip placed where surfaces meet, such as between walls and ceilings and around windows and doors.

Mudsill. See *Sill*.

Mullion. Vertical element separating a row of windows or doors.

Muntin. Member of a *sash* that divides it into individual glass panes, or *lights*. Windows with a single pane may have a snap-in grid to give the effect of muntins.

Nominal. Nominal dimensions of lumber are those used to describe a standard size, although the actual size may be smaller. For example, a 2 x 4 usually measures just $1\frac{1}{2}$ x $3\frac{1}{2}$ inches.

On center (O.C.). Term used to describe the distance from the center of one framing member to the center of the next.

Overhang. Portion of a roof that projects beyond the wall.

Payment schedule. In a contract, the breakdown of payments to be made to the *contractor*. Payments are made on specific dates or when the project reaches certain stages of completion.

Penny. Term used to describe nail length, represented by the lowercase letter d.

Pigtail. Wires twisted around each other that form a corkscrew reminiscent of a pig's tail. Frequently used in reference to short lengths of copper wire that are attached to aluminum house wiring to improve contacts at switches and receptacles.

Pitch. Steepness of a roof; also, one inclined side of a roof.

Plate. Horizontal member of a frame, running both below and above a course of *studs*. The lower plate is also known as a *sole plate* or bottom plate; the upper is also known as a top plate or ceiling plate.

Platform framing. Construction method in which the subfloor provides a surface upon which walls for the next story are erected.

Plumb. Exactly vertical (perpendicular) to the floor.

Plumb line, plumb bob. Weight suspended from a string to determine *plumb*.

Pocket door. Door that slides into a concealed pocket framed into the adjacent wall space.

Primer. Special form of paint or other finish; used to seal a surface and prepare it for one or more top coats of the standard product.

P-trap. Section of waste pipe, shaped like the letter P, that is located just below a plumbing fixture; by trapping a small amount of water, the P-trap prevents waste gases from backing up into the home.

Punch list. Written inventory of items still to be completed at the end of a construction job.

Quarter-round. A common form of *molding* shaped like one-quarter of a cylinder when viewed in cross section.

R-value. Index of the resistance of a medium to the transfer of heat.

Rabbet. A recess on the edge of a piece of lumber or plywood; see also *Dado*.

Rafter. Framing member that supports a roof.

Rafter tail. Portion of a *rafter* that extends over a wall, forming an overhang.

Rail. Horizontal member of a window *sash* or door.

Rake. The inclined edge of a roof; for example, the edge along a gable end.

Rebar. Abbreviated name for reinforcing bar, a metal rod placed within poured *concrete* for added strength.

Receptacle. Electrical wall fixture into which plugs are placed.

Reveal. The inside edge of a door or window frame left exposed when the *casing* is applied. Sometimes refers to any groove formed where different elements come together.

Ridge. The junction between two sloped roof sections; the apex.

Ridge board. Framing member that defines the *ridge*.

Rise. Height of a roof measured vertically from the base to the *ridge*.

Riser tube. Length of tube or pipe that connects a supply *stubout* to a faucet or toilet tank, often with a shutoff valve in between.

Roofing felt. Asphalt-impregnated paper used as a water barrier beneath finish roofing, wall siding, and flooring. Also called *building paper* or *tar paper.*

Rough opening. Space defined by framing members to be faced with trim or to receive a door or window frame.

Run. Span of a roof measured horizontally at the baseline from the lower edge to the point plumb with the *ridge.*

Sash. Framed window element containing one or more glass panes. A double-hung window has two sashes, both of which are operable.

Schematic design. Preliminary drawings and cost estimates for a project provided by an architect.

Screed. To level freshly poured concrete to a certain thickness; a device for leveling *concrete.*

Scribe. To mark the outline of an irregular cut.

Scribe edge. Strip at the edge of a cabinet that can be trimmed to fit tightly against the imperfect surface of a wall or ceiling.

Select. Term used in wood grading systems to describe the second best grade of material; see also *Clear* and *Common.*

Service head. Connecting post at which the main electrical service wires are attached to a house from a utility pole.

Service panel. Metal box into which the main electric service cable is connected and from which house wiring is routed via *circuit breakers,* or fuses.

Setback. Minimum distance between a structure and property lines, as specified by local regulations.

Sheathing. Layer of material applied directly to exterior wall or roof frames and to the top side of floor frames.

Shed. Type of roof having a single sloping side.

Shim. Thin strip or wedge of wood used to adjust and hold position of wood members.

Side jamb. Two vertical parts of a door or window frame.

Siding. Finish layer covering walls.

Sill. Horizontal framing member placed atop the foundation (also called a *mudsill*); lowest member of a door or window frame.

Sleepers. Rows of wood strips, usually 2 x 3 or 2 x 4 stock, attached to a concrete slab to inhibit moisture transfer from the slab to a finished floor.

Soffit. Underside of the roof *eave;* also a section of ceiling that drops lower than the main ceiling.

Softwood. Wood from a coniferous tree (one that doesn't shed its leaves).

Soil pipe, soil stack. Principal vertical waste pipe of plumbing system.

Sole plate. Horizontal member of a wall frame that runs below a course of *studs.*

Span. Distance between supports.

Square. Unit of measure, equaling 100 square feet, used to describe roofing and siding materials; layout tool, with arms set at right angles; description of two elements that are at right angles to one another.

Stack. Vertical section of a plumbing system's waste and vent lines.

Starter strip. A specially shaped piece of molding nailed to the lower edge of a wall to anchor the first strip of vinyl siding.

Stile. Vertical member of a window *sash* or door.

Stool. Horizontal piece of interior window trim attached to the *sill;* typically extends slightly into a room and beyond the ends of a window frame.

Stop and waste valve. Stop valve recommended for outdoor faucets that has a waste cleanout plug for draining standing water.

Strip flooring. Finished floor made of narrow strips of wood flooring, usually *hardwood.*

Stubouts. Short lengths of supply or waste pipe that protrude from walls and floors and to which plumbing fixtures are attached.

Stud. Vertical member used to frame walls.

Subcontractor. Independent tradesperson hired for specific parts of a building project, like roofing or plumbing.

Subfloor. Layer of *sheathing* over joists that is to be covered by a finished floor.

Subpanel. Secondary *service panel* installed to serve a specific zone of a house or an added space, thereby reducing the number of *circuits* and the amount of wiring routed to the main panel (called a *service panel*).

Tar paper. See *Roofing felt.*

Tee. A T-shaped plumbing fitting with three openings at 90 degrees to each other.

Tee-wye. A Y-shaped plumbing fitting with three openings, two of which form a straight line, while the third is angled at 45 degrees.

Threshold. Metal or wood strip attached to the floor beneath a door; bridges the gap between floor surfaces and provides a seal against air passage.

Timber. Lumber with *nominal* thickness of at least 5 inches.

Time and materials. Contract that stipulates you will pay a *contractor* or *subcontractor* a specific amount for the time to do a job, plus cover the contractor's actual cost for materials. Also referred to as cost plus.

Toenail. To nail at other than a right angle to a surface, either from necessity or to help better lock a joint.

Tongue and groove, T and G. Edge joint in which the tongue of one board or sheet is locked within the groove of the adjoining element.

Transition fitting. Plumbing fitting that connects one type of pipe material to another, for example, copper to PVC.

Transit level. Precision instrument for establishing level and square reference points when laying out a *foundation*.

Trap. Plumbing fitting that provides a water seal to prevent sewer gases from entering the house.

Trimmer. Reinforcing *stud* nailed directly to a common *stud*. It defines the side of a window or door opening and supports a header.

Underlayment. A thin layer of material, usually plywood, laid over the *subfloor* to provide a smooth surface for finish flooring like carpet or tile.

Vapor barrier. Sheet or applied coating that prevents water vapor or moisture from passing through a surface.

Variance. Exception to a *zoning ordinance* granted by a zoning board.

Volts. Standard unit for measuring the quantity of force of electrical currents; 120V and 240V are the standard voltages of house currents.

Wainscoting, wainscot. Paneling along the lower third or so of an interior wall.

Water hammer. Banging sound that results when water flow in supply lines is abruptly started or stopped.

Water level. Length of clear plastic tubing used to transfer an elevation mark from one point to another point that is level with the first.

Wire nut. Twist-on device used to join the ends of wires.

Working drawing. Drawing used in carpentry and cabinetry detailing exactly what is to be built and specific materials to be used.

Wye. A Y-shaped plumbing fitting with three openings.

Zone. Branch of a heating or cooling system, often with its own thermostat and pump or fan.

Zoning ordinance. Local rules that govern such things as the type, size, and location of building projects relative to street and property lines.

INDEX

370

372

373

**If you've enjoyed this book,
you may be interested in these other titles from Rodale Press.**

**THE WORKSHOP COMPANION:
FINISH CARPENTRY**
by Nick Engler
Whether you're installing windows, doors, floors, paneling, or trim, this book will show you how to produce results like the pros.
Hardcover   ISBN 0-87596-583-0

**THE WORKSHOP COMPANION:
MAKING BUILT-IN CABINETS**
by Nick Engler
This book shows how to combine plywood and solid wood to make awe-inspiring cabinets, entertainment centers, storage units, and bookcases.
Hardcover   ISBN 0-87596-139-8

THE WORKSHOP COMPANION: FINISHING
by Nick Engler
This comprehensive guide explains how furniture finishes differ, which ones work together, and how to apply them.
Hardcover   ISBN 0-87596-138-X

CABINETS AND BUILT-INS
**A Practical Guide to Building
Professional-Quality Cabinetry**
by Paul Levine
This book presents a simple, practical system for building fine wood cabinets and built-in furniture. Fourteen great projects show you how to apply the techniques.
Hardcover   ISBN 0-87596-590-3

OUTDOOR FURNITURE
30 Great Projects for the Deck, Lawn and Garden
by Bill Hylton, with Fred Matlack and Phil Gehret
With a project to suit every taste and to challenge every skill level, this is *the* book on making outdoor furniture.
Hardcover   ISBN 0-87596-105-3

DECKS
**How to Design and Build the Perfect Deck
for Your Home**
by Tim Snyder, coauthor of The New Yankee Workshop
From careful design to applying a protective finish, this book explains everything you need to know to build the deck of your dreams.
Paperback   ISBN 0-87857-955-9
Hardcover   ISBN 0-87857-949-4

UNDERSTANDING WOOD FINISHING
How to Select and Apply the Right Finish
by Bob Flexner
America's top finishing expert takes the mystery out of finishing and shows you how and why every finish behaves the way it does.
Hardcover   ISBN 0-87596-566-0

**THE BIG BOOK OF SMALL
HOUSEHOLD REPAIRS**
**Your Goof-Proof Guide to Fixing
over 200 Annoying Breakdowns**
by Charlie Wing
This engaging, step-by-step guide to 243 household repairs shows you inexpensive and frustration-free ways to repair everything from a broken light switch to a leaking sink.
Hardcover   ISBN 0-87596-649-7

**THE BACKYARD BUILDER:
PROJECTS FOR OUTDOOR LIVING**
edited by William Hylton
The detailed instructions and graphics in this book show you exactly how to build over 150 projects for your home and garden.
Hardcover   ISBN 0-87857-884-6

**BUILD-IT-BETTER-YOURSELF WOODWORKING
PROJECTS: BENCHES, SWINGS, AND GLIDERS**
by Nick Engler
Make the home and garden a showplace with patio furniture, porch swings, a deacon's bench, and more. The quick and beautiful projects are thoroughly explained.
Hardcover   ISBN 0-87857-943-5

For more information or to order a book, call 1-800-527-8200.